301.2

W9-AFM-813

KANSAS SCHOOL OF RELIGION
University of Kansas
1300 Oread Avenue
LAWRENCE, KANSAS 66044

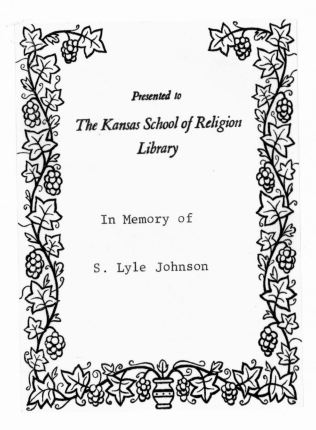

Presented to

The Kansas School of Religion
Library

In Memory of

S. Lyle Johnson

A.S.A. MONOGRAPHS

General Editor: MICHAEL BANTON

9

Witchcraft
Confessions & Accusations

WITCHCRAFT

CONFESSIONS & ACCUSATIONS

Edited by Mary Douglas

KANSAS SCHOOL OF RELIGION
University of Kansas
1300 Oread Avenue
LAWRENCE, KANSAS 66044

TAVISTOCK PUBLICATIONS

London · New York · Sydney · Toronto · Wellington

BF1563
.W56

First published in 1970
by Tavistock Publications Limited
11 New Fetter Lane, London EC4

This book has been set in Modern Series 7
and was printed by T. & A. Constable Limited,
Edinburgh

© *Association of Social Anthropologists of the Commonwealth*
1970

SBN 422 73200 1

This volume derives mainly from papers presented at the annual conference of the Association of Social Anthropologists of the Commonwealth on the theme of witchcraft. The conference was held at King's College, Cambridge, 3-6 April 1968, and the Association wishes to record its gratitude to the Provost and Fellows of King's College for their hospitality on that occasion.

ms – Witchcraft

Distributed in the U.S.A.
by Barnes & Noble, Inc.

The papers included in this volume
are offered as a tribute to
Professor E. E. Evans-Pritchard
Founder and First President of the
Association of Social Anthropologists

Contents

		page
Editor's Preface		xi

MARY DOUGLAS
Introduction: Thirty Years after *Witchcraft, Oracles and Magic* — xiii

Part I   The Context of Witchcraft in Europe

1   NORMAN COHN
The Myth of Satan and his Human Servants — 3

2   PETER BROWN
Sorcery, Demons, and the Rise of Christianity from Late Antiquity into the Middle Ages — 17

3   KEITH THOMAS
The Relevance of Social Anthropology to the Historical Study of English Witchcraft — 47

4   ALAN MACFARLANE
Witchcraft in Tudor and Stuart Essex — 81

Part II   Cleansing and Confession of Witches

5   ALISON REDMAYNE
Chikanga: An African Diviner with an International Reputation — 103

6   R. G. WILLIS
Instant Millennium: The Sociology of African Witch-cleansing Cults — 129

7   EDWIN ARDENER
Witchcraft, Economics, and the Continuity of Belief — 141

8   ROBERT BRAIN
Child-witches — 161

Contents

Part III Idioms of Power

9 JULIAN PITT-RIVERS
Spiritual Power in Central America: The Naguals of
Chiapas   183

10 ESTHER GOODY
Legitimate and Illegitimate Aggression in a West
African State   207

11 PETER RIVIÈRE
Factions and Exclusions in Two South American
Village Systems   245

12 ANTHONY FORGE
Prestige, Influence, and Sorcery: A New Guinea
Example   257

Part IV Alternative Interpretations of Misfortune

13 GODFREY LIENHARDT
The Situation of Death: An Aspect of Anuak
Philosophy   279

14 I. M. LEWIS
A Structural Approach to Witchcraft and Spirit-
possession   293

15 BRIAN SPOONER
The Evil Eye in the Middle East   311

16 G. I. JONES
A Boundary to Accusations   321

17 MALCOLM RUEL
Were-animals and the Introverted Witch   333

18 T. O. BEIDELMAN
Towards More Open Theoretical Interpretations   351

Notes on Contributors   357

Author Index   363

Subject Index   367

Contents

Maps

	page
The county of Essex, showing sample villages	85
Chikanga and surrounding area	104
The site of Chikanga	105
Eastern Region of Nigeria: differential concern with witchcraft	322

Editor's Preface

The Association of Social Anthropologists was founded in 1946 by Professor Evans-Pritchard. When the date of his retirement from the Chair of Anthropology at Oxford drew close, many of us were looking for ways to express our homage. At Professor Schapera's suggestion the A.S.A. decided to hold a conference in his honour. If it could have taken place in 1967 it would have fallen on the thirtieth anniversary of one of the most influential books in social anthropology, *Witchcraft, Oracles and Magic among the Azande*. Thus was the subject of the conference chosen, even if the conference had to take place in 1968.

As convener, I felt two responsibilities. The first was to salute Evans-Pritchard's achievement and the scope of his influence. This has been by no means confined to a narrow discipline. He has always had at heart the need of anthropology to use and understand historical disciplines. Witchcraft is a subject that concerns historians of certain periods. I was therefore delighted by the generous response of distinguished historians who joined the conference. Their papers in the first section of this volume add greatly to the weight and interest of the whole. They have carried, almost alone, the task of making this a cross-disciplinary exercise, since they have assimilated anthropological ideas and applied them to their own material.

My second responsibility was to draw as widely as possible from among anthropologists, so that the advances in understanding witch beliefs would not be presented in a parochial way. It would not do to let it seem that witchcraft is the private obsession of Africanists or that the original Azande study has influenced Africanists only. Though many contributors quickly offered themselves, they all happened to be concerned with Africa. I tried without success to find anthropologists with Melanesian, Indian, or American material, who would be able to extend the range of our discussions. At one point it seemed that I might face the dilemma of either ignoring the regional bias or trying to explain why an allegedly sociological set of insights applies only in a culturally defined region. Fortunately the conference itself corrected the bias. Several members have subsequently contributed papers so that Islamic culture, New Guinea, and Central and South America are represented. This extension very much increases the value of the book.

Several people who spoke or acted as chairmen at the conference, or led the discussions, are not represented in these pages. They should be mentioned because they gave us so much stimulus: Professor Raymond Firth, Professor Daryll Forde, Professor Christoph von Fürer-Haimendorf, Dr Francis Huxley, Dr Phyllis Kaberry, Professor Igor Kopytoff, Professor Jacques Maquet, and Dr Audrey Richards. It is a pity that the timing of the conference failed to realize the full ritualism of Professor Schapera's project, but I feel that we have responded enthusiastically to the essentials of his original idea.

INTRODUCTION

Mary Douglas

Thirty Years
after *Witchcraft, Oracles and Magic*[1]

Historians and anthropologists have a common interest in the subject of witchcraft, but until very recently their outlooks have diverged. Historians dealing with sixteenth- and seventeenth-century Europe or Massachusetts cannot but see witchcraft as part of a cumulative process with frequently a violent and tragic climax. Its scale may not have matched the religious persecutions of earlier times, but it is difficult not to see it in Europe as another scourge, a destructive belief liable to run away with reason, as Norman Cohn convincingly shows below. The anthropologists of the 1950s developed insights into the functioning of witch beliefs which seemed about as relevant to the European experience as if they came from another planet. Dangerous in Europe, the same beliefs in Melanesia or Africa appeared to be tame, even domesticated; they served useful functions and were not expected to run amuck.

Is the difference objectively valid? Does it really result from a difference in the social conditions, or is it due to prejudice in the eye of the observer? Formerly anthropologists used to emphasize the different quality of the information accessible to the two disciplines of research. Now this difference is being narrowed: the historians who have contributed to this volume have succeeded in delving into material very comparable to that used by anthropologists and the latter are gradually improving the time-scale of their observation. The moment has come for a survey of the subject.

For a good decade, between its publication in 1937 and the beginning of postwar research, *Witchcraft, Oracles and Magic among the Azande* had little influence. (Clyde Kluckhohn's *Navaho Witchcraft* (1944) was clearly written independently.) But in the next twenty years it came to dominate the writings of anthropologists in a remarkable way. As is the fate of any original work, it has been applied in directions not foreseen, nor even blessed, by its author. Evans-Pritchard denounces in no uncertain terms the crude functionalism to which witchcraft studies have contributed (Evans-Pritchard, 1965, p. 114). In the short run, much of the work which has derived from his book has seemed to frustrate his own wish to bring anthropologists and historians together. In asking how this happened we raise fundamental questions about the nature of scholarly research.

First and foremost this was a book about the sociology of knowledge. It showed how Azande, clever and sceptical as they were, could tolerate discrepancies in their beliefs and could limit the kinds of question they asked about the universe. It might have been expected to stimulate more studies on the social restraints upon perception. Instead it fathered studies of micropolitics. The relation between belief and society, instead of appearing as infinitely complex, subtle, and fluid, was presented as a control system with a negative feedback. Anthropologists strictly limited the questions they asked and restrained their natural curiosity. The assumptions of their model were no more critically examined than those underlying the Azande theory of witchcraft.

The change of interest from perception theory to political analysis was partly due to the interruption of the Second World War. When teaching and fieldwork were resumed Evans-Pritchard himself had started to publish his Nuer studies and was working also on *The Sanusi of Cyrenaica* (1949). His contemporaries were publishing important researches. Each new fieldworker produced new material, new ideas, and new technical problems. A new range of social institutions had to be analysed. A simplified approach was necessary for assimilating so much that was unfamiliar. If some of the lessons of the Azande book were overlaid with other ideas, remember also that Evans-Pritchard is deeply modest. He does not seek to dominate or to influence unduly a student's thought. It is impossible to imagine him complaining that there is more in his first book than has been noticed, or that he has been misinterpreted.

Perhaps it is necessary, before going on, to establish that the study of Azande witchcraft was indeed offered as a contribution to the sociology of perception. In his lectures on magic in the

Introduction

University of Cairo (1933, 1934), Evans-Pritchard discusses the 'intellectualist' interpretations favoured by the English anthropologists and takes them to task for supposing that patterns of thought can be explained by the working of the individual's mind. He applauds the French, especially Durkheim and Lévy-Bruhl, for their sociological approach. Indeed, he is our last direct link with the French sociologists of *L'Année Sociologique*, for the rest of us received Durkheim filtered through Radcliffe-Brown. At this stage he admits himself a disciple of Lévy-Bruhl:

> 'The criticisms of Lévy-Bruhl's theories are so obvious and so forcible that only books of exceptional brilliance and originality could have survived them. . . . Lévy-Bruhl is speaking of patterns or modes of thought which, after eliminating all individual variation, are the same among all the members of a primitive community and are what are called their beliefs. . . . Every individual is compelled to adopt these beliefs by pressure of social circumstances. . . . When Lévy-Bruhl says that a representation is collective, he means that it is a socially determined mode of thought and is therefore common to all members of a society or of a social segment' (1934, p. 9).

Evans-Pritchard went on to make the necessary link with contemporary perception theory:

> 'As James and Rignano and others have shown, any sound or sight may reach the brain of a person without entering into his consciousness. We may say that he "hears" or "sees" it but does not "notice" it. In a stream of sense impressions only a few become conscious and these are selected on account of their greater affectivity. A man's interests are the selective agents and these are to a great extent socially determined . . .' (ibid., p. 18).

Much earlier, Marx had argued that religious beliefs are influenced by social experience. There was no novelty in the twentieth century in inquiring how the choice between one kind of religion or another might be so determined. But the problem that Lévy-Bruhl set himself amounted to the broader one of asking how any religion at all could be accepted. Why should beliefs in invisible demons and gods, *mana* and *tabu*, have explanatory value? Phrased in Lévy-Bruhl's terms the question seems unanswerable, except by postulating a special 'primitive' cast of mind. But Evans-Pritchard solved it by broadening the question still further and considering it as part of the problem of explanation as such. He asked why any metaphysical system should be accepted. The difference between religious explanations and other explanations then fades into the background. In an inquiry into witchcraft as a principle of causation, no mysterious spiritual beings are postulated, only the mysterious powers of humans. The belief is on the same footing as belief in the conspiracy theory of history, in the baneful effects of fluoridation or the curative value of psychoanalysis – or any proposition that can be presented in an unverifiable form. The question then becomes one about rationality.

The witchcraft beliefs of the Azande were protected, Evans-Pritchard showed, not only by secondary elaborations of the main hypotheses but by a set of social processes. First, the witchcraft beliefs sustained Azande moral values and their institutions. Second, they were restricted so as never to apply in contexts in which conflicting sectors might have found an interest in denying them. For example, the belief that witchcraft was hereditary in the class of commoners, and that the ruling class had no taint of it, ensured that commoners would never accuse aristocrats. Equally, the domestic structure was upheld in so far as no son could accuse his own father without branding himself as heir to a tainted line of descent. Azande had worked out warily the social implications of hereditary and nonhereditary witchcraft, but were still able to ignore them when their own individual case pointed to relationships with witches. Where the beliefs seemed most vulnerable to intellectual challenge and had not been provided with protective mechanisms, the astutest Azande informants were incapable of spotting the problem. They could not see, for example, any difficulty with their theoretical view that every death was caused either by witchcraft or by vengeance magic against the guilty witch. In their practical experience every death was blamed on witchcraft. When the anthropologist wanted to tot up deaths of witches' victims against deaths of witches killed in vengeance, no one knew anything about the latter. But it was not difficult for him to discern the set of interests that blinkered believers and enabled them to remain content with an explanatory system that served so many practical needs. The source of his insight lay in examining beliefs always from the point of view of the actors in a given social situation. Thus he disclosed the areas of the greatest concern, and those in which their curiosity could lie dormant. Gaps and discrepancies could be tolerated without in the least disturbing the illusion of a completed circle of beliefs.

Evans-Pritchard's next book, *The Nuer* (1940a), extends further his interest in the social structuring of experience. His chapter on Nuer perception of time is such an exercise. The main theme of the book is a discussion of how a people can use an acceptable idiom to present their political system to themselves without worrying about how little it corresponds to the facts (1940b, p. 288). By the time he writes *Nuer Religion* (1956) he is much closer to Durkheim than to Lévy-Bruhl. But in the interval *The Sanusi of Cyrenaica* (1949) analyses the social structuring of conversion. So he has consistently followed his early interest in the social restraints on perception. It would be very much in the spirit of these books to note the social structuring of blind spots and insights in work derived from them.

Three main principles of the Azande analysis have been applied in later research. First, tolerance of foreign beliefs: Professor Seligman's introduction points out that the Azande were far from being oppressed by witchcraft fears (Evans-Pritchard, 1937, p. xix), and Evans-Pritchard points out the lubricant effect of allowing grudges to be brought out into the open and of providing a formula for action in misfortune.

Second, the hostilities that were expressed by witchcraft beliefs were clearly patterned. Accusations clustered in areas of ambiguous social relations. Where roles were buffered by unequal power, wealth, or other forms of social distance, witchcraft accusations were not made; they appeared where tensions between neighbouring rivals could not otherwise be resolved. The mechanism for producing this pattern of accusations lay in the way in which oracles were unconsciously manipulated.

Third, witch beliefs had a normative effect on behaviour. Thus the moral system and social codes were supported by the sanction of attracting suspicion of witchcraft, since witches were thought to be rude, mean, or snatching. Moreover, being bewitched was never accepted as an excuse for moral or technical defects where responsibility could be established.

Evans-Pritchard's main interest seems to have been in showing how a metaphysical system could compel belief by a variety of self-validating procedures. But the same approach was well adapted to a more simplistic functional hypothesis. The researches of Max Marwick (1952, 1965) and of Clyde Mitchell (1956) in Central Africa emphasized the morality-sustaining, normative, and explanatory functions of witchcraft. But they added a new level of insight.

Among the Azande, witchcraft beliefs seem to lie like static electricity activated by incidental friction, whereas in Yao and Ceŵa communities their power was mobilized for the cyclical changes the social system would periodically undergo. When the little village reached a size larger than its frail resources of authority could control, witchcraft accusations were an idiom in which the painful process of fission could be set going. The original Azande picture was of a social system permanently harbouring areas of ill-defined relationships in which witchcraft accusations flourished. Now this was developed by a new model which could take account of recurrent changes in time. At one point in the history of a small Central African village, witchcraft accusations would be rare, at another point they would intensify as rivals competed for factional advantage.

Fieldwork continued to dot the i's and cross the t's, confirming the usefulness of the general approach. Here witch accusations were used to challenge abuse of authority, there to strengthen it. Wherever belief in witchcraft was found to flourish, the hypothesis that accusations would tend to cluster in niches where social relations were ill defined and competitive could not fail to work, because competitiveness and ambiguity were identified by means of witch accusations. But inevitably the subject began to lose interest as the lack of predictive power in the irrefutable governing hypothesis was revealed. A turning-point is marked by Daryll Forde's discussion of the Yakö cosmology as a supernatural economy of means and ends (1958). Perhaps Turner's article in *Africa* (1964), in which he challenges the value of the so-called structural approach, marks the end.

The Azande study certainly contributed its share to the gulf between historians and anthropologists, since the idea of witchcraft as part of a homeostatic control system derived directly from it. Perhaps no one has gone further than Philip Mayer in implying that witchcraft beliefs (at least in Africa in its original untouched state before missionaries, cash, and colonists had disturbed the balance) were a fully domesticated species, not to be compared with the wild, European sort (1954):

> 'In a normally stable society the witchcraft is effectively controlled. It admittedly provides a vent for hatreds and anxieties that society cannot express, but this remains after all a controlled outlet: the frequency or severity of convictions is somehow kept within bounds' (1954, p. 15).

Max Gluckman was more ingenious in justifying the witchcraft accusation by showing that the witch is guilty of unchristian feelings:

> 'An Anglican anthem demands "See that ye love one another fervently". Beliefs in the malice of witchcraft and in the wrath of ancestral spirits do more than ask this as an act of grace; they affirm that if you do not love one another fervently, misfortune will come. Bad feeling is charged with mystical danger; virtue in itself produces order throughout the universe. Though a charge of witchcraft for causing a misfortune may exaggerate and exacerbate a quarrel, the belief emphasises the threat to the wider social order which is contained in immoral sentiments. Hence the beliefs exert some pressure on men and women to observe the social virtues, and to feel the right sentiments, lest they be suspected of being witches' (Gluckman, 1955, p. 94).

Starting from a homeostatic model of society in which witchcraft beliefs help to maintain the system, the natural way to account for witchcraft accusations getting out of control was by reference to a general breakdown of the society. Curiously, the link between European and African witchcraft was made by reference to the Industrial Revolution (Gluckman, op. cit., pp. 97, 101, 102; Mayer, op. cit., p. 15).

In the case of Africa it is the break-up of the small face-to-face community with the advent of missionaries, wage-labour, and town life that produces an unbalanced increase in witchcraft fears and accusations:

'We all feel that a society that gives excessive prominence to witchcraft must be a sick society, rather as a witch-ridden personality is a sick personality. This is confirmed by anthropological studies which in several cases have shown an increase in witch-phenomena in communities undergoing social breakdown. The native peoples of South Africa during the difficult phase of urbanisation provide several cases in point' (Mayer, 1954, p. 15).

This echoes Audrey Richards's remarks nearly twenty years earlier:

'Missionaries all over Africa are teaching a religion which casts out fear, but economic and social changes have so shattered tribal institutions and moral codes that the result of white contact is in many cases an actual increase in the dread of witchcraft, and therefore in the whole incidence of magic throughout the group' (1935, pp. 458, 460; see also Ward, 1956, p. 47).

The general proposition that an increase of witchcraft accusations occurs as a symptom of disorder and moral collapse was superbly untestable. Taken seriously it would have required some assessment of the level of accusations before and after the crucial point, and also an independent measure of the state of morals and the regularity of social relations. Only now, with sophisticated techniques of network analysis, would it be theoretically possible to attempt such an assessment, and the task is daunting. In fact the concept of moral health and sickness, central to this discussion, has never been analysed. Instead, it was taken as axiomatic that a high degree of witch accusations in itself indicated the moral breakdown, etc., that was expected to be correlated with it. Contrary evidence was ignored. Monica and Godfrey Wilson had long ago declared that their researches in the Copperbelt did not support the view that witchcraft fears increased in urban conditions (1945). More recently, a more detailed case-study suggests the same (Mitchell, 1965, p. 201).

If witchcraft accusations were indeed found to increase where social relations became more diffuse and more easily broken off, much of the field research of the 1950s and 1960s would have to be reinterpreted. For Clyde Mitchell (1956), Max Marwick (1952), John Middleton (1960), and Victor Turner (1954) (some of the best known) had interpreted the accusation of witch-craft primarily as an instrument for breaking off relations. The accuser was using a legitimate form of attack which absolved him of unwanted obligations. In so far as rootlessness and mobility and laxity of morals characterize town life, the weapon of witchcraft accusation would be redundant. It would also be ineffectual, for it depends for its success on a relatively closed circle of neighbours, in whose good opinion the accused is made to suffer. Thus the orthodoxy of the 1950s makes it unlikely that witchcraft accusations would increase in urban society, except within limited competitive sectors. Nor would they plausibly increase with the breakdown of social obligations and moral codes. It would seem difficult to move from the theory of the witchcraft belief functioning as an instrument of social health to the idea of it as a symptom of a sick society. For this the theory would have to be expanded. In stage one, in small-scale society, witchcraft would be under control; in stage two, with the dislocation of social life, it would run wild; in stage three, with the advent of large-scale society and impersonal relations, it would fade away. On this showing it should have been at stage two and well out of control when it was being observed in Africa in the 1940-60 period – precisely the time it was felt to slot so well into the homeostatic functional theory. It should have been out of control in England in the period leading up to the Industrial Revolution, that is in the later seventeenth century, the period when, according to Keith Thomas below, its decline was well begun. Further difficulties arise when the respective time-scales of anthropologists and historians are compared. Alan Macfarlane (below) analyses cases in Essex villages in a period of 120 years. No anthropologist can draw on case-material over such a long time. What appears to the anthropologist as part of a stable pattern of relations, to the historian is a mere point in time. If the Protestant Reformation and the Poor Law are new elements in the rural society of Tudor and Stuart Essex, so are Colonial rule and Christianity new in the African picture. The homeostatic model of society cannot deal with thorny problems of time-scale (Gellner, 1958).

Nor can a functional theory avoid importing crude ideas of normality which may gravely distort the analysis, as Dr Beidelman has cogently argued below (p. 351).

The anthropologists who let the homeostatic model govern their teaching and thinking, in spite of its many drawbacks, were accepting a scientific paradigm in much the same way as the natural scientists described by Kuhn in his book *The Structure of Scientific Revolutions* (1962). Once a single paradigm of concepts and theories gets adopted throughout the field, according to Kuhn, a period of 'normal science' follows, in which scientists accept the paradigm unquestioningly and limit themselves to developing and checking its implications. To new students it is presented as established dogma. Out-of-fashion concepts and problems are rarely discussed; students are trained to develop expertise within the accepted framework. Kuhn supposes that the method of teaching in the physical sciences is more likely to produce a rigid 'mental set' than that in the social sciences. But everything that he says about the use of paradigms in scientific thinking has strong relevance for British anthropology following the Second World War.

We are now at the predicted stage at which the accumulation of anomalies has forced us to recognize an existing paradigm as inadequate. S. B. Barnes (1968) has attempted to compare the thinking of scientists while applying their current paradigm with the thinking of Azande on the subject of witchcraft. Without seeking to identify primitiveness in scientific thought, he has narrowed the gulf between primitives and scientists which so impressed Lévy-Bruhl and is still important in the work of Lévi-Strauss. His seems to be the only study which has caught the spirit of the Azande book and applied its lessons. Let me therefore take this opportunity of applying one of his suggestions. Scientific paradigms, argues Barnes, can more easily be changed than social paradigms:

> 'Thus for the actor the social paradigm governs more action and more significant action than the scientific one. Abandoning, say, the molecular orbital theory of chemistry means a lot less than abandoning the notion of responsibility or, for example, abandoning belief in poison oracles if you are an Azande.'

However, the social scientist is not so well able to insulate his scientific from his social paradigms and will seek to achieve consonance between them.

If we ask why we anthropologists have been content with a theoretical scheme which combines so little explanatory value with so many discrepancies and gaps, we can refer to the dominant social paradigm of the time, liberal philosophy, and to the special position of the anthropologist as its representative and as mediator between his informants and their colonial rulers. Evans-Pritchard's article on 'Witchcraft' in *Africa* (1935) warned missionaries and administrators not to try to destroy other people's beliefs, even if they seem misguided. The responsibility to protect and to preach tolerance was widely echoed. To show witchcraft beliefs as performing a constructive role in a functioning social system has been one way of carrying out this responsibility. Evans-Pritchard's Azande study minimizes the gulf between European and primitive culture. One would suppose that any emphasis on the gulf would be at variance with the main principles of liberal philosophy. Yet in another sense anthropologists tended to exaggerate the dichotomy, since their enthusiasm for native cultures led them to take up a theoretical position which treated conflict as benign in primitive society, a position they would not extend to their own society. And so the whole argument about 'Their' mentality and 'Ours' has had to proceed as if the Azande study had no relevance to ourselves and our history. Another factor is the special position of African fieldwork in the history of anthropology. It is interesting to reflect on what would have happened in British anthropology if work in New Guinea had developed as quickly as in Africa. If a Melanesian equivalent of the International African Institute had been organized by an opposite number to Daryll Forde, the homeostasis theory could surely not have survived for so long unchallenged. In Africa, colonial rule had been established for over fifty years and tribal societies had no doubt adapted by producing control mechanisms within their traditional institutions. It was easier to overlook the significance of the poison ordeal (then disappeared) and witch-cleansing movements (successfully repressed) than it would be to overlook the challenge presented by cargo cults in those parts of Melanesia where violent millennial outbursts offer a continual challenge to colonial authority.

So much for how we came to adopt a paradigm and to find it satisfactory. And so much for its limitations. Kuhn regards the rigid application of a paradigm as a necessary and useful stage in science. To the credit of this one we should chalk up two benefits. By accepting conflict as a normal part of any social system we have developed a more realistic model. Anthropologists are henceforth convicted of naïveté when they report a conflict-free social system without adducing special evidence to prove its existence. The long years of microscopic attention to detail in social relations have given us further sophistication about the way in which ideology relates to social structure. Some kinds of mistakes and loose thinking will be ruled out even in the present period of paradigm confusion.

If we were to make a fresh start to the classifying of witchcraft beliefs, drawing on existing field reports, we would do well to begin with the class of ideas that attract belief but are inactive in human affairs. People may believe in the possibility of witchcraft, yet never make accusations of witchcraft. Several examples are given in this book. G. I. Jones maintains that the Ibo, during the period in which he knew them, though they believed in witchcraft, rarely felt themselves troubled by witches (p. 321 below); misfortune tended to be traced to ghosts or to breach of ritual. Malcolm Ruel, in his account of Banyang witch beliefs, remarks that Banyang rarely accuse one another (p. 333). The same has been said of the Dinka concept of witchcraft (Lienhardt, 1951). For other peoples we have a more dynamic picture: John Middleton (1960) has described the Lugbara keeping their witch beliefs inactive during the early phases of lineage growth but bringing them out in active form as a weapon of attack when political succession and the splitting of the lineage pose problems of role-definition. The Bakweri of West Cameroon, who once seemed to be dominated by jealousy and witchcraft, steadfastly put both aside when their economic position improved so much that competition was not deemed a threat to community. Yet Edwin Ardener (below) suggests that the beliefs remained in their cosmology, ready for active service should occasion require. We shall return later to these instances of quiescent beliefs.

Where witchcraft beliefs are active in social life, there are two levels of analysis, the individual and the community.

Individuals use the accusation of witchcraft as a weapon of attack where relationships are ambiguous, and this may be for one of two reasons. It may be that the relationships are normally competitive and unregulated. Thus Peter Brown (below) gives us a glimpse of jealous dons in the Late Roman Empire and of charioteers accusing each other: the accusation is just one more form of attack and counter-attack between rival factions. Or it may be that some class of persons comes into an altogether anomalous position of advantage or disadvantage so that the umbrella of community protection is withdrawn from them. Alan Macfarlane (below) finds that dependent widows begging from their neighbours were in this position in sixteenth-century Essex villages: to suspect of witchcraft was a means of justifying the withholding of alms. The analysis closely parallels White's account of Luvale widows accused of witchcraft (1961). Female money-lenders in rural India lay themselves open to the charge of witchcraft by their defaulting debtors because of the anomalous advantage they have gained (Epstein, 1959).

We can take it that animosity against witches is always activated at this individual level. How it intervenes at the community level depends on the local organization. The accusation amounts to a denial of common bonds and responsibility. What happens when an accusation has been made depends on the state of community politics and on what pattern of relationships needs redefining at the time. For witchcraft beliefs are essentially a means of clarifying and affirming social definitions.

Taking up Tom Beidelman's challenge to consider the symbolic levels of witchcraft beliefs, I would first and foremost relate these beliefs to dominant aspects of the social structure; for whereas I join anyone who criticizes blatant errors in functionalist assumptions, I also feel that the possibilities of functional analysis have not been exhausted. Like Christian ethics, it can be defended against its critics on the ground that it has never really been tried. Take away the rigidity and crudity of the homeostatic control model and it still provides an explanatory framework based on the idea of a communication system. People are trying to control one another, albeit with small success. The idea of the witch is used to whip their own consciences or those of their friends. The witch-image is as effective as the idea of the community is strong.

The witch is an attacker and deceiver. He uses what is impure and potent to harm what is pure and helpless. The symbols of what we recognize across the globe as witchcraft all build on the theme of vulnerable internal goodness attacked by external power. But these symbols vary according to local patterns of meaning and, above all, according to variations in the social structure. Not all witches ride broomsticks, not all have bilocation, not all keep familiars, not all suck the vital juices of their victims. To interpret these variations, psychoanalytic insights should wait upon social analysis. For the psyche common to us all cannot by its structure explain our differences. The themes of inside and outside, manifest in witch symbolism, are not exhausted by the child's experience of his body and his mother's, or by universally extending these experiences as an interpretative pattern. For inside and outside can be charged with more powerful meaning by the experience of a bounded social unit.

I find it useful to note two main patterns of witch belief: (a) where the witch is an outsider; (b) where he is the internal enemy.

(a) *The witch as an outsider*

Here one would expect the imputed form of attack to be the sending of long-range missiles, weapons that intrude into the body of the victim. One would associate the belief with a very small-scale and simple form of organization. The function of the accusation is to reaffirm group boundaries and solidarity. The witch would rarely be identified. More attention would be paid to curing the victim or practising long-range ritual vengeance. But sometimes the accusation is levelled at a member of the group who is forthwith denounced as an intruder from outside. This gives us two sub-types:

(i) Witch not identified or punished
Example: Navaho 'far-away' witch
who attacks with intrusive missiles
(Kluckhohn, 1944).

(ii) Witch expelled
Example: Trio witch whose weapons
are verbal, the curse (Rivière, below).

Function of accusation (i) and (ii):
to redefine boundary.

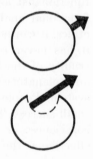

(b) *The witch as an internal enemy*

This appears with a slightly more complex form of social organization in which two or more factions are embraced within the community. But there are several ways of suspecting witches within the community. The symbols of the attack by witchcraft tend to make the body of the victim into an image of the betrayed community: its internal strength is sucked out or poisoned by someone who can get into very close contact.

(i) The witch as member of a rival faction
Examples: Shavante (Rivière, below),
Yao (Mitchell, 1956),
Ceŵa (Marwick, 1965).
Function of accusation: to
redefine faction boundaries

or realign faction hierarchy or split community. This is presumably where the accusations lodged against charioteers in the Later Roman Empire should be classed (Brown).

(ii) The witch as a dangerous deviant
Examples: dangerously powerful or rich –
Bakweri (Ardener, below),
Mysore usuress (Epstein, 1959);
dangerously demanding –
Essex in the sixteenth century
(Macfarlane, below),
Azande (Evans-Pritchard, 1937).
Function of accusation: to control deviants in the name of
community values.

(iii) The witch as an internal
enemy with outside liaisons
Example: Abelam (Forge).

Function of accusation: to
promote factional rivalry,
split community, and
redefine hierarchy.

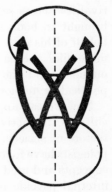

The Abelam are especially interesting in this series because of the precise play upon internal and external dangers in their symbolizing of witchcraft (see Forge, below). Each leader makes his way by powerful trade connections outside the village and is confronted by one or several rivals in his own village. Every death is interpreted as being caused by the treachery of an internal rival who has stolen some bodily rejects of the victim and sent them away to a foreign sorcerer who combines them fatally with magic paint. Paint, the essential expression of the outside, external façade and of conscious communication, has to be mixed with the leavings of the victim, especially with his or her sexual secretions. There could hardly be a more explicit statement of conscious attack from the outside upon the unconscious, unsuspecting, interior self. The Abelam leader, who is thought to have collected leavings from all the members of his own village, has them in his power as effectively as the Bakweri successful man had power over a hut full of zombies working for him. For all these people, their insides are at the mercy of the traitor.

So it would seem that the way the witch works, his sources of power, the nature of his attack on his victim, all these can be related to an image of the community and the kind of attack to which community values are subject.

Here we have part of the explanation sought by Esther Goody (below) as to why the Gonja condone the lethal magic of their menfolk and brutally punish witchcraft in women. By the Gonja system of succession, office circulates between dynastic segments. Suspicions of male witchcraft express rivalries across segment boundaries, and a male witch is not brought to book for alleged killings, since these are made on behalf of his own segment in the rival segment. The picture is more like the case of the Navaho above. The witch is an outsider, and the use of magic a mere extension of normal political aggression.

Now we can approach the difficult question of why, in some cultures, distinctive kinds of witchcraft are allocated to different sectors of society. To allow for this distinction many anthropologists have followed Evans-Pritchard's translation of Azande concepts and used 'sorcery' for black magic and 'witchcraft' for internal psychic power to harm. Whatever it may be in the language of the Azande, this usage is cumbersome in English since the verb 'to bewitch' is commonly used for either case. It is, moreover, difficult to maintain when discussing widely different cultures only some of which make the discrimination, and it is not easily translated into French.

On the face of it, a separate allocation of dangerous powers to separate social sectors is a way of insulating the latter from additional conflict. If we find that women use one kind of power and men are thought to use another, commoners one kind and royalty another, we can suppose that the distinction enters into the definition of the sexes and of political classes and expresses the separation of their roles. When we find that only one kind of witchcraft is believed, and that it is thought to be available to any man, woman, or child, we would suppose a lack of insulation, a total competitiveness running right through society. Alas, for that too facile answer! Gonja women are not normally in competition with men for chiefly office, and yet they are blamed for using the same kind of magic. Esther Goody convinces us that they would fare better by establishing  that they have no access to specifically male medicines. The Gonja case is an unusual one, and closer analysis shows that the kinds of medicine attributed to female witches differ from those used by men. In societies in which two kinds of witchcraft are recognized, from what has been said we would expect the forms of witchcraft to express something about the social situation. In the Congo, among the Bushong, men compete for political advantage in a very well-articulated system of offices: they are thought to use magic against one another in the normal course of affairs; to their women they attribute lethal psychic powers harnessed to jealousy between co-wives (Vansina, 1969). This situation is depicted in the diagram above, in which a thick arrow represents accusations between political rivals and a fine one accusations against women.

The same sociological distinction applies to the Abelam belief in two kinds of witchcraft: psychic power used by women, and external magic used by men in furtherance of acceptable political objectives. Peter Morton-Williams in a private communication tells me that the allocation of sinister psychic power and magic among the Yoruba follows the same lines. The same applies to the Azande. Trying to generalize from this I have drawn the preceding diagrams with thick and thin lines in an attempt to indicate the social niches appropriate to dangerous external magic and dangerous psychic power. I suggest, for further testing, that when the source of witchcraft power is thought to come from inside the witch, particularly from an area beyond conscious control, the social situation will correspond to type b(ii) above, where the witch is seen as an internal enemy, not as a member of a rival faction. This is well illustrated by Brian Spooner's summary of ideas about the Evil Eye (below). In Islamic communities, the stranger with evil eye, singular in appearance, apt to stare rather than to speak, in little control of his witchcraft powers, is not a member of any internal faction. His glance shoots out danger from inside him. In other words, the social symbolism of inside and outside is applied not only to the sufferings of the victim's body but to the body of the witch as well.

Now to return to the cultures in which witch beliefs are either inactive or totally absent. If witchcraft sharpens definition where roles are ill defined, we would expect it to be absent where there is no call for clear definition. Thus among people who have very sparse, irregular social contacts, the cosmos is likely to be less dominated by the idea of dangerous human beings than in a society in which human interaction is close. We would expect anthropomorphic ideas of power to dominate where humans press closely upon one another. And if these intensive social relations are well defined, we would expect the anthropomorphism of the cosmos to be regulative, to uphold the moral and social codes by just ancestral wrath; whereas, if intensive social interaction is ill defined, we would expect a witchcraft-dominated cosmos. This argument is suggested and beautifully illustrated in a little-known article by Godfrey Lienhardt, which we are glad to reproduce here. He compares the Nuer-Dinka world view, in which witchcraft matters very little, with that of the competitive, intrigue-loving Anuak.

The Nuer-Dinka social world is sparsely inhabited. Men are reliable, within the expected limits, while seasons and pastures are not. Their cosmos is dominated correspondingly by a distant (and not fully anthropomorphic) deity. On the other hand, the

Anuak, competing for the favour of capricious patrons in little village courts, have an entirely unreliable social world of palace revolutions, palace favourites, and enemy conspirators. Their cosmos is dominated by the idea of malicious human witches and vengeful ghosts.

Here, surely, are small tribal microcosms of the shift in cosmology which took place between the middle of the sixteenth and the middle of the seventeenth century among the intellectual leaders of Europe. Trevor-Roper, one of the most sociologically sensitive of our historians, has highlighted the apparent paradox that witch beliefs had the support of the most highly educated men at the end of the sixteenth century (1967, Chapter 3). Instead of being consistently and continually against a destructive superstition to which the ignorant subscribed, they upheld and ardently propagated it. Only in the mid-seventeenth century, with the triumph of the laity over the clergy, only with the waning of the ideological warfare between Christians, which inevitably nourished hate and fear, only then was it possible to entertain a modern idea of God operating in a mechanical universe stripped of angels as well as of demons. To Trevor-Roper's profound insights we may venture to offer one from the comparison of Nuer-Dinka and Anuak, for, as he insists in his introduction, the sixteenth century cannot be understood if the great witch craze is ignored. Each period must be seen as a whole. Therefore we should take his mocking account of how the minds of highly esteemed scholars were in thrall to the witchcraft cosmology along with his other chapter on the general crisis of the mid-seventeenth century (1967, pp. 46-89). Here he describes how the orderly, responsible cities of the early Renaissance were supplanted by the Renaissance princes, how the extravagance of the rulers was sustained by a system of official corruption which threatened to sap the prosperity of the people. As the seventeenth century approached, their increasing splendour heightened the intrigue-ridden atmosphere of the courts; great fortunes were made and spent, and great names met disaster. And in the wake of their patrons, even more precarious, he describes the growing train of clerics and court officials. These were the intellectuals who failed to shake themselves free of witch beliefs. These insecure competitors for patronage only too easily saw the universe as a counterpart of their society. Their cosmos was dominated, not by God as a spiritual equivalent of a mighty patron, but by other dangerous humans competing against them unfairly with demonic powers. We recognize an Anuak style of cosmology filling the minds of people in an Anuak style of social situation. The paradox of intellectual support for witchcraft beliefs is resolved, since it would be patently absurd to expect a Nuer-Dinka cosmology in an Anuak society. Only when the revolutions of the mid-century destroyed the late Renaissance states was a new kind of intellectual to emerge, proposing a new kind of cosmos to fit the new society. Trevor-Roper suggests that but for the Reformation and the Counter-reformation, which artificially sustained the earlier intellectual synthesis, the Renaissance might have led direct to the Enlightenment. The two great figures he especially singles out in this development are Erasmus and Descartes. How much more like the society of nomadic pastoralists were the immediate social worlds of these thinkers. Erasmus had his far-flung range of scholarly correspondents. He travelled as widely. The daily pressures of inescapable, long-term, face-to-face relations were not his problem. He knew the caprice of princes and cardinals but could evade its effects. In his turn, Descartes, in his chosen vocation of scholar among soldiers, lived in relative isolation. This above all seems to be the requirement for contemplating a clockwork cosmos not subject to anthropomorphic beings.

That sixteenth-century academics should have held more strongly to witch beliefs than the general run of the population is no longer a paradox. They recall their predecessors in Late Antiquity who copied out sorcery and anti-sorcery techniques and accused their rivals of maliciously destroying their eloquence. Peter Brown has found that the legacy of writings about sorcery from this period (see below) can be traced to a set of definable social niches – those of academics and insecure court officials. Charioteers also ranged themselves with competing factions and their status was also ill defined. In Late Antiquity the other areas of society enjoyed wave upon wave of expansion, so that donnish fears of persecution met no answering response in the wider population. But at the end of the sixteenth century a great period of expansion was coming to its close. The academics' experience of insecurity, human caprice, and unfair competition was widespread. Thus we may start to explain why their beliefs were not contained within their own circles but were unleashed with such destructive violence abroad.

It may be a gloomy conclusion that the people least likely to believe in witches are those whose level of social interaction is so low and so irregular that they have little need of social definition. The Mbuti pygmies neither believe in witches nor enjoy a richly organized set of cosmological ideas (Turnbull, 1966). Their case suggests that we should reject the compensatory theory of witchcraft proposed by Nadel (1952). According to this view, witchcraft is an alternative method of explaining misfortune, which substitutes for mythological or scientific explanations. But the pygmies prove that there is no reason to believe that if one declines the other will pop up in its place. People can do without explanations of misfortune. They can live in tolerance and amity and without metaphysical curiosity. The precondition is that they should be free to move away from each other whenever strains appear. The price of such a benign cosmology is a low level of organization.

But this is not the only way to control witch beliefs. Another is by means of a highly ordered system of ascribed roles. Yet if these are too inflexible, other grotesque beliefs appear. Ioan Lewis (below, p. 300), comparing beliefs in attack by identified witches with beliefs in attack by unidentified spirits, relates the latter to rigid role structures. He describes women who use their illnesses as a means of exacting more generous treatment from their husbands. This is half-way between attack and reconciliation. He indicates the role structure in which it would be an appropriate strategy – one where the weaker party in a relationship seeks, not to break it off, but to mitigate its rigour.

Where there is witchcraft there is usually witch-cleansing. One of Keith Thomas's insights into the post-Reformation increase in English witchcraft accusations points to the loss of religious techniques for dealing with personal problems: confession and absolution, exorcism and protective blessings having become unavailable, witchcraft fears were less easily controlled. In Africa in the Colonial period, while ordeals were outlawed, witchcraft was controlled to some extent by other means. Roy Willis (below) gives a brief overall perspective of these movements which arise and spread over vast areas of Africa and die

B   xxxiii

out. He compares them interestingly with millennial cults. Alison Redmayne (below) balances this long view by a close-up of the career of a particular diviner, famous still and for a long time to come in East Africa. Pilgrims came from hundreds of miles away to consult Chikanga about their families and their illnesses and to have their own names cleared of witchcraft suspicion.

Anthropologists have usually approached witchcraft from the point of view of the accuser, always assuming that the accusation is false. This has made it hard for us to interpret witchcraft confessions. Threats to practise witchcraft against an enemy, these we can interpret as empty boasting. But the idea that a person may sincerely believe himself a witch and go to a diviner to be cured of his state is difficult to understand within the terms of our analysis. This is no doubt why Barbara Ward's vivid description of witch-confession cults in Ashanti (1956) made so little impact at the time. Therefore I especially value three contributions to this volume which describe cultures in which it is impossible not to suppose oneself a potential witch. Robert Brain makes sense of the role that children play (bribed by promises of food) in maintaining the adult world view by their horrifying confessions of witchcraft. But confessions are not always extorted by bribes and threats. Julian Pitt-Rivers and Malcolm Ruel describe cosmologies, one in Central America, one in Africa, in which each human has one or several were-animal personalities attributed to him. The question at any time is only whether one's animal selves are peaceable or dangerous.

It seems that all the rich fantasy of Banyang were-animals does not normally result in witchcraft accusations. The direction in which the beliefs point is 'to personal responsibility and personal implication, and not (directly at least) to the hostility of others'. This echoes Godfrey Lienhardt's account of Dinka witchcraft (1951). Dinka witches are mainly anonymous and unidentified. The concept of the witch is none the less very explicit. It is used to remind each man of the dangers in himself:

'A man who thinks himself bewitched is interpreting what he takes to be the intentions of his neighbours towards him. If he thinks himself envied, hated or frustrated, then he readily

thinks himself bewitched. The reversible roles of the witch
and the victim in the ordeal and the Dinka's strong reluctance
to call any man a witch, seem to me to be a recognition that
a man who easily thinks himself hated is one who easily
hates, and that a man who sees others as bearing malice
towards himself is one who himself feels malice. This is the
situation of witches. . . . The night witch is an outlaw because
he embodies those appetites and passions in every man
which, if ungoverned, would destroy any moral law. The
night witch may thus be seen to correspond to the concealed
intention, the amorality and hence the opposition to shared
moral values which make community possible, of the unique
self, existing and acting as such. So although, understood in
one way, the night witch is a fantasy, understood in another
way he is indeed a reality which the Dinka know. It is
understandable that he should be associated with deformed
and imperfect creatures, who by their very nature cannot be
full members of society' (1951, pp. 317-318).

Thus Dinka witchcraft concepts represent an assessment of
normal human nature and self-appraisal. For them, hell can
lie within themselves. In witchcraft-dominated cosmologies, in
contrast, envy and malice and all evils are attributed to
abnormal neighbours. For them, hell is other people. Lévi-
Strauss has recently remarked that this famous dictum of
Sartre has no universal value but is merely an ethnographic
comment on a particular culture (1968, p. 422). Everything we
have said so far bears him out. Some cultures are prone to witch
beliefs, others are not. We are almost ready to state the pre-
disposing social structures. Where social interaction is intense
and ill defined, there we may expect to find witchcraft beliefs.
Where human relations are sparse and diffuse, or where roles
are very fully ascribed, we would not expect to find witchcraft
beliefs. After this, it is tempting to collect other instances of
witch-free cosmologies and seek to account for them by absence
of conflict, absence of competition, or absence of ambiguity in
roles or of contradiction in ultimate goals. The argument will
take us quite a long way, but not quite far enough; for the
Banyang of the West Cameroon use the idea of the witch more
as a mirror to their own conscience; and yet (unlike the Dinka)

they live with competition and ambiguity. I cherish their case as a warning against a too rigid social determinism.

The old paradigm has served its purpose. As far as witchcraft studies are concerned, the field is open to anyone who cares to enter it. Anthropologists need no longer fear the historian as 'a person whose job it is to destroy the other fellow's generalization' (Reisman, 1956, p. 79), and historians need not be warned against copying slavishly our methods and conclusions. The distinguished contributions of historians to this volume suggest raiding forays as much as tributary salutes. We can confidently expect that the full insights of the Azande book will be exploited in many other disciplines.

NOTE

1. In this introduction the term witchcraft is used to cover all forms of belief in spell-binding, fascination by evil eye, and bewitching. When it is necessary to discriminate between different kinds, descriptive phrases are used. In the substantive part of the book, however, most of the contributors have used 'witchcraft' to refer exclusively to internal psychic power to harm, and 'sorcery' for bewitching by means of external symbols, whether by spells, charms, or potions.

REFERENCES

BARNES, S. B. 1968. Paradigms, Scientific and Social. *Man* (n.s.) 4 (1): 94-102.

EPSTEIN, SCARLETT. 1959. A Sociological Analysis of Witch Beliefs in a Mysore Village. *Eastern Anthropologist* 12 (4): 234-251.

EVANS-PRITCHARD, E. E. 1933. The Intellectualist (English) Interpretation of Magic. *Bulletin of Faculty of Arts* 1 (2). Egyptian University, Cairo.

—— 1934. Lévy-Bruhl's Theory of Primitive Mentality. *Bulletin of Faculty of Arts* 2 (1). Egyptian University, Cairo.

—— 1935. Witchcraft. *Africa* 8 (4): 417-422.

—— 1937. *Witchcraft, Oracles and Magic among the Azande*. Oxford: Clarendon Press.

—— 1940a. *The Nuer: Political Institutions of a Nilotic People*. Oxford: Clarendon Press.

—— 1940b. The Nuer of the Southern Sudan. In M. Fortes & E. E. Evans-Pritchard (eds.), *African Political Systems*, pp. 272-296. London: Oxford University Press (for the International African Institute).

—— 1949. *The Sanusi of Cyrenaica*. London: Oxford University Press.

—— 1956. *Nuer Religion*. Oxford: Clarendon Press.

—— 1965. *Theories of Primitive Religion*. Oxford: Clarendon Press.

FORDE, DARYLL. 1958. Spirits, Witches and Sorcerers in the Supernatural Economy of the Yakö. *Journal of the Royal Anthropological Institute* **88** (2): 165-178.

GELLNER, E. 1958. Time and Theory in Social Anthropology. *Mind* **67** (266): 182-202.

GLUCKMAN, M. 1955. *Custom and Conflict in Africa*. Oxford: Blackwell.

KLUCKHOHN, CLYDE. 1944. *Navaho Witchcraft*. Peabody Museum Papers, Harvard University, 22 (no. 2).

KUHN, T. S. 1962. *The Structure of Scientific Revolutions*. Chicago: University of Chicago Press.

LÉVI-STRAUSS, C. 1968. *L'Origine des manières de table. Mythologiques III*. Paris: Plon.

LIENHARDT, R. G. 1951. Some Notions of Witchcraft among the Dinka. *Africa* **21** (4): 303-318.

MARWICK, M. G. 1952. The Social Context of Ceŵa Witch Beliefs. *Africa* **22** (2): 120-135, (3): 215-233.

—— 1965. *Sorcery in its Social Setting: A Study of the Northern Rhodesian Ceŵa*. Manchester: Manchester University Press.

MAYER, PHILIP. 1954. Witches. Inaugural Lecture, Rhodes University, Grahamstown.

MIDDLETON, JOHN. 1960. *Lugbara Religion*. London: Oxford University Press (for the International African Institute).

MITCHELL, CLYDE. 1956. *The Yao Village: A Study in the Social Structure of a Nyasaland Tribe*. Manchester: Manchester University Press.

—— 1965. The Meaning in Misfortune for Urban Africans. In M. Fortes & G. Dieterlen (eds.), *African Systems of Thought*. London: Oxford University Press (for the International African Institute).

NADEL, S. F. 1952. Witchcraft in Four African Societies: An Essay in Comparison. *American Anthropologist* **54** (1): 18-29.

REISMAN, DAVID. 1956. *Constraint and Variety in American Education*. Lincoln, Neb.: University of Nebraska Press.

RICHARDS, A. I. 1935. A Modern Movement of Witchfinders. *Africa* **8** (4): 448-461.

TREVOR-ROPER, H. 1967. *Religion, the Reformation, and Social Change*. London: Macmillan.

TURNBULL, COLIN M. 1966. *Wayward Servants*. London: Eyre & Spottiswoode.

TURNER, V. W. 1954. *Schism and Continuity in an African Society: A Study of Ndembu Village Life*. Manchester: Manchester University Press.

—— 1964. Witchcraft and Sorcery: Taxonomy versus Dynamics. *Africa* **34** (4): 314-325.

VANSINA, J. 1969. The Poison Ordeal of the Bushong. In P. M. Kaberry & M. Douglas (eds.), *Man in Africa*. London: Tavistock Publications.

WARD, BARBARA. 1956. Some Observations on Religious Cults in Ashanti. *Africa* **26** (1): 47-60.

WHITE, C. M. W. 1961. *Elements in Luvale Beliefs and Rituals*. Manchester: Manchester University Press (for the Rhodes-Livingstone Institute).

WILSON, BRYAN R. (ed.). 1967. *Patterns of Sectarianism*. London: Heinemann.

WILSON, GODFREY & MONICA. 1945. *The Analysis of Social Change. Based on Observations in Central Africa*. Cambridge: Cambridge University Press.

© Mary Douglas 1970

PART I

The Context of Witchcraft in Europe

Norman Cohn

The Myth of Satan and his Human Servants

This paper is concerned with a fantasy and the part it has played in European history. The fantasy is that there exists a category of human beings that is pledged to the service of Satan; a sect that worships Satan in secret conventicles and, on Satan's behalf, wages relentless war against Christendom and against individual Christians. At one time in the Middle Ages this fantasy became attached to certain heretical sects, and helped to legitimate and intensify their persecution. A couple of centuries later it gave the traditional witchcraft beliefs of Europe a twist which turned them into something new and strange – something quite different from, and vastly more lethal than, the witchcraft beliefs that anthropologists find and study in primitive societies today. And the fantasy has also frequently been attached to the Jews – and not only in far-off times but in the late nineteenth and early twentieth centuries, when it helped to prepare the way for the secular demonology of the Nazis. It is a long story but a perfectly coherent one, and it is excellently documented.

At the heart of the fantasy is the figure of Satan himself; and the history of this figure is established. As the great opponent of God and the supreme symbol of evil, Satan is less ancient than might be supposed. In the Old Testament he does not appear at all in that capacity. For the early Hebrews Yahveh was a tribal god; they thought of the gods of the neighbouring peoples as antagonistic to them and to Yahveh, and they felt no need for any more grandiose embodiment of evil. Later, of course, the tribal religion developed into a monotheism; but then the monotheism is so absolute, the omnipotence and omnipresence of God are so constantly affirmed, that the powers of evil seem insignificant by comparison. In all the books of the Old Testament these powers are in fact only hinted at in a few uncoordinated references. We are accustomed to regard the serpent, who deceived Eve in the Garden of Eden, as being Satan in disguise; but there is no warrant for this in the text, where the serpent is shown as being one of God's creatures, and therefore good, and is cursed only after, and because of, its disastrous intervention. Nor is there anything in the Old Testament or in the Gospels to warrant such an identification. Indeed, the first clear indication that the tempter in Paradise was Satan comes in non-canonical works from the first century after Christ.

For every monotheism the existence of evil constitutes, potentially, a problem: why, after all, should an omnipotent god tolerate suffering and evil-doing in his creation? But not every monotheism gives equal attention to the problem, and the religion of the ancient Hebrews seems to have given very little. Almost throughout the Old Testament, God is shown as responsible for all happenings, good and evil: 'I form the light, and create darkness: I make peace and create evil: I the Lord do all these things' (Isaiah 45:7). Misfortunes are simply punishments for those who transgress God's commandments; and for the fact that men do so transgress, no metaphysical explanation is offered. The Satan who appears in the prologue to the Book of Job has none of the functions that were later to be attributed to the Devil; on the contrary, he is shown as a courtier in the court of God, and his achievement is that he induces God himself to inflict suffering on a blameless man. To find any hint of a power systematically working against God one has to turn to the story of the numbering of Israel and Judah: 2 Samuel 24 tells how the Lord tempted David to carry out a census of the people, and then punished him for doing so by sending a plague to reduce their numbers; after which the Lord himself 'repented him of the evil'. The same story is told in 1 Chronicles 21, and in exactly the same words – except that here the responsibility for tempting David is transferred from God to Satan. This seems to be the one instance in the whole of the Old Testament that in any way suggests that Satan exists as a principle of evil, a power that tempts men to sin against God.

The Book of Chronicles is probably no older than the third century BC. And when one turns to the body of non-canonical apocalyptic literature which was produced by Jews between the second century before and the first century after Christ, one finds a fully developed demonology. Here, in some of the so-called Apocrypha and in some of the Dead Sea Scrolls, we learn for the first time how some of the angels rebelled against God and were cast out of heaven. To support this belief it was customary to invoke an obscure passage in Genesis 6, which tells how the sons of God took the daughters of men as wives, and produced a progeny of mighty men. Originally this passage probably reflected a popular legend about giants; and the apocryphal work known as 1 Enoch tells how the giants, in turn, bred evil spirits or demons who are still on earth, invisible and incorporeal, yet always at work to harm and destroy and kill. Moreover, these spirits are under the command of the chief of the fallen angels, who is sometimes called Mastema, sometimes Belial or Beliar, and sometimes Satan. This figure is imagined as a true adversary of God, and history and time will end when God finally defeats him.

Was the emergence of this complicated demonology due to Iranian influence? There certainly is a striking resemblance between these Jewish ideas and the tenets of Iranian religion, with which the Jews had been in contact ever since the Babylonian exile. For whatever may have been taught by Zoroaster himself (probably in the fifth century BC), the later Mazdean religion shows the universe as a battlefield between two spirits, Ahura Mazda (Ormazd), who is good, and Angra Mainyu (Ahriman), who is evil. Angra Mainyu, or Ahriman, commands a host of demons who spread sin, death, disease, and every kind of affliction among the human inhabitants of this earth. These beings are thought of almost as persons: they are marshalled in a hierarchical order, and their leader is a personification of aggressive evil; together they are incessantly at work to ruin the ordered universe which Ormazd struggles to uphold. But at the end of time Ormazd and the forces of good will triumph, and Ahriman will be cast out of the transfigured creation and will never be able to enter it again. Although it cannot be proved that these Mazdean teachings were responsible for the dramatic 'promotion of Satan' within Judaism, it seems unlikely that they had no part in it at all.

However that may be, Judaism at the time of Jesus had an elaborate demonology; and much of this was taken over by the new religion which was to become Christianity. In the Gospels it is taken for granted not only that Satan and his hosts of demons exist, but that they are more active than ever before, as though the presence of Jesus were stimulating them to a desperate counter-attack. We are told that Satan was the 'Lord of this world' until the coming of Jesus; now doomed to defeat, he will be finally cast down at the Second Coming and the Last Judgement. Meanwhile he is engaged in a desperate struggle to hinder the spread of the new religion. According to St Paul, Satan and the demonic hosts occupy the dark spaces of the heavens, and thence wage war upon the Christians. This is, in fact, the original meaning of the famous phrase 'spiritual wickedness in high places' (Ephesians 6:11, 2:2).

But it is one thing to speak of Satan and his demons and to point to the evil they are bringing about in this world, and it is quite another thing to argue that they have human allies. This idea – that Satan has his servants among living men and women – has never had any place in the central tradition of Judaism, but it is to be found in some of the apocryphal books, in some of the Dead Sea Scrolls, and in certain passages of the New Testament. Already in the second century BC the *Testament of Levi* says: 'Choose for yourselves either the light or the darkness, either the law of the Lord or the works of Beliar'[1] – that is, of Satan. About the time of Jesus, the Dead Sea sect were looking forward to a forty years' war in which they, 'the sons of light', would, with the aid of the celestial hosts, exterminate the heathen, whom they call 'the sons of darkness' or 'the sons of Belial'. In the Gospels those who plot against Jesus are called 'sons of the Devil' (John 8:44). The historical background of these utterances is known. In all these cases we find a small sect of intensely religious Jews, living in expectation of the end of this imperfect world and the beginning of the messianic age. In their eyes the sons of Satan, or Belial, or the Devil are those who deny that great consummation – the Romans, or the heathen in general, or the Jews of traditionalist outlook, or indeed all those who do not share their own apocalyptic faith. But in later centuries the idea of Satan's servants was to undergo a spectacular development and to serve very different purposes.

For the Fathers of the early Church the deities of the pagan

world were demons, and those who worshipped them were really
serving the purposes of Satan. Thus Tertullian writes: 'All the
operations of the demons tend to the ruination of man. . . .
Demons . . . so blind the souls of men that they themselves come
to be worshipped, and that sacrifices are offered to their statues
. . .'[2] Moreover, if a Christian ventured to criticize new practices
or beliefs, after they had received the official sanction of the
Church, this, too, must have been instigated by a pagan diety,
operating as a demon. When a monk called Vigilantius wrote
against the growing cult of the bones of the martyrs, St Jerome
retorted:

> 'The unclean spirit who makes you write these things has
> often been tormented by this humble dust [of the bones of
> the martyrs]. . . . Here is my advice to you. Go into the
> basilicas of the martyrs, and you will be cured. . . . Then you
> will confess, what you now deny, that it is Mercury who speaks
> through the mouth of Vigilantius.'[3]

At the same time, the attitude to magical practices changed
radically. In the pagan world such practices had been judged
according to the intention behind them: for instance, divination, or the foretelling of future events, was no offence, but
harmful sorcery was a crime under civil law. But the Fathers,
while convinced that magicians and sorcerers could indeed do
supernatural things, were also convinced that these powers
came from the old pagan gods. Any practice of magic – even
beneficent magic – was therefore regarded as a form of demon-
worship and a grave religious transgression, irrespective of
whether or not it was a civil crime. In these ways the teachings
of the early Church prepared the way for the great 'demoniza-
tion' of human beings that was to take place, many centuries
later, in Western Europe.

Yet this does not mean that the Church that gradually
christianized the Germanic and Celtic peoples was a fanatical
institution. The conversion of Europe was only rarely pursued
by means of fire and sword; in the main it was achieved by
preaching missionaries. Pagan observances were not always
ruthlessly suppressed; many were even incorporated, with
only the most superficial modification, into the practice of
the Church. In such matters the leaders of the Church often

gave evidence of much tolerance and common sense. This was true even of their attitude to sorcery. Like everybody else they believed in the possibility and reality of sorcery, but they certainly did not encourage mass persecution of suspected sorcerers.

But around the year 1100 a great change began to make itself felt. Up to the eleventh century there were no heretical sects in the area of Western Christendom, but from then onwards they began to spread along the trade routes from the Balkans and to proliferate in the developing urban civilizations of northern Italy, France, and the Rhine valley; finding their adherents first among the nobles and the clergy, and then among the merchants and artisans. The authorities, both ecclesiastical and secular, reacted sharply to these signs of organized dissent. The easy-going pragmatism of earlier centuries gave place to a growing intolerance and rigidity in matters of faith. Heretics were burned, but that was not enough; very soon they were being defamed as well. It was in the context of this struggle against heresy that, for the first time in Western Europe, groups of human beings were described as Satan-worshippers.

In 1022, a number of canons of the cathedral at Orléans were found guilty of heresy and burned. We know what their heresy really consisted in: they denied that the body and blood of Christ are really present in the eucharist, they denied that baptism with water has any supernatural efficacy, they regarded it as meaningless to invoke the intercession of the saints. Instead, they themselves claimed to receive the holy spirit through the laying-on of hands, and they also talked much of a certain 'heavenly food'. The reference to 'heavenly food' was sufficient to set imaginations working and tongues wagging. A contemporary chronicler, Adhémar de Chabannes, describes how these men were deceived by an unlettered layman, who gave them the ashes of dead children to eat and so bound them to his sect. Once they were initiated, the Devil would appear to them, sometimes as a Negro and sometimes in the guise of an angel of light. He would command them to deny Christ in their hearts, even while pretending publicly to be true followers of Christ. He would also instruct them to abandon themselves in secret to every kind of vice. Around the year 1100 this description was further elaborated by a monk of Chartres. Looking back to the incident of 1022, he says:

> 'They came together at night, each carrying a light. The demons were invoked with particular formulae, and appeared in the guise of animals. Thereupon the lights were extinguished, and fornication and incest followed. The children born as a result of this were burned and their ashes were treasured like a holy relic. These ashes had such diabolic power that anyone who tasted even the smallest bit of them was irrevocably bound to the sect. . . .'[4]

There was still one step to take: heretics had to be shown not simply as associated with demons but as actually worshipping Satan. This was accomplished by the end of the twelfth century. About 1190, the English chronicler Walter Map, or Mapes, who lived much in France, described the meetings of heretics which were supposed to be taking place in various French provinces, notably Aquitaine and Burgundy. He tells how a huge black cat would descend upon the meeting, using a rope suspended from the ceiling; at once the lights would be extinguished and everyone would hurry to adore the cat – which was, of course, Satan – by kissing it in an obscene manner. Henceforth this notion of the physical adoration of an embodied Satan was to be an integral part of the popular stereotype of the heretic. In 1233, Pope Gregory IX himself issued a bull describing how at heretical assemblies in Germany Satan would appear as a black cat, or as a frog or toad, or as a furry man; and how the company would give him obscene kisses and then embark on perverted orgies.

Yet, even after the Pope's pronouncement, another seventy years were to pass before such accusations figured in an actual trial – and then it was a trial not of real heretics but of the Knights Templars of France. The Knights Templars were an Order of warrior monks, which for two centuries fought to safeguard the conquests achieved by the crusades in the Near East. But the Order also became enormously wealthy, with estates and strongholds in every country from Armenia to Ireland. Moreover, the Templars acted as international financiers and bankers, with whom kings and popes deposited their revenues and from whom, on occasion, they would borrow money. Their stronghold in Paris became the centre of the world's money-market. And the privileges that they had acquired from kings and popes made them, in France at least, a state within a state. In 1307 the King of France, Philip IV, who had already despoiled and expelled the Jews and the Lombard bankers, decided to destroy the French Templars and to appropriate their wealth. The Templars were arrested and tortured so cruelly that many died under the torture. But others 'confessed'. They declared that, on their initiation into the Order, they had renounced Christ and spat upon the crucifix; that, under the statute law of the Order, they had taken part in nocturnal assemblies where the Devil was worshipped in the form of a black cat, or else as an idol called Baphomet (doubtless a corruption of Mahomet); that these assemblies involved sexual orgies, sometimes homosexual, sometimes with demons in the guise of women; that any children born were roasted, and their fat smeared on the idol Baphomet. On the strength of these accusations the Order of Knights Templars was dissolved, dozens of Templars were burned, and the King of France was relieved of some of his financial embarrassments.

In all this one hears relatively little of the professional hunters of heretics, the papal inquisitors. The Inquisition had been founded in 1230, and it was active throughout the thirteenth century, especially against the so-called Albigensian or Catharist sects of southern France. We possess the manuals which certain inquisitors wrote for the guidance of their fellows; we also possess the records of many hundreds of interrogations – and before the trial of the Templars they very seldom even mention Satan-worship. This does not mean that the inquisitors were lenient in their dealings with heretics. They employed torture to extract confessions, and those who confessed were handed over to the secular arm for punishment. A common punishment was imprisonment for life, in solitary confinement, on a diet of bread and water; while impenitent or relapsed heretics were invariably burned. But however ruthless they might be, most inquisitors were genuinely concerned to establish what the heretics really believed and did, and to get them condemned for that. The first time they began to pay serious attention to Satan-worship was a generation after the affair of the Templars. This was the moment, around 1335, when they began to concern themselves with witchcraft as well as with heresy.

Some anthropologists, studying primitive peoples of today, have found two kinds of belief about sorcery and witchcraft; and they have found them in the most diverse societies, which have never had any contact whatsoever with one another. On the one hand there is the belief in maleficent sorcery: the belief that people can, by magical means, cause harm to those they hate – whether by making them fall ill, or by killing them, or by harming their cattle or crops. On the other hand there is the belief in the night-witch: the belief that certain people fly through the air at night, assemble in distant places, and there indulge in cannibal feasts, usually with babies as their favourite victims. And these beliefs sometimes express themselves in action: in many societies individuals who are suspected of practising maleficent sorcery, or of being night-witches, or of both, are killed.

Now in Europe, too, these beliefs formed part of the body of traditional folk-belief; they were familiar to Graeco-Roman antiquity and to the Germanic and Celtic peoples of pre-Christian times, and they were still current in the Middle Ages. And in Europe, too, a few individuals in a town or village would occasionally be killed for practising sorcery or for being witches.

What the inquisitors did was to interpret these age-old popular beliefs in terms of Satan-worship. In doing so they created the stereotype of the witch as a man or woman who has voluntarily entered into Satan's service, and who has received in exchange the power to harm human beings in their property or their health or their lives. They also created the fantasy of the witches' sabbat: what some chroniclers had hitherto imputed to heretics – that they attended secret nocturnal assemblies, presided over by Satan, where sexual orgies were performed and babies roasted and eaten – was now officially imputed to witches; with the addition that, instead of going to these assemblies on foot, they flew to them on an animal or a broomstick. In this way the inquisitors built up a fantasy of a mysterious sect, endowed with supernatural powers, which at Satan's bidding was waging incessant war on Christians and on Christendom.

This sect was wholly imaginary. Whereas heretical sects did at least exist, there was no sect of witches. That is not to deny

11

that some individuals attempted various forms of sorcery – they certainly did; but they were not an organized body, they did not fly through the air, and they did not worship Satan. The sect of witches was a fantasy. To make it seem a reality, the inquisitors tortured people until they not only confessed that they themselves attended the sabbat but denounced others for attending it. In this way they created the preconditions for the great witch-hunt which was to sweep large areas of Continental Europe long after the Inquisition had ceased to function there. For the persecution that was begun by the Inquisition around 1335 reached its height much later, in the sixteenth and seventeenth centuries; by which time the persecutors were mostly secular lawyers, some Catholic, some Lutheran, some Calvinist. And at its height it was a vast holocaust; nobody knows how many people perished at the stake during those two centuries, but responsible estimates vary from 200,000 to a million.

How is one to relate this lurid picture to the relatively undramatic scene described by Mr Thomas and Dr Macfarlane in their papers on English witchcraft (pp. 47-99 below)? Why this great massacre on the Continent, while in England only a few hundreds were executed? The answer, I suggest, is that while English and Continental witchcraft share a common substructure, Continental witchcraft at the height of the great persecution possessed a superstructure that was all its own. The substructure consisted of the tensions, anxieties, and resentments of village life, expressed in terms of maleficent sorcery; and with certain minor variations these seem to have been much the same from Essex to Lorraine or Bavaria. The superstructure consisted of the myth of the Satanic set of witches, with the sabbat as its core. And whereas these fantasies never obtained official sanction or juridical expression in England, they did obtain them in certain Continental countries, notably France, Germany, and Switzerland.

In these countries, too, magistrates found, at the popular level, plenty of suspicions and accusations concerning maleficent sorcery. Where they differed from their English counterparts is in the extent to which they elaborated and distorted what they found, to fit their own demonological preconceptions. They were able to do this because, like the Inquisitors before them, they could use torture – something that was not permitted by the common law of England. And it is no doubt owing to this circumstance that, whereas English witches were almost all married women or widows, and of low social status, on the Continent anyone might be a witch – man, woman, or child, and of any status. For, forced by torture to name those whom she had seen at the sabbat, an obscure woman was as likely to name the town mayor and councillors and all their families as she was to name other obscure women. Wherever the prosecution of individuals turned into mass persecution one finds the myth of the Satanic sect at work, justifying torture, which in turn validated the myth.

By the eighteenth century the great European witch-hunt was over. Although from time to time, in remote and backward areas, the populace would still hunt down and kill individuals suspected of maleficent sorcery, the idea of a Satanic sect of witches had lost its appeal. But the myth of Satan's servants was not dead, and in the nineteenth century it reappeared in a new context, as the myth of the Jewish world-conspiracy. It is usual to think of the antisemitic obsession of the Nazis as being simply a particularly virulent form of racism, but this belief is mistaken. At the heart of Hitler's antisemitism is the fantasy that, for thousands of years, all Jews, everywhere, have been united in a ceaseless endeavour to undermine, ruin, and then dominate the rest of humanity. And although in Hitler's mind and in Nazi ideology this fantasy is dressed up in the pseudo-scientific garb of racism, the fantasy itself stems from quite another source.

During the early Middle Ages there was little serious propaganda against the Jewish religion, and Christians and Jews generally lived peacefully side by side. But at the time when heretics came to be regarded as servants of Satan – that is to say, around the year 1100 – a similar fate befell the Jews. It was in the twelfth century that Jews were for the first time accused of such things as ritually murdering Christian children, torturing the consecrated wafer, poisoning the wells. Above all, people began to say that Jews worshipped Satan and that Satan in return rewarded them by making them collectively masters of black magic. From this it followed that, however helpless individual Jews might seem, Jews collectively were regarded as possessing limitless powers for evil. It is true that the higher ecclesiastical authorities – the popes and bishops – had no time at all for these fabrications and fantasies, and indeed frequently and emphatically condemned them. But the lower clergy continued to propagate them, century after century, and in the end this decisively influenced the attitude of the laity. Over large areas of Europe the period from the twelfth to the eighteenth century was, for the Jews, a long martyrdom, during which they became what they had never been in the early Middle Ages: a wholly alien people within Christendom, compulsorily restricted to the most sordid trades, regarding the Gentile world with bitterness. And in the eyes of many Christians these strange creatures became demons in human form, endowed with uncanny and infinitely sinister powers.

The emancipation of the Jews began with the French Revolution; and in the course of the nineteenth century Jews were relieved of their legal disabilities in one country after another in Western and Central Europe. But in every country the prospect of Jewish emancipation produced a wave of panic. Partly, no doubt, this reaction was stimulated by the fact that in certain fields – such as banking, journalism, and radical politics – Jews quickly achieved an influence quite out of proportion to their numbers. But the roots of the panic lay much deeper. To see just where it lay, one has only to consider the book that became the fountainhead of modern, political antisemitism: *Le Juif, le judaïsme et la judaïsation des peuples chrétiens*, by Gougenot des Mousseaux, published in 1869.

Des Mousseaux was convinced that the world is in the grip of a mysterious body of Satan-worshippers, whom he calls 'Kabbalistic Jews'. He imagined that there existed a secret demonic religion, a systematic cult of evil which had been established by the Devil at the very beginning of the world. The grand masters of the cult were Jews, whom des Mousseaux calls 'the representatives on earth of the spirits of darkness'; and those who had helped the Jews in spreading the reign of the Devil throughout the world included the medieval heretics, the Templars, and, more recently, the Freemasons. The cult itself centred on the worship of Satan, symbolized by a serpent and the phallus; and its ritual consisted of erotic orgies of the wildest kind, interspersed with episodes when Jews murdered Christian

14

children in order to use their blood for magical purposes. The book claimed to unmask a Jewish plot to dominate the whole world through control of the banks, the press, and the political parties – and this, too, was supposed to be done on Satan's behalf and with Satan's help.

It was out of these frankly demonological fantasies that there emerged the *Protocols of the Elders of Zion*, the famous antisemitic forgery which was to obsess the mind of Adolf Hitler. Indeed, the man who launched the *Protocols* upon the world was a half-crazy Russian pseudo-mystic, Sergey Nilus; and the book in which he first printed them is a religious tract about the Second Coming of Christ and the final struggle against the demonic hosts. That was as late as 1905. At this point the myth of Satan and his human servants finally expired, but it left a deadly legacy. A generation later the Nazis were using the *Protocols* in a purely secular context, stripped of all overtly demonic associations, as a weapon in their political struggles and, eventually, as a warrant for the near-extermination of Europe's Jews.

The myth of Satan and his human servants has indeed played an extraordinary part in European history. Viewed sociologically, this story shows at least one thing: that one and the same myth can be made to serve a variety of purposes and can fulfil a variety of functions. The medieval sects were real groups and real opponents of the Church; the clergy who applied the myth to them were attacking potential rivals. The Templars also formed a real group, but one that desired only to serve the Church; the King of France who accused them of worshipping Satan was motivated simply by financial need or greed. The so-called witches, on the other hand, were not a real group; this is a case where the myth created, in the imagination of persecutors and populace, a dangerous organization which in reality did not exist at all. Just how this came about is still a matter that needs careful investigation. As for the Jews, the myth has affected their fate at various times and in various ways. A very real group, they were, nevertheless, not regarded as a dangerous one until the eleventh century, when the Church found itself threatened by heresy. At that point the myth was applied to them, and gradually turned them into a pariah-group. Many centuries later, as they were emerging from this situation

Norman Cohn

to rejoin the mainstream of European life, the myth was used again as a means of rejecting them.

It is a curiously complex story, but one generalization at least seems permissible. During some nine centuries in the history of Europe, to accuse people of being Satan's servants was a very effective way of releasing huge potentials of hatred, and of enabling people to support and engage in one-sided killing without qualms of conscience.

NOTES

1. Charles, Vol. II, p. 315.
2. Tertullian, cap. XXII, cols. 405-407.
3. Jerome, col. 348.
4. Paul, monk of Chartres, p. 112.

REFERENCES

CHARLES, R. H. 1913. *The Apocrypha and Pseudepigrapha of the Old Testament*, Vol. II. Oxford: Clarendon Press.
DES MOUSSEAUX, GOUGENOT. 1869. *Le Juif, le judaïsme et la judaïsation des peuples chrétiens*. Paris.
JEROME. Liber contra Vigilantium. In Migne, *Patrologiae cursus completus*. Latin series, Tom. XXII. Paris, 1845.
PAUL (Monk of Chartres). Liber Aganonis. In M. Guérard (ed.), *Cartulaire de l'abbaye de Saint-Père de Chartres*, Tom. I. Paris, 1840.
TERTULLIAN. Apologeticus. In Migne, *Patrologiae cursus completus*. Latin series, Tom. I. Paris, 1844.

© Norman Cohn, 1970

2

Peter Brown

Sorcery, Demons, and the Rise of Christianity from Late Antiquity into the Middle Ages

My concern, in this paper, is to re-examine a small facet of the religious history of the Late Antique period, and to show how the historian may be helped by an extensive literature by social anthropologists on the problems of sorcery and spirit-possession.

The need to link disciplines is frequently expressed among us. Discussion of this need takes place in an atmosphere, however, that suggests the observation of an African chieftain on a neighbouring tribe: 'They are our enemies. We marry them.' Matchmaking should be a cautious process. The would-be linker of disciplines must be prepared 'to sigh throughout the long delays of courtship': in attempts to link social and religious history, classical and theological studies, I have observed that the unwary, or the precipitate, suitor has often ended up with the elderly, ugly daughter. I can only say that I have tried to keep abreast of a recent literature in social anthropology which, beginning with Professor Evans-Pritchard's *Witchcraft, Oracles and Magic among the Azande* of 1937, represents one of the most remarkable attempts to study, with precision and sophistication, an aspect of the role of the irrational in society.

To look again, with an insight schooled on other human disciplines, at the religious history of the Late Antique world is one of the most urgent tasks facing the ancient and the medieval historian. We have long possessed an overwhelming erudition on the religious ideas of the period from AD 200 to 600. We have begun to refine our views on the structure and functioning of Late Roman society. Yet, somehow, the nexus between the religious and the social evolution of Late Antiquity escapes us: worse still, it is a gap papered over, in most accounts, by textbook rhetoric.

17

I

My first debt to the social anthropologists is that they have helped me to delimit the field of my inquiry. In his *Witchcraft, Oracles and Magic*, Evans-Pritchard has shown how fruitfully sorcery can be treated as 'a function of personal relations' and 'a function of situations of misfortune'.[1] Sorcery, therefore, need not be treated in isolation. It is not an unswept corner of odd beliefs surrounding unsavoury practices: the anthropologists have shown that belief in sorcery is an element in the way in which men have frequently attempted to conceptualize their social relationships and to relate themselves to the problem of evil.

The historian of sorcery in Late Antiquity begins, however, where the anthropologist leaves off. The anthropologist meets beliefs and accusations surrounding the human figure of the sorcerer. He has a clear idea of how such a man fits in among his fellows. The most interesting advances in this aspect of his discipline have been connected with those insights into the structure of a society which may be elicited from the study of the witch and the sorcerer in it. The rites of the sorcerer are usually hidden from him.[2] By contrast, the historian makes his first acquaintance with this subject in the form of a vast collection of texts, principally magical papyri[3] and leaden cursing-tablets,[4] that minutely illustrate the 'technology' of sorcery in the ancient world. These highly circumstantial descriptions of a divine and demonic society would present any anthropologist interested in possible correlations between the structure of the spirit-world and social change with an *embarras de richesses*: perhaps he would be less disturbed than many students of ancient religion by the appearance of 'Jesus great god of the Hebrews' on a spell, hardened as he is by phenomena such as the spirit which 'appeared in the curious guise of a small motor-car'.[5]

But in such manuals of the suprahuman world, the human agent is lost to view. One meets sorcery as a *belief*, not as an event in society. As a result, the study of sorcery in Late Antiquity – as, indeed, in early Medieval Islam and in the Medieval and Renaissance periods – has been engulfed in the study of religion and of the occult sciences.[6] More particularly, the topic has been harnessed to the problem of the 'decadence' of the ancient world. The occult sciences have been studied as marking the nadir of the downward curve of Greek scientific rationalism;[7] the rigmaroles of Gnostic demons, as a nadir in the decline of traditional Graeco-Roman religion;[8] and the widespread opinion of historians, that a 'terror of magic' was endemic in the fourth century AD, is held to illustrate a nadir in the morale and culture of the Roman governing classes.[9] It is assumed, therefore, that the 'decadence' of the Later Roman Empire is illustrated by a sharp increase in sorcery beliefs. The reasons usually given are of studious generality: the general misery and insecurity of the period; the confusion and decay of traditional religions; and, more specifically, for the fourth century AD, the rise to power in the Roman state of a class of 'semi-Christians', whose new faith in Christ was overshadowed by a superstitious fear of demons.[10]

To comment on these explanations briefly: In the first case, accusations against sorcerers occur in precisely those areas and classes which we know to have been the most effectively sheltered from brutal dislocation – the senatorial aristocracy, for instance, and the professors of the great Mediterranean cities. It was in just such stable and well-oriented groups that certain forms of misfortune (see below, p. 30) were explained by pinning blame on individuals. Public and continuous misfortune, by contrast, was habitually explained, in this age of bitter confessional hatreds, by the anger of the gods or of God at the existence of dissenting religious groups – Christians, pagans, or heretics.[11]

As for the last, it is an inverted anachronism common among historians of the Later Roman period to project an undifferentiated force of 'superstition' into the safe remoteness of the fourth century, and to endow this force with far greater potency in directing men's behaviour than can be observed among the *hommes moyens sensuels* of any contemporary society that still believes in suprahuman sanctions and dangers. Suffice to say that we have detailed descriptions of those emperors who followed up sorcery accusations, from the pen of a pagan, Ammianus Marcellinus. Now, Ammianus describes the Christian emperor Constantius II as showing 'an old wives' superstition' only when discussing the *minutiae* of the Christian Trinity;[12] but, faced by sorcery and illicit divination, he is judged for the

19

way he acted strictly as a politician, and not as a religious man – he was 'suspicious and over-precise'.[13] Taken altogether, the purges that followed accusations of sorcery and illicit divination point, not to any increase in a 'terror of magic', but to a more precise, if more prosaic, development – to an increase in the zeal and efficacy of the emperor's servants, and their greater ability to override the vested interests of the traditional aristocracies of the Empire, whether to collect taxes or to chastise the black arts.

Thus it is far from certain that there was any absolute increase in fear of sorcery or in sorcery practices in the Late Roman period. Nor is it certain that the religious and intellectual changes of Late Antiquity greatly changed the basic attitudes of ancient men to sorcery: in the first century AD, for instance, Pliny the Elder had already taken for granted that 'there is no one who is not afraid of becoming the object of lethal spells' (*Historia Naturalis*, XXVIII, 4, 9). All that can be said is that, in the fourth century AD, we happen to know more about sorcery because we are told more about it, in accounts of the politics of the Imperial court and in the careers of professors. We meet sorcery, therefore, in its *social* context.

My paper must take this fact as its starting-point. I shall have to ask the historian of the religious ideas of Late Antiquity to suspend belief for a moment. Sorcery accusations in Late Roman sources, I would suggest, need not be used exclusively to illustrate the regrettable ramifications of superstition in a 'post-classical' world: they point to social phenomena. My thesis, in the first part of this paper, is that a precise *malaise* in the structure of the governing classes of the Roman Empire (especially in its eastern, Greek-speaking half) forced the ubiquitous sorcery beliefs of ancient man to a flash-point of accusations in the mid-fourth century AD. The incidence of these accusations synchronizes with changes within the structure of the governing class: thus they reach a peak at a time of maximum uncertainty and conflict in the 'new' society of the mid-fourth century; they are substantially reduced as occasions for conflict and uncertainty are progressively restricted by a growth of political and social stability, whose results are best documented for the sixth century AD – the age of Justinian and of the first 'barbarian' kingdoms in the West.

The *malaise* to which I refer cannot be seized through the
conventional catalogue of catastrophes attending the fall of
the Roman Empire in the West, still less by laments on the
decline of Greek rationalism, but by an analysis of the points
of uncertainty and conflict in the structure of the governing
classes of the Empire. These strong and weak points can be
grasped most easily by contrasting the views of two schools of
modern social historians, describing the society of the fourth,
fifth, and sixth centuries AD.[14] One school saw in this period an
increase in 'vested' power and social rigidity: an oriental
despotism; an emperor raised above his subjects by theocratic
doctrines of divine right; his authority rendered impersonal by an
elaborate court ceremonial; his person surrounded by eunuchs;
Late Roman society, as a whole, stagnant and hierarchical –
divided into rigid castes with little hope of personal advancement, its culture directed towards producing a 'mandarinate' of
noblemen, 'reared above the common lot of men', by an archaic
literary language. The other, more recent, view has stressed the
fact that many individuals in this society enjoyed a remarkable
degree of social fluidity; that the emperor was open to constant
symbiosis with and impingement from a diffuse governing class,
ranging from traditional great landowners to Christian bishops;
that the educational system of this society was an area excep-
tionally favourable to social mobility; and that its dominant
religion, Christianity, had seeped triumphantly upwards, at
just this time, from the lower-middle classes into a court aristocracy of *parvenus*.

I would suggest that, far from the one view replacing the
other, we should work with both. Late Roman society was
dominated by the problem of the conflict between change and
stability in a traditional society.

It is here that we find a situation which has been observed
both to foster sorcery accusations and to offer scope for resort
to sorcery. This is when *two systems of power* are sensed to clash
within the one society. On the one hand, there is *articulate*
power, power defined and agreed upon by everyone (and
especially by its holders!): authority vested in precise persons;
admiration and success gained by recognized channels. Running counter to this there may be other forms of influence less
easy to pin down – *inarticulate* power: the disturbing intangibles

of social life; the imponderable advantages of certain groups; personal skills that succeed in a way that is unacceptable or difficult to understand. Where these two systems overlap, we may expect to find the sorcerer.

In some areas, where competition is not easily resolved by normal means, we find actual resort to sorcery. Far more important, however, in a situation where articulate and inarticulate power clash, we find greater fear of sorcery, and the reprobation and hunting-down of the sorcerer. In this situation, the accuser is usually the man with the Single Image. For him, there is one, single, recognized way of making one's way in the world. In rejecting sorcery, such a man has rejected any *additional* source of power. He has left the hidden potentialities of the occult untouched. He is *castus*. The sorcerer, by contrast, is seen as the man invested with the Double Image. There is more to him than meets the eye. He has brought in the unseen to redress the balance of the seen. His achievements may be admired, but they are, essentially, illegitimate.

To fear and suppress the sorcerer is an extreme assertion of the Single Image. Many societies that have sorcery beliefs do not go out of their way to iron out the sorcerer. The society, or the group within the society, that actually acts on its fears is usually the society that feels challenged, through conflict, to uphold an image of itself in which everything that happens, happens through *articulate* channels only – where power springs from vested authority, where admiration is gained by conforming to recognized norms of behaviour, where the gods are worshipped in public, and where wisdom is the exclusive preserve of the traditional educational machine.

The best-documented aspect of this problem is the conflict in the governing class of the Later Roman Empire between fixed vested roles, on the one hand, and the holders of ambiguous positions of personal power, on the other. This personal power was based largely on skills, such as rhetoric, which, in turn, associated the man of skill with the ill-defined, inherited prestige of the traditional aristocracies. Thus we find men whose positions in society were plainly delimited as servants of the emperor lodging accusations against men whose positions and whose successes were less easy to define, based as they were on the imponderable, almost numinous prestige of classical culture and aristocratic values in Late Roman society. This conflict passed through its most acute phase in the fourth century; and it is precisely in the areas marked out by it that we find the overwhelming majority of cases of sorcery.[15]

To take the governing class in its narrow sense and to view it from the hub outwards – that is, to analyse purges based largely on accusations of sorcery in the reigns of Constantius II, Valentinian I, and Valens.[16] The scene is usually the inner ring of the court: it is played out among officials, ex-officials, local notables. All of these men would have had personal contact with the emperor as a man, and not only as a remote figure of authority.

To rationalize such accusations as 'smears' is only half the truth.[17] They certainly were not pretexts for suppressing political conspiracies. Ammianus is firm on this point: the emperor knew only too well what an assassination plot was, and suppressed it as such.[18] Rather, these accusations indicate very faithfully a situation where organized political opposition was increasingly unthinkable: the days of a 'senatorial opposition', able to make itself felt by assassination, were gone for ever; the civilian governing class was overtly homogeneous, and stridently loyalist.[19] Thus, resentments and anomalous power on the edge of the court could be isolated only by the more intimate allegation – sorcery. Indeed, seen from the point of view of the emperor's image of himself, some sorcery was even a necessity: for to survive sorcery was to prove, in a manner intelligible to all Late Roman men, that the vested power of the emperor, his *fatum*, was above powers of evil directed by mere human agents.[20] A sorcerer's attack, indeed, is an obligatory preliminary, in biographies of the time, to demonstrating the divine power that protected the hero, whether this be the divine *daemon* of the pagan philosopher, Plotinus, or the guardian archangel of St Ambrose.[21] When we see them in this light, we can appreciate how the sorcery accusations of the fourth century mark a stage of conflict on the way to a greater definition of the secular governing class of the Eastern Empire as an aristocracy of service, formed under an emperor by divine right. In this way, as in so many others, Constantius II stands 'à la tête de la lignée des souverains de Byzance'.[22]

For these accusations are rarely made by the *parvenus* of the court among themselves: they are usually made by such groups against the holders of ill-defined, traditional status – to 'shake the pillars of the patrician class'.[23] In the fourth century, the boundary between the court and the traditional aristocracy coincided, generally, with a boundary between Christianity and paganism. It is often assumed that to accuse a pagan aristocrat of sorcery was a covert form of religious persecution. (To the Christian, who took for granted that a pagan *worshipped* demons, it was convenient to assume that he would also *manipulate* them, in sorcery;[24] and so the burning of books of magic, a traditional police action, is continued, in the Christian period, as a cover for the destruction of much of the religious literature of paganism.)[25] However, the boundary between court and aristocracy long survives the disappearance of the boundary between Christianity and paganism; in the sixth century, the falls of two great patricians, good Christians both – Boëthius in Italy and Mummolus of Bordeaux in Gaul – are accompanied by charges of sorcery.[26]

We can appreciate the urgency of the problem if we look at it from the rim of the wheel, as it were, in the works of Libanius of Antioch.[27] Here we have a man identified with the traditional aristocracy, whose status was an *achieved* status, based on his skill in rhetoric. In general, professors of rhetoric and philosophy, and poets (and, on a local level, in their own communities, the Jewish *rabbis*)[28] were the supreme examples of men whose status was not fixed.[29] They could become the *éminences grises* of the court; as the spokesmen of their cities, they could exert indefinable pressures on the central government; they were indispensable to the emperor as propagandists.[30] Their position among their colleagues was dependent on the fluctuation of their talents, in cities that had great zeal for such 'stars' but very little money left to give them a proper position. Any study of the *rhetors*, at any period of Late Roman history, takes us into situations of intense and insoluble rivalry,[31] between men who had not absorbed Homer for nothing, for whom 'shame' was worse than death. Not surprisingly, therefore, the life of Libanius was punctuated by accusations of sorcery: accusations by him and against him.[32] Rivalry, however, was not all. More precisely, the accusations against Libanius are, all of them, accusations that explain his ill-defined *power*: a rival 'went

24

around with the fairy-tale that he had been worsted by magic. I was intimate, so he said, with an astrologer who controlled the stars and through them could bring help or harm to men – just like a tyrant with his bodyguard';[33] and, later still, he had to face 'allegations that I had cut off the heads of a couple of girls and kept them for use in magic, one against the Caesar Gallus, the other against his senior colleague (Constantius II)'.[34] Throughout these accusations, therefore, we have something more than the occult measures which men in a competitive situation undeniably did take to increase their success and crush their rivals:[35] there is an attempt to explain a theme that still puzzles the historian of the Later Empire, the *je ne sais quoi* of the predominance of an ill-defined aristocracy of culture and inherited prestige, constantly pressing in upon an autocracy whose servants derived their status from membership of a meticulously graded bureaucracy.[36]

Sorcery beliefs in the Later Empire, therefore, may be used like radio-active traces in an x-ray: where these assemble, we have a hint of pockets of uncertainty and competition in a society increasingly committed to a vested hierarchy in church and state.

Take the charioteer. He owed his position to a personal skill which was both increased[37] and frequently attacked[38] by magic. Furthermore, a chariot race in a Late Roman town owed its importance to the fact that, in these firmly governed communities, increasingly dominated by a single religious leader, the orthodox bishop, the rivalry of racing factions marked a welcome *détente* in unity, an opportunity for bitter confrontations among the local aristocracies and their supporters.[39] As long as the successes of the charioteers were bound up in the public imagination with the 'Fortune' of the city, this usually remote and stable figure (who would be easily assimilated to the unmoved majesty of a Christian archangel) was thrown on to the 'open market' by the talents of a star.[40] The charioteer himself was an undefined mediator in urban society: he was both the client of local aristocracies[41] and the leader of organized groups of lower-class fans – and so, at times, a potential figure-head in urban rioting, that nightmare of Late Roman government.[42] Along with athletes and actors, he belonged to the *demi-monde* – a very important class in the imaginations (and, one would suspect, also in the daily life) of the studiously aristocratic society of the Later Empire.[43] Accusations of sorcery frequently take us from upper-class families into a world where charioteer and sorcerer are intimately associated.[44]

For it is in this *demi-monde*, in the wide sense, that we find the professional sorcerer. The cultivated man, it was believed, drew his power from absorbing a traditional culture. His soul, in becoming transcendent through traditional disciplines, was above the material world, and so was above sorcery.[45] He did not need the occult. We meet the sorcerer pressing upwards against this rigid barrier, as a man of uncontrolled occult 'skill'. One such, Albicerius of Carthage, would help the young Augustine to find a silver spoon, and could even 'thought-read' verses of Vergil in the mind of a proconsul; but both educated men agreed – Albicerius could never be 'good' because he could never be 'wise'; for he lacked the only proper training of a classical education.[46]

It is in this *demi-monde*, of course, that we meet the Christian Church. Previously, the Church had been the greatest challenge from below to traditional beliefs and organization: the powers of its founders, Jesus and Peter, and of its clergy, were regularly ascribed to sorcery.[47] Moreover, in the fourth and fifth centuries, the Church was a group which had harnessed the forces of social mobility to itself more effectively even than the teaching profession: its hierarchy was notably a *carrière ouverte aux talents*; and it played a decisive role in the 'democratization' of culture.[48]

Such a group pullulated saints and sorcerers. (In popular belief, the line between the two was very thin: St Ambrose, to name only one saint, was associated with twelve deaths – more deaths than stand to the credit of any Late Roman *maleficus*.) To take only one example: as a Christian bishop, Athanasius of Alexandria was able to manipulate Late Roman public opinion, in his career as an ecclesiastical politician, with far greater *éclat* than a *rhetor* such as Libanius. It was through the insistent opposition of Athanasius to his religious policies, for instance, that the autocracy of the Emperor Constantius II 'received' (in Gibbon's words) 'an invisible wound which he could neither heal nor revenge'. Athanasius reaped his due recognition from contemporaries in a reputation for sorcery.[49] The clergy followed their leaders. Sorcery was rife among the Syrian clergy

26

of the fifth century.[50] This is, of course, partly a tribute to their 'book learning' and so to their reputation as guardians of the occult.[51] But knowledge of sorcery was more precisely associated with a fluid group. Clients turned to the clergy for the same reason as they had turned to Albicerius: to men in touch with ill-defined 'skills', on the penumbra of a dominant educated aristocracy.

We shall come, later, to the sequel (see below, p. 35). We should note, however, in confirmation of this suggestion, that, as Late Roman society grew more stable and defined, in the course of the sixth century, so sorcery accusations seem to have waned. The marked increase in the political violence of the racing factions of Constantinople, for instance, is not, to the best of my present knowledge, accompanied by any notable increase in sorcery.[52] Among many reasons, this may be because the 'Fortune' of the city was more closely identified with supra-human figures, and, so, more clearly dissociated from human agents.[53] In the West, the triumph of the great landowners ensured that senatorial blood, episcopal office, and sanctity presented a formidable united front: any form of uncontrolled religious power received short shrift in the circle of Gregory of Tours.[54]

II

It was the particular merit of Professor Evans-Pritchard to have stressed the importance of witchcraft as an explanation of misfortune.[55] The historian of Late Antiquity must welcome this way of posing the problem. For he is acutely aware that the evidence for the political and social structure of the Empire will always remain fragmentary, while he finds himself the proud possessor of a body of religious literature of unparalleled richness and diversity, much of which deals directly with the problem of evil. So, he cannot avoid the challenge of the rise of Christianity in Late Antiquity, and its relation to sorcery beliefs.

In certain African tribes it has been noted that the rise of Christianity, by destroying many traditional explanations of misfortune (such as the anger of the ancestors), has led to an increased incidence in witchcraft accusations. Belief in human mystical agents of evil has had to take the full charge of explanations of misfortune that had, previously, been more widely distributed.[56] It could be argued that the opposite was true of the Late Roman period: Christianity mobilized a current drift, in the Late Antique world, towards explanations of misfortune through *supra*human agencies in such a way as to bypass the human agent.

For pagan and Christian alike, misfortune was unambiguously the work of suprahuman agents, the *daemones*. Whether these were the ambivalent 'spirits of the lower air' of much pagan belief, or actively hostile to the human race, as in Zoroastrianism, Christianity, and the Gnostic sects,[57] demons were the effective agents of all misfortune.[58] The sorcerer caused misfortune only by manipulating the demons,[59] the curser, by 'delivering over' his victim to their hostility.[60] In Late Antique literature, the human agent is pushed into a corner by the demon-host: 'If we believe that the myriad bacilli about us were each and all inspired by a conscious will to injure man, we might then gain a realisation of the constant menace that broods over human life in the biographies of Byzantine saints.'[61]

It may well be the case that the Christian Church effected a *détente* in sorcery beliefs in this period. But it did not do this through its repeated and ineffective injunctions against 'superstitious' practices:[62] rather, the Christian Church offered an explanation of misfortune that both embraced all the phenomena previously ascribed to sorcery, and armed the individual with weapons of satisfying precision and efficacy against its suprahuman agents. I would suggest that this change in the explanation of misfortune coincides with social changes in just those milieux where Christianity became dominant.

To take explanations of misfortune first: When we read the later works of Augustine, written to rally public opinion and deeply in touch with the sentiments of the average Christian,[63] we realize that his doctrine of the punishment of the human race for the sin of Adam has been widened so as to embrace all misfortune. Misfortune, indeed, has eclipsed voluntary sin as the object of the old man's bleak meditations. Because of Adam's sin, God had permitted the demons to act as His 'public executioners' – to use the phrase of an earlier Christian writer.[64] The human race was the 'plaything of demons':[65] damage to crops, disease, possession, incongruous behaviour (such as the lapse of holy men), gratuitous accidents, and, as an insistent

refrain, the untimely deaths of small children[66] – phenomena
that might characterize a society in which the sorcerer had been
given *carte blanche* to wreak his will – are ascribed by Augustine
to the abiding anger of God: *He has sent upon them the anger of
His indignation, indignation and rage and tribulation, and possession by evil spirits.*[67]

So much for the formal statement of views which became more
widespread in this period. What one must seize, however, are
the deep reasons that would lead a man like Libanius, almost
an exact contemporary of Augustine, to react to a bad dream
as an omen of '(magical) medicines, spells and attacks on me by
sorcerers',[68] while Augustine will say, of the terror of dreams,
that they 'show clearly that, from our first root in Adam, the
human race stands condemned to punishment'.[69]

I would suggest that part of the reason may lie in differing
attitudes to one's identity. Libanius and his colleagues were
men identified with their skill. Magical attacks were conceived
of as the most intimate possible attack on such a skill as
rhetoric – loss of memory invariably provoked accusations of
sorcery among such men;[70] for loss of memory damaged a man's
identity at just the point where he was most certain of himself –
in his mastery of classical literature through having memorized
it. We are dealing with incidents that are accompanied by
shame, by discrepancies in performance, such as have been
defined as 'when what is exposed is incongruous with, or glar-
ingly inappropriate to, the situation, or to our previous image
of ourselves in it'.[71] The misfortunes traditionally ascribed to
sorcery in the ancient world relate, precisely, to such an
experience of incongruity: a professor forgets his speech, a
chaste and noble woman falls in love,[72] a lover is impotent.[73]
Death by sorcery is also experienced as an incongruity between
the victim's death and his 'natural' span.[74]

Now incongruity assumes a very fixed image of a man's
identity. Augustine, by contrast, had a most acute sense of
discrepancies in behaviour,[75] but, for him, they fitted into a
view of man's identity which, unlike that of Libanius, has had
the bottom knocked out of it: 'For no one is known to another so
intimately as he is known to himself, and yet no one is so well-
known even to himself, that he can be sure as to his own conduct
on the morrow.'[76]

The two reactions may allow us to glimpse two different worlds. Libanius lived most of his life among the well-oriented upper classes of Antioch. When subjected to a misfortune ascribed to sorcery, he knew on whom he might pin blame; he would be blamed by others; he and his colleagues drew their identity from skills common to a traditionalist society. When such professors and civic notables competed among themselves, they trod a narrow stage whose backdrop had changed little. In so stable, well-oriented a world, a man would expect to be certain of his identity: he knew what was expected of him, and he knew that he could live up to these expectations. When an incongruity suddenly appears in his performance, he defends his image of himself by treating it as an intrusive element, placed there, from the outside, by some hostile agent. 'Misfortune' of the kind we are discussing is experienced as an attempt, from the outside, to sabotage the 'good fortune' to which a man's conscious control of his environment entitles him. And, in the world of Libanius, it is possible to identify the saboteur in the precise human figure of one's jealous colleague.

By contrast, the Christian communities in the third and fourth centuries had grown up in precisely those classes of the great cities of the Mediterranean that were most exposed to fluidity and uncertainty.[77] For the lower classes of these cities continued to be recruited by the immigration of rootless peasants from the country.[78] In the fourth century, just those groups whose attachment to the government service made them most mobile were, also, predominantly Christian.[79] More important still, perhaps, was the inner exile imposed on leaders of the Christian Church, Augustine included, by the ascetic movement: the monastic life was 'the life of a stranger';[80] the Christian community was described, not without justification, as a 'race of strangers'.[81]

In the fourth and fifth centuries, therefore, the sense of a fixed identity in a stable and well-oriented world, that would encourage the blaming of sorcerers and would single out incongruities in public behaviour as *the* misfortune *par excellence*, was being eroded in both the social milieu and the religious ideas associated with the leaders of Christian opinion. This situation changed as Late Roman society became more fixed. The stabilization of the local Christian communities and the elaboration of a finely articulated penitential system placed boundaries on Augustine's sense of the unidentifiable guilt of a bottomless identity. The idea of ill-defined guilt hardened into a sense of exposure to misfortune through the neglect of prescribed actions. At the end of the sixth century, it was plain to Gregory the Great that a woman who slept with her husband before a religious procession would risk demonic possession, just as the nun who ate a lettuce without first making the sign of the cross on it would swallow a demon perched on its leaves.[82]

In the earlier centuries, however, the Christian communities grew up through a belief in human 'vested' agents of good, endowed with inherent powers, as 'bearers of the Holy Spirit', to combat suprahuman agents of evil.[83] The confrontation of Saint and Devil stole the scene from the sorcerer. 'Our struggle', wrote St Paul, 'is not *with flesh and blood*, but against . . . the World-Rulers of the darkness of this existence, against spiritual forces of evil in the heavenly regions.'[84] A belief which, as Origen remarked, 'has led the rank and file of Christian believers to think that all human sins are due to the powers of the upper air: so that, to put it another way, if the Devil did not exist, no man would sin'.[85] From the New Testament onwards, the Christian mission was a mission of 'driving out' demons. Martyrdom, and later asceticism, was a 'spiritual prize-fight' with the demons.[86] The bishop's office was 'to tread down Satan under his feet'.[87] Full membership of the Christian Church, by baptism, was preceded by drastic exorcisms.[88] Once inside the Christian Church, the Christian enjoyed, if in a form that was being constantly qualified, the millennial sensations of a modern African anti-sorcery cult.[89] The Church was the community for whom Satan had been bound: his limitless powers had been bridled to permit the triumph of the Gospel;[90] more immediately, the practising Christian gained immunity from sorcery.[91]

Now it cannot be stressed often enough that the rise of Christianity in the third and fourth centuries was not merely the spread of certain doctrines in a society that already possessed its own principles of organization – as might well be the case in modern Africa:[92] it was an effort of, often, rootless men to create a society in miniature, a 'people of God'; its appeal lay in its exceptional degree of cohesion and, at a later time when this cohesion was diluted, at least in the greater precision with which a bishop or a holy man resolved the disputes of a community.[93] But a newly established group committed to mutual love, its leaders acutely sensitive to the 'worldly smoke' of rivalry, could hardly survive the interplay of blame and envy that accompanied a belief in human agents of misfortune. What we find instead is a 'humanizing' of the suprahuman agents of evil. In all Christian literature, the ambivalent and somewhat faceless *daemones* of pagan belief are invested with the precise, unambiguous negative attributes and motives that Libanius still saw in a professional rival who resorted to sorcery. The Devil was the 'rival' of the saint; envy, hatred, and the deadly spleen of a defeated expert mark his reactions to the human race. On Christian amulets we may be sure that *Invide*, 'O Envious One', refers, not to the Christian's neighbour, but to the Devil.[94] Where the teachings of the Fathers of the Church clash with popular belief, it is invariably in the direction of denying the *human* links involved in sorcery (they will deny, for instance, that it is the souls of the dead that are the agents of misfortune),[95] in order to emphazise the purely *demonic* nature of the misfortunes that might afflict their congregations.

One incident illustrates this tendency very clearly. A girl had been bewitched by a love-spell. The saint, Macedonius, was brought in to exorcise her. When abjured, the demon excused itself. It could not come out so easily, for it had entered under duress; and it named the sorcerer who had constrained it. Straightway, the girl's father lodged an accusation against the sorcerer in the governor's court. For a moment it seems as if the testimony of a demon interrogated by a saint would solve a problem of blame-pinning that had previously been left to the clumsy Roman method of examining under torture the servants and intimates of the sorcerer.[96] Macedonius, significantly, refused this role. He chased away the demon before it could involve the sorcerer in a further string of misfortunes, and converted the sorcerer; and so, with the exception of the case of the girl, he left the role of the sorcerer in mid-air as far as the human participants were concerned.[97]

It is interesting to note that this incident took place in Antioch, at almost exactly the same period as the life of Libanius. The girl's father and the governor plainly still thought of sorcery as Libanius did, in terms of blame-pinning, occasionally followed by a capital prosecution of the offender. The new holy man had refused to use his spiritual powers to relieve human uncertainties. His traditional enemy was the demon, not the sorcerer. *Exceptio probat regulam*: compared with the vast number of direct conflicts with demons in the popular literature of the Christian Church, cases of confrontation with demons in the service of sorcerers are notably few, and, of these few, in only two cases known to me does the abjuration of the demon lead back to relations with a human agent.[98] The usual attitude to a demon acting under a spell was 'I don't know how you got in, but I order you to get out . . .'.[99]

In the fourth and fifth centuries, therefore, the rise of Christianity should be seen as the rise of a new grouping of Roman society and as an attempt to suspend certain forms of human relations within the fold of the 'people of God'. If there are sorcerers, they are usually seen to work outside the Christian community (hence the pervasive identification of paganism and magic in Christian sources); if there is misfortune, it is divorced from a human reference and the blame is pinned firmly on the 'spiritual powers of evil'. Hence, perhaps, the snowball effect of the rapid rise of Christianity. Men joined the new community to be delivered from the demons; and the new community, in turn, resolved its tensions by projecting them in the form of an even greater demonic menace from outside.

III

The period I have been discussing, from around AD, 300 to 600 is a recognizable whole. I think that it is misleading to regard it, as many scholars have done, merely as a preview of the Middle Ages. Writing on an experience of Libanius, one has said: 'The incident heightens the impression made by all the other evidence, namely, that the fourth century was darkened by the most degrading superstitions in a manner that can only be compared to the benighted condition of Western Europe in the later Middle Ages.'[100] This reaction reflects the despair of the classical scholar: by falling away at all from the standards of an ideal ancient world, the Later Empire could hardly have fallen any *lower* than the Middle Ages! In fact, all recent research on the culture, the religion, and the institutions of the Later Empire has revealed it to be a period in which men worked (and most creatively) on an unbroken ancient legacy, and which is not to be reduced to a prelude of the Middle Ages.

This is particularly true of sorcery. For it is *sorcery* in the strict sense that I have been discussing throughout – an occult skill to which anyone can resort. Late Roman sorcery was an 'art'.[101] It was an art consigned to great books.[102] To possess or transcribe such books might jeopardize the owner;[103] but their destruction was accepted as sufficient guarantee of the change of heart of the sorcerer.[104] Knowledge of sorcery techniques could be widespread among the literate people that the historian meets;[105] but the knowledge tended to be specialized in professional practitioners.[106]

Now, as we have seen, the man accused of practising sorcery was a man of undefinable *power*. In extreme cases, the ideal type produced by the traditional 'vested' culture would wear this ambivalent halo: the philosopher Apollonius of Tyana was widely known as a *magus*;[107] many saints were spontaneously hailed as *magi*;[108] and it is, perhaps, not only a coincidence that, in popular Christian romances, the sorcerers should bear the same names as two of the greatest bishops in the Christian Church – Cyprian and Athanasius.[109] Therefore, when a Byzantine miniaturist wishes to portray a sorcerer, he shows an idealized portrait of a pagan philosopher.[110]

Above all, the sorcerer is a man who enjoys power *over* the demons, even over the gods. He can threaten the gods;[111] he works very largely by what the psychoanalyst would call 'introjective identification', that is, he *becomes* the god – 'for Thou art I and I am Thou: whatever I say must come to pass'.[112] In Christian sources, the demons act as the servants of the sorcerer: he is the servant of the Devil only in a very generalized sense, for he is free to abandon him by destroying the books of his trade and by accepting Christian baptism.[113] The contrast between the saint and the sorcerer is not that the saint commands the demons while the sorcerer is their agent: both can command; but the saint has an effective 'vested' power, whereas the sorcerer works with a technique that is unreliable and, above all, cumbersome.

Such sorcery is very much a *carrière ouverte aux talents*. A man of occult learning could placate, manipulate, even threaten

suprahuman powers to his advantage. If a society gets the
sorcery it deserves, then Late Antique sorcery is a tribute to the
learned and competitive spirit prevailing in the fluid areas of
society in which it was most rife.

This 'learned' sorcery, of course, will survive into the Middle
Ages, both in the West, in clerical circles,[114] and even more so
in the Eastern Mediterranean, among societies that had remained
in touch with their ancient roots – in Byzantium, Islam, and the
Jewish communities.[115] At the end of our period, however, it is
joined by another theme. We meet the *witch* in the full sense, a
person who either is born with or achieves an inherent character
of evil. In this case, it is not an unconscious mystical quality:
it is gained by a conscious act. But the power is gained by a
binding compact with the ultimate pole of evil – the Devil; and,
once this quality is gained, it is rare (outside pious stories) that
the Christian authorities accept the recantation of the new-style
witch. The contents of this new belief are well known. What
matters is to seize the exact date and milieu in which it comes
to the fore.

It is a Mediterranean phenomenon. We meet witches after
the heart of the ethnographer in the law-codes of the Northern
barbarians.[116] But these witches are already glimpsed at a
distance. They may not have long survived the process of rapid
de-tribalization that coincided with Christianization, which
marks the evolution of the barbarian ruling classes in Western
Europe.[117] The idea of the 'servant of Satan', I would suggest,
is a direct sequel of certain developments in Western and
Byzantine society at the end of the sixth century.

By the end of the sixth century, we are dealing with a society
which regards itself as totally Christian. The last occasions when
notable cases of sorcery can be associated with the worship of
the pagan gods belong to the Eastern Empire in the 570s.[118]
From then on, there is only one possible outsider in a Christian
world – the Jew. It is precisely at this time that we have the
first widespread movements presenting the Jewish communities
in Africa, Byzantium, Visigothic Spain, and, sporadically, Gaul,
with the choice of baptism or exile.[119]

Most important of all, perhaps, a man's conscious identity was
now deeply linked with his Christianity. In Christian popular
opinion, the sorcerer could no longer be tolerated in the

community on condition that he recanted his *art*: for he was now considered to have abandoned his *identity*; he had denied his Christian baptism.[120] Accusations of sorcery now take us into entirely Christian circles: bishops were implicated;[121] and, in the new stories, the sorcerer is no longer the pagan outside the community – the man who delivers his soul to the Devil is a bishop *manqué*.[122] The power of sorcery is gained, not by skill, but by a compact, a sealed document delivered over to the Devil, renouncing Christ, His Mother, and one's baptism.[123] Significantly, the Jew plays a part in these stories, not only because he is an outsider, but, more particularly, because he had always denied Christ – he was the 'apostate' *par excellence*.[124]

We have come to a world where the overt bonds are far more rigid. This can be seen more clearly, even, in Heaven than on earth. The correlation between Christian imagery and the social structure of the Later Empire is a fact almost too big to be seen: we meet it in every detail of the iconography of the Christian churches.[125] By the sixth century the image of the divine world had become exceedingly stable. Angels were the courtiers and bureaucrats of a remote Heavenly Emperor, and the saints, the *patroni*, the 'protectors', whose efficacious interventions at court channelled the benefits of a just autocrat to individuals and localities.[126] In the late sixth and early seventh century, sorcery is more often punished by the direct intervention of these divine governors: the sorcerer receives short shrift, as a traitor from a well-regimented celestial society.[127]

We have entered the tidy world of the Middle Ages. In Byzantium, an emperor conceived of as a 'servant of Christ', his person transparent to the image of Christ as King of Kings, will rule over a city where aristocracy and factions alike have been cowed.[128] At the other end of the Mediterranean, the Visigothic kings of Toledo are showing strident proof of their high level of 'civilization' by swearing oaths at their coronation to rid their land of the 'impiety of the Jews'.[129] And, at the far pole of men's minds, the Devil also has grown in majesty: he, also, is a great lord, a *patronos*;[130] he, also, can welcome his servants: 'Welcome, from this time forth, my own loyal friend.'[131]

NOTES

1. Evans-Pritchard (1937, esp. pp. 63-117).

2. Middleton & Winter (1963, pp. 3-4).

3. See, for example, Eitrem (1925); Preisendanz *et al.* (1928 and 1931). The evidence is so widely dispersed that the beginner should utilize monographs which have mobilized the baffling range of references, most notably Abt (1908). For a discussion of demonology and magic between two learned men of the second and third centuries, skilfully translated and commented, see Chadwick (1953). Radermacher (1927) is essential for the Christian image of the sorcerer.

4. See esp. Audollent (1904); Wünsch (1912).

5. Cited by Beattie in Middleton & Winter (1963, p. 54, n. 1).

6. See, most notably, Festugière (1944) and Abel (1957, pp. 291 ff.).

7. Festugière (1944, pp. 1-18).

8. Audollent (1904, pp. lxi and cxvii); Nock (1929, pp. 219 ff.); Nilsson (1948).

9. Maurice (1927, pp. 108 ff.); MacMullen (1967, pp. 124-127).

10. Notably Barb (1963, esp. pp. 105-108).

11. The Christians, see de Ste Croix (1963, p. 37, n. 136) and Courcelle (1964, pp. 67-77); Jews, Samaritans, pagans, and heretics, see Theodosius II, *Novella* III (438), c. 8.

12. Ammianus Marcellinus, *Res gestae*, XXI, xvi, 18.

13. Amm. Marc. XIX, xii, 5.

14. For a survey and discussion of all recent work, see Brown (1967a, esp. pp. 337-339).

15. For this perspective, I am particularly indebted to the fertile suggestions of Douglas (1966, esp. pp. 101-112).

16. Amm. Marc. XVI, viii, 1 ff.; XIX, xii, 3 ff.; XXVIII, i, 1 ff.; XXIX, i, 5 ff.

17. Amm. Marc. XXIX, i, 41; XXIX, ii, 3; Boëthius, *De consolatione philosophiae*, I, iv, 37. (The statements of the victims or of supporters of the victims.)

18. Amm. Marc. XXI, xvi, 10.

19. Jones (1964, esp. pp. 321-365). See Rubin (1960, pp. 168-224) for the sixth century.

20. Amm. Marc. XIX, xii, 16.

21. Porphyry, Life of Plotinus, 10 (transl. MacKenna, *Plotinus, The Enneads*, 2nd edn. 1956, 8); Paulinus, *Vita Ambrosii*, 20.

22. Piganiol (1947, pp. 107-109) is excellent on Constantius II.

23. Amm. Marc. XXIX, ii, 9.

24. Martroye (1930, pp. 669 ff.), an admirable study of the traditional anti-magic laws in the Christian period, underestimates the use to which these laws were put to victimize paganism in general. For a 'working misunderstanding' of the law, in the reverse direction, see John Beattie in Middleton & Winter (1963, p. 49): colonial laws directed against pagan 'impostures' used against sorcery, taken as 'real'.

25. Valens: Amm. Marc. XXIX, i, 41 (burning of magic books); cf. XXIX, ii, 4 (libraries burnt to protect their owners from accusations). The destruction of magic books to justify the raiding of pagan houses: Marc le Diacre, *Vie de Porphyre*, c. 71, ed. Grégoire-Kugener, 1930, p. 57 (Gaza); Barns (1964, pp. 153-154 and 157) (for Upper Egypt). A vivid description of a burning of magic books in sixth-century Beirut: Zachary the Scholastic, *Vie de Sévère*, *Patrologia orientalis*, II, pp. 69 ff.

26. Boëthius, *De consolatione philosophiae*, I, iv, 37. See, most recently, Wes (1967, pp. 181) and Gregory of Tours, *Historia Francorum*, VI, 35. On the Merovingian governing class, see Sprandel (1961, pp. 33 ff.).

27. Excellently translated and commented by Norman (1965). See Petit (1955).

28. Neusner (1966, p. 147).

29. See esp. Hopkins (1961, pp. 239 ff.).

30. Cameron (1965, pp. 470 ff.).

31. See Marwick (1952, p. 127) on such situations as bringing about accusations of sorcery.

32. Norman, *Libanius' Autobiography*, ss. 43 ff. (pp. 30-31); s. 50 (pp. 34-35); s. 62 (pp. 38-40); s. 71 (pp. 44-45); s. 98 (pp. 60-61); s. 162 (pp. 92-93); ss. 247-249 (pp. 128-129), and *oratio* xxxvi, *de veneficiis*, on which see Campbell-Bonner (1932, pp. 34 ff.).

33. Norman, *Libanius' Autobiography*, s. 41 (pp. 30-31).

34. Norman, *Libanius' Autobiography*, s. 98 (pp. 60-61).

35. See the material collected in Abt (1908, pp. 92 ff.) and Eitrem (1925, pp. 6, 35 ff.; 25, 35; 42-43). Given this literature, it cannot be said of Late Roman sorcery, as had been said of African, that 'such acts, although widely believed to be common, may in fact rarely, perhaps never, be performed' (Middleton & Winter, 1963, p. 4).

36. See Brown (1967a, p. 339).

37. Cassiodorus, *Variae*, III, 1.

38. See Audollent (1904, cxxviii, and *Index*, V, *Defixionum genera et causae*, D, p. 473).

39. Explicit in Jerome, *Vita Hilarionis* (*Patrologia Latina*, 23, 20).

40. Libanius, *Oratio*, xxxvi, 15.

41. See, most recently, Picard (1964, pp. 101 ff.); Pietri (1966, pp. 123 ff.).

42. See Macmullen (1967, p. 171, and nn. 10-12 at pp. 339-341).

43. See Amm. Marc. XXVIII, i, 1 ff., and Norman (1965, s. 150, pp. 90-91).

44. *Codex Theodosianus*, IX, xvi, 11 (389).

45. Chadwick (1953, p. 356, n. 1).

46. Augustine, *Contra Academicos*, I, vii, 19-21.

47. See Barb (1963, p. 164, n. 2) and *Origen*, VI, in Chadwick (1953, p. 340).

48. See Brown (1968a, p. 92).

49. See Amm. Marc. XV, vii, 7.

50. See the evidence amassed by Peterson (1959, pp. 333 ff.).

51. See Barb (1963, p. 124) on the transmission of spells in clerical circles, and Kayser (1888, pp. 456 ff.).

52. Apart from the reiteration of the law of 389 (cit. above, n. 44) in *Codex Justinianus* IX, xviii, 9, the reference to the magician Masades, patronized by sporting fans and local notables, is the only example known to me from the reign of Justinian: see John of Nikiou, *Chronique* s. 96, ed. Zotenberg, 509.

53. See Baynes (1960).

54. For instance, Gregory of Tours, *Hist. Franc.* VIII, 34; IX, 6; X, 25.

55. Evans-Pritchard (1937, pp. 63-83, 99-106).

56. Jean la Fontaine in Middleton & Winter (1953, p. 192).

57. Dodds (1965, esp. p. 17).

58. See Origen, *Contra Celsum* I, 31, in Chadwick (1953, pp. 30-31).

59. See the speech of the demon serving Cyprian the magician, in Radermacher (1927, pp. 86-88), and Libanius, *Declamatio* 41, 29.

60. Audollent (1904, 1-lix).

61. Dawes & Baynes (1948, p. xii).

62. Barb (1963, pp. 106-107, 122-123).

63. Brown (1967b, pp. 385-386).

64. Origen, *Contra Celsum* VIII, 31, in Chadwick (1953, pp. 474-475).

65. Augustine, *Contra Julianum*, VI, xxi, 67.

66. See esp. Augustine, *de civitate Dei*, XXII, 22.

67. Psalm 77, 49, in *Contra Julianum* V, iii, 8; also cited by Origen – Origen, *Contra Celsum* VIII, 32, in Chadwick (1953, p. 475). In general, see Brown (1967b, pp. 394-397).

68. Norman, *Libanius' Autobiography*, s. 245 (pp. 128-129).

69. Augustine, *de civitate Dei*, XXII, 22.

70. Cicero, *Brutus* 60, 217; Norman, *Libanius' Autobiography*, s. 50 (pp. 34-35); s. 71 (pp. 44-45).

71. Lynd (1958, p. 34).

72. For this period alone, see Amm. Marc. XXVIII, i, 50; Jerome, *Vita Hilarionis* (*Patrol. Lat.* 23, 39-40); Theodoret, *Historia Religiosa*, xiii (*Patrol. Graeca* 82, 1406 ff.); Amphilochius of Iconium, *Vita Basilii*, in Latin translation, *Patrologia Lat.* 73, 303 AB: Greek edition in Radermacher (1927, pp. 122-149); Gregory the Great, *Dialogues* I, 4 (*Patrol. Lat.* 77, 168 B).

73. Ovid, *Am. III*, vii, 27-28.

74. See esp. *Corpus Inscriptionum Latinarum* VIII, 2756. In comparison with African material, death is rarely ascribed to sorcery, though it was believed to be possible and to have been committed even by Christians; see Council of Elvira (311) canon 8. On the ideas surrounding untimely death, see esp. Dölger (1930, pp. 21 ff.).

75. See Brown (1967b, p. 405).

76. Augustine, *Letter* 130, ii, 4.

77. Clearly appreciated by Dodds (1965, p. 78, n. 1, and pp. 137-138).

78. See Mazzarino (1951, pp. 217-261).

79. See Jones (1963, esp. pp. 35-37).

80. Leclercq (1960, pp. 212 ff.).

81. Augustine, *Enarratio in Ps.* 136, 13: see Brown (1967b, pp. 323-324, esp. p. 323, n. 7).

82. Gregory the Great, *Dialogues,* I, 30 (*Patrol. Lat.* 77, 200-201) and I, 4 (ibid., 169).

83. See the abundant material collected by Tamborino (1909, pp. 27 ff.).

84. Ephesians 6: 12.

85. Origen, *de principiis* III, 2, 1 (*Patrol. Graeca* II, 205).

86. E.g. Brown (1967b, p. 244).

87. *Canones Hippolyti,* xvii (ed. Achelis, Texte und Untersuchungen, VI, 4, 1891).

88. Vividly described for North Africa by Poque (1965, pp. 27-29).

89. See Douglas (1963, pp. 247 and 257).

90. Augustine, *de civitate Dei,* XX, 8.

91. Origen, *Contra Celsum* VI, 41, in Chadwick (1953, pp. 356-357).

92. This would apply less to the governing class, who adopted Christianity after the conversion of the emperors. See, for example, Brown (1961, pp. 1 ff.) and (1968b, p. 101). For analogous cases in Africa, where the chief was the agent of conversion, see Schapera (1958).

93. See, for example, Brown (1967b, pp. 195-196).

94. Diehl, *Inscriptiones latinae christianae veteres,* I, 1961, no. 2388 (pp. 462-463).

95. Chrysostom, *Hom. 28 in Matthaeum* (*Patrol. Graeca* 57, 353).

96. E.g. Amm. Marc. XXVIII, i, 7, and Norman, *Libanius' Autobiography,* s. 41 (p. 26).

97. Theodoret, *Hist. religiosa,* xiii (*Patrol. Graeca* 82, 1405 ff.).

98. Theodoret, cit. above n. 97, and 'Life of Theodore of Sykeon', cc. 35 and 38, in Dawes & Baynes (1948, pp. 112 and 114-115).

99. Jerome, *Vita Hilarionis,* 22 (*Patrol. Lat.* 23, 41).

100. Campbell-Bonner (1932, p. 44).

101. See Abt (1908, pp. 104-105).

102. See Preisendanz (1950, pp. 226 ff.). See Zachary the Scholastic, *Vie de Sévère, Patrologia Orientalis* II, 58.

103. See, for instance, Amm. Marc. XXVIII, i, 27; Chrysostom, *Hom. 38 in Act. Apostolorum* (*Patrol. Graeca* 59, 273 ff.); Vie de Sévère, *Patrol. Orientalis* II, 65-66.

104. *Codex Theodosianus* IX, xvi, 12 (409); *Vie de Sévère, Patrol. Orientalis* II, 61-62; 'Life of Theodore of Sykeon', 38, ed. Dawes & Baynes (1948, p. 115); Radermacher (1927, p. 104).

105. E.g. *Vie de Sévère, Patrol. Orientalis* II, 37 (a book of invocations).

106. For instance, Audollent (1904, xliv ff.), on the professional execution and uniformity of leaden cursing-tablets.

107. See Chadwick (1953, p. 356, n. 3); MacMullen (1957, pp. 95-115); and, in general, Abt (1908, pp. 108-115) on the position of the magician as an ascetic and 'servant of God'.

108. For instance, Jerome, *Vita Hilarionis*, 20 and 23 (*Patrol. Lat.* 23, 37, and 48).

109. Radermacher (1927, p. 41).

110. See the Byzantine miniature of the ninth century illustrating Cyprian the Magician, Radermacher (1927, facing p. 234).

111. Now in Sodano (1958, pp. 61-63).

112. See E. R. Dodds (1965, pp. 72-73) and Festugière (1944, pp. 290-298).

113. See Radermacher (1927, p. 44): 'Denn dort ist der Zauberer Herr und Gebieter über die Dämonen. Von einem Vertrag ist keine Rede . . . Die Rolle Satans in der Historie ist kläglich.'

114. See Barb (1963, pp. 122-124) and d'Alverny, 1 (1962, pp. 155 ff.).

115. Kraus (1942); Ritter & Plessner (1962); and Golb (1967, pp. 12-15; 17, n. 26).

116. E.g. *Edictum* of Rothari c. 376: 'Nullus praesumat haldiam alienam aut ancillam quasi strigam, quem dicunt mascam, occidere: quod christianis mentibus nullatenus credendum est, nec possibile ut mulier hominem vivum intrinsecus possit comedere.'

117. See Thompson (1966, pp. 127-132) and Wallace-Hadrill (1962, p. 125). The cases of sorcery known to me at the Merovingian court, like so many other aspects of that society, strike me as quite definitely belonging to Late Antiquity, not to a 'barbarian' world.

118. Evagrius, *Historia Ecclesiastica*, V, 18; John of Ephesus, *Hist. Eccles.* III, 29-30.

119. See Blumencranz (1960, pp. 97-138) and Brown (1967a, p. 332).

120. Theophylact Simocatta, *Historiae* I, 11 (ed. Bonn Corpus, 56, line 10); and John of Nikiou c. 98 (ed. Zotenberg, 534-535).

121. Evagrius, *Hist. Eccles.* V, 18.

122. The story of Theophilus, in Radermacher (1927, pp. 164 ff.).

123. Radermacher (1927, p. 166).

124. Ibid., p. 165.

125. On this vast subject, see, for instance, Peterson (1935); Nordström (1953); Pietri (1961, pp. 275 ff.).

126. See, for example, de Ste Croix (1954, esp. pp. 46 ff.) and Wallace-Hadrill (1962, p. 127).

127. Moschus, *Pratum spirituale* c. 145 (Latin translation in *Patrol. Lat.* 74, 192); Evagrius, *Hist. Eccles.* V, 18 – the Virgin appears in dreams, demanding vengeance against 'traitors' to Her Son.

128. See esp. Breckenridge (1959).

129. VI Council of Toledo (638), can. 3 in Hefele & Leclercq (1909, p. 279).

130. Radermacher (1927, p. 168, line 17).

131. Ibid., p. 167.

REFERENCES

ABEL, A. 1957. La Place des sciences occultes dans la décadence. In *Classicisme et déclin dans l'histoire de l'Islam*. Paris.

ABT, A. 1908. *Die Apologie des Apuleius von Madaura und die antike Zauberei*. Naumburg.

ALVERNY, M.-T. D'. 1962. La Survivance de la magie antique. *Antike und Orient im Mittelalter, Miscellanea Medievalia I*. Berlin.

AUDOLLENT, A. 1904. *Defixionum Tabellae*. Paris.

BARB, A. 1963. The Survival of Magic Arts. In A. D. Momigliano (ed.), *The Conflict between Paganism and Christianity in the Fourth Century*. London: Oxford University Press.

BARNS, J. 1964. Schenute as an Historical Source. *Actes du Xème Congrès International des Papyrologues*. Warsaw.

BAYNES, N. H. 1960. The Supernatural Defenders of Constantinople. In *Byzantine Studies and other Essays*. London: Athlone Press (University of London).

BLUMENCRANZ, B. 1960. *Juifs et chrétiens dans le monde occidental, 430-1096*. Paris.

BRECKENRIDGE, J. D. 1959. *The Numismatic Iconography of Justinian II*. Numismatic Notes and Monographs 144. Harvard.

BROWN, PETER. 1961. Aspects of the Christianisation of the Roman Aristocracy. *Journal of Roman Studies 51*. London.

—— 1967a. The Later Roman Empire. Essays in Bibliography and Criticism LVI. *Economic History Review* (ser. 2) **20**. London.

—— 1967b. *Augustine of Hippo*. London: Faber.

—— 1968a. Christianity and Local Culture in Late Roman Africa. *Journal of Roman Studies* **58**. London.

—— 1968b. Pelagius and his Supporters: Aims and Environment. *Journal of Theological Studies* (n.s.) **19**. Oxford.

CAMERON, A. 1965. Wandering Poets. A Literary Movement in Egypt. *Historia* **14**. Wiesbaden.

CAMPBELL-BONNER, A. 1932. Witchcraft in the Lecture-room of Libanius. *Transactions of the American Philological Society* **63**. Connecticut.

CHADWICK, H. (ed.). 1953. *Origen: Contra Celsum*. Cambridge: Cambridge University Press.

COURCELLE, P. 1964. *Histoire littéraire des grandes invasions germaniques*. Paris.

DAWES, E. & BAYNES, N. H. 1948. *Three Byzantine Saints*. Oxford: Blackwell.

DODDS, E. R. 1965. *Pagan and Christian in an Age of Anxiety*. Cambridge: Cambridge University Press.

DÖLGER, F. 1930. Antike Parallelen zum leidenden Deinocrates. *Antike und Christentum* **2**. Münster-in-Westfalen.

DOUGLAS, MARY. 1963. *The Lele of the Kasai.* London: Oxford University Press (for the International African Institute).

—— 1966. *Purity and Danger.* London: Routledge & Kegan Paul; New York: Praeger.

EITREM, S. 1925. *Papyri Osloenses, fasc. I. Magical Papyri.* Oslo.

EVANS-PRITCHARD, E. E. 1937. *Witchcraft, Oracles and Magic among the Azande.* Oxford: Clarendon Press.

FESTUGIÈRE, A. J. 1944. *La Révélation d'Hermès Trismégiste I: L'Astrologie et les sciences occultes.* Paris.

GOLB, N. 1967. Aspects of the Historical Background of Jewish Life in Medieval Egypt. In A. Altmann (ed.), *Jewish Medieval and Renaissance Studies.* Cambridge, Mass.: Harvard University Press; London: Oxford University Press.

GRÉGOIRE-KUGENER, 1930. *Marc le Diacre. Vie de Porphyre.* Paris. Éditions Budé.

HEFELE, D. & LECLERCQ, J. 1909. *Histoire des Conciles*, Vol. III, 1. Paris.

HOPKINS, K. M. 1961. Social Mobility in the Later Empire: the Evidence of Ausonius. *Classical Quarterly* (n.s.) **11**. Oxford.

JONES, A. H. M. 1963. The Social Background of the Struggle between Paganism and Christianity. In A. D. Momigliano (ed.), *The Conflict between Paganism and Christianity in the Fourth Century.* London: Oxford University Press.

—— 1964. *The Later Empire.* 3 vols. Oxford: Blackwell.

KAYSER, G. 1888. Das Gebrauch von Psalmen zur Zauberei. *Zeitschrift der deutschen morgenländischen Gesellschaft* **42**. Leipzig.

KRAUS, P. 1942. *Jābir ibn Hayyān.* Cairo.

LECLERCQ, J. 1960. Mönchtum und Peregrinatio im Frühmittelalter. *Römische Quartalschrift* **55**. Rome.

LYND, H. M. 1958. *On Shame and the Search for Identity.* London: Routledge & Kegan Paul; New York: Harcourt, Brace.

MACMULLEN, R. 1967. *Enemies of the Roman Order.* Cambridge, Mass.: Harvard University Press; London: Oxford University Press.

MARTROYE, F. 1930. La Répression de la magie et le culte des gentils au IVe siècle. *Revue historique du droit français et étranger* (sér. iv) **9**. Paris.

MARWICK, M. G. 1952. The Social Context of Ceŵa Witch Beliefs. *Africa* **22** (2): 120-135, (3): 215-233.

MAURICE, J. 1927. La Terreur de la magie au IVe siècle. *Revue historique du droit français et étranger* **6**. Paris.

MAZZARINO, S. 1951. *Aspetti Sociali del quarto secolo.* Rome.

MIDDLETON, JOHN & WINTER, E. H. (eds.). 1963. *Witchcraft and Sorcery in East Africa.* London: Routledge & Kegan Paul.

NEUSNER, J. 1966. *A History of the Jews in Babylonia: II, The Early Sassanian Period.* Leiden.

NILSSON, M. P. 1948. Die Religion in der griechischen Zauberpapyri. *Bulletin de la Société de Lettres de Lund.* Lund.

NOCK, A. D. 1929. Greek Magical Papyri. *Journal of Egyptian Archaeology* 15. London.

NORDSTRÖM, E. 1953. *Ravennastudien.* Stockholm.

NORMAN, A. F. (ed.). 1965. *Libanius' Autobiography* (Oratio I). Hull.

PETERSON, E. 1935. *Monotheismus als politisches Problem.* Leipzig.

—— 1959. Die geheimen Praktiken eines syrischen Bischofs. *Frühkirche, Judentum und Gnosis.* Vienna.

PETIT, P. 1955. *Libanius et la vie municipale d'Antioche au IVe siècle.* Paris.

PICARD, G. C. 1964. Un Palais du IVe siècle à Carthage. *Comptes-Rendus de l'Académie des Inscriptions et Belles-Lettres.* Paris.

PIETRI, M. C. 1961. *Concordia apostolorum et renovatio urbis* (Culte du martyre et propagande papale). *Mélanges d'archéologie et d'histoire* 73. Paris.

—— 1966. Le Sénat, le peuple chrétien et les factions de cirque à Rome. *Mélanges d'archéologie et d'histoire* 78. Paris.

PIGANIOL, A. 1947. *L'Empire chrétien.* Paris.

POQUE, SUZANNE. 1965. *Augustin d'Hippone; Sermons pour la Pâque.* Sources chrétiennes 116. Paris.

PREISENDANZ, K. 1928 and 1931. *Papyri Graeci Magici: Die griechischen Zauberpapyri.* 2 vols. Leipzig/Berlin.

—— 1950. Zur Uberlieferungsgeschichte der spätantiker Magie. *Aus der Welt des Buches, Festgabe für G. Ley.* Leipzig.

RADERMACHER, L. 1927. Griechische Quellen zur Faustsage. *Sitzungsberichte der Wiener Akademie der Wissenschaften* 206 (4). Vienna.

RITTER, H. & PLESSNER, M. 1962. *Picatrix.* London: Warburg Institute (University of London).

RUBIN, B. 1960. *Das Zeitalter Justinians,* Vol. I. Berlin.

STE CROIX, G. E. M. DE. 1954. Suffragium: from Vote to Patronage. *British Journal of Sociology* 5. London.

—— 1963. Why were the Early Christians Persecuted? *Past and Present* 26. Kendal.

SCHAPERA, I. 1958. Christianity and the Tswana. *Journal of the Royal Anthropological Institute* 88. London.

SODANO, A. 1958. *Porfirio, Lettera ad Anebo.* Naples.

SPRANDEL, R. 1961. Struktur und Geschichte des merowingischen Adels. *Historische Zeitschrift* **192**. Munich.

TAMBORINO, J. 1909. *De antiquorum Daemonismo*. Naumburg.

THOMPSON, E. A. 1966. *The Visigoths in the Time of Ulfila*. London: Oxford University Press.

WALLACE-HADRILL, M. 1962. The Blood Feud of the Franks. In *The Long-Haired Kings*. London: Methuen.

WES, M. A. 1967. *Das Ende des Kaisertums im Westen des römischen Reiches*. The Hague.

WÜNSCH, R. 1912. *Antike Fluchtafeln* (Kleine Texte für Vorlesungen und Übungen 20). Bonn.

© Peter Brown 1970.

3

Keith Thomas

The Relevance of
Social Anthropology to the Historical
Study of English Witchcraft

INTRODUCTION [1]

During the past few years I have been engaged in a study of
some of the primitive beliefs that were current in sixteenth- and
seventeenth-century England. My sole qualifications are the
relatively narrow ones of the conventional academic historian,
and my knowledge of social anthropology is only that of the
amateur. Nevertheless, I have become convinced that many of
the insights of the social anthropologist can be profitably
applied to the study of history, and that this is nowhere more so
than in the case of the history of witchcraft – a topic which most
historians regard as peripheral, not to say bizarre, but which
has always been central to the British anthropological tradition.
The parallels between African and European witchcraft have
often been noticed, but they have not, so far as I know, yet
received any systematic examination. My aim in this paper,
therefore, will be to examine some of the basic features of
English witchcraft beliefs and accusations in the light of
anthropological studies of witchcraft elsewhere. For this reason
my approach will be primarily sociological, and I shall have to
omit any consideration of intellectual or psychological aspects
of the subject. Any fully satisfying explanation of English
witchcraft, would, of course, have to take account of them as
well. But here I shall merely try to indicate, as candidly as I
can, the points at which the historian can learn from the social
anthropologist, as well as those at which he is liable to find him
disappointingly unhelpful. In the process I shall also attempt
to sketch out an interpretation of English witchcraft beliefs
which I plan to develop more fully elsewhere. My substantial
indebtedness to the long flow of anthropological studies of

47

witchcraft set in motion by the pioneering investigations of Professor Evans-Pritchard will, I hope, be obvious.

DEFINITIONS

The term 'witchcraft' was used loosely in Tudor and Stuart England, and was at one time or another applied to virtually every kind of magical activity or ritual operation that worked by occult methods. Village diviners who foretold the future or who tracked down lost property were often called 'witches'; so were the 'wise women' who healed the sick by charms or prayers. Contemporary scientists whose operations baffled the ignorant were sometimes suspected of witchcraft, while the label was readily attached by Protestant polemicists to the ritual operations of the Catholic Church. Theologians invariably distrusted any claims to supernatural activity which their own religion did not authorize; a conjuror who invoked spirits to gain occult knowledge was a 'witch' so far as they were concerned, however innocent his own intentions.

The historian has, therefore, to impose his own classification upon the bewildering variety of semantic usage presented by the literature of the period. In this paper I propose to restrict the term 'witchcraft' to mean the employment (or presumed employment) of some supernatural means of doing harm to other people in a way that was generally disapproved of by the mass of society. (A Protestant who prayed successfully that God might blast the Catholic enemies of the English Church would not be a witch in the eyes of most of his fellow-citizens. But a Catholic who did the same in reverse might conceivably be so regarded.) A witch was thus a person of either sex (but in belief and practice more often female) who could mysteriously injure or kill other people. She could also molest farm animals and frustrate such domestic operations as making butter, cheese, and beer. In England her acts of damage – *maleficium*, as it was technically called – usually came under one of these heads. It was very rare for her to be accused of interfering with the weather or of frustrating sexual relations between man and wife, as was said to happen on the European Continent.

Many contemporary theologians, however, would not have agreed that the essence of witchcraft lay in the damage it did to other persons. For them witchcraft was not malevolent magic as such, but a heretical belief – Devil-worship. The witch owed any power she might possess to the pact she had made with Satan; and her primary offence was not injuring other people, but heresy. Indeed, whether or not she injured others, she deserved to die for her disloyalty to God. The lawyer, Sir Edward Coke, accordingly defined a witch as 'a person that hath conference with the Devil, to consult with him or to do some act'.[2] Around this notion was built up the extensive concept of ritual Devil-worship, involving the nocturnal sabbath at which the witches gathered to do homage to their master and to copulate with him.

From the sociological point of view, the problem presented by the concept of ritual Devil-worship is not the same as that raised by the popular belief in the existence of persons capable of doing harm by occult means. Much recent historical writing has concentrated exclusively on the origins of the idea of Devil-worship and attempted to establish the circumstances which led to its fabrication by the medieval Church and its adoption by many contemporary clergy and intellectuals. Most of the relevant material was collected by Lea (1939) and dazzlingly summarized by Trevor-Roper (1967, Chapter 3). But I intend to ignore this concept of witchcraft here because I think it was never as important in England as it is said to have been on the Continent. This is not to deny that many educated Englishmen imbibed the notion during the sixteenth and seventeenth centuries, or that it was reflected in many contemporary treatises and in the actual working of the criminal law: when an accusation of *maleficium* reached the courts it could easily turn into one of Devil-worship, if it happened to fall into the hands of interested lawyers or clergy. But, so far as the beliefs of the uneducated populace and the mass of actual witch accusations are concerned, there is every reason to think that the idea of Devil-worship was essentially peripheral. Contemporary intellectuals may have assimilated the idea, but it made much less impact at the village level, where most of these accusations originated. Even the Acts of Parliament which made witchcraft a statutory offence reflected the popular emphasis on damage (*maleficium*) rather than Devil-worship. There were three Acts – 1542 (repealed 1547), 1563 (repealed 1604), and 1604 (repealed

1736). Neither of the first two contained any reference to the diabolical compact, although the second forbade the invocation of evil spirits for any purpose. The 1604 Act made it a capital offence to covenant with, or to entertain, evil spirits, but it still displayed the earlier preoccupation with *maleficium* by making it a felony to kill anyone by witchcraft, while imposing a lesser penalty for less serious types of injury.

Most of the actual prosecutions under these Acts, moreover, related to alleged acts of damage and seldom involved allegations of Devil-worship. Thus, of the approximately 200 persons who are known to have been convicted under the Acts on the Home Circuit (Essex, Hertfordshire, Kent, Surrey, Sussex) between 1558 and 1736, there were (if we except the highly untypical prosecutions initiated in 1645 by the witch-finder Matthew Hopkins) only seven, or possibly eight, who were not found guilty of having inflicted mysterious acts of damage upon their neighbours or their goods. Even half of those convicted, under Hopkins's influence, of keeping evil spirits were also found guilty of killing other people or their animals (Ewen, 1929, *passim*). For most men, therefore, 'witchcraft' remained essentially the power to do supernatural harm to others. As one contemporary observed, 'In common account none are reputed to be witches, but only such who are thought to have both will and skill to hurt man and beast.'[3] English witch beliefs are thus more suitable for comparison with African ones than is sometimes appreciated.[4] The essential preoccupation with *maleficium* makes the differences arising from the English religious tradition less important.

How was damage by witchcraft thought to have been inflicted? And does the English evidence justify the well-known anthropological distinction between 'witchcraft' (a psychic, imaginary, and often involuntary act) and 'sorcery' (the employment of destructive spells, charms, and medicines)? These are difficult questions to answer. Contemporary witch trials suggest that the witch was believed to exercise her power in a variety of ways. She could touch her victim, or give out a potent but invisible fascination from her eyes: in this case he was said to have been 'fascinated' or 'overlooked'. She could pronounce a curse or malediction: then he would be 'forspoken'. Less commonly, she might use technical aids – making a wax image of the victim and sticking pins into it, writing his name on a piece of paper and then burning it, and so forth. My overall impression is that contemporaries were less interested in the mechanics of the operation than in the fact of the witch's malice. Once this was proved, it mattered less whether evidence of the means employed was forthcoming.

Some case can, however, be made for applying the distinction between 'witchcraft' and 'sorcery' to England, even though its relevance to many African societies other than the Azande is nowadays much disputed.[5] There was at least one type of unintentional witch in the shape of the person whose eyes were thought to have a special power of fascination, like the man who accidentally killed his own cattle by looking at them: one JP actually called such persons 'involuntary witches' (Ewen, 1933, p. 356). But these figures were primarily creations of folklore, and seldom appeared in the actual trials. There was also some suggestion that witches might have physical peculiarities, in addition to the witch's 'mark', or protuberance, to which her animal familiar might attach itself so as to suck her blood. In 1599 a judge said that he had heard that a witch's hair could not be cut off; others asserted that she would leave no shadow in the sunshine.[6] Many suspected that witchcraft might be hereditary.

Closest of all to the well-known anthropological distinction was the difference perceived by a few writers between 'witchcraft', which was an occult power given by the Devil, and 'sorcery', which involved the use of images, poisons, etc. Thus one author declared in 1653 that sorcery was

'a thing or mischief which is distinct from witchcraft, as thus, witchcraft being performed by the Devil's insinuation of himself with witches, . . . sorcery being performed by mere sophistication and wicked abuse of nature in things of nature's own production, by sympathy and antipathy'.

When nature was exploited for a good purpose, this was legitimate: 'it is the evil of the end which is sorcery'. This comes very close to the anthropologist's description of sorcery as 'that division of destructive magic that is socially disapproved or deemed illegitimate'.[7] Francis Bacon similarly anticipated Professor Evans-Pritchard when he noted that a magical technique like tying knots to prevent the consummation of a marriage had 'less affinity with witchcraft, because not *peculiar persons only* (*such as witches are*), but anybody may do it'.[8]

Despite such passages in the writings of contemporary intellectuals, I doubt if the witchcraft/sorcery distinction can ultimately be sustained when applied to the English ethnographic context.[9] The supposed Devil-worshipping witch frequently employed curses and imprecations, and sometimes even image-magic. Nor did anyone think of her activities as involuntary. She was bound by her pact with Satan, it was true, but she had begun life as a free agent, and some authorities held that it was still possible for godly ministers to reclaim her to society. When all the voluminous evidence for English witch accusations has been digested, it does not seem that any very illuminating distinction can be drawn on the basis of the presence or absence of magical techniques. Such a distinction would be crucial if we were investigating contemporary intellectual magicians in the Neoplatonist tradition, like John Dee. But when we are concerned with allegations of damage made in witch trials, it seems largely irrelevant. It has some intellectual interest, but not, I suggest, much sociological importance. In any case, the contemporary evidence is so diverse and conflicting that no firm distinction between witches and sorcerers can ultimately be sustained. We cannot even say that sorcerers sometimes existed, whereas witches were imaginary, for, as I shall suggest later, there really were persons who thought they could harm others merely by ill-wishing, just as there were some who felt they had gone over to the Devil.

EVIDENCE

The nature of English witchcraft beliefs has to be established by an analysis of the surviving literature of the period. In practice almost any writing, from drama to theology, can throw light on the subject. The evidence for the witchcraft accusations themselves is more restricted. Only some of the once voluminous judicial records still survive, and the majority of these are only bald indictments made at Quarter Sessions or Assizes. A good deal can also be learnt from the defamation cases brought before both secular and ecclesiastical courts by persons who felt they had been wrongly accused of witchcraft; while incidental light is thrown on magical practices in general by the prosecutions of charmers and diviners before the Church courts. But it is only when detailed depositions by witnesses can be found, either in their original form or in the versions contained in the contemporary pamphlet accounts of celebrated trials, that the social context of the accusations can be discovered.[10]

Judicial cases of all kinds, however, represent only the tip of the iceberg, and it is at the lower reaches that the historian, by comparison with the anthropologist, is most hampered, since, unless an accusation reached the law-courts, it is unlikely to have left any mark on the surviving evidence. The only substantial exception to this rule is constituted by the case-books of the contemporary doctors and astrologers who were consulted by persons who believed themselves to have been bewitched. The evidence they contain is sufficient to confirm that formal accusations of witchcraft represented only a small proportion of the suspicions and allegations made in everyday life.

This dependence upon surviving documents does not of itself distinguish history from anthropology, so far as witchcraft is concerned. One of the most recent anthropological studies of the subject (Crawford, 1967) is itself largely founded upon the records of the Rhodesian Attorney-General, and uses evidence very much like that of the English Assize depositions. Mr Crawford was, however, able to supplement his research by drawing upon local oral information and observation. I agree with his view that the combination of record sources and fieldwork is better than sole reliance upon either. But I think the historian can get a very long way on the basis of records alone, provided he is prepared to interpret them in the light of the insight derived from anthropological field studies, even from those made in a different environment. Indeed, the historian can aspire to answer some questions which fieldwork alone will never resolve. Information about the chronology and extent of witchcraft accusations, for example, is essential to their understanding. But until recently, anthropological writings on witchcraft have been markedly unstatistical; and even the studies of Mr Crawford and Professor Marwick are founded upon a

relatively minute number of cases, compared with those potentially available for historical study; though it must be admitted
that the evidence they have relating to those cases is often
much fuller.[11]

At present there is a great deal of historical research waiting
to be done upon the scale and number of European witchcraft
prosecutions. By comparison with recent work in England,
Continental studies have neglected judicial records and depended
largely upon the accounts given by contemporary demonolo-
gists. They therefore have little statistical value. Even in
England there are many records of Quarter Sessions and local
courts still waiting to be examined, though the data relating to
Assize prosecutions have by now been fairly thoroughly sifted.
The quantification of beliefs, suspicions, and informal allegations is an impossibility. But at least one can attempt to count
and measure the actual trials. The careful listing and plotting
of formal prosecutions, however, is a matter for conventional
historical research, and it is only when it has been fully completed that an anthropological interpretation can be effectively
made. As John Selden remarked,

> 'The reason of a thing is not to be enquired after, till you are
> sure the thing itself be so. We commonly are at *What's the
> reason of it?* before we are sure of the thing.'[12]

The ensuing remarks are thus in a sense premature.

THE EXPLANATORY ROLE OF WITCH BELIEFS

After several generations of anthropological writing it is hardly
necessary to stress that English witch beliefs, like those elsewhere, helped to account for the misfortunes of daily life. The
sudden death of a child, the loss of a cow, the failure of some
routine operation to achieve its result – such unexpected disasters could all, in default of any more obvious explanation, be
attributed to the influence of some malevolent neighbour.
Particularly in the field of medicine, where professional advice
was scarce, expensive, and largely worthless, there was a standing disposition to attribute to witchcraft many diseases which
would cause us no intellectual problem today. Indeed, Justices
of the Peace were instructed in a contemporary handbook

that the first likely sign of witchcraft was 'when a healthful body shall be suddenly taken . . . without probable reason or natural cause appearing' (Ewen, 1929, p. 269).

Any otherwise inexplicable event was therefore susceptible of explanation in such terms. Charges of diabolical aid were freely thrown around by politicians baffled by the success of their rivals, whether Cardinal Wolsey, who (like Anne Boleyn) was believed to have bewitched Henry VIII, or Oliver Cromwell, who was well known to have made a contract with the Devil on the eve of the Battle of Worcester.[13] This 'face-saving function' of witchcraft, as it has been called, was not, I think, typical of the average accusation. Witch beliefs were occasionally invoked to account for a commercial rival's success or to explain some particularly blatant example of that social mobility to which Tudor Englishmen could never adjust themselves. But witch-craft beliefs did not usually have an egalitarian function or provide a check upon individual effort in the way they have been known to do elsewhere.[14] 'Face-saving' allegations of this kind were rare in England; and disingenuous charges made by those seeking to excuse their own incompetence or to discredit some enemy were essentially parasitic to the main corpus of witch accusations. Even so, many accusations emanated from servants or children seeking to excuse their own negligence, sometimes by deliberate lying, sometimes by an unconscious desire to exculpate themselves. The Elizabethan Vicar of Brenchley, Kent, who kept losing his voice when conducting the service in Church, chose to blame this upon the sorceries of one of his parishioners, but the wiser members of the congrega-tion were unconvinced, for they knew he had the French pox.[15]

It is thus important to recognize that many accusations were dishonest. It must also be remembered that there were many different levels of belief and intellectual sophistication coexisting in England at this period. This means that general-izations of the kind made by anthropologists about small homogeneous societies are extremely difficult to handle when applied to fit a country of five million inhabitants, with a developing economy, and an intellectual life capable of throw-ing up giants of the stature of Shakespeare, Wren, or Newton. Scepticism about the existence of witchcraft is, I understand, not unknown in African societies,[16] but it is clearly marginal or unimportant in most of the work of most leading anthropological studies. The meaning and function of witchcraft are bound to be different in a society like seventeenth-century England, where scepticism of varying degrees was widespread. They are also different when a printed literature in several different languages brings accounts of witchcraft in other societies to the knowledge of the better-educated inhabitants. Continental accounts of witch trials influenced English thought in this period, just as today the Bible and Shakespeare help to sustain the belief in spirits among modern Africans (Crawford, 1967, p. 93). Social anthropologists are primarily concerned to study witchcraft in relationship to social structure, but the student of English witchcraft has also to consider the impact of a great number of different cultural traditions at a variety of different levels, social, intellectual, and regional.

A further difference between England and Africa is that Tudor Englishmen did not find it necessary to explain all misfortunes in terms of some supernatural belief, whether witchcraft or anything else. There seem to be many primitive societies where virtually all deaths are attributed to witchcraft or to ancestral spirits or to some similar phenomenon.[17] In England, by contrast, it seems that the possibility of 'accident' and 'misadventure' was fully recognized, as was that of death by purely natural causes. It is true that academic theologians resolutely denied the existence of chance and insisted that all otherwise unexplained natural events were the direct work of divine Providence, but the role which this idea played in the lives of the population at large is problematical.

Nevertheless, witchcraft in England, as elsewhere, had to compete with other supernatural explanations of misfortune. Explanations in terms of unlucky days, unlucky stars, or the neglect of some elementary ritual precaution were also prevalent. So was the disposition to attribute disasters of certain kinds to the activities of secret enemies of society, notably the Papists. But most important was the theological idea that the disaster had been caused by God, either to punish sin or to try the believer, or for some other unknown but undoubtedly just purpose. This theological explanation of misfortune was not, however, strictly speaking, an alternative to an explanation in terms of witchcraft, but an additional gloss upon it. Theologians upheld the reality of the Devil and the existence of witches. They usually agreed that God might try or punish his servants through the activities of witches no less than by any other means.[18]

Why was it, therefore, that a man sometimes turned to the occult malevolence of his neighbour rather than to some other supernatural or natural explanation of his misfortune? The answer to this question obviously depends in part upon the education and intellectual equipment of the individual concerned. But it also depends, as the anthropologists have shown, upon the social context in which the suspicion originated.

One prior attraction of witch beliefs, however, is obvious. A man who decided that God was responsible for his illness could do little about it. He could pray that it might be cured, but with no very certain prospect of success, for God's ways were mysterious, and, though he could be supplicated, he could not be coerced. Protestant theologians taught that Christians should suffer stoically like Job, but this doctrine was not a comfortable one. The attraction of witch beliefs, by contrast, was that they held out precisely that certainty of redress which the theologians denied. A man who feared that a witch might attack him could invoke a number of magical preservatives in order to ensure his self-protection. If the witch had already struck, it was still open for him to practise counter-magic against his supposed persecutor. By burning a piece of thatch off the witch's roof, or by burying a bottle of urine, he could force the witch to come hurrying to the scene of her crime. Once she appeared, the victim could put an end to his illness by scratching her and drawing blood; this was 'the most infallible cure', said the witnesses in a Leicester witch trial in 1717 (Ewen, 1929, p. 315). Best of all, the victim could have the witch prosecuted and executed. For the point of such witch trials was not merely that they afforded the gratification of revenge, but that, according to contemporary belief, they positively relieved the victim. 'The malefice', wrote one authority, 'is prevented or cured in the execution of the witch.'[19] Or, as James I put it, the destruction of the witch was 'a salutary sacrifice for the patient'.[20]

Witch beliefs thus seemed preferable to a theological explanation of misfortune; for although the divines recognized the possibility of *maleficium* they strenuously denied that the

Christian could lawfully employ counter-magic to rid himself of it; even scratching the witch was a diabolical action, as they saw it. Before the Reformation the Catholic Church had provided an elaborate repertoire of ritual precautions designed to ward off evil spirits and malevolent magic. This, I think, is why so few cases of misfortune in England are known to have been blamed upon witches before the mid-sixteenth century, even though legal machinery, both ecclesiastical and secular, undoubtedly existed for their prosecution. A man who fell victim to witchcraft did not need to take his case to the courts since there was a variety of alternative procedures available. Indeed, a good Christian who used holy water, the sign of the cross, and the aid of the priest ought not to be so afflicted at all. After the Reformation, by contrast, Protestant preachers strenuously denied that such aids could have any effect. They reaffirmed the power of evil, but left believers disarmed before the old enemy. The only way out in these circumstances was recourse to counter-magic (and this had to be clandestine) or, better still, to the now approved method of legal prosecution. Hence the multiplication of witch trials during the following century. On the Continent, by contrast, theologians seem to have lost faith in the curative power of religious symbols long before the Reformation; and trials were accordingly initiated much earlier.

In England most trials can be shown to have originated at a local level and to have reflected local animosities rather than to have been initiated from above. The only parallel to the African witch-finding campaigns of modern times was the crusade conducted by Matthew Hopkins in the Eastern Counties between 1645 and 1647.[21] This drive unearthed several hundred witches and led to many executions. It may have had its millenarian aspects, but the evidence suggests that Hopkins merely exploited local tensions in such a way as to bring accusations into the courts at an unprecedented rate. Like the African witch-finding movements, the campaign had a protective purpose, but, unlike them, it does not ever seem to have implied that sorcery was the cause of all evils or that, once the witches had been hanged, everyone's troubles would be over. But the problems presented by Hopkins's brief career are still not solved, and more may yet be learned by comparing the reaction of local communities to his arrival with that aroused in Central Africa by the coming of the Mcape in the 1930s or of Bwanali and Mpulumutsi in 1947.[22]

THE IDENTIFICATION OF THE WITCH

So far, the English evidence has confirmed the anthropological truism that the most satisfactory interpretation of misfortune is that which allows effective action to be taken against it. But why were witch beliefs invoked at one moment rather than another, and what were the circumstances that brought them into play? The answer to these questions can be discovered only by studying the relationships between the witch, her victim, and her accuser. This is an approach which has been successfully pioneered by the social anthropologists, and it is worth applying to the English data.

The first feature that emerges from a scrutiny of surviving witchcraft accusations is an obvious one, but is nevertheless important. This is that it was excessively rare for men to decide that they had been the victims of witchcraft without also having a particular suspect in mind. Once they had diagnosed witch-craft as the cause of their sufferings, it seldom took them long to identify the probable source. Usually they knew at once who it must have been. Sometimes they even had the suspect in mind before the witchcraft had been committed. 'I have a suspicion in thee,' said Mary Dingley to Margery Singleton in 1573, 'and if any in my house should miscarry thou shalt answer for it.'[23]

This feature is admittedly difficult to establish in all cases, since the first extant evidence is usually the formal indictment, in which the offence and the accused are named simultaneously, and it is impossible to reconstruct the thought-processes which had previously gone on in the victim's mind. But even these bald statements show us that the accused did not operate from a distance against strangers, but lived in the same neighbour-hood, usually the same village, and was already in some sort of social relationship with her victim before she had begun to practise her malice.

The depositions show that the witch's identity was estab-lished in one of various standard ways. The victim might recall the person with whom he had quarrelled before the misfortune had occurred, sometimes denouncing him on his death-bed. Alternatively, he might have nocturnal visions of the witch, or cry out in his fits against her. Very often he would invoke the assistance of a diviner – a 'white witch', 'cunning man', or 'wise woman', as such people were called. The client would go to the wizard, describe his symptoms, and invite a diagnosis. The action he subsequently took might be considerably determined by the advice he received.

This is the point at which the historian can only envy the anthropologist's ability to be present at some of these critical moments. But the surviving accounts of the process of Tudor and Stuart divination can be suggestively interpreted in the light of what has been found out about the cunning man's modern African counterparts. We know that most forms of divination are capable of manipulation, that diviners are sensitive to the reactions of their audience, that they often proceed on a trial-and-error basis, and that in many cases they merely confirm the suspicions in the client's own mind by serving them back to him as the supposed product of their magical skill.[24] The English evidence suggests that diviners sometimes created suspicions which would not otherwise have arisen; they may have been less statesmanlike than those of their African counterparts who act as a brake on public opinion (Douglas, 1963a, pp. 225-226, 232-233). It was in their interest to diagnose witchcraft, after all, because they had a near-monopoly of the techniques necessary for dealing with it. In England, as among the Azande, the belief in malevolent witches could not have existed without the parallel existence of witch-doctors ready to confirm their presence.[25]

But my overall impression, and it can, alas, never be more than an impression, is that usually the client suspected witchcraft before he ever went to the diviner, and that it was he who did the actual identification, by recognizing a face in a mirror or polished stone, or by supplying a list of suspects to be narrowed down by divination. As a contemporary summarized the procedure:

'A man is taken lame; he suspecteth that he is bewitched; he sendeth to the cunning man; (who) demandeth whom they suspect, and then sheweth the image of the party in a glass.'[26]

In 1579 an ostler of Windsor developed a back-ache after a quarrel with an old woman, Mother Stile. So he went to a wise man, who

'told him that he was bewitched, and that there was many ill women in Windsor, and asked him whom he did mistrust; and the said ostler answered, "Mother Stile". . . . "Well", said the wise man, "if you can meet her and . . . scratch her, so that you draw blood of her, you shall presently mend." '

In another case a worried mother consulted a wizard as to who was the cause of her child's illness. Back came the answer, via a servant: 'Your mistress knows as well who hath wronged her child as I.'[27] In these and many similar cases, we can see how it was the function of the cunning man to make the victim face up to the suspicions he had already formed, to strengthen them by the addition of a magical *imprimatur*, and thus to create the circumstances necessary for converting a mere suspicion into a positive accusation.[28] Yet the diviner's role has been virtually ignored in most historical writing about witchcraft, and without some acquaintance with anthropological studies of African divination I doubt whether I should ever have thought about it.

So far, I have suggested that the witch was always a person known to her accuser. A further fact emerges from the depositions and pamphlet accounts and that is that she was almost always believed to bear a grudge against him. This may be obvious, but it does at least rule out the possibility of motiveless malignity. Contemporaries were horrified by the witch's activities, but they seldom denied that she had some genuine reason for wishing ill upon her victim. Here the English situation is neater than that in some African societies, where witches are sometimes believed to be largely capricious in their motivation.

The crucial question, therefore, is that of the prior animosity believed to exist between the English witch and her victim. Did it usually conform to a pattern or was every type of grudge liable to be involved? The answer can be extracted only from those cases where the depositions or pamphlet accounts are sufficiently detailed, and is therefore difficult to represent statistically. But one fact seems to be clear. The charge of witchcraft was normally levelled, not just when the accuser felt

that the witch bore a grudge against the victim (or his family),
but when he felt that the grudge was a *justifiable* one. The witch,
in other words, was not merely being vindictive. She was thought
to be avenging a definite injury. This is a situation that Professor Marwick has found in 60 per cent of his Ceŵa cases.[29]
Any figure finally produced for England would, I think, be a
good deal higher.

Just as among the Ceŵa, the type of misdemeanour attributed
to the victim varied. He might have refused to pay some legitimate debt or have behaved with unjustifiable churlishness to
the witch or her children. He might have failed to invite her to
some communal celebration – a wedding, a sheep-shearing, or a
harvest-home. (It will be remembered that the classic malevolence of the wicked fairy sprang from the failure of the Sleeping
Beauty's parents to invite her to the christening.) Or he might
have used unjustified violence against some old woman or her
dependants. Thus when John Orkton struck Mary Smith's son
in 1616 he found himself growing 'distempered in stomach', and
his fingers and toes began to rot; and when a servant snatched a
pair of gloves from the pocket of Mother Nokes's daughter in
1579 he suddenly lost the use of his limbs and was bedridden
for eight days (Ewen, 1933, pp. 229, 152).

But the most common situation of all was when the victim
(or his parents) had turned away empty-handed an old neighbour who had come to the door to beg or borrow some food or
drink, or the loan of some household utensil. The overwhelming
majority of English witch cases fell into this simple pattern. The
witch was sent away, perhaps mumbling a malediction, and in
due course something went wrong with the household or one of
its members, for which she was immediately held responsible.
The requests made by the witch varied, but they were usually
for food or drink – butter, cheese, yeast, milk, or beer. Sometimes
she asked for money or a piece of equipment. In all cases denial
was followed by retribution, and the punishment often fitted the
crime. Thus at Castle Cary around 1530, Isabel Turner denied
Christian Shirston a quart of ale, whereupon 'a stand of ale of
twelve gallons began to boil as fast as a crock on the fire'. Joan
Vicars would give her no milk, and thereafter her cow yielded
nothing but blood and water. Henry Russe also refused her milk,
only to find himself unable to make cheese until Michaelmas.[30]

These depressing peregrinations from door to door were the background to most witchcraft accusations. They are not to be confused with simple begging. Rather, they illustrate the breakdown of the tradition of mutual help upon which many English village communities were based. The loan of equipment or the giving of food and drink were normal neighbourly activities. What was notable in these cases was that they should have been refused. The fact that Christian Shirston was accused of witchcraft by the very people who had failed to fulfil their accepted social obligations to her illustrates the essential conflict between neighbourliness and individualism which generated the tensions from which the accusations of witchcraft were most likely to arise. When shutting the door in Christian Shirston's face, her neighbours were only too well aware of having departed from the accepted ethical code. They knew they had put their selfish interests before their social duty. When some minor accident overtook them or their children it was their guilty conscience that told them where to look to find the source of their misfortunes.

Two essential features thus made up the background to most of the allegations of witchcraft levied in sixteenth- and seventeenth-century England. The first was the occurrence of a personal misfortune for which no natural explanation was forthcoming. The second was an awareness on the victim's part of having given offence to a neighbour, usually by having failed to discharge some customary social obligation. As often as not the link between the misfortune incurred and the obligation neglected was furnished by the frank expression of malignity on the part of the suspected witch. Old women (most accused witches were women, and it is likely, but unprovable, that they tended to be elderly) did not like being turned away from the door, and made no bones about their malevolence. The court books of the Anglican Church abound in reports of men and women who prayed or cursed in a highly ritual way that God would shorten the lives of their enemies, burn their homes, kill their children, destroy their goods, and blast them and their descendants.

But in many cases it was not necessary for the suspected witch to have given evidence of her malevolence. The victim's guilty conscience was sufficient to provoke an accusation, since, when a misfortune occurred, his first reaction, like that of most primitives, was to ask what he had done to deserve it. When, in 1589, a Southampton tanner's pigs expired, after having 'danced and leaped in a most strange sort, as if they had been bewitched', he recalled how on the previous day Widow Wells had come to his door on two occasions, 'there sitting (and) asking nothing; at length, having not anything given unto her [we may underline his assumption that something should have been], she departed'. On the basis of the next day's occurrences, he warned her that 'if he took any hurt by her afterwards he would have her burned for a witch'. Yet there is no evidence of any expressed malevolence on her part at all.[31]

THE WITCH'S POINT OF VIEW

A few words ought to be said about the position of the accused witch. We have seen that she was usually a relatively dependent member of society and this explains, I think, why witches were so often women and especially widows, whose means of subsistence were often inadequate without neighbourly support. The position of such people had been weakened by the decline of customary manorial arrangements for the support of the elderly; and it is this, rather than any sexual tensions, that accounts for the frequency with which old women were cast by society for the role of witch. Many were dependent upon their neighbours, while lacking the institutional recognition afforded to those in receipt of poor relief. It was the ambiguity in their situation that was their downfall.

Something about the feelings of these unfortunates can be inferred from the confessions extracted at the trials, and from their other *obiter dicta*. The veracity of such confessions has been the subject of much historical controversy, and anthropologists have often found them equally embarrassing, choosing to put them down to 'malnutrition', or 'depression' (Crawford, 1967, p. 65; Field, 1960, pp. 149 ff.), just as seventeenth-century intellectuals attributed them to 'melancholy'. But some anthropological insight on this subject is extremely illuminating; for example, Dr Douglas's observation that, among the Lele, suspects sometimes welcome the chance to submit themselves voluntarily to tests for witchcraft in order to clear their name in the community (Douglas, 1963a, p. 249; 1963b, pp. 133-135). This makes good sense when applied to the unsolicited examinees who came forward during the Hopkins crusade.

Confessions of relations with the Devil are more difficult to interpret, and I doubt if social anthropologists can help the historian much here.[32] But in principle there seems no reason why alienated individuals, filled with genuine malice for their neighbours, may not have personified their evil desires in this way. Contemporary religious teaching portrayed the Devil as the symbol of everything evil and antisocial; indeed, it was common for Devil-worship to be one of the temptations experienced by those undergoing the depressive state that usually preceded a Puritan religious conversion. If many felt the temptation, there is no reason to doubt that some may have succumbed.

It is also certain that malevolent magic was often practised, just like sorcery in Africa – extant magical formulae and the observation of witnesses both confirm this. But witches' sabbaths were almost certainly non-existent, and their alleged devotees present problems similar to those raised by the African 'night-witches', of whose existence anthropologists remain in doubt, even after long residence in a community.[33] The most important point about the witch's resort to curses, black magic, or even Devil-worship, seems to be that it sprang from frustration. She was too weak to avenge herself against the community by physical force; and she could not take her persecutors to law. Magic was a substitute for impotence. The only alternative was arson, and this secret and indiscriminate means of wreaking vengeance on a community was occasionally practised, and even more often threatened, by persons in positions similar to those of accused witches. I do not wish to suggest that all those accused of witchcraft had malicious thoughts about their neighbours. But some certainly did, though we shall never know what proportion. This was why some of the most powerful intellects of the day believed in punishing witches, though totally sceptical about their powers. Thomas Hobbes wrote:

'As for witches, I think not that their witchcraft is any real power; but yet that they are justly punished, for the false belief they have that they can do such mischief, joined with their purpose to do it if they can.'[34]

65

To have a reputation for witchcraft, indeed, could be an old woman's last form of defence. 'These miserable wretches are so odious unto all their neighbours,' wrote Reginald Scot, 'and so feared, as few dare offend them, or deny them any thing they ask.'[35] The belief in witchcraft helped to ensure that neighbourly obligations were not neglected, and that an old woman's requests were not automatically denied. As the Chartist, William Lovett, recalled from his Cornish childhood, a reputed witch was treated with respect: 'Anything that Aunt Tammy took a fancy to, few who feared her dared to refuse.'[36]

THE FUNCTION OF WITCH BELIEFS

The essentially village context of witchcraft accusations determined their main character in England. They were seldom made between members of the same family or between close relations. The preoccupation with different types of kinship system, which has dominated so much anthropological writing about witch beliefs, is thus largely irrelevant in the English context; though no doubt the absence of many witchcraft accusations within the English family is itself a subject calling for comment. It may be that, as in African towns today, the family was more tightly integrated, so that members who suffered misfortune would look outside for the source of mystical evil-doing (Mitchell, 1965, pp. 195-196; Gluckman, 1955, pp. 97, 101-102). But other signs of hostility within the family, like homicide and violence, were not unknown, so the explanation may be more complicated than this.

Most English witch accusations can, therefore, be understood only within the structure of the English village community, and here there is much historical research waiting to be done. At first glance, however, it seems that the primary function of witch beliefs was a conservative one. They reinforced accepted moral standards by postulating that a breach in the norms of neighbourly behaviour would be followed by material repercussions. As Professor Evans-Pritchard wrote of the Azande, 'belief in witchcraft is a valuable corrective to uncharitable impulses, because a show of spleen or meanness or hostility may bring serious consequences in its train'.[37] Witch beliefs, like the parallel belief in divine Providence, were a manifestation of the primitive assumption that a likely cause of material misfortune is to be found in some breach of moral behaviour – that the natural order and the moral order are related to each other. They made men hesitate before departing from the traditional norms of neighbourly conduct. 'I am loath to displease my neighbour, Allridge,' said an Elizabethan husbandman, 'for I can never displease him, but I have one mischance or another amongst my cattle.'[38] Conversely, the fear of being accused of witchcraft made old women think twice before giving vent to curses and other expressions of malignity. From this point of view, witch beliefs may be fairly described as 'conservative social forces' (Marwick, 1965a, p. 221), upholding the norms of village life, and worthy to be studied alongside such other props to traditional behaviour as gossip, the lack of privacy, and the risk of denunciation as a scold or troublemaker to the ecclesiastical courts.

But there is another side to the picture. Witch beliefs also had a function which may be described as radical. They arose at a time when the old tradition of mutual charity was being sapped by the introduction of a national Poor Law. This made the model householder's role essentially ambiguous. The clergy still insisted on the duty of local charity, whereas local authorities were beginning to forbid householders to give indiscriminate alms at the door. It is this unhappy conjunction of private and public charity that accounts for the uncertain light in which contemporaries viewed the poor. On the one hand, they hated them as a burden to the community and a threat to public order. On the other, they still recognized that it was their Christian duty to give them help. The conflict between resentment and a sense of obligation produced the ambivalence which made it possible for men to turn begging women brusquely from the door and yet to suffer torments of conscience after having done so.[39] This ensuing guilt was fertile ground for witchcraft accusations, since subsequent misfortune could be seen as retaliation on the part of the witch. The tensions that produced witchcraft allegations were thus those generated by a society which no longer held a clear view as to how its dependent members should be treated; they reflected the ethical conflict between the twin and opposing doctrines that those who did not work should not eat, and that it was blessed for the rich to support the poor.

In these circumstances witch beliefs assumed their radical function. For although most writers warned men to be charitable, so as to avoid supernatural retaliation, there were others who stressed that it was dangerous to give anything to a suspected witch and advised that she should be ostracized by the community. These two notions did not really conflict, for it was only the person already suspected of witchcraft who was to be turned away; and such a suspicion was unlikely to arise so long as she was treated in a neighbourly way. Witch beliefs thus upheld the old conventions of village life, but, once these conventions had broken down, they also justified the breach, and made it possible for the uncharitable to divert attention from their own guilt by focusing attention on that of the witch. The fear of being subsequently accused of witchcraft would similarly deter a person from knocking at an unfriendly door. In England, as in Africa, therefore, the belief in witchcraft could help to dissolve 'social relations which become redundant'.[40]

Witch beliefs are thus of interest to the social historian, no less than the social anthropologist, for the light they throw upon weak points in the social structure. The witch and her victim existed in a state of concealed hostility for which society provided no legitimate outlet. They could not take each other to law, neither could they have recourse to open violence.[41] It was the particular social context that explained why witchcraft was invoked to explain some misfortunes but not others. Witches were not interchangeable with such other bogeys as Jews or Catholics. Paranoia about Popery might suggest an explanation for a disaster like the Fire of London, which affected a whole community; but it was seldom employed to explain why a mysterious fire should have burned down the barn of one individual but not that of his neighbour. Papists were the enemies of society as a whole; witches were the enemies of individuals. Only those who thought of witches as an organized sect of Devil-worshippers could plausibly blame them for misfortunes common to everyone.[42] Nor was the belief in witchcraft interchangeable with that in divine Providence, though theologians tried to make it so. Providence was most likely to be invoked when the victim felt he had sinned against God; witchcraft when he was more conscious of having sinned against his neighbour.

THE DECLINE OF WITCHCRAFT

The later seventeenth century saw the decline of witchcraft prosecutions in England. The last execution was in 1685 and the last known trial in 1717. In 1736 the Witchcraft Act of 1604 was repealed and replaced by a measure which permitted no more accusations of witchcraft, but imposed minor penalties for fortune-telling and similar frauds. Among intellectuals, the belief in the possibility of witchcraft had declined in the later seventeenth century. Judges and juries had shown a growing reluctance to convict, long before the passage of the 1736 Act, and this reflected a changed attitude on the part of the educated classes. In the countryside, however, witch beliefs lingered on until the late nineteenth century.

Why did this change occur? Here, if I may be forgiven for saying so, anthropologists seem least helpful. Perhaps this is because a functional approach to any primitive belief is notoriously difficult to reconcile with a theory of social and intellectual change. I know of few anthropological writings which offer more than a couple of sentences on the reasons for the growth of scepticism and the decline of witchcraft accusations. Yet many stress how difficult it is for men to break out of a self-confirming system of this kind. Such remarks about the reasons for the decline as I have been able to discover are suggestive, but too brief to be very persuasive. In the first place, the overall assumption that changes in beliefs must necessarily be bound up with changes in social structure, and particularly with changes in kinship,[43] seems to have generated a disposition to discount any explanation for the decline of witchcraft which relies primarily upon the rise of science and the new philosophy. Thus Professor Marwick says that the decline cannot 'be attributed entirely to the rise of rationalism', though he gives no reason for this opinion. Mr Crawford similarly states that 'increasing scientific knowledge does not necessarily destroy beliefs in wizardry'.[44]

Yet when we look at seventeenth-century England it seems impossible to brush aside the influence of the scientific and philosophical innovations of the period. Inevitably they affected the attitude of the lawyers, jurymen, and legislators. Changing intellectual fashions involved the debunking of the belief in spirits and occult influences, making possible both the collapse of formal prosecutions and ultimately the repeal of the Act upon which those prosecutions rested. In the sixteenth century, by contrast, most intellectuals had held a view of the world in which the belief in witchcraft made good sense. It had fitted in especially well with Neoplatonic assumptions about vital influences and a universe of unseen spirits, and it could also be reconciled with older assumptions about the microcosm and macrocosm. But in the seventeenth century the new mechanical philosophy destroyed all this; and the contemporary mathematicians who evolved laws of chance gradually revealed that even the incidence of misfortune was predictable. Much has yet to be discovered about the diffusion and influence of these changes. Indeed, their direct impact upon the witch trials is by no means clear. But if we are to explain why the prosecutions ended we have to take account of them.

Unfortunately, the removal of the legal machinery of prosecution after 1736 makes it impossible for the modern historian to plot the exact chronology and distribution of subsequent informal witch accusations and suspicions. But, despite the many instances which are known to have occurred throughout the eighteenth and nineteenth centuries, my impression is that the bulk of these suspicions also began to decline during the later seventeenth century. If this impression is correct, how are we to explain the change? It can hardly be argued that Cartesian philosophy or Newtonian science had already reached the village level, and it seems more sensible to look for some sociological explanation instead.

Here the anthropologists are ready with their answers. One favoured interpretation is that invoked by Professor Gluckman when he states rather boldly that 'in our own history accusations of witchcraft were ruled illegal when the industrial revolution began to develop'.[45] This is the approach sketched out by the Wilsons and reiterated by many more recent writers. Witch beliefs, it is said, are the product of small-scale societies. But the growth of large-scale societies, where relationships are 'impersonal and segmental', precludes the need for such concepts. For then, says Professor Marwick, 'disturbances in those relationships that remain personal and total may be isolated, compartmentalized and expressed in forms that do not necessarily require a belief in mystical personal influence'.[46]

Allied with theories of this kind is the assumption that superior technology ultimately makes magic superfluous. This is presumably a development of the view originally stated by Malinowski. It is echoed by Mr Reynolds, when he says that 'no doubt, as twin standards of health and education rise', the African belief in witchcraft will dwindle; and by Mr Crawford, who remarks that 'as long as children and young people continue to die it is unlikely that belief in wizardry will be abandoned'.[47]

Finally, there is the view that witch beliefs dwindle when men find alternative methods of expressing the same tensions. Such methods include arson, abuse, and homicide in the villages; radicalism and the open expression of hostility in the towns.[48]

All these interpretations are extremely suggestive, yet I think, with respect, that they all call for more scrutiny before they can be confidently applied to England. Large-scale communities, for example, had existed long before 1736. London, in particular, had several hundred thousand inhabitants by 1600, but it was not free from witchcraft accusations. Of course, neighbourly communities can subsist within very large urban complexes, but I doubt whether any great change took place in the texture of metropolitan living during the critical transitional period of the late seventeenth and early eighteenth centuries. Nor can it be said that technology had made magic superfluous by 1700. Medical therapy, which is the technique most obviously relevant to our subject, made no advance (smallpox inoculation apart) that substantially affected the expectation of life before the nineteenth century; some say even later. There is no reason to believe that the level of infant mortality or the general vulnerability to inexplicable disease was so much less in 1750 than it had been in 1550 as to account for the decline in witchcraft suspicions between the two dates. The remarkable fact in the history of medicine is that supernatural theories went out before modern techniques came in. Men somehow became prepared to combine impotence in the face of current misfortune with the faith that a technical solution would one day be found, much in the spirit with which we regard cancer today.

Instead of these highly generalized explanations, I would

suggest that an essential circumstance underlying the decline of witchcraft accusations in England was the changing situation of the dependent members of the community. In the Middle Ages the tensions arising from the inadequate discharge of neighbourly duties seldom produced accusations of witchcraft, since prevailing religious beliefs did not allow this to happen. The Reformation made such accusations possible, while also coinciding with a deterioration in the position of widows and the dependent. But by the later seventeenth century the conflict between charity and individualism, which had generated so many witch accusations in the past, was fast on the way to being resolved. With the development of the national Poor Law, the support of the indigent became a legal obligation and gradually ceased to be regarded as a private moral duty. The Poor Law was established in Tudor times, but it was at first invoked only as a last resort to supplement private charity, and it took time for men to grow accustomed to its implications. It was inevitable, however, that their everyday standards of conduct should ultimately have been affected. The merchants and gentry who established the large charitable foundations did not give food away at the door; neither did old women come to ask them for it. Even the clergy began to teach that charity should be prudent and calculated, and that the poor were largely responsible for their own misfortunes.

In such circumstances many of the old tensions and feelings of guilt withered away. A man who turned his neighbour from the door could do so with a clearer conscience, for he knew that other ways now existed of dealing with the problem. The period when witch accusations were at their height was the time when the conflict between the communal norms of mutual aid and the individualistic ethic of self-help was probably at its most acute. By the end of the seventeenth century this conflict was on its way to being resolved by the disappearance of the old norms and their supersession by a new individualistic morality.

In many village communities, however, the conventions of neighbourliness and mutual help survived into the nineteenth century. Women still came to the door to beg and borrow, and the man who turned them away empty-handed did so with mixed feelings. But the abolition of the Witchcraft Act meant that the possibility of formal accusation was no longer open.

Instead, villagers turned to informal violence, counter-magic, and the occasional lynching. The tensions reflected by these isolated acts of violence, which, it must be remembered, continued all through the nineteenth century, remained much the same. It was no accident that Ruth Osborne, who was lynched for witchcraft by a Hertfordshire mob in 1751, had been previously refused butter-milk by a farmer, whose subsequent mysterious illness was the basis of the accusation against her.[49] But acts of violence of this kind were now treated by the authorities as cases of murder. The position of English villagers in the century after 1736 may thus be compared to that of the modern African, deprived of his poison ordeals, and subject to Witchcraft Suppression Acts. In these circumstances, witch beliefs inevitably declined, for, as Mr Crawford stresses (1967, pp. 281-282), it is not the accusation of witchcraft that has the cathartic effect, but its acceptance and *proof*; and after 1736 proof became difficult and means of redress illegal. In these circumstances a different attitude to misfortune was ultimately to arise.

CONCLUSION

I therefore suggest that a functional interpretation of the role of witch beliefs in English villages during the sixteenth and seventeenth centuries can be simultaneously combined with a theory of social and intellectual change. The tensions expressed in witchcraft accusations had existed long before the witch trials started in the mid-sixteenth century. But they had had to be expressed and resolved in other ways. Witchcraft was something against which the English medieval Church provided a satisfactory ritual means of protection and, if necessary, a cure. This is why misfortune was so seldom attributed to witchcraft before the Reformation. Such cases as we know of usually relate to allegations of *attempted maleficium*, not to damage actually caused. But, once the Protestant Reformers took this religious counter-magic away, open accusations and legal prosecutions became necessary. In the later seventeenth century, however, the educated classes lost faith in the intellectual presuppositions upon which witch beliefs depended. The trials therefore came to an end. Informal allegations continued to be made in some village communities, but only in those where the conflict between individualism and neighbourliness was still a real one. In the country at large this conflict was steadily diminishing.

I claim no finality for these suggestions, and it will be obvious that I have had to telescope my argument at many points. Nor am I unaware of the difficulties and inconsistencies it presents. But I hope to have shown that anthropological insights can illuminate the study of historical records in an English context; and I have no doubt that much of the Continental evidence is susceptible to the same kind of treatment. It is pleasant, therefore, to have the opportunity of expressing my indebtedness to the many social anthropologists without whose patient labours my own less cautious speculations would have been impossible. There are certain key points that only observation in the field can resolve, and for the historian such observation is impossible. But there is much to be learnt from those who have witnessed similar phenomena elsewhere, even though they have done so in the present rather than in the past, and in Africa rather than in England.

NOTES

1. This paper has been left in substantially the same form as that in which it was presented to the Conference. But many valuable suggestions and criticisms were offered during the ensuing discussion and I have tried to take account of them in a book entitled *Religion and the Decline of Magic*, which I plan to publish shortly. My investigations throughout have been greatly stimulated by talks with Dr Alan Macfarlane, whose Oxford D.Phil. thesis, Witchcraft Prosecutions in Essex, 1560-1680: A Sociological Analysis' (1967), has appeared under the title *Witchcraft in Tudor and Stuart England* (London: Routledge, 1970). In order to avoid over-burdening the footnotes to this paper I have confined most of my references to the anthropological literature. The evidence for the historical argument is presented in my book.

2. Sir E. Coke, *The Third Part of the Institutes of the Laws of England*, Chapter 6 (at p. 43 in the 1817 edn).

3. E. Poeton, 'The Winnowing of White Witchcraft' (British Museum, Sloane MS. 1954), fol. 163v.

4. *Pace* Lienhardt, 1964, p. 151.

5. The original distinction was made by Evans-Pritchard, 1937, pp. 21 and 387, and has recently been amplified by Marwick, 1965b, pp. 23-24. For its limitations in other contexts see, for example, Middleton & Winter, 1963, pp. 2-3; Beidelman, 1963, p. 61, n. 2; Turner, 1964, pp. 318-324; Douglas, 1967; Crawford, 1967, p. 95.

6. Ewen, 1933, p. 190; 'A Touchstone or Triall of Witches discoveringe them by Scripture' (British Museum, Royal MS. 17 C XXIII), fol. 13r.

7. W. Freeman, 'Artificiall Alligations and Suspentions shewing the Conjunction of Art and Nature' (1653) (Bodleian Library, Ashmole MS. 1807), fol. 82v; Marwick, 1965b, p. 22.

8. *The Works of Francis Bacon*, ed. J. Spedding, R. L. Ellis, and D. D. Heath (1857-59), Vol. II, p. 660.

9. *Pace* Gluckman, 1965, p. 266, n. 2.

10. The most systematic account of the Assize records and depositions at present available is provided by Ewen (1929 and 1933). Dr Macfarlane's thesis (see note 1) has refined and corrected Ewen's findings for the county of Essex.

11. Marwick, 1965a, p. 17 (101 cases); Crawford, 1967, appendix I (103 cases). E. J. & J. D. Krige, 1943, pp. 264-267, cite 50 cases; Wilson, 1951, has 38; and Schapera, 1952, p. 49, refers to 90. Cf. the comments of Turner, 1964, p. 316.

12. J. Selden, *Table Talk* (Temple Classics edn), p. 125. I cannot echo Professor Trevor-Roper's optimistic allusion to 'this whole episode, whose basic facts, thanks to the work of our predecessors, are not in dispute' (Trevor-Roper, 1967, pp. 100-101).

13. A. F. Pollard, *Wolsey* (1929), p. 101; *Letters and Papers, Foreign and Domestic, of the Reign of Henry VIII*, ed. J. Gairdner (1887), Vol. X, p. 70; W. C. Abbott, *The Writings and Speeches of Oliver Cromwell* (1937-47), Vol. II, p. 458.

14. As described by Gluckman, 1955, Chapter 4, and 1965, p. 59. The point was originally made by Frazer, 1936, pp. 1-3.

15. R. Scot, *The Discoverie of Witchcraft* (1584), 1964 edn, pp. 28-29.

16. For example, Hunter, 1936, p. 347; Hulstaert, 1965, pp. 167-168; Crawford, 1967, p. 67. But Marwick, 1965a, pp. 3 and 72, says that 'virtually all', or 'close on 100 per cent', of the Ceŵa believe in it.

17. Only four of the forty-seven tribes discussed by Simmons, 1945, regard death as entirely natural (pp. 219-220).

18. I am puzzled by the assertion in Gluckman, 1965, p. 263, that 'universalistic religions like Christianity exclude . . . reference of misfortunes to personal mystical evil doing'.

19. J. Gaule, *The Mag-astro-mancer, or the Magicall-astrologicall-diviner Posed, and Puzzled* (1652), p. 197.

20. James VI, *Daemonologie, in Forme of a Dialogue* (Edinburgh, 1597), p. 49.

21. General accounts are given in Notestein, 1965, Chapter 8, and Ewen, 1933, pp. 254-314.

22. For these and similar campaigns see Richards, 1935; Marwick, 1950; Douglas, 1963b, p. 136; Marwick, 1965a, p. 94; Willis, 1968.

23. Winchester Diocesan Records, Court Book 37, p. 216.

24. See, for example, Hunter, 1936, pp. 308-309; Krige & Krige, 1943, p. 260; Mitchell, 1956, p. 153n; Reynolds, 1963, pp. 126-127; Beattie, 1964; Crawford, 1967, pp. 179-208. In England astrological divination was ultimately as subjective in its interpretation as is African astralagomancy, which has rules of comparable intricacy (Krige & Krige, 1943, p. 227).

25. Evans-Pritchard, 1937, p. 257. The contemporary sceptic, Thomas Ady,

unhesitatingly listed the existence of cunning men as one of the causes of the belief in witchcraft; T. Ady, *A Perfect Discovery of Witches* (1661), p. 169.

26. G. Gifford, *Two Sermons upon 1 Peter 5, vers. 8 and 9* (1597), pp. 67-68.

27. *A Rehearsall both Straung and True of Hainous Actes committed by Elizabeth Stile* (1579), Biv-Biir; M. Moore, *Wonderfull News from the North* (1650), p. 7.

28. 'I believe that in most cases the majority of the inquirers have decided in their own minds who is guilty, and that person is named by the diviner' (Hunter, 1936, pp. 308-309). It should be added that English diviners were usually expected to establish or deny the presence of witchcraft as opposed to purely natural causes, and were less concerned to adjudicate between different kinds of mystical cause than were their African counterparts.

29. Marwick, 1965a, pp. vii-viii, 8, 241-246, and the valuable Table XXV, listing the various types of previous misdemeanour attributed to the victims or their associates.

30. Wells Diocesan Records (Somerset Record Office), D 1.

31. *Books of Examinations and Depositions, 1570-1594*, ed. G. H. Hamilton (Pubs. of the Southampton Record Soc.), Southampton, 1914, pp. 158-159. It should be added that the same pattern of social relationship between witch and accuser can be traced in many of the trials initiated by Matthew Hopkins and can also be found in much of the material relating to witchcraft accusations on the Continent and in New England.

32. At least so long as they regard it as unimportant to decide whether witches exist or not (Firth, 1964, p. 237).

33. For example, Beidelman, 1963, pp. 62-63.

34. T. Hobbes, *Leviathan* (1651), Chapter 2.

35. Scot, *The Discoverie of Witchcraft* (1584), 1964 edn, p. 29.

36. *Life and Struggles of William Lovett*, ed. R. H. Tawney (1920), Vol. I, p. 18.

37. Evans-Pritchard, 1937, p. 117. Cf. Gluckman, 1955, p. 94, and 1962, p. 29; Beattie, 1963, pp. 51-52; Marwick, 1965a, pp. 281-282.

38. Winchester Diocesan Records, Court Book 50, p. 449. A character in G. Gifford's *A Dialogue concerning Witches and Witchcraftes* (1593) remarks of a local suspect that 'I have been as careful to please her as ever I was to please mine own mother, and to give her ever anon one thing or other' (Blr).

39. For a marvellously vivid account of this ambivalence, see the passage from A. Coppe, *A Fiery Flying Roll* (1649), printed in N. Cohn, *The Pursuit of the Millennium* (Mercury Books edn, 1962), pp. 371-374.

40. Marwick, 1952, p. 232. Cf. Gluckman, 1955, p. 98 ('The charge of witchcraft enables the rupture of the disturbed relationship to be effected with social approval').

41. 'One of the conditions for the resolution of tension in terms of sorcery is that alternative ways of expressing it are not available' (Marwick, 1965a, p. 294).

42. Trevor-Roper, 1967, by contrast, appears to regard Jews, witches, and Papists as interchangeable at will.

43. See, for example, Middleton & Winter, 1963.

44. Marwick, 1965a, pp. 295-296; Crawford, 1967, p. 67. Middleton & Winter, 1963, are similarly cautious about the impact of Western education unaccompanied by other changes (pp. 19-20).

45. Gluckman, 1965, p. 59. He also attributes the emergence of the concept of chance to 'the full flowering of the industrial revolution' (p. 218).

46. G. & M. Wilson, 1945, pp. 104, 162; Marwick, 1965a, pp. 295-296.

47. Reynolds, 1963, p. 165; Crawford, 1967, p. 285. A few suggestive criticisms of Malinowski's ideas on this subject are made in Kroeber, 1948, pp. 308-310.

48. Marwick, 1965a, p. 295; Mitchell, 1965, p. 201. The three general factors singled out by Horton, 1967, as helping to effect the transition from a traditional ('closed') to a scientifically oriented ('open') society are the development of the written transmission of beliefs, the growth of culturally heterogeneous communities, and the rise of trade, travel, and exploration (pp. 180-185). But all had been under way long before the decline of English witch beliefs.

49. Robbins, 1960, pp. 368-369. The same principle can be seen at work in a twentieth-century case quoted in Martin, 1965, pp. 72-73. An account of the better-known cases of informal violence against witches after 1736 is given in Summers, 1958, pp. 167-179.

REFERENCES

BEATTIE, JOHN. 1963. Sorcery in Bunyoro. In J. Middleton & E. H. Winter (eds.), *Witchcraft and Sorcery in East Africa*. London: Routledge & Kegan Paul.

—— 1964. Divination in Bunyoro, Uganda. *Sociologus* (n.s.) **14**: 44-62.

BEIDELMAN, T. O. 1963. Witchcraft in Ukaguru. In J. Middleton & E. H. Winter (eds.), *Witchcraft and Sorcery in East Africa*. London: Routledge & Kegan Paul.

CRAWFORD, J. R. 1967. *Witchcraft and Sorcery in Rhodesia*. London: Oxford University Press (for the International African Institute).

DOUGLAS, MARY. 1963a. *The Lele of the Kasai*. London: Oxford University Press (for the International African Institute).

—— 1963b. Techniques of Sorcery Control in Central Africa. In J. Middleton & E. H. Winter (eds.), *Witchcraft and Sorcery in East Africa*. London: Routledge & Kegan Paul.

—— 1967. Witch Beliefs in Central Africa. *Africa* **37** (1): 72-80.

EVANS-PRITCHARD, E. E. 1937. *Witchcraft, Oracles and Magic among the Azande*. Oxford: Clarendon Press.

EWEN, C. L'ESTRANGE. 1929. *Witch Hunting and Witch Trials. The Indictments for Witchcraft from the Records of 1373 Assizes held for the Home Circuit AD 1559-1736*. London: Kegan Paul, Trench, Trubner.

EWEN, C. L'ESTRANGE. 1933. *Witchcraft and Demonianism. A Concise Account Derived from Sworn Depositions and Confessions Obtained in the Courts of England and Wales*. London: Heath Cranton.

FIELD, M. J. 1960. *Search for Security: An Ethno-psychiatric Study of Rural Ghana*. London: Faber.

FIRTH, RAYMOND. 1964. *Essays on Social Organization and Values*. London: Athlone Press.

FRAZER, SIR JAMES GEORGE. 1936. *Aftermath: A Supplement to the Golden Bough*. London: Macmillan.

GLUCKMAN, MAX. 1955. *Custom and Conflict in Africa*. Oxford: Blackwell.

—— 1962. Les Rites de Passage. In M. Gluckman (ed.). *Essays on the Ritual of Social Relations*. Manchester: Manchester University Press.

—— 1965. *Politics, Law and Ritual in Tribal Society*. Oxford: Blackwell; Chicago: Aldine.

HORTON, ROBIN. 1967. African Traditional Thought and Western Science. *Africa* **37** (1): 50-71, (2): 155-187.

HULSTAERT, G. 1965. La Sorcellerie chez les Mongo. In M. Fortes & G. Dieterlen (eds.), *African Systems of Thought*. London: Oxford University Press (for the International African Institute).

HUNTER, MONICA. 1936. *Reaction to Conquest: Effects of Contact with Europeans on the Pondo of South Africa*. London: Oxford University Press (for the International Institute of African Languages and Cultures).

KRIGE, E. J. & J. D. 1943. *The Realm of a Rain-Queen: A Study of the Pattern of Lovedu Society*. London: Oxford University Press (for the International Institute of African Languages and Cultures).

KROEBER, A. L. 1948. *Anthropology*. (New edition.) New York: Harcourt, Brace.

LEA, H. C. 1939. *Materials towards a History of Witchcraft*. (Edited by A. C. Howland.) Philadelphia: University of Pennsylvania Press.

LIENHARDT, GODFREY. 1964. *Social Anthropology*. London: Oxford University Press.

MARTIN, E. W. 1965. *The Shearers and the Shorn: A Study of Life in a Devon Community*. London: Routledge & Kegan Paul.

MARWICK, M. G. 1950. Another Modern Anti-Witchcraft Movement in East Central Africa. *Africa* **20** (2): 100-112.

—— 1952. The Social Context of Ceŵa Witch Beliefs. *Africa* **22** (2): 120-135.

—— 1965a. *Sorcery in its Social Setting: A Study of the Northern Rhodesian Ceŵa*. Manchester: Manchester University Press.

MARWICK M. G. 1965b. Comment. In M. Fortes & G. Dieterlen (eds.), *African Systems of Thought*. London: Oxford University Press (for the International African Institute).

MIDDLETON, J. & WINTER, E. H. (eds.). 1963. Introduction to *Witchcraft and Sorcery in East Africa*. London: Routledge & Kegan Paul.

MITCHELL, J. CLYDE. 1956. *The Yao Village: A Study in the Social Structure of a Nyasaland Tribe*. Manchester: Manchester University Press.

— 1965. The Meaning in Misfortune for Urban Africans. In M. Fortes & G. Dieterlen (eds.), *African Systems of Thought*. London: Oxford University Press (for the International African Institute).

NOTESTEIN, WALLACE. 1911. *A History of Witchcraft in England from 1558 to 1718*. Reprinted, New York: Russell & Russell, 1965.

REYNOLDS, BARRIE. 1963. *Magic, Divination and Witchcraft among the Barotse of Northern Rhodesia*. London: Chatto & Windus.

RICHARDS, AUDREY I. 1935. A Modern Movement of Witch-Finders. *Africa* 8 (4): 448-461.

ROBBINS, ROSSELL HOPE. 1960. *The Encyclopaedia of Witchcraft and Demonology*. (Second printing.) London: Peter Nevill; New York: Crown Publishers.

SCHAPERA, ISAAC. 1952. Sorcery and Witchcraft in Bechuanaland. *African Affairs* **51**: 41-52.

SIMMONS, LEO W. 1945. *The Role of the Aged in Primitive Society*. New Haven, Conn.: Yale University Press.

SUMMERS, MONTAGUE. 1958. *The Geography of Witchcraft*. (First published in 1927.) Evanston and New York: University Books.

TREVOR-ROPER, H. R. 1967. *Religion, the Reformation and Social Change*. London: Macmillan.

TURNER, VICTOR W. 1964. Witchcraft and Sorcery: Taxonomy versus Dynamics. *Africa* **34** (4): 314-324.

WILLIS, R. G. 1968. Kamcape: An Anti-sorcery Movement in South-West Tanzania. *Africa* **38** (1): 1-15.

WILSON, GODFREY & MONICA. 1945. *The Analysis of Social Change*. Cambridge: Cambridge University Press.

WILSON, MONICA. 1951. *Good Company: A Study of Nyakyusa Age-Villages*. London: Oxford University Press (for the International African Institute).

© Keith Thomas, 1970

4

Alan Macfarlane

Witchcraft in Tudor and Stuart Essex[1]

INTRODUCTION

This paper will assume a knowledge of the historical background
to witchcraft prosecutions in sixteenth- and seventeenth-century
England. (The best general studies of English witchcraft are
Ewen, 1929, and Notestein, 1911.) It will also assume a general
knowledge of current anthropological interpretations of witchcraft and sorcery.[2] Its more general aim is to show by a concrete
example the way in which the disciplines of history and social
anthropology may benefit each other.

There are many topics that, like witchcraft, need serious investigation by the historian of pre-industrial England equipped
with contemporary anthropological ideas. An exchange of ideas
would also benefit anthropologists. Historical material provides
information which is different from and often more extensive
than that used by anthropologists. For example, the following
account of Essex witchcraft is based on over 700 cases of witchcraft in one county in England over a period of 120 years. This
is a far greater number than has ever been assembled by an
anthropologist.[3] The historian also has the advantage of being
able to study change in beliefs. He is able to watch the rise and
decline of accusations and may seek to correlate such changes
with other contemporary movements. He is able to recognize
that witchcraft accusations may be a far more radical and disruptive force than they sometimes appear in anthropological
analysis.

In the year 1593 a literary character was made to say concerning witches:

> 'I heare of much harme done by them: they lame men and
> kill their cattle, yea they destroy both men and children. They
> say there is scarce any towne or village in all this shire, but
> there is one or two witches at the least in it' (Gifford, 1593,
> sig. A4^v).

The first object of this paper will be to see how far the assertion that there was 'scarce any towne or village' without its witch was true. If it was accurate, it seems evident that we cannot understand Elizabethan village society without taking witchcraft beliefs into account. In the latter part of the paper two theories will be suggested to account for the phenomena outlined in the first part. It will be seen how far witchcraft beliefs helped to explain events for which religious and medical knowledge were unable to provide a satisfactory answer. An attempt, albeit superficial in the limited space available, will also be made to relate witchcraft accusations and beliefs to certain types of conflict in society, particularly that between an ideal of neighbourliness and the practical necessities enforced by economic and social change. Because my knowledge is limited to that area, this discussion will be confined to the county of Essex. On a number of occasions, where even more detailed research is needed, I have confined myself to three adjacent villages, Hatfield Peverel, Boreham, and Little Baddow, which lay approximately five miles to the east of Chelmsford (see map on p. 85). Most of the analysis will be centred on the forty years after the passing of the Witchcraft Statute of 1563. The problems of how far Essex was exceptional within England, how far England differed from the Continent, and to what extent witchcraft beliefs changed after 1603 or originated before 1563, crucial as they are, cannot be discussed here.

The meaning given to the term 'witchcraft' will emerge during this paper, but it may be given a preliminary definition as supernatural activity, believed to be the result of power given by the Devil, and causing physical damage, for instance death. 'White witchcraft' is roughly similar to this, except that the aim is healing rather than hurting.

THE DIMENSIONS OF WITCHCRAFT IN ESSEX

Court records, principally those of the Assize and ecclesiastical courts, provide the bulk of the actual prosecutions for witchcraft in Essex. From them we learn the names and villages of approximately 545 people who were accused of witchcraft, black or white, between 1560 and 1680. Over two-thirds of these were accused of 'black' witchcraft, and many were imprisoned or

executed; for instance, some seventy-four persons are known to
have been executed at the Essex Assizes. Of the 426 villages in
Essex at this time, some 227 are known to have been connected
with witchcraft prosecutions in some way or other. At the peak
period of prosecutions some 13 per cent of the indictments for
all offences over a ten-year period at the Essex Assizes were for
witchcraft; this offence was second only to theft in its frequency.
Witches were accused of bewitching humans on 341 occasions
and animals on eighty occasions at this court.

At the village level, Hatfield Peverel, with a total population
of roughly 500, over a period of twenty-five years, harboured
fifteen suspected witches; another thirty persons were directly
involved as husbands or victims of witches. In Boreham, a
village of seventy-eight households in 1575, there were at least
four suspected witches. Seen as a proportion of all known
offences at the Quarter Sessions and Assize courts from these
villages during Elizabeth's reign, witchcraft accusations also
appear important. Thus, in Hatfield Peverel, there were roughly
twenty-six assault cases, two murders, one suicide, eleven cases
of theft, and fourteen cases of witchcraft; in Boreham, the
proportion of witchcraft cases was a good deal lower – five
assaults, one murder, twenty thefts, and four witchcraft. In the
three villages together there were five times as many known
cases of witchcraft as of murder.

Yet even these numbers seriously underestimate the amount
of interest in witchcraft. Comparison of the court records with
other sources suggests that loss of records means that under
75 per cent of the suspected witches brought to court are known
to us. Moreover, it seems that approximately one in four of
those strongly suspected of witchcraft in the villages were never
formally accused. Fear of the witch, the migration of the suspect, and other factors tended to curb accusations. It further
appears that only the more serious offences at the Assizes were
recorded; thus the actual total of 490 indictments for black
witchcraft represents only some one-third of the accusations
made at the court. To take one example: from court records we
learn of a woman tried at Quarter Sessions and Assizes for
bewitching a gelding to death; she was acquitted at the latter
court. The court records alone would give a picture of a mild
prosecution. But from the pamphlet account of the same trial

we learn of a web of suspicions behind this one official accusation. Among the misfortunes supposedly inflicted by this suspect were: tormenting a man, killing chickens, causing a woman to swell so that she looked pregnant and nearly burst, making cattle give 'gore stynking blood' instead of milk, making a child ill, and tormenting another so that it 'fell unto suche shrickyng and staryng, wringyng and writhyng of the bodie to an fro, that all that sawe it, were doubtful of the life of it'. If we take all these underestimates into account and multiply the total of known prosecutions, it seems that roughly 2,500 individuals were involved directly in black witchcraft accusations, either as witch or victim, between 1560 and 1680. These accusations occurred within a county with a population of approximately 100,000 persons.

The distribution of the actual prosecutions may be analysed in various ways. Temporally, the peak of trials at both ecclesiastical and Assize courts was in the 1580s and 1590s – with a final outburst in 1645 (see graph on p. 86). The prosecutions died away long before the repeal of the Witchcraft Act in 1736. Although certain years saw peaks, accusations continued year in and year out during Elizabeth's reign.

By geographical area, again, prosecutions were spread all over Essex (see map facing). They seem to have started in the area around Chelmsford and were, to a certain extent, concentrated in the central and northern strip of Essex. The northeastern Tendring Hundred was practically free except for the two most notorious trials, those of 1582 and 1645, when a group of adjoining villages became the centre of prosecutions. All broad attempts to correlate the distribution with economic, social, or religious factors have, so far, been unsuccessful. For example, there seems to be no particular relationship to areas of population density, the new draperies, enclosure, or forest land.

By sex, it is apparent that witches were usually women. Of 270 suspected witches at the Assizes, all but twenty-three were women. Women, also, were slightly more likely to be bewitched; thus, at the same court, indictments stated that 103 males had been bewitched to death, 116 females. Neither in this, nor in the myths and types of injury inflicted, does there seem to have been any marked sexual element in Essex witchcraft.

By occupation and status, it appears that witches were usually from a slightly lower economic level than their accusers. Thus, of fifty husbands of witches whose status is given in the Assize records, twenty-three were 'labourer' and four were yeomen; while of forty-five victims whose status was given, only six were labourers and sixteen yeomen. Twenty per cent of the suspects were connected with non-agricultural occupations, and 40 per cent of the victims; the totals are, however, very small. Evidence

The county of Essex, showing sample villages

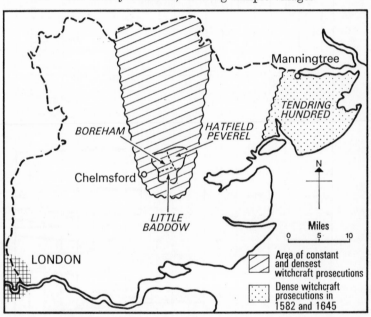

from the pamphlet accounts of trials, and from the study of the three villages, suggests that the suspects, although poorer than their victims, were not the poorest in the village. For instance, in Boreham, of the ten people receiving aid from the overseers of the poor, none were witches – despite the presence of four suspected witches in the village. Rather, Margaret Poole of that village, a suspected witch, was married to a man who was constable of the village, and who, in 1566, was one of the assessors of the lay subsidy and himself the sixteenth highest contributor.

As regards marriage and age, it does not seem that witches were necessarily unmarried, either widows or spinsters. Thus,

Number of persons accused of witchcraft at the Essex Assizes, 1560–1680,
and number of Assize files surviving

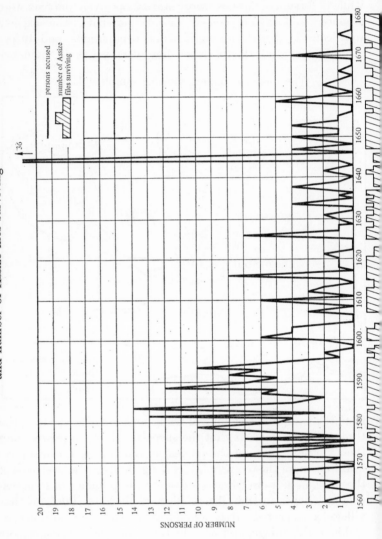

of fifteen women whose marital status we know in the three sample villages, only one was unmarried, while eight were widowed. From the Assize records we know that, of 117 persons whose marital status was given, 40 per cent were widows. This figure is clearly interlinked with the age of those involved. It is difficult to get statistical information on this problem, but coroners' inquisitions on five imprisoned witches in 1645 show them to have been aged 40, 'about 50', 70, 70, and 'about 84' years, respectively. Tracing individuals in local records also suggests that older women, that is women over about 50 years of age, were more powerful witches, though it was believed that they tried to impart their witchcraft to their young children.

Detailed analysis of the kinship structure in the three villages has given the negative conclusion that witches were hardly ever related by blood to their victims, though they occasionally confessed to bewitching their husband or relations by marriage. On the other hand, almost all bewitchings occurred within a village and within groups of neighbours. Thus, of 460 cases of bewitching property or persons tried at the Assizes, only fifty occurred between villages; the rest were within the village. This inter-neighbour bewitching is clearly shown in the pamphlets. In Hatfield Peverel, one witch gave her familiar 'to mother Waterhouse her neighbour' and she in turn 'falling out wyth another of her neybours' killed three geese and 'falling out with another of her neybours and his wife' killed the husband. In this village it is even beginning to appear that nearly all the accusations took place between the tenants of one manor and not those of another. This manor was composed of a dissolved priory, but there seems to be no general correlation between dissolved monastic foundations and witchcraft tensions. Nor has any connection been found between manors with partible inheritance, or ultimogeniture, and accusations.

Finally, those involved may be analysed to see whether there is any connection between witchcraft suspicions, religious groupings, and deviant behaviour of other kinds. The distribution of prosecutions shows no obvious correlation with Puritan centres or with Roman Catholic strongholds. Nor does a detailed study of church attendance and the religious formula of wills in the three sample villages show any marked relationship between religious attitudes and attitudes to witchcraft. Thus, in Hatfield

Peverel, none of the ten women presented between 1584 and 1600 for not attending church were suspected witches. In fact it was recognized by contemporaries that witches might be outwardly godly people; those 'which seemed to be very religious people, and would constantly repair to Sermons near them' might be witches (Stearne, 1648, p. 39). Nor does comparison of those known to be witches and those accused of thefts, suicide, murder, breaking the sabbath, quarrelling, scolding, or sexual offences show any clear correlation in the three villages. Thus in Boreham, where there were roughly thirteen bastardy cases, six cases of premarital intercourse, and seventeen miscellaneous cases of sexual misbehaviour between 1570 and 1600, there is only one possible overlap with a suspected witch. Although witches were thought of as quarrelsome and unpleasant people they were not usually formally accused of other offences.

WITCHCRAFT AS AN EXPLANATION OF MISFORTUNE IN VILLAGE LIFE

One theory for the existence of witchcraft beliefs is that they are, in certain respects, the most satisfactory explanation of misfortune or strange events. If medicine failed to heal and God seemed to turn a deaf ear to prayer, then the individual, it is suggested, could at least busy himself in hunting down the witch and countering her magic, occupations which both took the mind off the grief and held out a partial hope of recovery. So attractive, in fact, was the witchcraft explanation, that some authorities believed that people related almost every injury to a witch. Reginald Scot argued

> 'that fewe or none can (nowadaies) with patience indure the hand and correction of God. For if any adversitie, greefe, sicknesse, losse of children, corne, cattell, or libertie happen unto them; by and by they exclaime uppon witches' (Scot, 1584, p. 25).

On the other hand, it is quite evident from the three-village study that only a small proportion of the many accidents in an Elizabethan village *were* interpreted as the result of the evil will of a neighbour. In Boreham between 1560 and 1603 witches were accused of killing one child and making one man ill. Even if this was only a small part of the actual suspicions against them, it must have been a tiny proportion of the total illness and 351 known deaths during this period in the village. In the same village, coroner's inquests were held on the bodies of two young men who were squashed to death by a landslide while digging in a sand pit, and on another inhabitant who fell into a stream and drowned. There is no suggestion that they were believed to have been bewitched; the verdict was 'death by misfortune'. Since it seems, therefore, that death or injury could be explained in other ways, we are left with the problem of why certain injuries were ascribed to witches and not others.

To a limited extent the answer lies in the nature of the injury. To begin with, witchcraft explained only individual misfortunes, not general phenomena such as major climatic changes or the burning down of a whole town. Witches were accused in Essex courts of burning down a *particular* barn, nearly blowing down a *particular* house, and sinking a *particular* ship. There was also an emphasis on the strangeness of an event: for instance when a huge tree suddenly fell down on a windless day; or when a normally clean woman 'was on a sudden so filled with Lice, that they might have been swept off her cloaths with a stick', especially when the lice were 'long, and lean, and not like other Lice' (Pamphlet, 1645, p. 23). Again, the amount of pain, physical or emotional, involved and the ability of physicians to deal with it, were partly relevant. Thus witches were, above all, suspected of killing human beings, and those whose death was ascribed to witches characteristically languished some time before they died. Of 214 people stated at the Assizes to have been bewitched to death where the length of time they were ill is given, only seventeen were said to have died immediately, while seventy were ill for between one and three months.

It is very difficult to know whether certain illnesses were always ascribed to witches, and other types never. It does seem that the plague was infrequently blamed on specific witches; thus in the three sample villages, years of high mortality in the parish registers did not coincide with an increase in supposed deaths by witchcraft. Nor does it seem to have been death at childbirth that was automatically blamed on witches. Of 233 deaths by witchcraft recorded at the Assizes, only seven are known to have been those of infants under three months old.

Even children seem to have been less frequently the objects of witches' attacks than mature people: in Hatfield Peverel, nine out of ten of those supposedly bewitched to death were adults. Thus witchcraft was characteristically a relationship between two fully grown people. If, as sometimes was alleged to happen, the witch was unable to bewitch her enemy because of his godly life, she bewitched his children or animals instead.

Some sceptics argued that witchcraft was used as an explanation only where medical knowledge fell short, that physicians themselves blamed witches if they could find no 'naturall distemperature of the body'. This seems only partly to have been true, and the conclusion drawn from it, that witchcraft beliefs and accusations declined because of an alleged advance in medical techniques during the seventeenth century, seems even less likely. Such a theory is *not* based on any demonstrable advance in medical knowledge at the village or practical level during this period, nor does it account for the many injuries to animals and property – such as beer and butter – blamed on witches. At a more sophisticated level, both Sir Thomas Browne and William Perkins stressed that, even if an illness was explicable by medical theory, it might still originate in the evil will of another person. Here they were making the distinction between a cause in the mechanistic sense – *how* a certain person was injured – and cause in the purposive sense – *why* this person and not another was injured. When people blamed witches they did it not out of mere ignorance, but because it explained why a certain misfortune had happened to *them*, despite all their precautions; why, for example, their butter did not 'come'. Thus we have an account of a woman who could not have success with her butter; she tried feeding the cows on better food, tried scalding her butter pans, and finally, in desperation, used the old counter-witchcraft charm of sticking in a red-hot horseshoe. The butter came (Pamphlet, 1582, sig. E8^v).

A very complex, yet vital, problem is whether people suffered some misfortune and then looked round for a witch, or whether they disliked a person and then blamed subsequent misfortunes on him. There is evidence for both processes, but the more normal form seems to have been for the quarrel to precede the injury, for the suspicion to be present before the accident. The way in which suspicions grew up, intermingling injuries with tensions, is excellently illustrated in the words of George Gifford, writing in 1587:

'Some woman doth fal out bitterly with her neighbour: there followeth some great hurt, either that God hath permitted the devil to vex him: or otherwise. There is a suspicion conceived. Within fewe yeares after shee is in some iarre with an other. Hee is also plagued. This is noted of all. Great fame is spread of the matter. Mother W is a witch. She hath bewitched goodman B. Two hogges which died strangely: or else hee is taken lame. Wel, mother W doth begin to bee very odious and terrible unto many. Her neighbours, dare say nothing but yet in their heartes they wish shee were hanged. Shortly after an other falleth sicke and doth pine, hee can have no stomacke unto his meate, nowe he can not sleepe. The neighbours come to visit him. Well neighbour, sayth one, do ye not suspect some naughty dealing: did ye never anger mother W? truly neighbour (sayth he) I have not liked the woman a long tyme. I can not tell how I should displease her, unlesse it were this other day, my wife prayed her, and so did I, that shee would keepe her hennes out of my garden. Wee spake her as fayre as wee could for our lives. I thinke verely shee hath bewitched me. Every body sayth now that mother W is a witch in deede, and hath bewitched the good man E. Hee cannot eate his meate. It is out of all doubt: for there were (those) which saw a weasil runne from her house-ward into his yard even a little before hee fell sicke. The sicke man dieth, and taketh it upon his death that he is bewitched: then is mother W apprehended, and sent to prison' (Gifford, 1587, sigs. G4-G4ᵛ).

This account is amply substantiated in the Essex pamphlets. How there was a gradual growth of feeling over a long period, although no event was ascribed to the witch for several years at a time, and then how more and more disaster was laid at her door, are graphically illustrated. Gifford shows how the whole village community became involved in the gossip and tension. He also shows the process whereby a person cast around in his mind to see who might have bewitched him: in this case he selected a person with whom he felt uneasy and against whom he had offended. Mounting bitterness against an individual could not find an outlet until proof of her witchcraft had been discovered; then she was either forced to confess her guilt and promise amendment of life at the ecclesiastical courts, or removed from the community by imprisonment or death at the Assizes. The stress throughout the account is on neither the strangeness nor the painfulness of the injuries, but rather on the social relationship preceding the injury. It would seem, there-fore, that the key to understanding Essex prosecutions does not lie primarily in the amount of pain and in explanations of suffer-ing current in Elizabethan villages, but rather in strains between villagers.

WITCHCRAFT AS A METHOD OF
DEALING WITH CONFLICT

Witchcraft prosecutions, we have seen, usually occurred between village neighbours. They almost always arose from quarrels over gifts and loans, when the victim refused the witch some small article, heard her muttering under her breath or threatening him, and subsequently suffered some misfortune. This sequence is particularly well illustrated in the witchcraft pamphlets. The following are some of the motives suggested either by confessing witches or by their accusers in the 1582 Assize trial. The witch acted because she was: refused the nurs-ing of a child; refused a loan of 'scouring sand'; refused 12*d*. for her sick husband; denied mault at the price she wanted; refused a 'mess of milk'; denied mutton. If we examine the motives of a single witch, Joan Robinson, we see that her various acts of witchcraft were precipitated by the following acts of her neigh-bours: she was denied an implement for making hay, the hire of a pasture, the sale of a pig, a cheese, a pig she had been promised, and payment for goods 'at her own reckoning'.

Another illustration of the fact that witchcraft was seen as a reply to unneighbourly behaviour is provided by the various counter-activities that were believed to be efficacious against witches. It was noted by contemporaries that it was those who refused gifts and other neighbourly charity who incurred the wrath of witches. Thus an Elizabethan preacher, Francis Trigge, told his congregation that

'we may see how experience, and the very confessions of witches, agree that the merciful lenders and givers are preserved of God, and unmerciful and covetous Nabals are vexed and troubled of Satan' (Haweis, 1844, p. 224).

Thus it begins to seem as if it was those who offended against the ideals of a cooperative society by refusing to help their neighbours who found themselves bewitched. The continued force of the old ideals of neighbourliness, as well as the belief that a moral offence would bring physical affliction, is excellently illustrated in the words of an Essex writer in 1656:

' "God hath given it as a strict Command to all men to relieve the poor" he told his audience, then he quoted from Leviticus that "Whosoever hearkeneth not to all the Commandements of the Lord to do them (whereof relieving the poor is one) the Lord will send several crosses and afflictions, and diseases upon them, as followeth in the Chapter" and continued that "therefore men should look into the Scriptures, and search what sins bring afflictions from Gods hand, and not say presently, what old man or woman was last at my door, that I may hang him or her for a Witch; yea, we should rather say, Because I did not relieve such a poor body that was lately at my door, but gave him harsh and bitter words, therefore God hath laid his Affliction upon me, for God saith, Exod. 22.23. If thou any way afflict widows, and fatherless, and they at all cry unto me, I will surely hear their cry, and my wrath shall wax hot against thee" ' (Ady, 1656, p. 130).

Physical afflictions, he suggested, could be punishment for failure to uphold the social code, and men might well tremble when they heard a neighbour's curse, backed, as it might be, by power from God, or, as they preferred to think, from the Devil.

Cursing was one of the most important methods supposedly employed by witches to injure their victims; often their familiars first appeared when an angry woman cursed or swore revenge on a neighbour. It seems, then, that a sanction which had long been effective in making people live up to social obligations was still felt to be powerful. Thus when Thomas Cooper warned the godly in 1617 to forgo indiscriminate charity and especially to be hard on suspected witches, 'to bee straight-handed towards them, not to entertaine them in our houses not to relieve them

93

with our morsels', he had to counsel his audience to 'use a Christian courage in all our Actions, not to feare their curses, nor seeke for their blessings' (Cooper, 1617, p. 288). It was considered necessary to shun overtures of friendliness on the part of suspected witches, for gifts of food might be the vehicle of witchcraft. In 1579 a witch bewitched two neighbours in gifts of a drink and an apple-pie. Witchcraft beliefs thus provided a mechanism for severing unwanted relationships; a person could be cut off 'because' he or she was a witch. Moreover, since people still felt guilt at such a break with the traditional ideals, witchcraft explained to them their feeling of anxiety – no wonder they were worried since they were in peril of being bewitched, likely to be repaid on the supernatural plane for their lack of charity. Although the outwardly accepted village ethic was still one of mutual aid and intimate neighbourly links, people were constantly forced into situations where they were made to depart from such an ideal. Hence we find people especially sensitive to witchcraft attacks on those occasions when neighbourly sentiments are most openly shown, during festivities such as weddings, or during illness. Suspected witches were often those who went round inquiring about their neighbours' health.

When a person was forced into a situation – by pressures it is beyond the scope of this paper to discuss – where he had to break with a neighbour, there must have been considerable difficulties in an Elizabethan village. There was no code to which he could appeal for justification; Christianity still upheld communal values. But through the mechanism of the witchcraft laws, and the informal channels of village opinion, support in a dispute over neighbourly obligations was given to the bewitched person rather than to the witch, who had, in fact, suffered under the older social ideals. Thus it could be argued that the emotion that lay behind witchcraft accusations arose largely from discord within individuals, within people who felt the demands of the old communal values and the power of the old sanctions, while also realizing the practical necessity of cutting down, or re-directing, their relationships. By means of witchcraft prosecutions the older values were undermined or changed while, on the surface, they were still, apparently, subscribed to.

Since some Essex villages seem to have been free from accusations, it is clear that witchcraft was not the necessary or only solution to such a conflict. Nor does it seem probable that disputes were absent before 1560 or suddenly ended in the middle of the seventeenth century. This suggests that alternative methods of settling village tensions were available, both in Elizabethan society and in the periods before and after. This is a huge topic and cannot be treated here. All that can be suggested is that earlier conflict may not have risen to such a pitch since there was a universal standard of behaviour to which appeal could be made, and that during the seventeenth century a new ethic and new institutions, centring on the treatment of poverty and one's obligations to neighbours, emerged and were established.

In Elizabeth's reign we may be witnessing a transitional stage. Such a clash of values could not be settled by most other normal methods of settling disputes. Religious guidance was split, and any comfort given by the ritualization of conflict or the confessional was destroyed at the Reformation. Various escapes such as suicide, mental breakdown, compulsive work or organization, alcoholism, and aggression, physical or verbal, seem to have been limited both in availability and in effectiveness. Thus, tentative as such conclusions must be because of the records, there do seem to have been comparatively low rates of crime, suicide, and mental breakdown in the three sample villages. It is even more difficult to decide how useful informal methods of settling disputes between and within villages were – gossip, joking, work and leisure activities, the advice of elders, and so on. The only positive evidence is that witchcraft *did* provide many acceptable mechanisms for overcoming uncertainty and anxiety. Physical attack on the witch was encouraged by the popular belief that an effective cure was to draw the witch's blood; a whole detailed set of counter-witchcraft rituals, and myths about the evil doings of witches, gave ample scope for activities and outlet for repressed fears and worries. Probably this all seems very highflown in the context of the historian's usual picture of an Elizabethan village. Perhaps, therefore, I could end by showing the sort of insight into village mentality that witchcraft evidence provides. Not only does it reveal some of the mental concomitants of economic and social change, but it also reveals a much less stable and simple 'popular mentality' than one might expect from the usual local sources.

On the surface, the villagers of Hatfield Peverel were practical, 'rational', farmers and craftsmen. Their seventy-five Elizabethan wills, extensive manor court rolls, criminal and ecclesiastical records show little sign, beyond the witchcraft prosecutions already mentioned, of oddness or tension. Yet, quite by chance, we are enabled to see, through the series of confessions recorded for the Assizes of 1566 and 1579, some of their secret fears and thoughts. The result is extraordinary. It immediately becomes clear that overlapping with the ordinary physical world was a sphere inhabited by strange, evil creatures, half-animal, half-demon. A world full of 'power', both good and evil. This cannot be dismissed as a delusion or fantasy of a minority; it appears to have been fully credible to all the villagers and to the presiding magistrates, who included the Queen's Attorney, Sir John Fortescue (later Chancellor of the Exchequer), and Thomas Cole, Archdeacon of Essex.

Only one example of the beliefs circulating in this village can be quoted here, one of the more extraordinary, but not exceptional. A girl was questioned by the Queen's Attorney and answered that while she was churning butter

> 'there came to her a thynge like a black dogge with a face like an ape, a short taile, a cheine and sylver whystle (to her thinking) about his neck, and a peyre of hornes on his head, and brought in his mouth the key of the milkehouse doore';

the animal demanded some butter from the milkhouse and then departed. When the girl told her aunt of this encounter, she sent for the priest who 'bad her to praye to God, and cal on the name of Jesus'. This manoeuvre caused only a momentary diversion, and the familiar reappeared several times. The Queen's Attorney then turned to Agnes Waterhouse, the suspected witch, and asked her, 'can you make it come before us nowe, if ye can we will dispatche you out of prison by and by', but she replied that she could not call him;

> 'then saide the queenes atturneye, Agnes Waterhouse when dyd thye cat suck of thy bloud never saide she, no saide hee, let me se, and then the jayler lifted up her kercher on her heade, and there was diverse spottes in her face and one on her nose, then sayde the quenes atturney, in good faith Agnes

when dydde he sucke of thy bloud laste, by my fayth my lord sayde she, not this fortynyght' (Pamphlet, 1566, pp. 322-323).

Agnes Waterhouse was duly executed; she was one of the first of a minimum of 110 Essex inhabitants who were to die, either of prison fever or by execution, on a charge of witchcraft, within the next hundred years.

The above study is based on the records of one English county. Until the remaining counties have been investigated we will not know how exceptional Essex is. It is hoped that some historically minded anthropologists will help in this immense task. The other even greater need is for general analysis of the social background within which witchcraft prosecutions occurred in Tudor and Stuart England. Many of the most important problems in this field have already been brilliantly outlined (Thomas, 1963). Until we know far more about the social impact of illness and high mortality, about conflict and tension between groups and between ideals, about kinship and neighbourliness, it is very difficult to make more than tentative suggestions concerning English witchcraft. If we study witchcraft in this period using anthropological studies as a model, it is as if Professor Evans-Pritchard had tried to write his book on witchcraft among the Azande in 1900, instead of 1937.

NOTES

1. This paper derives from my *Witchcraft in Tudor and Stuart England* (1970), which gives fuller consideration to sources and statistics. Research was carried out between 1964 and 1966 in the Essex and Public Record Offices. Thanks are due to all those at these Offices who made the research possible. I am especially grateful to my former supervisor, Mr Keith Thomas of St John's College, Oxford, many of whose ideas have been borrowed unacknowledged. His forthcoming work, entitled *Religion and the Decline of Magic*, provides a fuller discussion of many of the issues merely hinted at in this paper. Finally, this analysis would have been impossible without the help of my nuclear family, who aided in the laborious task of reconstructing the village background to prosecutions.

2. My enormous debt to anthropological analyses, particularly to those works included in the list of references below, will be apparent from this treatment of English witchcraft. It would have been quite useless to study English witchcraft prosecutions – as it is futile to study many other topics in pre-industrial England – without having absorbed the stimulating anthropological literature.

3. As White points out (1961, p. 65), most anthropological studies of witchcraft have 'made use of comparatively small quantities of case material', and

his thirty-five cases constitute a relatively large sample. Among anthropologists, M. G. Marwick appears to have drawn on the largest number of witchcraft cases as the basis for his statistics (Marwick, 1965, pp. 15, 17): thirty or forty informants described 194 cases; 107 of these were ascribed to sorcerers, and in 79 instances both victim and sorcerer are identifiable.

ACKNOWLEDGEMENT

The map of Essex and the graph of accused persons included in this paper are reproduced from the author's *Witchcraft in Tudor and Stuart England* (1970) by kind permission of the publisher, Routledge & Kegan Paul Ltd., London.

REFERENCES

ADY, THOMAS. 1656. *A Candle in the Dark: or, A Treatise Concerning the Nature of Witches and Witchcraft*. London.

COOPER, THOMAS. 1617. *The Mystery of Witchcraft*. London.

EVANS-PRITCHARD, E. E. 1937. *Witchcraft, Oracles and Magic among the Azande*. Oxford: Clarendon Press.

EWEN, C. L. 1929. *Witch Hunting and Witch Trials*. London: Kegan Paul, Trench, Trubner.

GIFFORD, GEORGE. 1587. *A Discourse of the Subtill Practises of Devilles by Witches and Sorcerers*. London.

—— 1593. *A Dialogue concerning Witches and Witchcrafts*. London.

GLUCKMAN, MAX. 1955. *Custom and Conflict in Africa*, Chapter IV. Oxford: Blackwell.

HAWEIS, J. O. W. 1844. *Sketches of the Reformation and Elizabethan Age*. London.

KLUCKHOHN, C. 1944. *Navaho Witchcraft*. Peabody Museum Papers, Harvard University, 22 (no. 2).

MACFARLANE, A. 1970. *Witchcraft in Tudor and Stuart England*. London: Routledge & Kegan Paul.

MARWICK, M. G. 1965. *Sorcery in its Social Setting: A Study of the Northern Rhodesian Ceŵa*. Manchester: Manchester University Press.

MIDDLETON, J. & WINTER, E. H. (eds.) 1963. *Witchcraft and Sorcery in East Africa*. London: Routledge & Kegan Paul.

NADEL, S. F. 1954. *Nupe Religion*, Chapter VI. London: Routledge & Kegan Paul.

NOTESTEIN, W. 1911. *A History of Witchcraft in England from 1558 to 1718*. Reprinted, New York: Russell & Russell, 1965.

PAMPHLET. 1566. *The Examination and Confession of Certain Witches at Chensford*. (Reprinted in Ewen, 1929, pp. 317-324.)

PAMPHLET. 1582. *A True and Just Recorde of the Information, Examination and Confession of All the Witches, Taken at St. Oses in the Countie of Essex,* by W. W.

—— 1645. *A True and Exact Relation . . . of Witches, Arraigned and Executed in the County of Essex..*

STEARNE, JOHN. 1648. *A Confirmation and Discovery of Witchcraft.* London.

SCOT, REGINALD. 1584. *The Discoverie of Witchcraft.* Page references are to the 1964 edition, preface by H. R. Williamson. Slough, Bucks.: Centaur Books.

THOMAS, KEITH. 1963. History and Anthropology. *Past and Present* **24**: 3-24.

WHITE, C. M. N. 1961. *Elements in Luvale Beliefs and Rituals.* Manchester: Manchester University Press (for the Rhodes-Livingstone Institute).

WILSON, M. 1951. Witch Beliefs and Social Structure. *American Journal of Sociology* **56**: 307-313.

© Alan Macfarlane 1970

PART II

Cleansing and Confession of Witches

Alison Redmayne

Chikanga: An African Diviner with an International Reputation[1]

This paper is about an African in Nyasaland[2] who was active as a diviner from about 1956 to 1964 and during that time attracted a large clientele from at least four different countries. Its purpose is threefold: first, to record briefly what is known about him, about his methods of divination and the spread of his influence; second, to discuss some of the factors that enabled him to be so influential, particularly among the Hehe of Tanganyika, a people who speak a Bantu language and who, from the time that they resisted the German conquest, have been regarded as one of the most important peoples in the country;[3] third, to suggest that the way his influence spread and the way in which different people interpreted his work may illuminate the study of similar phenomena which have occurred at other times and in other places.

CHIKANGA'S CALLING AND WORK[4]

Lighton Chunda, a Henga man, who was living at Ihete village in the south Rumpi hills, Rumpi District, northern Nyasaland, was an ordinary peasant but he was a relatively well-educated member of the community because he had had seven years' primary education. He was also a member of the Church of Central Africa Presbyterian. In about 1956 he was afflicted by an illness and went to see a medicine man called Muzegeva Simwaka, who treated him. This illness was thought to be a sign that he had been called to be a diviner, and when he recovered from his immediate physical danger he began to practise his new craft, curing the type of illness with which he had been smitten and discovering witches and sorcerers; for this he was suspended by the Presbyterian Church. These facts alone do not suggest that he was remarkable, and relatively few people have

103

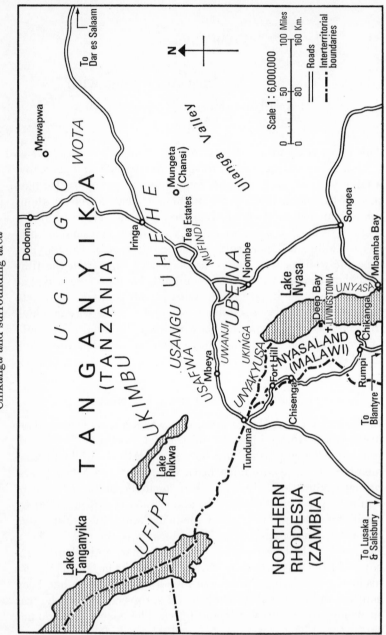

Chikanga and surrounding area

The site of Chikanga

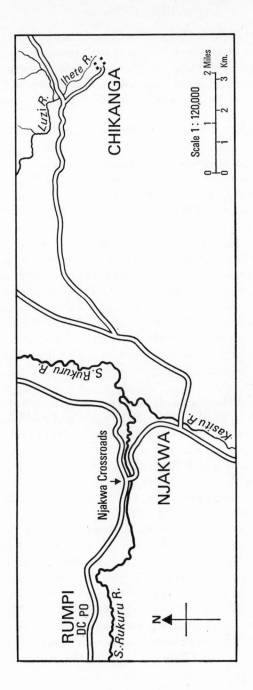

Most settlements are given the name of the headman, and the village where
Chikanga lived was actually called Chikanga.

heard about Lighton Chunda yet millions know about Chikanga, whose fame and influence spread in Nyasaland, Tanganyika, and Northern and Southern Rhodesia. Chikanga is a nickname meaning 'courage' which Lighton Chunda took when he began to practise as a diviner, a career in which he was extraordinarily successful.

At first he may have worked only spasmodically and drawn clients from near by, but by 1961 he was attracting a large number of people from the areas of Tanganyika nearest to the lake-shore, particularly among those in Songea District who are often referred to as Nyasa; by mid-1962 people from Mufindi in southern Uhehe had been to consult him; he became generally well known in northern Uhehe around Iringa town in about April 1963; and, during 1964, a significant number of Hehe from an isolated group at Wota in Mpwapwa District, central Tanganyika, visited him. His extraordinary ability as a diviner, drawing large crowds from four countries, would make a detailed investigation of his career worth while if anyone could attempt a study involving such diverse sources. This account, however, is limited because it is based mainly on the experience of observing his effect upon the Hehe and on a little knowledge gained from those who knew him, or who knew of his influence, in Nyasaland.[5]

Among the Hehe some diviners are made aware of their calling through an illness, in much the same way as Chikanga was, but the Hehe did not seem aware that Chikanga's power of divination had come to him in this way. There were a number of stories about how he started his career, yet no Hehe seemed concerned with the details. It might have mattered to some of his clients at the beginning, but it did not seem to later. He was reputed to have gone to South Africa to work and after some sort of quarrel with his brother he became ill, died, was buried, and rose from the dead.[6] When he arose he had acquired a mission. He had been sent by God[7] to cleanse Africa of witchcraft and sorcery, a formidable task, but one which, if he succeeded, would greatly diminish the frequency of sickness and death.

There was an impressive general agreement among a variety of his clients over an enormous area about everything involved in going to consult Chikanga – about the journey, about his

village, what happened there, Chikanga's appearance, food
supplies, cooking, language problems, transport, the way in
which divination sessions were organized, and how he delivered
his verdict. This story, told by one Hehe man who consulted
him, will serve to describe what happened.

This man – we shall call him John, a common name among
both Christian and pagan Hehe – had a chronic hernia, and in
January 1963 when he was unable to walk he had gone to
Iringa hospital and spent six days there being examined. He
had signed a paper agreeing to an operation and then managed to walk nine miles home on the day before the operation
was supposed to take place, because he had been told by a
sweeper that a dresser had been bribed by one of his enemies
to poison him. He then said that he was saving money to go
to be operated on in Dar es Salaam over 300 miles away
where he knew he would be safe. About five months later,
when the whole business of going to Chikanga was better
known, he decided instead to spend his money going there in
order to find out what had caused his illness.

John had a relation who also wished to consult Chikanga,
so they set off in the dark one morning and walked to Iringa
where they caught the 7.30 a.m. bus to Mbeya, about 230
miles away. They had never been so far away from Iringa
before, but they knew that Chikanga lived somewhere in
Nyasaland, and at Mbeya they would find plenty of people
who could tell them the way. As they had expected, they
found themselves in a crowd going to Chikanga, some Bena
and many Hehe, and with them they caught a bus going to
Tunduma on the Northern Rhodesian border, where they
arrived during the middle of the night. They passed through
the customs, where there was a door with a Tanganyika flag
over it, and waited until just before dawn when they got into
a bus which took them to Fort Hill. There it stopped for a
little while; they got out and bought bananas, and then the
bus went on to Chisenga and, after another stop, on again to
Rumpi, which they reached in the middle of the next night;
then on to the crossroads at Njakwa, which was the terminus
for this bus. They got out and hung around until about 4.0
a.m., when they went on in a different private bus, and just

before dawn they reached Chikanga's village. There they saw a number of long grass-roofed huts and Chikanga's own round hut. The bus-drivers then showed them the way to the huts where they could stay. There were people sleeping all over the floor, and at dawn some of them began to cook the food they had brought with them, for they had had no cooked food since they left home. In the morning they went to a clerk who spoke bad Swahili and better English, and he wrote down their headman's name and their chief's name, but not their own names. Then began their long wait.

The master of ceremonies was rumoured to be an ex-Tanganyika policeman. He was called Pilatu. Twice every day he used to blow a whistle to assemble the people and then announce a date; those who had arrived on that date would queue to consult Chikanga, while the others retired to another day of waiting around and discussing each other's troubles. At the evening whistle, which went after dark, each man had to take some leaves and a stick of firewood because Chikanga used to divine half the night by firelight. John claimed to have been luckier than most, since his day of arrival was called out on the sixth day after he reached Chikanga's village. He and his brother-in-law, who had accompanied him, stood in one of the long lines of people waiting to go into Chikanga. The first was a double line of those who had confessed their harmful activities, together with those whom they had afflicted, and the other five lines were single ones, of people seeking only the cause of their troubles. In turn they went into Chikanga's hut, where those who had been cleansed of their wrong-doing the day before were standing behind Chikanga's couch singing. In many rites or in games or when story-telling the Hehe consider it good manners to 'agree' (*kwidika*), that is to join in even if it means nothing to you, so John and his companion joined in when they had heard the songs through a few times, even though they did not understand them.

Chikanga was not an old man; he was, perhaps, in his mid-thirties, and he was not of striking appearance. He lay back on a European-type of couch and was wearing good European clothes, but he was unshaven. With his right hand he took hold of John and with his left he took hold of John's com-

panion, gripping each by his shirt at the throat, and declared
them both to be good men, that is they were not witches or
sorcerers. Some evil men were thought to go to Chikanga in
order to take suspicion away from themselves. He told them
to go to have small cuts made on their thumbs, neck, and
feet, and to come to hear the answer to their inquiries the
day after next.

The day after next they stood in the long lines at the first
morning whistle, and remained there passing the time by
talking to their neighbours. About an hour before the sun
set, they were called into Chikanga, who once more grabbed
their clothes at their throats and said to John with the hernia,
'You want to know about somebody's death?' He agreed.
'The one who died is not your relation but the child of your
brother-in-law.' He agreed. 'That child did not just die by the
will of *nguluvi* (the supreme being), he was killed by somebody.' John asked, 'Who has killed him?' Chikanga said
'Fundi Hassan mwaKipala. Do you know him?' He agreed
that he did. Then Chikanga, speaking to his companion, went
on to name a number of other people who had died, the
mother of another brother-in-law with her four children, two
of whom had died in one year and the other two the next,
together with their grandmother, who had been killed by another man. John and his companion asked why this sorcerer
should have killed his own close relations and affines, and
Chikanga explained that he had borrowed two head of cattle
from the brother-in-law and that the brother-in-law's mother
was the witness. Her death meant that there was no witness
to help him to claim his cattle back. The kinship of all these
in-laws is complicated because this man himself had four
wives and many full- and half-siblings.

The third matter discussed was John's own illness. Chikanga
told him that he was also seeking to know the cause of his
illness and that it did not come from *nguluvi*, the supreme
being, but from another brother-in-law. The client asked
'Who?' and Chikanga gave a Kihehe child's name, which he
did not immediately recognize, so Chikanga then gave the
name by which the man was known as an adult, and John
agreed that he knew him, but said that he could not understand why that brother-in-law should harm him. Chikanga

said it was because he wanted one of his wives. John, still very surprised, asked why he should particularly pick on *him* and *his* wife, and Chikanga's answer was, 'Why *not* you? He killed even his own brother.' John saw the point, so he then went with his companion to one of Chikanga's two clerks to get letters summoning the two sorcerers named by Chikanga. The clerk stamped the summonses with Chikanga's rubber stamp and then obtained what may have been his signature.

Such letters were usually addressed to the headmen of the areas from which the clients came and they were sometimes pinned up on the walls of local courts to put pressure on those named to visit Chikanga. Most had much the same theme. One, exhibited in a court, read thus:

'Ihete Village, P.O. Rumpi, Nyasaland. 18.4.63. Dear Sir, That one woman which you have sent here her name is Anjerinsa she very witching and another is very good her name Sismon Silonge. Chikanga (rubber stamp).'

The language of the Swahili versions was usually worse than this, but Chikanga understood that he must have a clerk capable of writing Swahili for his large Swahili-speaking clientele. The Swahili letters usually read something like this, '*Fulani ametakiwa hapa sana, sana. Halaka, Halaka Asicheriwe. Wasamu mimi* Chikanga (rubber stamp)', that is, 'So and so is wanted here very much, Hurry, hurry, he should not delay. Greetings me Chikanga.'

After receiving their letters the men were able to get into a privately owned Land Rover with a Tanganyika number plate, which journeyed through the night and the following day as far as the Tanganyika frontier, where the people were turned out because the driver was afraid of the Tanganyika police. In the evening they got into an Indian-owned bus, which for some reason – presumably because it had no lights – was not allowed to travel at night, so they slept in it and it moved off the next morning. They reached home on foot late that night. The dates John gave do not add up consistently, but the whole expedition took either two weeks or two weeks and two days, and this was considered very quick compared with the time spent by most other people, who had to wait for longer before Chikanga attended to their concerns. After some time the man who was supposed to have caused the hernia agreed to go to be cleansed, and John then said that he felt his health was improving.

It is difficult to imagine how bus-loads of people could have kept pouring into Chikanga's village and sustaining themselves there, often for weeks before they could obtain an audience, without the occurrence of an epidemic, social disorder, or severe food shortage. From 1960 there was a 'Chikanga bus' which ran on demand between Tunduma and Rumpi, and administrative officers feared that an epidemic might break out among the crowds of people living at Ihete in temporary huts in un-hygienic conditions. Eventually, the agricultural production of the surrounding area became geared to feeding the crowds that converged on Chikanga's village. Many people from other countries went enormous distances to consult him and were excited and impressed by what they saw. An administrative officer once had to arrange for the feeding, shelter, and repatri-ation of a vast crowd of Tanganyikans gathered at Deep Bay, who were hungry, penniless, and exuberant after seeing Chikanga.

Some have suggested that Chikanga kept his clients waiting a long time so that his assistants could mingle with them and find out what they wanted him to say and thus enable him to impress them with his uncanny knowledge of their affairs. However, sceptics who saw the gatherings at his village agree that the crowds were so large and of such diverse origins that this could not possibly have happened. Among the languages spoken by his clients and staff were Swahili, Chinyanja, English, and Chilapalapa (kitchen kaffir). Pilatu was a well-known figure as general organizer and head of the staff who made incisions in the clients. As Chikanga's popularity increased, so did the number and severity of Pilatu's incisions, until some Tonga people from the lake-shore complained and caused him to moderate the procedure.

Chikanga also impressed a number of Europeans by his obvious authority and confidence. One, employed in construct-ing roads in Tanganyika, had had trouble with the labourers

111

and, on the advice of the African foreman, visited Chikanga to obtain his verdict and assistance. Some doctors are said to have told a few of their patients to go to Chikanga, while he in turn sometimes advised his clients to obtain European medicine. The administrative officers who had the difficult task of administering Rumpi District found no evidence that could be used for prosecuting Chikanga; he himself demanded no payment for his services, and the administrators believed that he never named witches or sorcerers but merely requested that people should go to see him. The Churches collectively, particularly the local Presbyterian Church, which had a big mission station at Livingstonia only about sixty miles away from Ihete, regarded Chikanga with marked disapproval; yet among both European and African clergy there were many shades of opinion about how to regard him and how to deal with him. Officials of the Presbyterian Church once went to conduct a mission among the crowds waiting to consult him, and Chikanga made no attempt to resist or counteract this. Among his followers were some militant members of the Malawi Congress Party, who in the years before Independence attempted to disrupt the administration, but Chikanga joined the party only in 1960 and then probably with reluctance. Again, he himself could not be held responsible for the behaviour of others who intimidated their enemies into going to consult him. One District Commissioner who met him was impressed by his combination of modesty and serene confidence, and this view coincides with the impression given by the Hehe who consulted him. He was apolitical, not nativist, and, while telling some people that he was a member of the Church of Scotland and definitely not intending to be anti-Christian, appealed to those who recognized spiritual forces not acknowledged by the Church. He merely claimed to have the power of divination with which he wished to help good people.

There is thus evidence that the Hehe gave a substantially correct account of Chikanga and his work, but in order to assess the significance of his impact on the Hehe it is necessary to see it within the context of their beliefs concerning sickness and death, divination and sorcery – important matters in the daily life of the majority of Hehe, yet about which there is no detailed, readily available account.[8]

112

DIVINATION, SORCERY, AND MEDICINE
AMONG THE HEHE

Compared with the neighbouring peoples the Hehe are not particularly unhealthy and they appear to be rather more fertile,[9] but, like the members of any poor society without easy access to effective medical treatment, a high proportion of them are unwell most of the time. Adults are frequently involved in dealing with their own complaints and those of their children and relations. Many Hehe spend a significant amount of time seeking the advice of diviners, obtaining medicine, visiting the sick, and attending funerals. Common complaints are usually treated with herbal remedies, which people often make for themselves or for their friends and relatives, and there are other curative and protective medicines known only to professional medicine men or women. It is impossible to estimate how frequently most people procure medicine, but there are very few Hehe indeed whose bodies do not somewhere bear the scars of incisions made for administering medicine, which is rubbed into the cuts. There are common complaints such as scabies, tape worms, and ordinary wounds which are treated at their face value unless they become much more troublesome than they are expected to. However, there are also diseases about which many Hehe will consult a diviner because they believe that they must be told the cause of the complaint before the diviner will be able to advise them about the correct treatment.

Among the Hehe there are a considerable number of people who practise divination in a small way by rubbing sticks, shaking bottles containing foam, or putting the palms of their hands on boiling water. Generally, they attract clients who have minor concerns – who wish to detect a petty thief or to know which ancestral spirit is supposed to be causing a baby to cry for a name. However, the matters of most serious concern about which the Hehe consult diviners are likely to be severe illness and death. It is generally acknowledged that the most effective diviners are those possessed by a spirit (singular *lisoka*, plural *masoka*) and they often deliver a verdict by calling out, making odd noises, or speaking during their dreams. It is thought that the supreme being has looked kindly upon them and allowed

113

them to be possessed by a spirit which seeks responsibility in divination and so enables them to become rich. The Hehe also believe that there is a spirit living in a tree or a rock at Mungeta in the Ulanga valley, which they have consulted since before the German conquest.[10] This spirit is called Chansi and its messages are interpreted by a human servant whose name is Chavala. Chansi is unique but the Hehe consult it for much the same reasons as they would consult any other diviner who is reputed to be possessed by a perceptive spirit.

When a diviner has discovered sickness, infertility, or death to be the object of his client's inquiry there are a number of types of advice he may give. On rare occasions he may tell the client that his misfortune has been caused by the supreme being, or that a death was the result of *manga*, the type of extreme sadness and disappointment one may feel after being grossly mistreated by a relation, and that nothing can be done about it; more often he may tell him that he himself will make medicine for him or he may direct him to go to some particular medicine man; again, he may decide that the client has offended some particular ancestral spirit and that the best course of action is to make an offering to the spirit that has been offended; or he may decide that *wuhavi* (sorcery) is the cause of the misfortune and name the sorcerer.

Once a person has obtained harmful medicines or implements of sorcery, the Hehe believe that in order to make his medicines really powerful he must do something nasty, like committing incest or killing someone and eating the flesh. When the sorcerer uses his medicine to bring misfortune to others he enters into a relationship with it, so that if he wishes to change his ways and live once more as an ordinary person it is not enough for him to destroy his evil medicine; he must confess and be shaved (*kumogwa*). This process does not consist of shaving the hair but of making a series of little cuts on the temples, down the sides of the face, and sometimes also on the throat and hands, and then rubbing medicine into them.

Putting poison in someone's beer or burying harmful medicine in the path or hiding it in the eaves of one's enemy's hut are all alike described by the Hehe as *wuhavi*. It is impossible to distinguish exactly between what Hehe believe that others do and what they actually do. People accused of sorcery often

114

make extravagant confessions claiming to have done impossible things, but it is clear that a certain amount of poisoning, or attempted poisoning, does take place and that many Hehe keep medicines in their huts. Some of these are probably obtained with the intention of harming others and some for self-protection. There are medicines that fall into both categories, such as one believed to harm anyone who commits adultery with one's wife. How a Hehe regards this type of medicine will depend mainly on his position in relation to a particular case. A man possessing medicine intended to harm another who has wronged him will describe it as *litego* (a medicine trap), which he and his friends consider is legitimate self-protection or revenge. Those who believe themselves to have been harmed by that medicine, on the other hand, will probably describe its owner as a sorcerer.

There is no neatly structured pattern of sorcery accusations among the Hehe. This may be because their identity as one people with a common name is of relatively recent origin. Hehe society is an open society which developed rapidly between *c.* 1860 and 1890 when a number of small chiefdoms were amalgamated by an able chief and his successor, who also conquered many other peoples and imported a large number of war captives.[11] There are very few areas where the Hehe live in distinct settlements. Most live in dispersed homesteads whereever the land is sufficiently fertile and the water supply convenient. There is no standard pattern for the social composition of the neighbourhood and there are many different reasons why a man might become a headman. Those who suspect each other of sorcery may be of the same sex or of different sexes, they may be of the same generation or of proximate generations, they may be kin or affines or neighbours or completely unrelated people. Sorcerers may be men or women, but Hehe say that they are more often men because men have less pity than women. Perhaps the most significant relationship in which accusations of sorcery may occur is that between unrelated holders of political office, yet such accusations must be a very small proportion of the total.

Severe misfortune is not distributed evenly in the community and it does happen that a number of closely related people may become very ill or die within a short space of time. It is impossible to know what proportion of the total number of misfortunes is attributed to sorcery, because some matters are not dealt with until years after they occurred; yet it is certain that belief in sorcery and fear of it are important factors in Hehe society and that they have a significant influence on where people decide to live.

When a diviner has named a particular person as the cause of the illness about which he has been consulted, the client will attempt to persuade the sorcerer to be shaved by the diviner or by some other medicine man whom the diviner has named. The client hopes that, having eradicated the cause of his illness in this way, he will recover, and he will also be avenged by having induced the sorcerer to submit to the pain, humiliation, and expense of being treated. When a sorcerer has been named as the cause of a death or deaths the Hehe know that taking him to be shaved will not bring the dead person(s) back to life but the bereaved relations hope that it will prevent him killing anyone else; moreover, they may be able to persuade him to pay them substantial compensation and they may derive satisfaction from knowing that their enemy has had to submit to being shaved. Before the German conquest, ordeals were used to detect sorcerers and those found guilty were killed, but today accusations of sorcery and the punishment of supposed sorcerers are strictly forbidden by law.[12] People fear that some sorcerers may return to their evil ways even after they have been shaved. One educated Hehe wrote this of the beliefs of other members of his society:

> '(after being shaved) the particular *muhavi* may have learnt his lesson and decide to stop his devilish practice. However, some, with demonish audacity, decide to rearm themselves with the medicines at the possible risk of their own lives. They are usually the ones who have waded too far in blood and can hardly live out of it.'

There is also the problem of the person whom a diviner has named as a sorcerer, but who denies it and refuses to be shaved. The one who believes he has been attacked will then probably try to obtain stronger medicines to revenge himself and if the two are well matched the Hehe say that they may kill each other's relations. This type of sustained revenge is known as *wukole*.

The sheer quantity of misfortune, particularly sickness, infertility, and death, and the mental uneasiness caused by smouldering quarrels, mean that in Uhehe any new diviner who proved himself to be possessed by an effective spirit would be likely to attract many clients. However, there are certain features of the response of the Hehe to Chikanga which cannot be accounted for merely in these terms.

Ordinarily, if a Hehe has a problem which he deems is beyond the powers of some local diviner, he might travel to a more famous one in a neighbouring area or go to consult the spirit Chansi in the Ulanga valley. When the Hehe want medicine rather than divination they may consult local medicine men or those among neighbouring peoples. Likewise, if they want European medicine they may try the inadequate free District Council dispensaries, the unimpressive mission dispensaries in Uhehe, or the overcrowded government hospital in Iringa; and only if they have enough money, a particularly serious concern, and a very strong belief in the possibility of being healed do they go to one of the three good mission hospitals in neighbouring districts.

It is clear, then, that the journey people had to make in order to consult Chikanga was far longer than those which they would normally make in the quest for divination or healing, and for many of them it was the first time they had been outside Tanganyika. The return journey from anywhere in Uhehe was at least 800 miles by road, and for those from the isolated groups in central Tanganyika it was as much as 1,500 miles. The cost was also high, the bus fares being between about 120/- (£6) and 180/- (£9) return,[13] depending on the particular buses used as well as on the place from which one started. If, in addition, one had to buy food on the journey or at Chikanga's village, the expedition would be much more expensive. For the majority of the people who undertook the journey, these costs represented a very large outlay, not infrequently equal to their normal annual cash income; this is especially true where someone paid his own fare and then the fare of the person Chikanga had named as the cause of his misfortunes when he or she

agreed to go to be cleansed. Some people paid as much as 700/-
(£35) to accompany four named sorcerers who agreed to go.
This is an enormous price for poor agriculturalists to pay, the
equivalent of roofing a small hut with corrugated iron. However,
many people were not deterred; they borrowed from friends and
relations who presumably felt it in their own interests to be of
assistance, partly because if the illness or death concerned had
indeed been caused by a sorcerer they themselves might later
be attacked in the same manner, and partly because anyone who
was willing to lend money for this purpose would not be suspected of having caused the misfortunes in question. Some
probably had a genuine desire to help their friends who wished
to go. There was also the hope that once a sorcerer had been
named, had confessed, and had agreed to go to be shaved, he or
she would repay all the fares. In fact this matter of reclaiming
fares caused a lot of litigation, and headmen and Primary Court
magistrates were frequently troubled with such cases. In
Njombe District, on the southern borders of Uhehe, a rule had
to be made that no local court could hear a case concerned with
the expenses involved in visiting Chikanga.

The physical hardship of the journey was also likely to be far
greater than that usually involved in the pursuit of divination
or healing. Other famous diviners have drawn people from as
far as four or five days' walk away, and sometimes clients have
had to wait several days for an audience once they have arrived,
but the two or three days and nights in buses each way, and
then anything from a few days' to a month's wait at Chikanga's
village, required greater endurance than usual. Chikanga is
reputed to have told the local inhabitants around his village
not to charge high prices for food needed by his clients; some of
them, nevertheless, after nearly one month's sojourn there,
were weak, having finished their food and money, so they
went to tell Pilatu that if Chikanga could not see them that
day or the next day they would have to return home without
seeing him. Pilatu then arranged for Chikanga to see them
quickly.

There was one quality of Chikanga himself which set him
apart from, and above, all other diviners: he did not charge for
his services. For the Hehe the cost of visiting him was indeed
far greater than that of visiting and paying any ordinary diviner,

and cynical Europeans suggest that Chikanga was probably getting commission from the bus-owners who brought his clients to him, or that he owned a bus himself, and that he received many presents. The Hehe, however, were obviously impressed that he did not charge, and they therefore believed that he acted without any motive of personal gain.

It was also felt that Chikanga had an abnormal power over sorcerers, which ordinary diviners do not have. Those who resisted his summons were compelled to go to him by extra-ordinary means: bicycles came flying through the air to collect them; one man gave birth to a child; one who attempted to leave a bus bound for Chikanga was overcome with such pain that he pleaded to be put back, and the pain then left him. Sceptics could point to one man who resisted a summons in May 1963 and who is still alive and well, but others could reply that a well-known woman summoned at the same time refused to go and one year later she suddenly dropped dead. It was further believed that Chikanga was more effective than ordinary diviners because any sorcerer who agreed to be shaved and on his return did not immediately destroy his evil medicines would be destroyed by them.

One other remarkable feature of Chikanga's work, different from that of any other diviners ever known to the Hehe, was its wide inter-tribal and international appeal. It is clear that his influence extended throughout most of northern and central Nyasaland, north-eastern Northern Rhodesia, and south-western Tanganyika among peoples who speak different languages, which are not mutually intelligible, and whose social organization and beliefs about witchcraft and divination vary considerably. Some Hehe were impressed because it was said that Chikanga had a mission to cleanse *Africa* of sorcery and because they met a much greater variety of people going to consult him than they had known going to consult any other diviner. It is worth quoting again the words of an educated Hehe who has drawn attention to most of these points:

'In Swahili we have a proverb that says: *Kipya ni kinyemi ingawa ni kidonda*. The English equivalent of it is, "A novelty is pleasing even though it be a sore". This partly answers

119

your question as to why people went to Kiganga in multitudes. Coupled with this was the fact that Kiganga did not stand for any one particular tribe. He was a "universal diviner". Chansi was mainly for the Hehe, just as "Mkwenzulo" was, or is, for the Kinga. It was therefore natural that Kiganga should be looked upon as a "greater diviner" than Chansi. Hence people's expenses were well rewarded. And many people preferred him because he did not encourage revenge. He just shaved the *muhavi*. He did not help the bewitched make a counter-attack on his oppressor.'

The years 1963 and 1964, when the Hehe were most interested in visiting Chikanga, were a time of particular social and political stress. In 1962 Chief Adam Sapi Mkwawa of Uhehe was relieved of his administrative duties in the local government of Iringa District and was appointed Chairman of the Civil Service Commission, and, later, Speaker in the Tanganyika Parliament. In the pre-colonial period, Hehe chiefs had ordered the execution of people believed to be sorcerers but Chief Adam himself had always discouraged his subjects from accusing each other of sorcery. However, some of his people felt that various misfortunes were related to his absence and to the far-reaching reorganization of local government which took place at the same time. Thus, at the time when Chikanga's fame was spreading, the Hehe may have been unusually ready to accept some new way of coping with their difficulties.

The whole period of Chikanga's career was one of political and social unrest, especially in Rumpi District, where resistance to the Federation of Rhodesia and Nyasaland was particularly strong. The strikingly unusual idea expressed by some Hehe that Chikanga's mission was to cleanse *Africa* may have been a reflection of the language of nationalism and pan-Africanism with which most of his clients were becoming acquainted.

Northern Nyasaland is an area with a long history of witch-cleansing movements, diviners, prophets, and separatist sects, and the ideas underlying these had often spread to neighbouring regions. The high rate of labour migration from northern Nyasaland was also a factor in spreading Chikanga's fame. There were Nyasalanders among his clients who came from as far away as

Salisbury in Southern Rhodesia and Dodoma in central Tanganyika. These migrants were often better educated than most of the people in the areas to which they went to work and therefore their beliefs in Chikanga's powers may have carried some weight.

A final point is that Ihete village had been extremely difficult to reach until 1958, when a new road was made to facilitate the transport of the coffee crop; this road was used by most of Chikanga's clients.

FEATURES OF CHIKANGA'S SUCCESS IN UHEHE

All these factors, although contributing to the spread of Chikanga's fame, do not explain why, apparently for the first time, events of this type in Nyasaland should affect Uhehe. However, from a detailed knowledge of Chikanga's influence among the Hehe it is possible to show that there were certain interesting features about the way in which his work was interpreted and his fame spread – features that may be relevant to the study of the careers of diviners and miracle-workers, and to the appeal of the extraordinary, in other societies.

Because Chikanga did not define his role precisely, many different groups of people could find in him what they wanted. The stories that circulated suggested that, although he avoided claiming political or religious authority, a lot of his clients might have accepted him as a political or religious leader. In northern Nyasaland and Northern Rhodesia there had been a history of religious separatism and, in a Church of Scotland Foreign Mission Committee report, it was noted that at the ceremony of cleansing people hymns were sung in which Chikanga was praised (Church of Scotland, 1961, p. 14). In other areas, among them southern Nyasaland and the corridor area between Lakes Tanganyika and Nyasa, the inhabitants did not go to visit Chikanga but there were a number of people who claimed to have come from him with the power to detect witches and sorcerers. In Ufipa, and presumably also in the adjacent areas, the activities of these people were associated with an outbreak of the Kamcape witch-detecting and witch-cleansing movement which had flourished before on at least three occasions, each about ten years apart.[14] Agents claiming to have come

121

from Chikanga went from village to village in order to detect witches and sorcerers, to cause them to bring their harmful implements and medicines out of their huts, and then to submit to being cleansed by having cuts made on their brows and elsewhere into which medicines were rubbed.

The more the people of Uhehe were questioned about Chikanga's activities the more they insisted that through him the amount of sickness and death was decreasing. In August 1963 one Bena, who had worked for fifteen years in Uhehe, claimed that in his home area of Ubena very few people had died recently because nearly all the sorcerers had been summoned to Chikanga. He saw no difficulty in understanding why Chikanga's fame was spreading in such a large area among people of diverse tribes and tongues, for he believed that the benefits of ridding the community of the forces which cause sickness and death were self-evident.

From the Tanganyika sources it is impossible to know how Chikanga first established his reputation, which is presumably always the most difficult part of this type of mission, but once he had acquired his initial reputation it is clear how a belief in his powers spread further and further among the Hehe. Before the Hehe had heard of him Chikanga's reputation was well established among the Kinga, Wanji, and Bena to the south, and therefore the Hehe were able to hear from them how many had benefited from his work. This meant that knowledge of Chikanga came to the Hehe when there was already a widespread belief in his extraordinary powers.

Many of Chikanga's clients probably had lingering, but not severe, illnesses and the sufferer would feel better from the mental relief he obtained by going to Chikanga and learning the cause of his complaint, whether it came from the supreme being or from a sorcerer. In Africa it is possible to see a crippled child who does not walk and who has never been encouraged to try, yet, when it is put into his head that he should try, onlookers see to their astonishment that he can do much better than was expected. Chikanga may have had success with this type of person. There were also remarkable and impressive cases like that of a young barren woman who had been married for three years. She and her husband had sought fertility medicine locally without success, then she went to Chikanga. He named no sorcerer but applied what some say was his standard test for barren women: he told her to run, balancing a pot on her head, which she succeeded in doing without dropping it. He then told her to go home and in time she would bear a child, which, *mirabile dictu,* she did.[15]

It seems that a diviner with the right approach does not need many extraordinary successes in order to acquire a reputation, and once a reputation like this has grown it needs a large amount of contrary evidence to destroy it. Once a number of people from Uhehe had visited Chikanga and had found satisfaction, the news travelled great distances in general gossip and in popular ditties. The Hehe comment on many bits of interesting news by composing brief two- or three-line repetitive songs which are often spread by children who do not understand what they are about. There were a number of these about Chikanga.[16] Within not more than two years his reputation was established and accepted throughout Uhehe, an area of about 14,000 square miles, with a population of just over a quarter of a million. Some of the reasons why people accepted his effectiveness closely resemble those given by Tylor to explain why the falseness of the claims of magic can be undetected for so long (Tylor, 1891, pp. 133-136).

One other point perhaps not so well recognized is the way in which stories about any remarkable happenings grow and reinforce themselves. The credibility of a mildly extraordinary story is thought to be demonstrated by a more extraordinary one, and after a time even those near the source of the story cannot tell the difference between what really happened and what many people have said has happened.

Another striking feature of the spread of Chikanga's fame in Uhehe, which may have parallels elsewhere, was the way in which the Hehe refused to see that Chikanga's activities could possibly conflict with political or religious authority. All British colonial governments had been exercised about how to deal with accusations of witchcraft or sorcery and had drawn up strict regulations about it. In Tanganyika, the Witchcraft Ordinance forbade local courts to deal with any cases concerned with witchcraft or sorcery and those who went to court to accuse others of being witches or sorcerers usually found the case turned round so that they themselves were judged guilty of abusing those they had accused. In spite of this the majority of people believed that Chikanga was helping the government because he had a clerk with a rubber stamp and because they thought it was obviously important for the welfare of the whole country that sorcerers should be identified and shaved. Headmen in receipt of government salaries gave people notes which they could use as a form of identification on their way to Chikanga, and headmen, District Council messengers, and newly appointed Primary Court magistrates were all involved in finding those who had been named in Chikanga's letters and persuading them to go to be cleansed.

There was, indeed, some tension between mission teaching and the desire of many Christians to go to Chikanga. The small group of Lutherans took the most rigorous line against those who went to see him, yet one man insisted that he had seen a Finnish Lutheran missionary in a bus on his way back from Chikanga and that this missionary had cuts on his brow because he had agreed to be shaved. The story is all the more extraordinary when it is remembered that normally the Hehe do not believe that Europeans practise sorcery. The Italian Roman Catholic missionaries naturally disapproved of their Christians visiting Chikanga but most had the realism to accept that they could do little to prevent it. They were bound to find it hard to convince Africans that Church exorcism or unction was effective and good whereas to be shaved or healed by Chikanga was ineffective and wicked. It is not known how many Christians were prevented from going because the Church told them not to, but it is certain that a number of long-established Christians who were mission employees living on mission lands *did* go.

THE FALL OF CHIKANGA

In 1963 it was difficult to imagine how a decline in Chikanga's popularity could be brought about. He appeared to satisfy a popular demand, and very many people, at least in Tanganyika, felt that his work was beneficial to society as a whole. The end of his career came when President Hastings Banda summoned him to Blantyre, told him to stop his activities, and ordered him to live near Blantyre where he could be kept under observation. This was mainly the result of a complaint made by the General

Synod of the Church of Central Africa Presbyterian in 1964. The synod stated that:

1. He was undermining the authority of the chiefs because many cases were taken to him for judgement instead of to the chiefs.
2. His presence stirred up belief in witchcraft and therefore all the fear and animosity which go with it in village life.
3. His village, where hundreds congregated with an inadequate water supply and sanitation, was a menace to public health.

Tanganyikans were also prevented from visiting Chikanga when stricter border controls were applied because of the unfriendly relations between the governments of Malawi and Tanzania. It seems probable that his popularity would have declined a little anyway when so many people had consulted him and therefore his potential clients were fewer; moreover, in spite of the fact that a large number of people had been cleansed by him, there was no evidence that the amount of misfortune among the Hehe had been permanently reduced. In 1965 rumours were being spread around that Chikanga had started cheating people and those who gave credence to them thought that he could no longer help people in the way his earlier clients had believed he did.

CONCLUSION

In any one society beliefs concerning the cause of misfortune and accusations of witchcraft or sorcery do not necessarily fall into a neatly structured pattern. Change is always possible, and this is especially true where some members of a particular society are involved in the affairs of other groups. Presumably all that Chikanga's clients needed to have in common was a desire for some type of diagnosis of the cause of their various misfortunes and a feeling that Chikanga possessed some extraordinary spiritual power of universal validity which would enable him to help them. Beyond this it was possible for each person individually, and for the members of each society collectively, to perceive and interpret Chikanga's activities in terms of their preconceived ideas and their own particular needs; everyone, therefore, could find what he wanted in Chikanga's work.

NOTES

1. I acknowledge gratefully the support I received for my research from the following sources: The Worshipful Company of Goldsmiths, The Emslie Horniman Scholarship Fund, The British Institute of History and Archaeology in East Africa, and Nuffield College, Oxford.

2. I refer to Nyasaland, Northern and Southern Rhodesia, and Tanganyika because most of the events described in this paper took place before Malawi and Zambia achieved Independence and before the union of Tanganyika and Zanzibar.

3. There are two brief monographs on the Hehe, Nigmann (1908) and Brown & Hutt (1935).

4. Chikanga is the form of this name used in northern Nyasaland. The Hehe called him Kiganga and most other peoples adapted the name in some way to make it easy for them to pronounce in their own language.

5. I worked in Uhehe from October 1961 to September 1963, and again in Uhehe and the surrounding areas from April 1965 to September 1966, and thus I knew many members of the communities in which I lived both before and after they had been to Chikanga.

My knowledge of what happened in Nyasaland is derived from conversations and correspondence with the following people who had been there: Rev. George H. Campbell, Roy Fitzhenry, Griffith B. Jones, Rev. Stewart McCullough, Donald Moxon, Rev. Andrew Ross, and Robin Rowland. I learnt about Chikanga's influence in other parts of Tanganyika from John Arnold, Wilfred Christen, Patrick Ellis, Rev. Aylward Shorter, and Roy Willis. I am grateful to all these people, and also to Clement mwaNdulute, a Hehe, who read drafts of this paper, and to the numerous Hehe who helped me in my inquiries.

6. Dr Roy Willis, who worked among the Fipa, was also told that Chikanga had risen from the dead (Willis, 1968, pp. 6-7). There is no Kihehe word which means 'to rise from the dead'. When a congregation of the Lutheran Church say the creed in Kihehe they use the verb *kusilibuka*, but originally this verb meant only 'to recover from being in a coma in which one appeared to be dead'. It is therefore difficult to know exactly what the Hehe thought had happened to Chikanga when they said '*afwe, neke vamusile neke asilibuke*', literally, 'he died, then they buried him, then he came out of a coma'.

7. The Kihehe word *nguluvi* is used by Christians, Muslims, and pagans to refer to the divine spirit which all acknowledge in some way to be the creator of the universe and controller of events.

8. Nigmann has described Hehe beliefs about *nguluvi* (the supreme being), ancestral spirits, and sorcery, and some of their medical and surgical techniques (1908, pp. 29, 99-100); Brown has also discussed all these matters (Brown & Hutt, 1935, pp. 167-172, 175-184); and a certain amount can be learnt from some of the texts collected by Dempwolff (1913), from various reports in *M.StB-G.*, and from an article by the German military doctor, Weck (1910).

9. According to official census data the Hehe appear to have shown a proportionately greater increase in population than any other tribe between 1948 and 1957.

10. There is a passage about Chansi in *M.StB-G.*, June, 1908, pp. 129-134. This states that Chief Mkwawa used to send messengers to consult Chansi, and today many older Hehe believe that he did so.

11. The most detailed and readily available accounts of the history of the Hehe are my two articles (Redmayne, 1968 a and b).

12. Three types of ordeal were described by Nigmann (1908, pp. 71-72); see also Hofbauer (1909, pp. 23-24) and Dempwolff (1913, pp. 109-110). The Witchcraft Ordinance made it illegal for any indigenous rulers to deal with any matters concerning witchcraft and sorcery themselves. They were supposed to report all matters of this type to the District Office.

13. These prices were those paid in 1963 and 1964. The equivalents given in brackets were correct until the devaluation of United Kingdom currency in November 1967.

14. See Willis, 1968. There is evidence that these movements also affected Ukimbu. I am grateful to the Rev. Aylward Shorter for giving me this information from the Gua Mission Reports for 1954, 1963, and 1966.

15. This is a particularly well-documented case. I knew the woman's husband well in 1962-63 when he was searching for fertility medicine from local medicine men and from the newly formed Tanganyika African Medicine Company. I lived near them again in 1965 and saw the baby. There is no proof that her husband was the father of the child, but I heard no local gossip to suggest that he was not, and he and his family had accepted the child. This is important to the Hehe, who are extremely concerned about physical paternity and in doubtful cases go to considerable trouble to investigate the matter. See Brown (1932, pp. 185-193). Also Kalenga Appeal Court Records, civil cases nos. 28 and 38, 1942 (National Archives of Tanzania), where disputes about paternity were judged on the evidence given by the woman and on the resemblance the children appeared to bear to the possible genitors.

16. I recorded examples of two of these short songs. Copies of my recordings can be heard at the British Institute of Recorded Sound, 29 Exhibition Road, London, S.W.7. Reel 6, sung by Mama Anton seMunyifuna at Tanangosi on 11.6.1965, and Reel 21, sung by Wailes Kahemele mwaMbaya and his companions at Mugololo on 2.9.1965.

REFERENCES

BROWN, G. GORDON. 1932. Legitimacy and Paternity among the Hehe. *American Journal of Sociology* **38**: 185-193.

BROWN, G. GORDON & HUTT, A. MCD. BRUCE. 1935. *Anthropology in Action*. London: Oxford University Press.

CHURCH OF SCOTLAND. 1961. *Report of the Foreign Mission Committee for 1960*. Edinburgh.

DEMPWOLFF, OTTO. 1913. Beiträge zur Volksbescheibung der Hehe. *Baessler Archiv* **4** (3): 87-163.

EAST AFRICAN STATISTICAL DEPARTMENT. 1958. *Tanganyika Population Census 1957: General African Census, August 1957, Tribal Analysis Part I* and *Analysis by Sex and Age for Province, District and Territorial Census Areas.* Nairobi: East African Statistical Department.

HOFBAUER, (PATER) S. 1909. Das Zauberwesen der Wahehe. *M.StB-G.* 23-24.

MISSIONSBLÄTTER DER ST BENEDICTUS-GENOSSENSCHAFT (*M.StB-G.*). St Ottilien. (Various short notes.)

NATIONAL ARCHIVES OF TANZANIA. Iringa Local Court Records and Iringa District Office Files. Dar es Salaam.

NIGMANN, ERNST. 1908. *Die Wahehe: Ihre Geschichte, Kult-, Rechts-, Kriegs- und Jagd-Gebräuche.* Berlin: E. S. Mittler.

REDMAYNE, ALISON. 1964. *The Wahehe People of Tanganyika.* (Unpublished D. Phil. thesis, Oxford.)

—— 1965-66. Tape-recordings of songs of the Hehe. Available at the British Institute of Recorded Sound, 29 Exhibition Road, London, S.W.7.

—— 1968a. Mkwawa and the Hehe Wars. *Journal of African History* 9 (3): 409-436.

—— 1968b. The Hehe. In A. Roberts (ed.), (*Tanzania before 1900: Seven Area Histories.* Nairobi: East African Publishing House.

—— 1969. Hehe Medicine. *Tanzania Notes and Records* 70: 29-40. (An annotated translation of Weck's article.)

ROBERTS, ANDREW (ed.). 1968. *Tanzania before 1900: Seven Area Histories.* Nairobi: East African Publishing House.

TYLOR, EDWARD B. 1891. *Primitive Culture*, Vol. I. (Third edition.) London: John Murray.

WECK, (DR). 1910. Der Wahehe Arzt und seine Wissenschaft. *Deutsches Kolonialblatt*: 1104-1151. (For translation, see Redmayne, 1969.)

WILLIS, R. G. 1968. Kamcape: An Anti-sorcery Movement in South-West Tanzania. *Africa* 38 (1): 1-15.

© Alison Redmayne 1970

6

R. G. Willis

Instant Millennium
The Sociology of African Witch-cleansing Cults

Witch-cleansing cults have been reported from many parts of sub-Saharan Africa, and the time appears ripe to give them comparative consideration.

In most African societies, witchcraft (here used as synonymous with sorcery) is a putative cause of what is seen by the sufferer as unmerited misfortune. Usually, magical means of defence are available to individuals who feel themselves threatened by witchcraft. Such prophylactics are dispensed to their clients by local specialists, the witch-doctors of traditional Africa.

Occasionally, whole communities, as distinct from separate individuals, seem to become conscious of a need for protection against witchcraft: this is the emotional climate in which witch-cleansing cults arise and spread. These cults purport to go to the root of the trouble by neutralizing the witch himself. There is evidence that such collective apprehensions, and the cults that minister to them, occur in fairly regular cycles (cf. Douglas, 1963b, pp. 136 and 141; Willis, 1968a, pp. 8-9).

If we look at the recorded descriptions of witch-cleansing cults in various parts of Africa it becomes apparent that they all share certain basic characteristics, namely:

use of a relatively simple ritual procedure, intended to detect witches and neutralize them, at the same time giving protection against mystical attack to the supposedly innocent;
lack of a formal organizational structure, though there may be nominal recognition of a remote, semi-mythical founder-head;
handing-on of cult secrets and ritual from initiate to acolyte as the cult spreads;
ability to cross ethnic boundaries, at the same time adapting

ritual and ideology to the traditional ideas and institutions of each ethnic area.

What happens on those exceptional but recurrent occasions when local communities embrace witch-cleansing cults? Again, the pattern is remarkably similar all over Africa. First, there is the arrival of the cult's representatives, who initiate negotiations, usually in secret, with the local headman. The latter generally appears willing to see his village benefit from the new cult, notwithstanding the expense involved. He is under pressure, for to refuse to receive witch-cleansers could have sinister implications for himself, particularly if neighbouring villages are eagerly adopting the new ritual.

Next comes the cleansing operation itself. The first phase is witch detection. The cult organizers usually have their own way of doing this: traditional methods of divination are not favoured, and novel procedures are often reported. Among the Bemba and Fipa of Central Africa and in Dahomey, cultists have at various times used hand-mirrors to pick out witches from lines of villagers passing behind them.[1] The descriptions suggest that accusations are often pre-arranged.

Then comes the central part of the ritual, the confessions of the accused witches. These are almost invariably forthcoming, and correspond to local notions about witch behaviour. Thus Yoruba mothers admit devouring their own children (Morton-Williams, 1956, p. 322); Ashanti describe in detail the process of removing their victims' internal organs to make medicine (Ward, 1956, pp. 55ff.); and Fipa confess to murders committed in accordance with traditional ideas about the manipulation of noxious substances (Willis, 1968a, p. 5).

The moral pressure to confess is enormous. For the accused, the choice is between outlawry and reintegration into the community. Not surprisingly, most do what is wanted. Whether and in what sense the alleged witches also believe their confessions is another and difficult question which need not detain us here. For the cult, the confessions are crucial because they provide seemingly incontestable proof of its effectiveness: they at once confirm the accuracy of the cult's divinatory procedure, and endorse the truth and relevance of the local witch-image.

Instant Millennium

The final act in the ritual drama of witch-cleansing is usually an administration of medicine by the cult officiants to all members of the community. This medicine is customarily credited with the dual power of protecting the innocent against mystical attack and killing any who attempt to revert to their evil ways. Secure in this assurance, the past can be forgotten. Most reports suggest that the self-confessed witches immediately resume their accustomed places in the community, without any hint of ostracism. Supposedly, a new and morally regenerated life then begins for everyone.

Such is the implicit doctrine of every witch-cleansing cult. For a certain time, further cases of sickness and death can be explained, in terms of the cult ideology, as the medicine striking down would-be witches. But this explanation eventually wears thin. Faith in the efficacy of the cult declines and is finally extinguished. In due course the community will be ready to try again, to adopt a new cult. Some such cyclical evolution in communal attitudes towards witch-cleansing cults can surely be inferred from their repeated recurrence, at roughly ten-year intervals, in the Congo and in other parts of Central Africa.

What triggers off these successive attempts by whole communities to make a wholesale and permanent end of witchcraft? The fact that cults often spread over vast areas (the Mcape cult of the 'thirties spread from Nyasaland into Mozambique, Northern and Southern Rhodesia, south-west Tanganyika, and the Belgian Congo) suggests a possible connection between cults and even wider social currents: the religious, political, and economic changes associated with colonial rule. Such a connection has been posited by several authorities, notably Richards (1935) and Ward (1956); the difficulties of the theory have been emphasized by Goody (1957). Bohannan (1958) notes that witch-cleansing cults among the Tiv are reported in oral tradition from about the middle of the nineteenth century, well before the first appearance of colonial agents in Tivland. A similar point is made by Douglas (1963b) in discussing witch-cleansing cults in the Congo. To my mind these pertinent observations do not invalidate the essence of the social change hypothesis, but they do necessitate its reformulation in a wider perspective. Such a reformulation would take account of the fact

F* 131

that African societies were changing in pre-colonial times, and that innovative and adaptive mechanisms were developed to cope with change.

In terms of organization and ideology, witch-cleansing cults are probably the most rudimentary of these innovative and adaptive mechanisms developed in pre-colonial Africa. Examples of other and more complex mechanisms are the institution of the spirit-possessed prophet or *ngunza* among the Kongo peoples (Andersson, 1958, p. 3) and the tradition of religious revivalism in Ghana (cf. Baëta, 1962, p. 6).

Witch-cleansing cults are often misinterpreted by anthropologists and others because of their inherent ambiguity, a feature Balandier (1955) has discerned in many social phenomena of modern Africa. On the one hand they seem to aim solely at restoring a traditional ideal of social unity and harmony; on the other, by spreading as they do across tribal and ethnic boundaries, they tend to foster a new sense of unity transcending traditional social divisions. During field research among the Fipa of south-west Tanzania I observed a widespread tendency for a new cult, which originated in Malawi, to invest temporary political and social power at the village level in a few enterprising young people, giving an impression of incipient revolution. Bohannan (1958) noticed an analogous tendency during the operations of the Tiv cults, and Morton-Williams (1956, p. 332) speaks of the Atinga cult in Yorubaland in like terms. Parkin (1968) has also noted the innovative power in these cults.

Admittedly, cult-induced social change at the local-group level usually remains symbolic, embalmed in a brief ritual. But cults may in certain circumstances become transformed into more effective mediators of social action. There is evidence that the supra-tribal Maji-Maji rising against German rule in East Africa in 1905-06 originated in a witch-cleansing cult (cf. Iliffe, 1967).[2] Several Congolese cults, such as Lukusu in the early 1930s, were directed against whites as well as witches. The Kamcape cult among the Fipa and neighbouring peoples of south-west Tanzania in 1963-64 had a shadowy organizational structure headed by the renowned diviner and healer, Chikanga of Malawi (see Redmayne, above). Cults are potential generators of new social institutions, but only in exceptional conditions of crisis does this power escape from the prison of symbolic thought and behaviour. But, even though unrealized, the innovative potential remains, constantly recreating itself in new cults.

African witch-cleansing cults have a discernible common pattern, which I have tried to outline. Yet they are not institutionalized, and so are hardly accessible to the ordinary tools of sociological analysis. A similar problem has been noted recently by Father Johannes Fabian (Fabian, 1967, p. 146) in a paper on the Jamaa movement in Katanga. Yet it may well be that important new advances in the theory of social change will follow intensive comparative study of such *proto-institutions*, as they could be called.

One pointer to the significance of witch-cleansing cults is their comparative incidence. For by no means all African societies are subject to them. Cults of the kind described in this paper have never been reported, for instance, among the Azande of the south-west Sudan, in the Interlacustrine states of East Africa, or among the Luo and Kikuyu of Kenya; nor do they appear to have affected the Bantu peoples of South Africa, in spite of the importance of witchcraft as an explanation of misfortune in most of them. It is probably significant that these are all societies and areas that have been directly and intensively affected by the political and economic changes associated with colonialism; whereas the evidence suggests that witch-cleansing cults arise and spread in those parts of Africa that are relatively remote from the centres of urbanization and direct Western influence. In the more developed areas one encounters more complex and enduring kinds of reformative movement, such as independent churches and political parties.

On a broader scale, it may be instructive to look for parallels to African witch-cleansing cults elsewhere in the world, particularly among colonized peoples. There are significant resemblances to the cargo cults of Melanesia: for instance, both kinds of cult are attempts to reorder society by symbolic means and both are essentially rural phenomena (cf. Worsley, 1957, p. 48). Also, like witch-cleansing cults, cargo cults tend to break down traditional social barriers and to create new and more inclusive forms of social consciousness. They are similarly transient and recurrent.

There is, however, a significant difference in ideology. Where cargo cults belong to the classical category of millenarian movements, including those of medieval Europe, in prescribing certain procedures to be followed in anticipation of a coming new world, African witch-cleansing cults go as far as to inaugurate the millennium, the 'age of bliss . . . in which pain, disease, untimely death, violence and strife, war and hunger will be unknown' (Cohn, 1962, p. 5). The cheerful self-confidence of this approach gives a peculiarly African flavour to these rituals of social regeneration.

NOTES

1. Cf. the following description of the procedures of the Mcape witch-cleansers in East Africa in the early 1930s, by Mr J. B. Lawrence, District Officer, Songea, Tanganyika:

'The cult is spread by peripatetic bands of leaders, generally consisting of three or four to a band . . . On arrival in a village they call on the head of the community . . . and arrange a time and place for the meeting. To this meeting the whole community, male and female, comes without exception . . . They all sit round to form the three sides of a square with the "Mcapi" leader and his assistants in the middle, he then explains his object and starts on his "smelling out" process. For this he employs an ordinary looking-glass, and standing with his back to the people looks in the glass over his left shoulder, and points out such and such a person as having bad medicine in his house, this person goes to his house and brings out what he has and throws it in the centre. If the "Mcapi" leader decides this is all he has he is then given the "Mcapi" medicine, if not he must go back and get all the other remaining medicines. According to the heinousness of his offence, he is adjudged to pay cash from 10/- upwards; he may even be told he will have to buy medicine to the value of 2/- or more as he will need a great many doses to cure his "evil" '(National Archives of Tanzania, Dar es Salaam, File 61/128/Vol. I).

Cf. also similar accounts in Richards, 1935 (Bemba, Northern Rhodesia); Morton-Williams, 1956 (Yoruba, Nigeria); Tait, 1963 (Dagomba, Ghana); and Willis, 1968a (Fipa, Tanzania).

2. Cf. the following extract from a letter dated 12 September 1933 from the District Officer at Tunduru, southern Tanganyika, to his Provincial Commissioner, about the Mcape witch-cleansing cult:

'. . . Whilst on tour I discussed with the elders and headmen these people [the Mcape cultists] and they almost unanimously requested the Government to forbid their activities, as they stated that activities similar to this ensued before the "Maji-Maji". It appears that the people were told that if they drank the "mchape" medicine this would render them immune from any further disease, so that on the face of it there appears to be some resemblance . . .' (National Archives of Tanzania, Dar es Salaam, File 61/128/Vol. I).

BIBLIOGRAPHY

ANDERSSON, E. 1958. *Messianic Popular Movements in the Lower Congo.* Uppsala: Studia Ethnographica Upsaliensia XIV.

AQUINA, M. 1967. The People of the Spirit: An Independent Church in Rhodesia. *Africa* **37** (2): 203-219.

BAËTA, C. G. 1962. *Prophetism in Ghana: A Study of Some 'Spiritual' Churches.* London: SCM Press.

BALANDIER, G. 1951. La Situation coloniale: Approche théorique. *Cahiers internationaux de Sociologie* **11**: 44-79.

—— 1955. *Sociologie actuelle de l'Afrique noire: Dynamique de changements sociaux en Afrique centrale.* Paris: Presses Universitaires de France.

—— 1958. Brèves Remarques sur les 'Messianismes' de l'Afrique congolaise. *Archives de Sociologie des Religions* **5**: 91-95.

BANTON, M. 1963. African Prophets. *Race* **5** (2): 42-55.

BASTIDE, R. 1961. Messianisme et Développement économique et social. *Cahiers internationaux de Sociologie* (n.s.) 8: 3-14.

BOHANNAN, L. & P. 1953. *The Tiv of Central Nigeria.* Ethnographic Survey of Africa: Western Africa, Part VIII. London: International African Institute.

BOHANNAN, P. 1958. Extra-processual Events in Tiv Political Institutions. *American Anthropologist* **60** (1): 1-12.

BURRIDGE, K. 1960. *Mambu: A Melanesian Millennium.* London: Methuen.

COHN, N. 1957. *The Pursuit of the Millennium.* London: Secker & Warburg.

—— 1962. Medieval Millenarianism: Its Bearing on the Comparative Study of Millenarian Movements. *Comparative Studies in Society and History,* Supplement II: 31-43.

COMHAIRE, J. 1955. Sociétés secrètes et mouvements prophétiques au Congo Belge. *Africa* **25** (1): 54-59.

CRAWFORD, J. R. 1967. *Witchcraft and Sorcery in Rhodesia.* London: Oxford University Press.

DOUGLAS, M. 1963a. *The Lele of the Kasai.* London: Oxford University Press (for the International African Institute).

—— 1963b. Techniques of Sorcery Control in Central Africa. In J. Middleton & E. H. Winter (eds.), *Witchcraft and Sorcery in East Africa.* London: Routledge & Kegan Paul.

—— 1967. Witch beliefs in Central Africa. *Africa* **37** (1): 72-80.

DOUTRELOUX, A. 1965. Prophétisme et culture. In M. Fortes & G. Dieterlen (eds.), *African Systems of Thought.* Studies presented and discussed at the Third International African Seminar held in Salisbury, Rhodesia, December 1960. London: Oxford University Press (for the International African Institute).

EAST, R. 1939. *Akiga's Story: The Tiv Tribe as Seen by One of its Members*. London: International African Institute.

EVANS-PRITCHARD, E. E. 1937. *Witchcraft, Oracles and Magic among the Azande*. Oxford: Clarendon Press.

FABIAN, J. 1967. Tod dem Propheten: ein Dokument zur einer prophetischen Situation. *Sociologus* (n.s.) **17** (2): 131-146.

FERNANDEZ, J. W. 1964. The Lumpa Uprising: Why? *Africa Report*, November: 30-32.

—— 1965. Symbolic Consensus in a Fang Reformative Cult. *American Anthropologist* **67** (4): 902-929.

GAMITTO, A. C. P. 1960. *King Kazembe*. (Translated by I. Cunnison.) Lisbon: Junta de Investigaçoes do Ultramar.

GLUCKMAN, M. 1955. *Custom and Conflict in Africa*. Oxford: Blackwell.

GOODY, J. 1957. Anomie in Ashanti? *Africa* **27** (4): 356-363.

HOLAS, B. 1965. *Le Séparatisme religieux en Afrique noire: l'Exemple de la Côte d'Ivoire*. Paris: Presses Universitaires de France.

ILIFFE, J. 1967. The Organization of the Maji-Maji Rebellion. *Journal of African History* **8** (3): 495-512.

JONGHE, ÉD. DE. 1936. Formations récentes de sociétés secrètes au Congo Belge. *Africa* **9**: 56-63.

JUNOD, H. P. 1936. Notes on the Ethnological Situation in Portuguese East Africa on the South of the Zambesi. *Bantu Studies* **10**: 293-311.

KENNEDY, J. G. 1967. Psychological and Social Explanations of Witchcraft. *Man* (n.s.) **2**: 216-225.

KÖBBEN, A. J. F. 1960. Prophetic Movements as an Expression of Social Protest. *International Archives of Ethnography* **49**. Leiden.

LANTERNARI, V. 1963. *The Religions of the Oppressed: A Study of Modern Messianic Cults*. (Translated by L. Sergio.) London: MacGibbon & Kee.

LAWRENCE, P. 1964. *Road Belong Cargo: A Study of the Cargo Movement in the Southern Madang District, New Guinea*. Manchester: Manchester University Press.

LIENHARDT, R. G. 1951. Some Notions of Witchcraft among the Dinka. *Africa* **21** (4): 303-318.

LINTON, R. 1943. Nativistic Movements. *American Anthropologist* **45**: 230-240.

LONSDALE, J. M. 1968. Some Origins of Nationalism in East Africa. *Journal of African History* **9** (1): 119-146.

MAIR, L. P. 1959. Independent Religious Movements in Three Continents. *Comparative Studies in Society and History* 1 (2): 113-136.

MARWICK, M. G. 1950. Another Modern Anti-witchcraft Movement in East Central Africa. *Africa* 20 (1): 100-112.

—— 1965. *Sorcery in its Social Setting; A Study of the Northern Rhodesian Ceŵa*. Manchester: Manchester University Press.

MAYER, P. 1954. Witches. Grahamstown: Inaugural Lecture delivered at Rhodes University.

MELLAND, F. H. 1923. *In Witchbound Africa; An Account of the Primitive Kaonde Tribe and their Beliefs*. London: Seeley, Service.

MIDDLETON, J. 1963. The Yakan or Allah Water Cult among the Lugbara. *Journal of the Royal Anthropological Institute* 93 (1): 80-108.

MIDDLETON, J. & WINTER, E. H. (eds.). 1963. *Witchcraft and Sorcery in East Africa*. London: Routledge & Kegan Paul.

MITCHELL, J. C. 1956. *The Yao Village; A Study in the Social Structure of a Nyasaland Tribe*. Manchester: Manchester University Press.

MORTON-WILLIAMS, P. 1956. The Atinga Cult among the South-western Yoruba: A Sociological Analysis of a Witch-finding Movement. *Bulletin de l'Institut français d'Afrique noire* 18 (3-4): 315-334.

NADEL, S. F. 1952. Witchcraft in Four African Societies: An Essay in Comparison. *American Anthropologist* 54 (1): 18-29.

ODINGA, O. 1967. *Not Yet Uhuru*. London: Heinemann.

OGOT, B. A. 1963. British Administration in the Central Nyasa District of Kenya 1900-60. *Journal of African History* 4 (2): 249-273.

PARKIN, D. 1968. Medicines and Men of Influence. *Man* (n.s.) 3: 424-439.

PAULME, D. 1962. Une Religion syncrétique en Côte d'Ivoire: le Culte *deima*. *Cahiers d'Études Africaines* 3 (9): 5-90.

PEREIRA DE QUEIROZ, M. I. 1958. L'Influence du milieu social interne sur les mouvements messianiques brésiliens. *Archives de Sociologie des Religions* 5: 3-30.

RANGER, T. O. 1967. *Revolt in Southern Rhodesia 1896-7: A Study in African Resistance*. London: Heinemann.

—— 1968. Connexions between 'Primary Resistance' Movements and Modern Mass Nationalism in East and Central Africa. *Journal of African History* 9 (3): 437-453, (4): 631-641.

RICHARDS, A. I. 1935. A Modern Movement of Witch-finders. *Africa* 8 (4): 448-461.

—— 1939. *Land, Labour and Diet in Northern Rhodesia: An Economic Study of the Bemba Tribe*. London: Oxford University Press.

ROTBERG, R. 1961. The Lenshina Movement of Northern Rhodesia. *Rhodes-Livingstone Institute Journal* 29: 63-78.

SCHLOSSER, K. 1949. *Propheten in Afrika*. Braunschweig: Albert Limbach Verlag.

SHEPPERSON, G. 1962. Nyasaland and the Millennium. *Comparative Studies in Society and History*, Supplement II: 144-159.

SHEPPERSON, G. & PRICE, T. 1958. *Independent African: John Chilembwe and the Origins, Setting and Significance of the Nyasaland Native Rising of 1915*. Edinburgh: Edinburgh University Press.

SMITH, M. W. 1959. Towards a Classification of Cult Movements. *Man* 59 (1): 8-12, (2): 28.

SUNDKLER, B. G. M. 1961. *Bantu Prophets in South Africa*. London: Oxford University Press.

—— 1965. Chief and Prophet in Zululand and Swaziland. In M. Fortes & G. Dieterlen (eds.), *African Systems of Thought*. London: Oxford University Press (for the International African Institute).

TAIT, D. 1963. A Sorcery Hunt in Dagomba. *Africa* 33 (2): 136-147.

THEUSS, D. 1961. Le Mouvement 'Jamaa' au Katanga. *Rythmes du Monde* 8 (3-4): 201-212.

TURNER, H. W. 1967. *History of an African Independent Church*. Oxford: Clarendon Press.

TURNER, V. W. 1957. *Schism and Continuity in an African Society: A Study of Ndembu Village Life*. Manchester: Manchester University Press.

VAN WING, J. 1959. *Études Bakongo: Sociologie, religion et magie*. Bruges: Desclée de Brouwer, Museum Lessianum.

—— 1960. Les Mouvements messianiques populaires dans le Bas-Congo: Notes marginales. *Zaïre* 14 (2-3): 225-237.

WALLACE, A. F. C. 1956. Revitalization Movements. *American Anthropologist* 58 (2): 264-281.

WARD, B. E. 1956. Some Observations on Religious Cults in Ashanti. *Africa* 26 (1): 47-61.

WELBOURN, F. B. 1961. *East African Rebels: A Study of Some Independent Churches*. London: SCM Press.

WELBOURN, F. B. & OGOT, B. A. 1966. *A Place to Feel at Home: A Study of Two Independent Churches in Western Kenya*. London: Oxford University Press.

WILLIS, R. G. 1968a. Kamcape: An Anti-sorcery Movement in South-West Tanzania. *Africa* **38** (1): 1-15.

—— 1968b. Changes in Mystical Concepts and Practices among the Fipa. *Ethnology* **7** (2): 139-157.

WILSON, M. 1951. Witch Beliefs and Social Structure. *American Journal of Sociology* **56**: 307-313.

WISHLADE, R. L. 1965. *Sectarianism in Southern Nyasaland.* London: Oxford University Press.

WORSLEY, P. 1957. *The Trumpet Shall Sound: A Study of 'Cargo' Cults in Melanesia.* London: MacGibbon & Kee.

© R. G. Willis 1970

7

Edwin Ardener

Witchcraft, Economics, and the
Continuity of Belief

This paper[1] is about the interrelations of the witchcraft beliefs
of a certain African people and the various social and economic
pressures that they were subject to over a period of fifty years
or more. The story will show that the content of witchcraft
beliefs may be subject to fashions: the beliefs change, as the
world to which they refer changes. Among this people the particular and unusual form of the beliefs was associated with
economic stagnation, and many of their neighbours blamed the
stagnation on the failure of the people to move in some sense
into the modern world. Yet, when the opportunity for economic
expansion arrived, there was a skilful, if unconscious, adjust-
ment of their beliefs which made it possible for the people to
take advantage of the expansion, without shaking the basis of
the beliefs themselves. In telling this story, and it is a very
interesting one in itself, we shall come upon some sidelights on
the nature of witchcraft beliefs, and also perhaps draw some
lessons on how far one can blame a people's economic failure
upon its cherished beliefs. Such lessons may even have relevance
for populations of much greater size. The question of continuity
in the structure of belief will also be raised.

The Bakweri[2] of West Cameroon are Bantu-speaking – the
Bantu languages reach with them almost their farthest northern
and western extension. Their population is not much greater than
16,000. Before the German conquest of 1894, they were living
in scattered settlements round the southern slopes of Mount
Cameroon. There are very few mountains in West Africa, and
none is as high as this (more than 13,000 feet). It is also unusual
in that it stands right on the coast, descending through a maze
of foothills to the sea. At four degrees north of the equator,
it is not quite high enough for permanent snow. Instead,
winds loaded with moisture from 4,000 miles of Atlantic travel

precipitate copious rains, and swathe the slopes in mist and drizzle for many months of the year. Inside the clouded summit is an active volcano from which new craters burst out every few decades. The rain and the volcanic soil have made the mountain area one of the most fertile in Africa, and forest covers the mountain up to 6,000 feet. The Bakweri lived (and live) in thickest concentration in a belt of villages between 1,500 and 3,000 feet above sea level, but they occupied the whole base of the mountain below this very thinly, as far as the sea. With the advent of German rule the fertility of the soils was quickly recognized, and the area was developed as plantations – initially for tobacco and cocoa, and then (with the failure of these) for various other crops of which bananas, rubber, oil-palm products, and tea remain important to the present day.

The acquisition of plantation land began through negotiation with village heads and the like, but after 1894, with the conquest of the mountain villages by the *laissez-faire* governor, von Puttkamer, alienation increased rapidly. In the 1900s, the process came under some official restraints, and reservations were established for the Bakweri on a fixed number of hectares of land per hut. Before the establishment of the plantations, Bakweri settlements had been dispersed through the mountain forest in clusters of bark-walled huts occupied by close patrilineal kinsmen and their families. These clusters were grouped territorially into what may be called 'villages', but on the lower slopes of the mountain, the Bakweri desire for elbow-room resulted in some of these villages occupying large territories. One, for example, occupied fifty square miles – the same size as Berlin, as one German noted – but with a population of only a few hundreds. On the upper slopes in the more densely inhabited belt the settlements were more compact and had less room for manoeuvre. The village was the normal political unit, under the control of the village head and lineage elders, sometimes aided, or even superseded, by regulatory associations containing most of the male membership of the village.

The Bakweri cultivated a number of tubers, together with the coarse variety of banana which in West Africa is generally known as the plantain. In addition, the villagers in the upper belt of settlement were able to climb to the grassy higher slopes of Mount Cameroon, to hunt antelope and small game. The forest itself supported elephant, which were trapped in pits. While most agriculture was women's work, the originally staple plantain crop was a male concern. By 1890, the Bakweri economy had already changed considerably from what it must have been some forty years before. For one thing, the plantain as a source of food had been completely overshadowed by a new food crop, the *Xanthosoma* cocoyam, an American plant which had been introduced at the coast in the period after 1845 by a small missionary settlement from the neighbouring island of Fernando Po.[3] The xanthosoma flourished in Bakweri country like Jack's beanstalk. The rich soils and the absence of any drought made it throw up huge stems, and leaves under which a tall man could shelter. The 'mother' corm in the soil was not dug up annually as it is in drier conditions. It continued to throw out knob-like cormels from itself for a period of years, and these were cut off regularly while the main plant still grew. This women's crop solved the problem of food supply, and diminished the incentive of Bakweri men to farm. Large quantities of small livestock flourished on the rich vegetation. Pigs grew fat on the cocoyam waste.

Between 1850 and 1890 the Bakweri became rich in other ways. By trading foodstuffs to the coast, and blocking the way of expeditions into the interior, they had acquired considerable trade goods and an armament of flint-lock guns. The largest village, Buea (later less than 1,000 in population),[4] had begun to instigate small raids which the German government began to advertise as a threat to the coastal establishments. By 1891 the Bakweri were at a peak: in that year Buea defeated a German expedition. The misty, forested mountain was a barrier which reduced the Germans to small importance in Bakweri eyes. The German colonial government was starved of funds at this time.[5]

All this was shattered at a blow in December 1894.[6] A well-mounted expedition found the Bakweri now unprepared; the commander, von Stetten, looked round in disbelief for the source of the threat. He saw a timid people living in small huts in the forest surrounded by fences to keep the flourishing livestock away from the even more flourishing cocoyams. In the next decade the Bakweri were systematically tidied up. Scattered huts were grouped in lines and lands alienated for plantations. Von Puttkamer enthused over the neat settlement he had made out of a village called Soppo: all that is now required, he said with full Prussian sentiment, is the village postman going from door to door.[7]

The plantations found it difficult to find adequate local labour. The Bakweri were neither numerous enough nor used to the work. So began an influx of labourers from outside, who came, over the decades, to outnumber the Bakweri by three or more to one. The predominance of males among the migrants began a drift of Bakweri women into concubinage and prostitution, which became a byword. The Germans were succeeded in 1914 by the British, who did not dismantle the plantation industry. They did pursue for several decades a 'pro-Bakweri' policy – reserves were enlarged and after the Second World War a land policy was suggested whereby plantation lands might be excised for Bakweri use.

By then, however, the Bakweri had acquired an unprogressive reputation. The term then in public use was 'apathetic'. Far from requiring more land (it was said) they wasted what they had; they let it out to strangers at a profit, or (worse) they were even too apathetic to make a profit. They did not respond to government exhortations. They were said by one observer to be 'unindustrious but grasping'. The women ran away from the men because they had to do all the work. The Bakweri men were too apathetic to control the women. They were about to die out. They lived with pigs, in huts that were falling down. This view of the Bakweri was heartily endorsed by the large numbers of industrious migrants working in the plantation industry – which after 1949 was nationalized and feeding its profits to the government. The territory itself became in 1954 partly autonomous, with an elected legislature. There was to be no putting back the clock, and the present Federated State of West Cameroon needs every franc it can get from its only major industry. But in the later 'fifties the Bakweri suddenly stopped being apathetic, and made fortunes in peasant banana-growing (Ardener *et al.*, 1960, pp. 329-332).

So what happened? It is in this context that one must turn to the witchcraft beliefs of the Bakweri. First of all, in the whole Cameroon forest zone in which the Bakweri live, there is an ancient and general belief in witchcraft. This kind is known under the name *liemba*, and the term itself goes back to a common

Bantu word-form (it may therefore date from the Bantu dispersion). The belief in *liemba* was deeply seated just before the German conquest, we know, because the first German expedition, which the Bakweri defeated in 1891, was believed by them to have been sent because they had just hanged two women for *liemba*. The names of these two women were given to me over sixty years later. Of course, coastal Christians, both black and white, were known to object to witch-hangings. It was common knowledge among the Bakweri that the missionary settlement of Victoria at the coast had gained its convert population from escaped witches and other malefactors from their own villages. *Liemba* is a 'classical' form of witchcraft. It is generally regarded as inborn, although it can sometimes be passed on to a person who is without it. Witches may be of either sex and are said to leave their bodies at night and 'eat' people so that they become ill and die. What is eaten is the *elinge*: the word means 'reflection' and 'shadow'. Many sicknesses would be attributed to witchcraft; but the essential diagnosis was always made by a diviner. In the milder cases a treatment was prescribed that would defeat the witch. In serious cases the suspected witch would be named and made to drink sasswood medicine. If the suspect vomited it he was innocent; if not he was guilty and was hanged. Every village had a witch-hanging tree (Ardener, 1956, p. 105).[8]

The Bakweri were not greater believers in *liemba* than were their neighbours; indeed, they lacked some of the elaborations of many of the forest peoples, in which there was a post-mortem examination in order to determine, from the position of blood clots, the actual kind of witchcraft from which a person died. However, the Bakweri belief partook somewhat of their misty mountainous environment. With plenty of room to move in, they came to believe that they were moving into scattered hamlets to avoid witches. It was well known that you should never live too near your patrilineal relatives for they suffered from that chief Bakweri vice: *inona*. This word may be translated 'envy', but the flavour is of the most ignorant, ill-wishing envy. Where *inona* was, there too was *liemba*. As among the Tiv, there were grounds for the belief that close patrilineal relatives would be the most envious, for relations with these would be influenced by the rules of inheritance by which a man's brothers and half-brothers had a substantial claim over his property at his death, prior to his own sons.

The Bakweri were very conscious of *inona*. The accumulation of property – chiefly in goats, pigs, and dwarf cattle – was the chief means of establishing status in this jealously egalitarian society. Yet it was collected mainly to be destroyed. At a potlatch ceremony known as *ngbaya*, performed only by the very rich, hecatombs of goats, fowls, and cows of a tsetse-free dwarf breed would be killed and distributed among those attending. To receive a great share at *ngbaya* was a mark of status, and also a severe blow, for the recipients would be expected to ruin themselves even more splendidly. As a fascinating by-product, it was only at a *ngbaya* ceremony that boys with certain mysterious headaches could be cured. The cured boys often went on to be medicine men. The extraordinary psychic energies bound up in the acquisition of property, and the twin emotion of *inona*, give Bakweri beliefs an interesting flavour of their own. The envy of relatives was further stimulated and assuaged by making any riches in livestock that survived a man's death the subject of another *ngbaya*-like ceremony, known as *eyû*. Here again the goats stood trembling, tethered in rows, their heads to be cut off one by one. The last prize sacrifice (if possible, a slave) was the subject of a special dance called *motio*, and the head was to be felled at a blow (Ardener, 1956, pp. 76-77, 89-90).

It seems, then, that the Bakweri attitudes to property, to envy, and to *liemba* witchcraft were closely bound up in a highly emotional knot. One should imagine an essentially proud, but rather inward-looking people, on average rather slight in build, shivering in a damp and foggy climate and dwelling in bark-walled huts; but having also enjoyed, for many decades, an environment where livestock and the cocoyam thrived, where extra food could be obtained from hunting on the isolated mountain top, and where trade goods arrived from the coast – a strange mixture of deprivation and riches. The conquest and the establishment of the plantations must have come as a great shock. The first carpet-bagger Bakweri interpreters and other servants of the Germans moved in, and many quaint iron houses were built in the villages by the new rich. Most of the Bakweri in the villages presented a dull, lifeless impression to the German administrators, the women now clad in colonial cotton frocks, the men timid and withdrawn. We now embark upon that period of Bakweri apathy to which reference was to be made so often for fifty years of this century.

I first went to Bakweri country in 1953 and by then they had for decades worried themselves with the problem of how to control the entry of their women into prostitution and concubinage with the large migrant population. They were convinced that they were dying out. Villages were dwindling. The spread of venereal disease from the plantation centres to the villages must have been responsible for the undoubted degree of reproductive disturbance among them, possibly exacerbated by environmental factors (Ardener, 1962). Anyone entering a Bakweri village in those years could not but be impressed by the lack of those hordes of children which are so typical of West Africa, and by the empty tin houses of the early Bakweri carpet-baggers. Empty, that is, except for the zombies.

For in the intervening years the Bakweri had come to believe in a new kind of witchcraft compared with which the old *liemba* was regarded as almost a harmless trifle. This new kind was called *nyongo*. It was believed to have been brought in from outside by 'wicked people' at about the time of the First World War. It took a peculiar form. A person with *nyongo* was always prosperous, for he was a member of a witch association that had the power of causing its closest relatives, even its children, to appear to die. But in truth they were taken away to work for their witch-masters on another mountain sixty or seventy miles to the north: Mount Kupe in the territory of the Bakossi people. On Mount Kupe, the *nyongo* people were believed to have a town and all modern conveniences, including, as will be seen, motor-lorries. *Nyongo* people could best be recognized by their tin houses which they had been able to build with the zombie labour force of their dead relatives. How this belief grew up, and by what processes the association of dying children and the ownership of tin houses became so firmly fixed, cannot easily be traced. But by 1953 the belief had taken such a hold that no one would build a modern house for fear of being accused of possessing *nyongo*. Dying people who were being taken in *nyongo* were expected to be able to see the witch and to name him. I knew an old tailor, trained in German times, who lived in a plantation camp while his tin house in his home village was shunned, and people were dying with his name on their lips. A *nyongo* witch himself was not safe, it was believed, for one day his fellow *nyongo* people would come to him and take him too, and his house would stand empty. In this atmosphere, *any* conspicuous material success became suspect. Men with no deaths in their families, who built their houses visibly with their own hands, could hope to still the worst accusations, but most people were slow to exhibit the fruits of success for fear of suffering (or being accused of) *nyongo*.

The ancillary ornaments to the belief in *nyongo* were rich and circumstantial. When a person was taken in *nyongo* he was not really dead; the *nyongo* witch, acting as one of an association, would insert a dead rat under the body so that the corpse would appear to smell badly and would be quickly buried. Then he would invisibly abstract the body from the grave. Wherever the *nyongo* witches and their victims were, they manifested themselves as *vekongi*: zombie spirits. They occupied the tin houses, causing lights to be seen and noises to be heard. There would be unexplained knocks on doors in the night. A *nyongo* witch when dead was known to leave his grave himself as *ekongi*. To obviate this, known *nyongo* witches were buried face downward so that they would move deeper into the earth. Sometimes the head was severed.

In 1953 the belief in *nyongo* was deep-seated in all classes of the population, and there is no doubt that all 'economic' initiative was much affected by the climate of that belief. The non-Bakweri origin of some of its content can be confirmed. The name (=*nyungu*) is a foreign word, meaning 'rainbow' in the language of the neighbouring Duala people, among whom persons of unusual prosperity are supposed to have captured the magical python which manifests itself in the rainbow. Yet the Bakweri did not take over this belief in the rainbow source of the *nyongo* power. Again, the localization of the zombie town in another tribe, on a mountain they may not have heard of before the colonial period, tends to confirm the Bakweri belief that *nyongo* was a new witchcraft. It is, however, interesting that although the belief in zombies is found in East and Central Africa, it is not commonly found in West Africa. Its occurrence in the West Indies has been supposed by some to be a spontaneous growth. It is of some linguistic interest that the Bakweri word for the act of giving a relative to *nyongo* is *sómbà*, 'to pledge' or 'pawn', and in the tense used takes the form *sómbî*. For example, *à mò sómbî ô nyòngò*: 'he has pledged him in *nyongo*'. Possibly we should look somewhere in our area for the African transmission point of the Caribbean belief. Even if the circumstantial *realien* of the *nyongo* witchcraft were new to the Bakweri, an underlying belief in the possibility of witchcraft 'pawns' or 'pledges' may have long existed – an idea that could have become flesh on either side of the Atlantic. Once more, in any event, the property-gathering connotations of the 'pledge' may be noted.[9]

The whole tale in its extraordinary detail must be viewed as an exaggeration of those trends already marked in Bakweri belief: the powerful ambivalence towards riches and property; the sudden breach of the isolation of the society, accompanied, as is all too commonly the case with the victims of decline in power or status, by a sense of collective guilt; the low fertility, and the fear of dying out. Perhaps all this turned against those who were thought to have benefited by the events which had caused so much damage. Envy, disaster, property, and witchcraft were once more in close association. So much for Bakweri apathy. To anyone who knew them well, the quiet exterior seemed to cover a dangerously explosive mixture.

In 1954 things began to happen. After many years of rejecting all avenues of economic profit, the Bakweri had begun to take up commercial banana-farming. Things began very slowly at first, the stimulus coming from a group of educated Bakweri and from government officials. The idea was that individuals should not corner any economic markets, but that the villages themselves should work as cooperative units. There would be an office and organization: the old and the young would all gain. The commercial banana was a crop not dissimilar to the traditional plantain. The first steps were shaky and not free from *inona*. What clinched the operation was the immediate and disproportionate monetary return at the end of the first full year (1953). It had coincided with the great banana boom of the 'fifties. An *embarras de richesses* poured in: sums of the order of £100 per farmer entered Bakweri villages, with their tumbling huts and empty tin houses.[10] By common tacit consent the making of small improvements, such as cementing a floor, began to be taken as not necessarily of *nyongo* origin. Then, in 1955

149

and 1956, a masked figure called Obasi Njom began to glide about the villages. Bakweri villagers had used over £2,000 of the first banana revenue to purchase the secrets of a witch-finding association from the remote Banyang tribe. With the new advanced ritual technology they began to clear the *nyongo* witchcraft from the villages. The extraordinary logic of this behaviour makes one almost feel that it could have been done only by conscious reasoning. Jarvie (1963) would doubtless contend that this was so. For with the *nyongo* threat removed, obviously the next revenue could be spent on self-advancement, and yes, even on tin houses. Yet the change came like this:

On 9 January 1955, in the village of Lisoka, a young man named Emange Isongo was found dead at the foot of a palm tree which he had climbed to tap palm wine. His climbing rope, it was said, was unbroken. The village was shocked. Soon after, the story spread that Emange's father was one of the *nyongo* people, and that it had been his turn to supply a victim. Emange, it seemed, had fought the *nyongo* people at the foot of the tree, but his own father had clubbed him to death. It was Emange's sisters and a surviving brother who came back from a diviner with this story. Somehow, this particular event greatly upset the youth of the village, and they held meetings, at which the proverb was often quoted, *mèfondo mekpâ mὲὲsͻ mìikìsὲnὲ*: 'When the hair falls from the top of the head the temples take over'. This means that it was natural for the old to die before the young: whereas the reverse had been happening. Prominent in the succeeding period was a middle-aged traditional doctor named Njombe, who dealt with dangerous *nyongo* cases. As he put it to me in his own words in the local Cameroon creole:

'So Emange died. So everyone vex and the young men say they want to run out for town as he be young man too. So we begin to give advice to all young men: they can't run outside, so they begin cool their temper. From January, going February, March, April, dreams for sleep. People begin cry, time no dey, and man die on waking.'

In June new events began to happen. On a Sunday, 3 June 1955, a youth named Njie Evele was attacked in broad daylight by *vekongi* zombie spirits who were hiding in the village Presbyterian chapel. Njombe, the *nyongo* doctor, was called in (as

Njie put it) to 'doct him'. Njie was in a delirious state. What did he see? asked the doctor. He saw thirty-six *vekongi*, he said. Who led them? Njie called out 'Efukani!' Njombe put it rather charmingly: 'When he called Efukani, we say who is Efukani as we no get any Efukani.' Njie said this was the secret name of a man called Mbaki. Now Mbaki was a man with a large inguinal hernia which made it difficult for him to get about. But, Njie said, he had actually been driving the *nyongo* lorry, which was to take him away. Mbaki and three others who were also named were dragged to Njie's bedside, where they were ordered to let Njie go. The accused old men meekly did as they were ordered by the doctor Njombe. Njie made an excellent recovery.

The next day another young man, Manga ma Vekonje, suffered a similar experience. He gladly dictated to me his account. He had had a primary school education.

'I was working under Ekona Costains. Then it was payday of 4th of Juni [*sic*] of 1955. When I received my pay, when coming back to Lisoka I saw some little men of three feet high, black with white shirts and white trousers. They were plenty and I couldn't count them. They said we should go to Mpundu and sing *elonge*' [a kind of part-song].

But Manga managed to get back to his mother's hut. She gave him a dish of mashed cassava meal. The *vekongi* were still outside, climbing about in a small mango tree in front of his mother's door. (It is an interesting sidelight that probably under the influence of the local schoolteacher he called these *vekongi* 'eskimos'.) Manga was eating, but the little men ran in and ate up his cassava meal, and took him off to Mpundu and made him dance. They ran away at the approach of Njombe the *nyongo* doctor. Manga woke up on his bed, naming a suitable Lisoka adult who had been with the 'eskimos', and who duly confessed, after being found hiding under the bed in his own hut. Manga recovered with no ill effect except that the *vekongi* had escaped with his money and a long bar of washing soap.

On the following day, 5 June, there was a big meeting in Lisoka to protest against the conditions in the town. Njombe was prominent at the debate. The need for a really good medicine was stressed. 'So dey make a price 1/-, 1/- general, man, woman, big man, small boy, 1/-. We was collect on that day

151

£17 14*s*. 0*d*.' Two days later, the decision was made that only among the Banyang people, 150 miles away, did an appropriate medicine exist. After a further whip round, three delegates left for Banyang country with £30. On the 16th they returned with the news that the Banyang men would come, but that their price was £100. The town meeting nevertheless agreed: part of the banana fund was subscribed. And so, on 10 August, the Banyang people came with their medicine and their masked dancer: Obasi Njom. The marvels of the succeeding days passed expectation. Witches were flushed out in large numbers. The father of the dead Emange of the palm tree was pointed out by the medicine. He confessed that he had killed his son, but swore repentance. He was made to dance a rhythm at the request of the Banyang visitors, which they identified as a *nyongo* dance, which he clearly knew quite well. Other revelations followed. A by-product was the exposure of an ordinary (*liemba*) witch: a woman, Namondo, who was accused of having sexual intercourse with other women in witch form. Before the Banyang people left they trained thirty doctors capable of performing Obasi Njom. They also left a powerful fetish in the bush to protect the village.

They left on 7 September. It was like a great load off the village mind. By 1956 the news had spread from village to village. Emissaries flowed to Banyang country from a long roll-call of Bakweri settlements. Approximately £2,000 of the new banana money, as I have said, went to Banyang doctors. The newly constituted Obasi Njom lodges continued their anti-*nyongo* work for a year or more. Through 1956 and 1957 they came into conflict with the Churches and the law. In Wova, eight people were fined £5 apiece for digging up the floor of a wooden chapel, when the Obasi Njom masked figure indicated that the evil witchcraft medicine would be found there. As indeed it was: like all the others it was a latex rubber ball of nail-pairings and witchcraft symbols. Meanwhile, the villages resounded with the hammering as the new houses went up. On a visit at this time I could hardly hear what Njombe the *nyongo* doctor was saying, for the noise of the tin going on his enormous new house. We must leave this happy scene and reluctantly not pursue more of the details of the exorcising of *nyongo* from Bakweri land. Suffice it to say that from now on the new banana income was spent on village 'betterment'; the zombies retired and, as Njombe said, 'From there we no get trouble. They no die the same die. Plenty women conceived.' *Nyongo* was gone; there was Obasi Njom instead.[10a]

DISCUSSION

The general points I want to make are as follows. We clearly have three main elements in this situation: the questions of (1) a change in morale among the Bakweri; (2) a change in economic circumstances; and (3) a change in the supernatural situation. Of these only one, the economic change, was documentable or measurable by any 'objective' criteria. The economic change moved, indeed, from strength to strength, and began to show a downturn only about 1960 when, as we shall see, because of the weakening of the banana market, combined with certain political and economic factors that affected Cameroon particularly, the peasant cooperative movement in bananas began to lose money. The other two changes, the change in morale and the change in the supernatural situation, were, in rather different ways, what development economists would regard firmly as 'subjective'. Any Bakweri would, of course, have judged the change in the supernatural situation to be more important than either of the others. The change in the economic situation merely provided the means to rectify the supernatural situation. The change in morale followed this. The logic is perfect.

There are of course other logics. Here was a people who associated economic ambition with powerful forces of destruction which were supposed to be destroying the youth and fertility of the people. Suddenly, the attempt at communal betterment through cooperative exporting succeeds richly. Was not the previous body of hypotheses disproved? Such might be the neo-Popperian view. As Professor Evans-Pritchard has taught us to see, witchcraft beliefs express numerous situations of conflict and tension. While these conditions exist, and especially while individuals are thought to be able to project their wishes on reality and thus to change it, witchcraft beliefs are largely immune to disproof. The Bakweri hypotheses were not disproved. When the people were shaken by the shocks of fifty years, the pre-existing witchcraft beliefs took on a darker and more morbid form. When the 'objective' circumstances changed,

153

they did not abandon the beliefs: they acted as we have seen according to the logic of those beliefs; they exorcized the zombies but the zombies were, to them, no less real: they were now power-less.[11]

When one reflects on this material certain coincidences seem to be worth exploring. The experience of the Bakweri in 1954 of the influx of cash from commercial banana-farming must have been of the same kind as the earlier experience in the second half of the nineteenth century. Then, too, there was a striking rise in material wellbeing with the new xanthosoma cocoyam, and the flow of trade goods into the otherwise isolated economy. We can thus recognize the following phases of economics and belief.

Phase	Date	Economy	Belief
I	Pre–1850	Pre-xanthosoma; isolated	?
II	1850–1894	Xanthosoma; trade goods	No *nyongo*
III	1894–1954	Marginal to plantations	*Nyongo*
IV	1954–1961	Banana boom	*Nyongo* controlled

Some indication of a possible pattern has emerged since the decline of the banana boom. After 1961 the massive profits of cooperative banana production were reduced. The Bakweri who, during part of Phase IV, had even supplied a Premier to West Cameroon, suffered political setbacks in addition. They had generally been lukewarm to the unification of the two Cameroons. By 1963 the peasant economy was set back to a lower level than that of the end of the 'fifties, but not back to the level of Phase III. In that year a rumour spread from Bakweri villages on the mountain that the elders had ordered that no money should be picked up from the ground, since it was being scattered as a lure to entice men to the waterside. There, 'Frenchmen' would use them to work as zombies on a new deep-sea harbour, or use them to appease the water-spirits. For a number of months it was commonplace to see coins and even low-value notes lying about the streets of the capital. In June of that year the Chief of Buea pointed out to me with a significant gesture a disturb-ingly shiny 50 franc piece, lying in the garden of the British

Consulate, during a gathering of notables for the celebration of the Queen's birthday. These interesting events merit more than this brief mention. It is enough here, however, to note the revival of the zombie theme with totally new *realien*.[12] We may then set up tentatively:

Phase V   1961 +   Economic setback   *Nyongo*-like resurgence

The old *nyongo* spirits still remained exorcised: Bakweri were firm on this. Since 1963 no more striking events have occurred. It now seems to me, however, that Bakweri statements about the novelty of the zombie witch beliefs are to be taken to refer to the incidental, 'syncretistic' dress in which they appeared. Taken together with the linguistic evidence, which suggests a longer history for the *somba* witch-pledge than the Bakweri are aware of, it seems likely that the 'template' for new versions of this belief is permanently in existence. Replication occurs, perhaps, when general prosperity (*inona* low) is replaced by times in which individuals of property begin to stand out and to attract *inona*. Perhaps this speculative graph[13] may contain some truth:

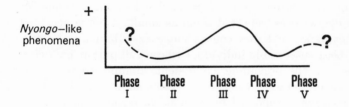

Perhaps the ambiguity of Phase V derives in part from the decline of the potlatch controls which may have helped to stabilize the property-versus-*inona* conflict during the great Phase II period of prosperity. The first (and still I think the only) *eyû* mortuary potlatches for a generation were performed in 1955 and 1960 during Phase IV, but no attempt has been made to revive *ngbaya*. There has been some discussion among psychologically minded economists as to whether some societies have innovating ideologies and others not. Such a distinction becomes unreal when one sees that the 'non-innovating' Bakweri have at least twice been supremely 'innovative': when they accepted the xanthosoma and when they accepted coopera-tives.[14]

I have used the idea of the 'template' to express the persist-ence of certain themes in belief, from which 'replication' occurs only when other elements in the social and physical environ-ment combine to permit this. The *realien*, the circumstantial details of 'content' through which the replicated element is expressed, may be different on every occasion – assembled, it may be, by that unconscious process of *bricolage* to which Lévi-Strauss (1962) has drawn our attention, and by that resolution of opposites upon which he (1964, 1966) as well as Needham (e.g. 1967) and others have worked to such effect.[15] When the Bakweri beliefs were 'live' during the critical months of 1955 the creation of new *realien* could be observed. For example, the novel and rather peculiar form of the zombies as lively little men of multi-coloured appearance is in striking agreement with a syndrome known as 'Lilliputian hallucinations' (a term in-vented by Leroy in 1909). It is found in Europe in combination with many states ranging from schizophrenia to relatively mild conditions – including measles.[16] In this connection it is interest-ing to note that the doctor Njombe had told me independently that the zombie spirits were twelve feet high. When Manga, an eye-witness, reported them as small, Njombe accepted this as evidence that they could change size. Manga, at least, I take to be a susceptible individual whose Lilliputian hallucinations were, in the prevailing excitement, assimilated to the general terms of Bakweri belief. Field (1960) shows how Lilliputianism is commonly reported by patients in terms of cultural beliefs, such as, for example, that in fairies.

Many will be struck by a fellowship in literary atmosphere of the Bakweri beliefs with those of the more remote parts of central Europe. The emergence of *nyongo* witches from their graves, and their general preying on the young, recall the whole complex of vampire beliefs. And the heroic position of *nyongo*-fighting doctors like Njombe, who braved the thick of the fray, rescuing victims at great spiritual risk to themselves – enabled perhaps to see the invisible conflict by tying a seed of Aframo-mum, the so-called 'Grain of Paradise', to the brow – all this has the sound of Tolkien's *Lord of the Rings*. Such men knew themselves to be fated to succumb at death to the evil. *Nyongo* doctors too were specially treated at burial, for there was the danger that they themselves would rise from their graves. Njombe died a few years ago, in his own view, and in that of the people, fatally weakened. He had only one eye, a disability which was taken as a wound. Witchcraft beliefs are all too often ignoble and sordid. On the contrary, the mundane troubles of the small and insignificant Bakweri people gained a certain grandeur from their projection into the spiritual conflict.

NOTES

1. An earlier version of this paper was given at Dr Mary Douglas's Seminar in London on 26 October 1967. An earlier version still was given for the Oxford University Delegacy of Extra-mural Studies on 27 January 1965.

2. The following can be amplified from Ardener (1956, 1961, 1962) and Ardener, Ardener & Warmington (1960). The Bakweri call themselves *Vakpe* and (with the removal of the Bantu prefix) they are also referred to in the literature as *Kpe*. I have now published (1970) the history of the mountain Bakweri in the nineteenth century.

3. Baptist missionaries landed at Fernando Po in 1841 and founded settlements at Bimbia (1844), Douala (1845), and Victoria (1858), finally evacuating Fernando Po itself. They often proudly claimed to have introduced the new crops. Saker (*Missionary Herald*, 1871, pp. 56-57) recalled that harvests on the coast had formerly provided only for three months' consumption. The xanthosoma bears in Bakweri and Duala the same name as the island of Fernando Po (Bk. *Likao*, Du. *Dikabo*); the Duala plural form *makabo* was later borrowed by inland peoples together with the crop.

4. Bakweri population of Buea (1953): 914. Preuss (*DKB*, II, 1891, p. 517) assessed the population in 1891 at 1,500 of whom 600 were men capable of bearing arms, 400 being provided with guns. Later, 600 guns were said to have taken part in the battle of Buea.

5. See *DKB*, III, 1892, pp. 14-18; Ardener, 1956, pp. 24-25. Von Gravenreuth, von Schuckmann, von Stetten, Dr Richter, and the gardener Pfeil, 150 African mercenaries, 10 Kru policemen, and a Maxim gun were halted at a barricaded ravine. Gravenreuth was shot dead, the Maxim gun jammed, and the expedition returned to the coast bearing its buried leader's head and heart.

6. *DKB*, VI, 1895, pp. 134, 321, 382-383. Dominic (1901, pp. 105-106) describes the unearthing of the rest of Gravenreuth's bones, finding them still clad, he says (as if echoing some grotesque advertisement), '*in den wohler-haltenen gelben, festen, nägelbeschlagenen Schnürschuhen*'! The remarkable obsequies of von Gravenreuth illustrate the peculiar muffling effect of belief on behaviour between foreign peoples. With Gravenreuth dead, the German belief system sought as if by antennae for the belief system of the Bakweri. The latter, as 'savages', were expected to prize a victim's head and heart: the Germans spared their leader's body the ignominy of losing those parts to the Bakweri by removing them themselves. Any explanation of the German behaviour must be found, then, in German belief, not in the belief of the Bakweri, for whom the events, had they been aware of them (and possibly

they were), would merely have suggested (on the contrary) that it was the Germans who prized the heads and hearts of the dead. By such a dialectic, no doubt, colonizers and the colonized may come in time to produce a body of shared beliefs which differ sharply from either of the parent systems. For the possibility that the Germans shot Gravenreuth by accident, see now Ardener, 1970.

7. Most of this report appears in *DKB*, X, 1899, p. 513.

8. The sasswood mixture was not thought of as in itself killing the witch.

9. For some of the closely comparable elements to be found in the beliefs of peoples neighbouring the Bakweri, see, for example: Talbot (1912), Ittmann (1953). The Haitian vocabulary of West African origin (Huxley, 1966, pp. 237-241) seems to contain some other coastal Cameroon elements. We may compare Bakweri *lova*, 'god', 'sky', Haitian *loa*, 'gods', 'spirits'; more securely: Bk. *nganga*, 'doctor', Ha. *gangan*, 'magician'; Bk. *gbanga*, Duala *bwanga*, 'medicine', Ha. *wanga*, 'a magical charm used for selfish ends'; Bk. *mwana*, Du. *muna*, 'child', Ha. *ti moun*, 'a child'; Bk. *ngole*, Du. *ngokolo*, 'millipede', Ha. *gangolo*, 'centipede'; Bk. *maese*, Du. *mawasa*, Ha. *marassa*, 'twins'.

10. For the detailed history of the Bakweri Cooperative Union of Farmers, see Ardener, S. (1958) and Ardener *et al.* (1960, pp. 329-332). The roots of the Union lay in a meeting of 5 August 1951. In 1952 it had an initial membership of only 73, yet in that year it shipped 8,000 stems of bananas valued at £2,500. There was a dramatic increase in membership. In 1953, the first full year of operations, it shipped 34,000 stems valued at £13,410. In 1958 the cooperators shipped 1,350,000 stems valued at nearly £1 million. In that year the villagers on the mountain received a net income of £300,000, about £150 per member. The 182 members at Lisoka (a village which looms large in this account) received £39,000 gross: an average of £216 gross each, about £75 net (Ardener *et al.*, 1960, p. 330 and Table 81).

10a. For Obasi Njom among the Banyang themselves (Basinjom), see now Ruel, 1969, pp. 210-213.

11. It is noteworthy that the cooperative nature of the venture enabled individual ambition to be achieved through collective endeavour. The higher and the more general the level of prosperity, the less likely may be the stimulation of *inona*. Whether all societies that lay great stress upon economic 'justice' tend to react in a Bakweri way (that is, with the sensitivity to individual success increasing when the economy is stagnant, thus increasing the tendency to stagnation) is a good economic question.

12. Or a new arrangement of *realien*. The water-spirits are part of a different section of Bakweri belief: in *liengu* (pl. *maengu*), appropriate to the deep-sea wharf environment (Ardener, 1956, pp. 93-94, 98-100). A surprising linkage of all the themes occurs, however, in the account of Bakweri folklore given to the administrator B. G. Stone, whose MS report (1929) leans heavily on the work of the late Mr Steane, a Bakweri teacher of Victoria. He says (paragraph 110) that there is a powerful spirit 'at the bottom of the lake near the summit of Mount Kupe in Kumba Division. In the latter lake there is a great spirit market and spirits from all over the world are thought to meet there and barter their goods. *The new Nigerian coinage and paper money* were said first to have been introduced in this spirit market, and to have been distributed thence to the people' (my italics). Mount Kupe is, of course, the *nyongo* mountain.

13. Phases III-V are documented. Phase II (no *nyongo*) rests on the statement of the Bakweri, the relatively modern *realien* of the *nyongo* belief, and the

saliency of the old *liemba* at the time of the colonial occupation. Phase I is merely a symmetrical speculation, aided by my guess that *sómbà* (*sómbì*) = Caribbean *zombi*. The transmission would have to occur before the almost total cessation of the slave-trade from this area after 1840 (the peak was from *c.* 1785 to 1830). The pre-xanthosoma economy is assumed not to be expanding, and to be based on the former plantain staple cultivated by men. There are some ritual hints of a yam staple before the plantain, based on the *D. dumetorum* species (Ardener, 1956, p. 46). A shadowy economic 'Phase minus I' is perhaps remotely conceivable.

14. The Bakweri 'innovations' were group borrowings which differed from 'non-innovative' borrowings mainly in their unforeseen effects. Yet the second innovation is ideologically connected with the first: it restored the place of the banana (man's crop) which the xanthosoma (woman's crop) had overwhelmed. Whatever the reinforcing effect of the 'jackpot' consequence, the earliest steps towards acceptance of export banana-farming were aided by its being a 'man's' crop.

15. Lévi-Strauss, particularly in his latest studies (1964, 1966), analyses brilliantly the constant rearrangements of themes and motifs, and transformations in myth. He uses the term *bricolage* (1962) to indicate the impression of new structures being 'bodged up' out of pieces of other structures. In his terminology: every so often, by a process of *bricolage*, a new Bakweri myth is created out of old and new elements embodying a statement involving economics with zombie-like phenomena. Something is repeated and revived over time through these successive replications. Whatever 'it' is, it is to be considered at a different level of analysis from that used in even the sophisticated analysis of content. I call it the 'template'. Its simple meaning of a 'form' or 'shape' used for copying is self-evident. I have in mind, however, the word's use in molecular biology, in the description of the process whereby the genetic material (DNA) continuously replicates itself from the chemical materials that are presented to it. The analogy I wish to bring out is that the molecules that replicate do so because their structures are logically limited in such a way that the chemical reactions they can take part in always compel the same end: the repetition of the original structures. They are like puzzles whose lengthy solution is finally in the form of the same puzzle. I suggest, merely on the loosest analogy, that in systems of belief over time certain configurations continually recur. Across time, 'synchronically', they may from time to time be absent. The metaphor of the 'template' is a way of visualizing that diachronic continuity perceived in the phrase: *plus ça change, plus c'est la même chose*. So we see the ideological template of the father-despot replicated in Russian history through totally different (even 'reversed') *realien* in Tsarist and Stalinist times. In French ideology two templates in particular replicate with monotonous regularity: one summarized by '*l'état c'est moi*' and one by 'the barricades'.

16. '[T]he patient sees very small, perfectly formed figures, usually active and mobile, gaily coloured, and pleasant to look upon.' In a case of scarlet fever, a child reported them as tiny 'clowns' who seemed to be moving across and under his bed. They reappeared at fifteen-minute intervals (Leroy, 1922; Savitsky & Tarachow, 1941).

REFERENCES

ARDENER, EDWIN. 1956. *Coastal Bantu of the Cameroons*. London: International African Institute.

Edwin Ardener

ARDENER, EDWIN. 1961. Social and Demographic problems of the Southern Cameroons Plantation Area. In A. Southall (ed.), *Social Change in Modern Africa*, pp. 83-97. London: Oxford University Press.

— 1962. *Divorce and Fertility*. London: Oxford University Press.

— 1970. *Kingdom on Mount Cameroon: Documents for the History of Buea, 1844-1898*. West Cameroon: Government Press.

ARDENER, EDWIN, ARDENER, SHIRLEY & WARMINGTON, W. A. 1960. *Plantation and Village in the Cameroons*. London: Oxford University Press.

ARDENER, SHIRLEY. 1958. Banana Co-operatives in the Southern Cameroons. *Nigerian Institute of Social and Economic Research: Conference Proceedings*, pp. 10-25. Ibadan.

Deutsches Kolonialblatt (DKB). Berlin (series).

DOMINIC, H. 1901. *Kamerun: Sechs Kriegs- und Friedensjahre in deutschen Tropen*. Berlin.

FIELD, M. J. 1960. *Search for Security*. London: Faber.

HUXLEY, F. 1966. *The Invisibles*. London: Hart-Davis.

ITTMANN, J. 1953. *Volkskundliche und religiöse Begriffe im nördlichen Waldland von Kamerun*. Berlin.

JARVIE, I. C. 1963. *The Revolution in Anthropology*. London: Routledge & Kegan Paul.

LEROY, R. 1922. Syndrome of Lilliputian Hallucinations. *Journal of Nervous and Mental Disease* **56**: 325.

LÉVI-STRAUSS, C. 1962. *La Pensée sauvage*. Paris: Plon.

— 1964. *Mythologiques: Le Cru et le cuit*. Paris: Plon.

— 1966. *Mythologiques: Du Miel aux cendres*. Paris: Plon.

Missionary Herald. Baptist Missionary Society, London (series).

NEEDHAM, R. 1967. Right and Left in Nyoro Symbolic Classification. *Africa* **37** (4): 425-452.

RUEL, M. 1969. *Leopards and Leaders: Constitutional Politics among a Cross River People*. London: Tavistock Publications.

SAVITSKY, N. & TARACHOW, S. 1941. Lilliputian Hallucinations during Convalescence of Scarlet Fever. *Journal of Nervous and Mental Disease* **93**: 310-312.

STONE, B. G. 1929. Notes on the Buea District. (MS.) Victoria, Cameroon.

TALBOT, P. A. 1912. *In the Shadow of the Bush*. London: Heinemann.

© Edwin Ardener 1970

8

Robert Brain

Child-witches

In Europe and Massachusetts in the sixteenth and seventeenth centuries children were used for 'crying out' witches, and their accusations were taken as gospel by priests, judges, and respectable members of the community. Young girls became officials of witch courts where their supposedly unbiased confessions and accusations were accepted as fact. Innumerable people were sent to their death because of the wanton mischief of unruly children. Girls accused priests of gross immorality. Sometimes they were coached by interested parties. In Bangwa, Cameroon,[1] children are frequently accused of witchcraft. They also confess to witching others, giving the names of their victims and incriminating other children and adults. Although accusations are never made in Bangwa with the same degree of irresponsibility as they were in Europe, the parallels between the European child-accusers of witches and the Bangwa confessed child-witches are clear. In Bangwa and Europe some of the children involved were little exhibitionists, confessing to witchcraft in order to get attention. In both cases it seems that deprivation (in the one case protein, in the other sexual) played an important role. In Europe and Bangwa children have been used by professional witch-hunters for political ends, and the child's accusation against adults is taken at face value. In Bangwa a child's evidence could be used by a chief against a wealthy political opponent. The onus is always on the accused to clear his name; in Bangwa it was formerly through a sasswood poison ordeal from which few escaped.

This paper explores the psychology of child witchcraft among the Bangwa, avoiding global structural-functionalist explanations, although the complex ethnography of Bangwa witchcraft, of which this is a small part, supports the usual hypotheses and counter-hypotheses: witchcraft explains misfortunes; it also explains good fortune. It is both 'good for the Bangwa' (resolving tensions, dissolving redundant obligations); and 'bad for the Bangwa' (bringing individual distress and exaggerating social dysphoria). It emanates both from the inarticulate and the articulate points of the social structure (witches are chiefs as well as children and lonely old ladies). On the whole, Bangwa witchcraft offers no perfect logic; it operates situationally, within a context of individual enmity and jealousy, or group disharmony and competition.

Although Marwick (in Fortes & Dieterlen, 1965) suggests that beliefs in sorcery and witchcraft may provide an outlet for repressed hostility, frustration, and anxiety, he gives a warning that psychological hypotheses such as this are outside the scope of sociological analysis. It is not scientific because it is not testable; we have no means of measuring frustration, aggression, or anxiety that could be used in establishing a relationship between these large subjective conditions and their release in the standardized delusions of witchcraft. I am not as optimistic as Marwick about the possibility of measuring such things as social tension by statistical science. Nor are my psychological suggestions ambitious; but I feel that the ethnographer has something to offer in the study of personality; witchcraft, in particular, is a pointer to personal problems as well as social problems. Lack of expertise handicaps me in presenting psychological hypotheses but I hope an attempt to abstract qualities such as fear, guilt, aggression, and subconscious desires may be useful.

CHILDREN OF THE GODS

Various supernatural explanations are given to account for the illness and death of children, a subject that concerns the Bangwa greatly. The vast majority are said to result from the sins and misdeeds of their parents, or from conflicts carried out in the adult sphere. They include illnesses inflicted on children through vengeance, magic, and sorcery; through the effects of pollution; by matrilateral and patrilineal ancestors; and through adult witchcraft. Today, most misfortunes are explained through the maleficence of adult witchcraft. But in this paper I am concerned only with misfortune brought about through the sins or misdeeds of the children themselves. There are two aspects:

one concerns children affected by the gods of the earth (known as 'children of the gods'); the other involves children supernaturally punished for the crime of witchcraft (known as 'children of the sky'). Children of the gods and children of the sky are categories set off from the rest of Bangwa children; they are, in a sense, abnormal children, subject to mystical dangers which are only removed through ritual.

Children of the gods are extraordinary beings, little gods themselves, whose attachment to the world is tenuous. They are recognized both before and after birth. They include twins, and children born with physical deformities, by breech birth, or with a caul. Twinness is also attributed to older children who show signs of psychological disturbance or chronic illness. Children of the gods have the capacity to return to the world of unborn children (*efeng*), a vast cave inhabited by spirit-children who wander around in pairs, rather disdainfully looking for a possible reincarnation on earth. The Bangwa recognize that their world has little to offer compared with the security and comforts of the spirit-world.

Illnesses of children of the gods are attributed either to their own desire to return to the earth, or to the blandishments of their unborn friends. To prevent their return (that is, their death), rites are performed by a ritual expert, the priest of the earth (*tanyi*, himself a father of twins). If the unborn twins are blamed, an effigy of the sick child is made and buried inside a grave; in this way the spirits are fooled and cease preying on the child. Other rituals for children of the gods who attempt to flee the insecurity of this world are more elaborate. These rites are called in Bangwa 'rubbing' or 'anointing' rites, and in pidgin English 'fattening'. They are commonly carried out for young girls at the time they are due to take up residence with a husband to whom they have been betrothed since birth. The girl's 'illness' (usually due to awkwardness about her marriage, adolescent depression or retarded nubility) is attributed, by the diviner, to her being a child of the gods. After long weeks of seclusion during which she is fed nourishing food and rubbed with a mixture of oil, camwood, and medicine, there is a 'coming-out' ceremony in which blood from a sacrificed goat is rubbed in her eyes: to prevent her seeing her way back to the happy world of *efeng*.

G*   163

This summary account of children of the gods must suffice, since this paper is concerned with witch-children; I shall return to the subject of godly children in a brief comparison of these two methods of blaming children's misfortunes on their own supernatural misdemeanours.

CHILDREN OF THE SKY

Bangwa witchcraft (*lekang*) is associated with shape-changing. Men, women, and children (even the occasional dog) transform themselves into wild animals, natural phenomena such as rainbows, and mythical beings, in order to harm their kith and kin. Witchcraft is inherited: through the father to his successor and heir; through the mother to all her children. Powers associated with witch-shapes are ambivalent: a chief-leopard is good; a child-leopard is evil. Were-animals are used to excel at playing the xylophone or ruling the country; they are also used to eat children, burn compounds, or destroy crops. Witches may be male or female, young or old, wealthy or poor. The subject of Bangwa witchcraft is complex, involving cosmological beliefs and political theory. Child witchcraft, as I have said, is only one aspect of it.

Apart from an emphasis on 'going to the sky', the mechanics of child witchcraft are not so different from those of adult witchcraft. A witch activates his were-animals at night. The 'bush-soul' leaves his sleeping body and enters his chosen shape to indulge with friends and associates a lust for food, usually human flesh. Membership of a coven is obtained by payment of a victim. Witchcraft orgies take place in the 'bush' (*mbæ*), the word given to the non-humanized (uncultured or uncultivated) area of the Bangwa landscape. It is not only the forest, but river deeps, waterfalls, holes, and caves. It is also the sky, hence the name 'sky children' given to child-witches. During the time a child's bush-soul is merged with the were-animal he is in a state of danger. If the animal is shot, gets lost, or is affected by anti-witchcraft medicines, the sleeping child falls ill, the illness and consequent death being attributed to the accident that befell the were-animal.

There are many ways of discovering whether a child is a witch: through the pronouncements of a diviner, the evidence of an autopsy or a post-mortem, his own confession, incriminations in other people's confessions, or through the particular symptoms of his illness. A child may be declared a witch before he is born: foetus witches are seen as snakes and chameleons who wander the sky, dying at birth and returning continually to annoy the same or different mothers. They are recognized at autopsies by their 'short ribs'. Such a child is mutilated and ritual precautions are taken to prevent further reincarnation.

Autopsies indicate whether a child died through witchcraft. The organs of the stomach, chest, and throat are investigated by a specialist. A government ban has never been enforced and post-mortems are still carried out. If there are no witch-signs, it is suspected that death was caused by another kind of supernatural agency and something is done about it in order to protect the child's surviving brothers and sisters. The child may be discovered to have been a sky child, a witch. The diviner, handling the stomach organs, declares to the assembled kin that the child has a rainbow (seen in the large intestines), or a bruised 'elephant-liver' (through being slapped in the witch-bush). If he announces the presence of human beings on the heart or in the throat, a cry of disgust rises up from the onlookers. The 'corpses' (in the form of clots of blood or tiny sinews) are removed and buried below a plantain in an attempt to revive those people at the point of death as a result of the attacks of the dead child. The burial is made quickly and the funeral is curtailed. The mother is comforted by kinsfolk who tell her that an evil child has been taken away. Even babies are investigated in this way, showing a capacity for supernatural crime beyond their years. There is a psychological mechanism here, since there is an immediate change in the emotional climate, making it easier for the mother to suffer the loss of her child.

ILLNESS AND CONFESSION

Supernatural explanations supplement natural ones in determining the causes of a child's illness. Blaming the invalid's own witchcraft is one of them. Some illnesses are automatically attributed to this (dropsy, jaundice, madness, are some examples). In other cases children confess to witchcraft. Diviners also attribute illness to a sick child's witchcraft. The only means of effecting a cure is for a child of the sky to confess the details of his crime so that the proper ritual remedies may complement those of the herbalist. Children do confess; even small children of five or six. Most often the confession is of a very mild nature; for example the child says that he changed himself into a monkey and caught a fever while in the cold plains of the highlands; or that his were-antelope tripped on a liana in the forest and gave him a pain in the leg. These confessions do not always involve ritual action but serve as a kind of explanation for minor illnesses. Other confessions are more serious: they may involve victims and incriminate other children and adults. Even the worst kind of witches – those who cause their victims' death – may be cured. Emetics and purges are given to remove the swallowed person from the child's stomach, in the shape of vague forms in bile and excreta; their removal ensures the recovery of the witch and also the victims. If the illness continues and the child refuses to confess, other supernatural causes are sought. Wasting illnesses, however, are sure proof of incurable witchcraft; in this case it is better to let the child succumb.

The usual route to the sky is via a plantain and an invisible black thread or spider's web. Before the child can be cured of an illness brought out by his witchcraft he must be brought back from the sky. In most cases a simple do-it-yourself rite (involving the sacrifice and eating of a chicken) suffices. In other cases a complicated ritual is performed, at the compound's plantain clump, in order to seduce the child or his bush-soul back from the delights of the witch-bush. Some children are seduced there by the blandishments of powerful elders – rather in the way that small girls are believed to be seduced for lechery by the promise of lollypops. Witchcraft has its attractive aspects; it is a land of plenty: meat, wine, dancing, and fine clothes. In the same way as the small girl is an innocent victim of the old man's lechery, children are on the whole considered blameless. Nevertheless, there are the occasional Lolitas. And whatever the blame attached to the child, the danger is always present, particularly from the innumerable anti-witchcraft medicines planted across the countryside. Other rites are performed to remove children from the clutches of the witch Humbert Humbert. Children are fed money to buy him off; or he is shot, from a plantain, with medicated gunpowder.

THE SOCIAL CONTEXT OF WITCHCRAFT

Witches attack close kin. The victims of child-witches are usually
the inhabitants of one compound or neighbourhood. Bangwa
compounds consist of a single nuclear or compound family. In a
polygynous compound each wife has her own house, her own
stores, her own farms, her own cash profits from trading. She
forms with children a semi-independent corporate unit; such
units compete against each other, particularly for the favours of
the compound head. A strict etiquette is observed between co-
wives, among whom the possibility of serious enmity is recognized. The compound head remains on formal terms with his
wives and children; he is emotionally distant and the dispas-
sionate arbitrator in disputes between mother-children units.
Hostility between half-siblings shows itself early, usually as an
extension or reflection of conflicts between co-wives. Agnates
do not live together after adulthood; brothers separate to build
their own compounds, often far away from the parental home.
The sense of disunity between half-siblings, and corresponding
co-wife jealousies, find their wildest expression on the death of
the compound head when mother and children units fight for
property and for the succession of one of them to property and
titles. These half-sibling antagonisms are reflected in many
witchcraft accusations and confessions among children. As one
child conveniently said when I told him that I did not believe
in witchcraft: 'Europeans do not know jealousy; they don't hate
their brothers so they do not need witchcraft to harm them.'
Children harm not only half-siblings: I have heard a youth confess to causing his father's death (he pushed him off the sky).
Full sibling attacks occur rarely and are considered particularly
heinous. I have not heard of a child attacking his mother.

A CHILD'S CONFESSION

Here is a rather bald account of a case concerning a twelve-year-
old child called Asung. In one polygynous compound (a man,
his fifteen wives, and his innumerable progeny) two wives had a
minor quarrel over the feeding of the compound's pigs. The
quarrel developed out of hand, other wives taking sides. The

matter was brought to the notice of their husband only when Asung's mother bragged in front of witnesses of her large farms, implying that she had more mouths to feed. In doing so she broke a taboo forbidding men or women to mention each other's children or lack of children in personal quarrels. A meeting of the wives was called and the woman was fined six large bundles of firewood for the compound meeting-house. Soon afterwards the other woman's three-month-old baby fell ill and the herbalist's attempt to cure it failed. Then Asung fell ill and the inevitable whispering campaign began. Was he a witch? His illness became serious; he suffered from a severe fever, delirium, and physical contractions; he had tetanus. As he grew worse his first confessions were heard with a sigh of relief on the part of all members of the compound, his mother excepted. The confession became more ornate and circumstantial. He had changed himself into a deer. Then he had 'taken out' his snake in order to eat his half-brother. This snake had been wounded on a piece of broken bottle on its way back to the compound; this explained his body cramps. His liver (his elephant) was caught in a swamp in the forest and could not get out; his large intestine (rainbow) was swelling like a vast water-filled bladder inside his stomach – it had drunk from the anti-witchcraft bowl in the compound – so that he felt he would burst. He confessed to eating another child who had recently died in the compound; this child was wrapping itself around his throat so that he could no longer turn his neck. The child confessed that his excursion to the sky resulted from his wish to help his mother in her quarrel.

The attitude of the co-wives was one of fear and indignation. The father's attitude remained neutral, until Asung confessed to the murder of a child; he then declared that Asung should neither be taken to hospital nor cured by a Bangwa expert, although the confession indicated how this might be done. The child was a favourite of his; but in a large compound 'polygyny politics' would not allow him openly to cure him. The case became an issue in Bangwa. The paramount chief and other important nobles made the long trek to the child's sick-bed to hear the remarkable confession. There were two camps: should the child be cured or not? The mother and her close kin stood by the child; eventually it was arranged that he should be taken to hospital, the father even giving money secretly. This was in 1965, before there was a mission hospital in Bangwa and the child died on arrival thirty miles away. At home the anti-witch group rejoiced at the death of a witch; the funeral was curtailed, but people streamed to the compound to congratulate the father and mother on the loss of the sky child. They nodded their wise heads at the anthropologist who had tried to cure a witch. Even a year later, the death of another child (a daughter of the enemy co-wife) was blamed on the depredations caused by Asung.

Cases like this are not so rare. Not all fathers, however, would refuse to cure such a child. Monogamous fathers with fewer children often attempt to cure confessed witch-murderers in spite of public opinion or the hostility of their chiefs. They run the risk, however, of bringing an accusation of witchcraft on the whole family. Who but a witch would cure a witch? In the case of Asung, the head of the polygynous compound had his hands tied; the anger of his wives, jealous for the safety of their children, would not permit him to cure a child who had confessed to causing the death of one or more of them. Even chiefs, however, may send a favourite child away to be cured secretly.

Confessions can cause considerable distress, particularly among the maternal kinsfolk of the child. Full brothers may become estranged. Even children declare that they would leave their devoted brothers to die if they confessed to such a horrible crime. Some children are ostracized: one child was sent to the south where it was expected that a few months' contact with electricity would cure his witchcraft. Children driven from their compounds can usually find a haven with their mother's kinsfolk. Among adults, of course, the incidence of distress arising from witchcraft accusations or confessions is far higher. I witnessed cases of madness leading to suicide resulting from public accusations.

REASONS FOR CONFESSION

What prompts children to confess? Some children say they confess because they want to please their parents. Others say they confess because they wish to escape the pestering of elders who loom around the sick-bed. Children confess because they believe it will provoke a cure. For the past few years there has been a hospital in Bangwa; in some cases parents still insist that their child should confess before attending the hospital. In this way the natural and supernatural symptoms may be allayed. Other children say they confess so that they can eat meat: the cure of a sky child involves a meal of chicken. Some children seem to enjoy confessing horrible details of the witch-bush: they are little exhibitionists who know how to play the system, stopping short at the mention of serious crimes. Sometimes confessions are wrung from children in the form of monosyllabic answers to leading questions. Feelings of guilt may come into it. Confessions also have a cathartic effect: they work as psychotherapy, many illnesses appearing to clear up miraculously after a confession.

The atmosphere of the sick-room is conducive to confession. Disturbed by pain, delirious with fever, a child stops distinguishing between reality and hallucination. A sick person is never left alone: crowds of kin and sympathizers pester him with well-meaning inquiries; he repeats his symptoms over and over again. What the visitors want to know, of course, are the real, the supernatural, causes of the illness. Veiled and not so veiled questions are put to the child: Where did you go? Did you change into a were-animal? Confess! Confess! In such an atmosphere confession may bring peace, and relief to a disordered mind. Throughout the illness the normal domestic activities of the one-roomed Bangwa hut continue for fifteen to twenty hours a day: small children crawl around the floor, visitors are fed, chickens fly over the raised threshold. The mother prepares food, or goods to sell in the market. The sick child shares a bed with his brothers or sisters, or, if he is the last-born, with his mother; she copulates with her husband on the same bed. It is not only the European who finds the crowded, disturbed room oppressive during illness. Children who fell ill in my house preferred its relative anonymity to the busy compound. Sick men avoid the press of visitors by placing taboo signs outside their sick-room. Chiefs are always put away privily, often in the house of a retainer.

SOURCES OF CONFESSION MATERIAL

In this section I should like to make some tentative suggestions about the contents of confessions and their sources. Children in

Bangwa are not sheltered from the hard facts of life; they have plenty of opportunities to acquire knowledge of witchcraft beliefs, to which they add embellishment from their own imaginations. Children attend witchcraft exorcizations. Tiny children are included in blanket accusations made by diviners against categories of kin. They join with their elders to stand over the corpse of a child killed by witchcraft and swear their innocence. They attend all-night dances when possessed twin-mothers or twin-fathers smell out witches. They witness accusations against their parents, even their mothers accusing their fathers. One man told me how he was made to witness his mother being administered the poison ordeal. Children are told gruesome folk tales involving shape-changing, bloodthirsty witchcraft, and bogeymen. Their world is a mixture of reality and unreality: a bathing pool in the daytime becomes an abode of witches at night; a clap of thunder is the dying breath of an old diviner; the forest is filled with mysterious breezes, shapes, and sounds – manifestations of witchcraft and evil. There is plenty of material for confessions.

Dreams and disturbed sleep

Dreams and disturbed sleep are taken seriously by the Bangwa. Even in tiny children moaning and talking are credited to witchcraft or other supernatural attacks. Children who suffer semipermanently from disturbed sleep are declared by the diviner to be children of the gods, and appropriate curing rites are carried out. A very deep sleep is a sign of possible witchcraft; for this reason there is a strong taboo on waking a child abruptly: this may alienate irrevocably his travelling bush-soul. Dreams fascinate the Bangwa: they are used for purposes of divination; they are also recounted in confessions and accusations of witchcraft, since they are given the same half-reality of witchcraft. Thus a mother of twins dreamt that a pangolin was nibbling her twins; two years later her children fell ill; she recalled the dream and made an open accusation against her pangolin brother-in-law. There is one snag here: the ability to see witchcraft in a dream involves oneself in suspicion.

The contents of children's dreams are the expression of their normal imagination. Some dreams are wilder. Children have told me of witches, not usually identified, who attack them in their sleep. The witch grips them by the throat, sitting on their chest and suffocating them. The similarity between this and the classic description of the European nightmare is striking. The meaning of nightmare is 'succubus or incubus of the night'. The Bangwa were-shape is not a sex-fiend but a black, suffocating, bird-like shape which springs down from the trees onto sleeping children. The Bangwa call it *ndem abonga*. Nightmares have been analysed as the expression of repressed sexual desires. This does not seem borne out by Bangwa accounts. As far as witchcraft is concerned, nightmares and dreams give a feeling of reality to witchcraft beliefs and provide gaudy material for the most exotic confessions. Psychoanalysts agree that nightmares, particularly, give an acute impression of reality.

Sex

This brings us to sex: my suggestions here are mostly negative. I bring up the subject since it is a classic, not because children's confessions have much to offer in terms of sexual symbolism. Bangwa witchcraft is free of the gaudier fantasies of European witchcraft involving incubi and succubi. Adults do, however, confess to supernatural sexuality: women admit to mystical unions with bush-pigs; young men to the possession of a 'night-penis' by which they have intercourse with other men's wives in the witch-bush. These sexual fantasies probably reflect the frustrations of young women married to elderly polygynists; and those of young men who rarely have the opportunity of regular sex until they marry in their thirties. Psychological disturbance at adolescence occurs among young girls; these disturbances, however, are attributed to the actions of the gods, such a girl being converted into the twin category of child of the gods. One girl confessed that she was threatened (in a dream) by a male kinsman in the form of a snake. Significantly, this girl is one of two girls who have entered the first class of a new Bangwa secondary school, where strict segregation has been instituted; there is an onus on the girl to restrict her sexuality until she achieves the momentous distinction of passing out of college in six years' time. Meanwhile her age-mates, many of whom did not even attend primary school, are married with children, and have, presumably, a complete sex life.

Food

If sex is not a good avenue of inquiry, food is. As far as children are concerned (and possibly many adults), a protein-deprivation theory is more to the point than one involving sexual deprivation. The confessions of the Bangwa sky children are always very meaty. The orgies of the witch-bush are orgies of eating. The meat is human, but it is not described as disgusting either by the witch or by the accusers. The plump are preferred to the skinny, and the young to the old. The meat is cooked by the coven's servants, with great care. Cannibalism was never institutionalized in Bangwa, although during recent wars with their southern Mbo neighbours the Bangwa learnt to enjoy human flesh. Children were given the soup, anally. Today the domestic supplies of meat fluctuate. Pork is sold in the market; goats and sheep are sacrificed at rituals; game is smoked and stored. Chiefs and wealthy men eat meat regularly, but women and children may go without for long periods. Children have their own preserves: snails, crabs, frogs, beetles, grasshoppers, giant rats. They are forbidden such high-protein delicacies as eggs, liver, chicken (except at rites). On the whole, Bangwa children are undernourished. This may have something to do with the fact that Bangwa men, preoccupied with trading and (in the past) warfare, leave agriculture and the care of livestock entirely to their wives.

It is, therefore, significant that a confession of witchcraft usually leads to a good meal: chickens are brought by relatives and given to the child as part of the ritual of bringing him back from the sky. It is also significant that psychological disturbances associated with twinness and the gods should involve 'fattening': copious feeding with nourishing food.

A clear example of the protein aspect of witchcraft is given in the following example. On my arrival in Bangwa everyone was talking about an incident that had occurred in the market. A young boy of about fourteen confessed to his father that he and his witch-associates (children and adults of the same neighbourhood) had been to the sky where they had been eating his small sister. This girl was at the time very ill and had been taken to the palace of the paramount chief, who was her marriage guardian. The chief was told of the confession. Next market-day his retainers summoned the boy and his accomplices to attend the palace. A goat was brought, and butchered; the boy gave precise instructions as to how his sister had been shared in the witch-bush. The goat was divided accordingly, and to the accompaniment of hoots from the spectators the witches were told to go home and eat their meat, and leave the child alone. Not one of the group protested, but took his share and quietly went away. The girl, of course, recovered.

Another child confessed to eating a small baby; the baby died. The corpse was tied around the neck of the confessed witch by the desperate mother who cried 'Why should I bury valuable meat? Eat him. Eat him.'

Environment

These are, as I said, suggestions. On the same level we should mention environmental factors. I could not, however, go so far as Trevor-Roper (1967) who, in discussing the origins of European witchcraft, says that the thin air of the mountains breeds hallucinations, and the exaggerated phenomena of nature (electric storms and avalanches) easily lead men to believe in demonic activity. He presumes that the superstitions of the mountains are exaggerations of the beliefs of the plains, and places the origin of medieval European witchcraft in these thin-aired pockets. Bangwa beliefs, however, do not vary much in cultural content from those of the malarial, thick-aired forests. Nevertheless it is certain that witchcraft beliefs are influenced by the fact that some Bangwa live on peaks over six thousand feet and that a depressive wet season lasts for eight months. During the rains, food is scarce, communal activities are almost nil, and communications between compounds and neighbour-hoods are rendered difficult by swollen rivers and dangerous landslides. Tensions and witchcraft accusations always build up towards the end of the hungry, rainy season; I used to feel peculiar myself. The Bangwa put it differently: in September, after weeks of cold, misty rain, there come bursts of hot sun; the unaccustomed heat melts the protective fat around the stomach's were-animals and the escaping beasts cause innumerable painful deaths after their long, hungry hibernation.

Aggressive feelings

Frustrated aggressions are expressed in dreams and witchcraft confessions. Only at a very early age are children permitted to indulge freely their aggressions: five- and six-year-olds may beat their older brothers and sisters without fear of punishment, and destroy objects without reprimand. As they become older, aggressive urges are curbed; at the same time, taboos are placed on infantile sexuality. Children learn an elaborate etiquette: correct behaviour between the young and the old, the poor and the rich, the normal and the abnormal. The taboo against violence is particularly strong: I came across only one case of physical assault, which was a matter of grave, public concern. Children of ten or eleven appear very adult. They have no toys, no games; they are not encouraged to be creative, even in the telling of stories. Play involves a serious imitation of adult activities: farming, hunting, carving, etc. From an early age their responsibilities are heavy: small children act as nursemaids while their mothers and elder siblings are away at distant farms. Guilt concerning aggressive feelings towards one's close kin is reflected in confessions.

Guilt about illness

Personal guilt feelings about illness are part of Bangwa thinking. A fever is not caused by mosquitoes or a sudden change of temperature; jaundice is not an infection. If the malevolence of a witch or other supernatural agency is not suspected, then the invalid is guilty. This guilt is manifested in confession and the confession itself may be cathartic in this context. Samuel Butler in *Erewhon* (1872) presents an imaginary society in which people who get sick are treated as criminals. The judge, a kind and thoughtful person of magnificent and benign presence, sums up in a case against a consumptive:

'It pains me to see one who is so young and whose prospects of life are otherwise excellent, brought to this distressing condition by a constitution which I can only regard as radically

175

vicious. . . . This is not your first offence . . . you were accused
of bronchitis last year. . . . It is all very well for you to say
that you had unhealthy parents and a severe accident in
childhood permanently undermined your constitution; excuses
such as these are the ordinary refuge of the criminal. . . . You
are a bad and dangerous person and stand branded in the
eyes of your fellow countrymen of one of the most heinous
known offences.'

He was sentenced to life imprisonment, the death penalty having
recently been abolished. 'Your presence', said the judge, 'in the
society of respectable people would lead the less able-bodied to
think more lightly of all forms of illness.' Although there was no
show of violence towards the guilty man, there was hooting from
the bystanders. This scene could easily represent a kind Bangwa
father blaming a confessed witch for his illness, with a horrified
'public opinion' looking on. Misfortunes and illnesses are placed
at the door of the victim; and confession to some extent ex-
punges the guilt.

FUNCTIONS OF CHILD WITCHCRAFT

The most important function of children's accusations and confessions (both Anglo-Saxon and Bangwa) is to confirm in a clear,
matter-of-fact fashion the vague beliefs of adults. Out of the
mouths of innocent babes come minute descriptions of un-
believable witchcraft excesses. Children do not lie; how can it
be in their interest to fabricate such circumstantial stories?
This explains why the delusions of the Bangwa children and
the fantasies of the Salem girls are taken seriously; the adults
need their inchoate beliefs substantialized. In an analysis of
one Zuñi case of sorcery accusation against a youth, Lévi-
Strauss points out (1963) that a confession of guilt reconstructs
the system for his elders. In the same way, the wild fantasies
of the European children and the expressive confessions of
the Bangwa children add logic to beliefs that need constant but-
tressing. A good way out for a Bangwa child who is suspected
of witchcraft is to confess with as much intriguing detail as
possible; the Zuñi boy, accused of sorcery, furthers his cause by
presenting successive versions of his supernatural exploits, each

more ornate than the rest. A confession of guilt is more effective than persistent protestations of innocence. This may be so. However, one should not forget the tragedies: some children know how to play the system in this way; others, as in the case of Asung, become martyrs to it.

The fantasies of childhood, blocked in real life, are given free rein in confession; the more way-out they are the better. Children's imaginations, notoriously more fertile than adults, are used to sustain witchcraft beliefs. Children cull exotic material from the half-real world of dreams and nightmares; and from their own perception of the adult world of witchcraft. When a particularly lurid confession has been made people come to hear it from the child's lips; chiefs make formal processions to the bedside of a small child who has come out with a particularly realistic account. Schoolchildren add foreign elements to the content of witchcraft beliefs; strange material from Roman Catholic dogma and Western science merges with traditional beliefs in shape-changing. In this way children's confessions also correspond to the fluctuating nature of witchcraft beliefs. Witchcraft has no fixed dogma, no single logic; it is utilized in many different kinds of situation as a means of explaining misfortune and expressing social tension. Constant reformulations through confessions are very important. For this reason alone it is clear that the confessions of Bangwa witch-children are not the fantasies of neurotics. Children show signs of temporary depression or psychological disturbance; but their confessions are normal to Bangwa society at the present. Whether Bangwa society (like European society in the sixteenth century) is normal is another question.

WITCHES AND GODS

I can now refer back to the children of the gods, the twin-children I mentioned at the beginning of the paper. The hypothesis is that witchcraft accusations, particularly against children, are increasing in a time of swift social change. In Bangwa now the traditional political system is breaking down. Commoners, former slaves, and servants are challenging the chiefs' authority and their monopoly of political power and wealth. Individual rather than corporate interests are being emphasized. The situation is analogous to that in medieval Europe when witch-craft became the refuge of traditionalists, representatives of the old order fighting against the inevitability of the industrial revolution. The Bangwa believe that misfortunes have been getting out of hand since the arrival of the Europeans (their industrial revolution). Witchcraft, rather than the traditional gods, explains epidemics of meningitis and yaws (real), and the increasing infertility of soil and women (presumably imagined). The traditional belief system, associated with the earth, the gods, the ancestors, personal spirit-guardians, has failed to cope with the new situation. The forces of the sky are winning over the forces of the earth. This is not just an anthropologist's conjecture: diviners today explain misfortune through the activities of witches rather than those of the ancestors, the gods, and the spirit-guardians. Children of the gods, associated with the earth, are becoming rare phenomena. Child-witches, associated with the sky, are everywhere.

Witchcraft accusations and exorcization rites are ten a penny; I had to wait months and walk miles to see the 'fattening' of a child of the gods. The explanation of misfortune has been personalized, replacing older beliefs in the 'will of the gods' and the divine punishment of ancestors. People cause evil now, not gods. Sky children may even be a new phenomenon.[2] Just before his death (in 1952) one paramount chief called a meeting of the country's priests, healers, and ritual experts, asking them to explain the phenomenon of sky children to him and why they seemed to have taken over from the children of the gods. He was himself a twin. No answer has been recorded; but the chief declared that activities against the rising tide of witchcraft, and child-witches in particular, should be hotted up.

Throughout Bangwa the attitude to witchcraft has changed; old men complain that witchcraft, once the elegant pastime of princes and their cronies, has now become entirely evil and the province of upstarts and children. These attitudes receive strange support from the missionaries in their own attempts to move religion from the earth to the sky; chiefs and fathers join forces in a common attack on witchcraft. A mission was not opened in Bangwa until 1966. Missionaries have shown themselves scornful of exotic beliefs concerning the earth and the ancestors: they dismiss them as superstitious beliefs associated with 'animism' and 'fetishes'. On the other hand, they are fascinated by witchcraft. Children attending the new secondary school present Bangwa witchcraft in a lively and realistic form, in the father's parlour and also, presumably, in the confessional! A local priest has his own witch stories; he can tell the children how he himself killed a witch lurking around his house at night. I have seen a priest give holy water to protect people fearful of witch-craft attack. Demonism (witchcraft), in its modern, evil aspect, gives the new religion (Christianity) something to fight. And it gives the chiefs a tool with which to attempt to shore up an old system, which shows serious signs of cracking.

NOTES

1. The Bangwa are a group of Bamileke chiefdoms situated in the Mamfe Division, West Cameroon. Fieldwork among them (1964-65, 1967) was aided by grants from the Wenner-Gren Foundation for Anthropological Research, the Trustees of the Horniman Fund, and the Central Research Fund. I thank Miss Penny Wright for additional material collected in 1968.

2. On this point I should note that beliefs associated with witchcraft are very similar to those held by neighbouring forest tribes, particularly the Banyang; the Bangwa word for sky is *lebu*, which is the Banyang word for witchcraft. Beliefs associated with the earth, the ancestors, and children of the gods are, on the other hand, similar to those held in the Bamileke highlands. Banyang beliefs are described by Malcolm Ruel in another essay in this volume.

REFERENCES

BUTLER, SAMUEL. 1872. *Erewhon.* (The extract quoted in the text is from pp. 81ff. of the Penguin Books edition, 1935.)

FORTES, M. & DIETERLEN, G. (eds.). *African Systems of Thought.* London: Oxford University Press (for the International African Institute).

LÉVI-STRAUSS, C. 1963. The Sorcerer and his Magic. In *Structural Anthropology.* New York: Basic Books.

TREVOR-ROPER, H. 1967. Witches and Witchcraft. *Encounter,* May.

© Robert Brain 1970.

PART III

Idioms of Power

9

Julian Pitt-Rivers

Spiritual Power in Central America
The Naguals of Chiapas

I

Evans-Pritchard has suggested that witchcraft and religion are alternative modes of dealing with the predicament of personal fate: the Azande blame their fellow-men for their misfortunes and seek vengeance, the Nuer blame themselves and seek atonement. The distinction is one that may be made in other parts of the world, though clearly not with any great precision, since to evaluate the relative importance of religion or witchcraft is necessarily a somewhat arbitrary task. In the case of the indians of Chiapas in southern Mexico, however, it would appear virtually impossible, for while they spend much of their lives praying, and even more working to acquire the wealth necessary to enable them to hold office in a religious sodality, their concern in witchcraft is as great as that of any people of the world. Moreover, as will be shown, the dividing line between witchcraft and religion is not easily drawn. The two fields of activity are in fact better viewed as aspects of a single conceptual system offering two courses of conduct to deal with the problem of personal fate, which may be pursued either alternatively or simultaneously. June Nash has suggested that a community in Chiapas may pass through a period of crisis in which the number of persons murdered as witches rises far above the norm, but even in quieter times the homicide rate is high and the victim is, in the great majority of cases, a witch. Allegations of witchcraft are continual in the daily life of the indians.[1]

One might wonder how it can be that so many people acquire the reputation of a witch and why they are not more careful to ensure themselves against an accusation which so often leads to their violent and premature end. It has perhaps been understressed in writings on the subject that if a witch is sometimes to some extent a social outcast, he is far from always being so, for through the fear he inspires he may well receive more respect than a reputation for virtue would earn him. He would not, in fact, be thought so evil were he not credited with power and, as Hobbes observed,[2] to be credited with power *is* power. Those who can cure can kill, and vice versa, but to be believed capable of either entitles a person to a privileged position in comparison with ordinary mortals. Hence it is that the lure of power tempts men, in their efforts to achieve predominance, not only to claim the ability to cure, but even to court the accusation of witchcraft and to boast of having effected the destruction of their enemies. The stakes may be high, but the prize is dear.

Therefore I believe that the threat to bewitch, if not made openly as in Chiapas as the parting shot in a quarrel, is made by implication more often than ethnographers have recorded. The hint of supernatural reprisals has a greater effect upon those who believe in witchcraft than a demonstration of natural force, and it provides the ambitious with a short-cut to power – a short-cut that may be taken in good faith, moreover, for those who believe in witchcraft easily believe themselves capable of it and confess to it; it is as easy to become convinced of the effective power of hate as to believe that love conquers all.

The ambivalence attaching to such power, a common feature of so-called primitive societies, is particularly acute in Chiapas, since witchcraft, so far from being an activity practised on the margins of social life, occupies a central position among the preoccupations of the indians and interlocks so intimately with their religion that it is not possible to discuss one without reference to the other. Spiritual power is the crux of the social system and spiritual sanctions dwarf all others in people's minds. A witch is merely someone who has misused his otherwise legitimate powers.[3] Hence, all powerful men end their lives murdered in revenge for their witchcraft or their demise is attributed to defeat in some spiritual encounter. In the indian view they are murdered either physically *as* a witch or spiritually *by* one.

The formal courtesy of the indians' manners, their studied claims to modesty, the ethical concerns which prompt them to practise confession and submit to whipping, their self-sacrificing response to the call of civic duty – all reflect in reverse an invisible world where power is what counts and small mercy is shown to the weak. Events on earth are entailed by actions at the celestial level where the human hierarchy is established and the fate of individuals determined. Judgements of conduct at the terrestrial level[4] are clearly formulated by the elders, and public opinion follows their lead, but in the spiritual realms events are clouded by uncertainty and regarding individual responsibilities there consensus is not easily reached on earth; it is not patent who has caused a given sickness or misfortune or whether it represents the victim's just deserts or an abuse of spiritual power. The curer's techniques of diagnosis aim precisely to resolve this point. A fine line distinguishes the licit punishment meted out by a spiritual guardian (saint, spirit, or elder of the community) from the malevolence of a witch.[5] Misfortune is the result of misdeeds which offend the spiritual powers, and no punishment can be inflicted without divine connivance, yet this ethically simplistic universe loses its logical cohesion when it is admitted that guiltless people can still suffer. Is this not proof of the existence of Evil? And where does Evil come from if not from envy, the universal inspiration of the witch? The belief in witchcraft therefore provides the exonerating clause which preserves the moral determinism of indian religion from the hazards of life.

Spiritual power is manifest in health and success, since these are thought to result from it. Sickness and misfortune are caused by the castigation of a more powerful spirit, divine or human. The spirit is conceived as a personal vital force whose strength will determine the destiny of the individual. Spiritual power accretes with age, so that longevity alone suffices to demonstrate it in some degree; those with weak spirits do not survive since they are not capable of defending themselves at the celestial level. The spirit is represented in various ways: as heat (*k'al*), more exactly burning power than physical heat;[6] it is also figured as understanding revealed through dreams and spiritual insight – the strong spirits are those 'who see how the world is'. This capacity is frequently related to another criterion of spiritual strength, that of height: those who fly high see how the world is. These qualities of heat, insight, and height have significance in relation to other aspects of the conceptual world into which it is not necessary to go, but they are no more than means of representing, as the occasion demands, the relative preponderance of individuals in relation to one another. At the terrestrial level, society is governed according to a strict etiquette of precedence, expressed in the order in which men salute each other, drink, or pass in procession. The same notion of precedence rules at the spiritual level, with this difference: it is a matter of conjecture rather than conduct and observation.

The central figure in the struggle for spiritual power is the *nagual*,[7] which has been described variously in Chiapas and Guatemala as the 'destiny-animal', 'animal-companion', 'animal-soul', 'guardian-spirit', 'spirit-counterpart', etc., and even, by those who have understood nothing of its nature, as 'the familiar spirit'. It is also recognized in Mexico north of the Isthmus of Tehuantepec as 'witch' or 'transforming witch', 'shaman' or 'pagan priest'. The word is of Nahuatl origin, from the root meaning to disguise, but it is used south of the Isthmus with a somewhat different meaning. The same concept is referred to in the Mayan languages by a number of other words: *lab'* or *wayohel* in Tzeltal, *wayihel* or *chanul* in Toztzil; but *nagual* is in general use and it is also the word used by Spanish-speakers. It has caused the greatest perplexity to ethnographers from earliest times. This essay aims to clarify its nature, dispel some of the misconceptions that surround it, and perhaps assist thereby in interpreting accounts of it in the historical literature. Its form varies from place to place (though perhaps not as much as the interpretations that have been applied to it). I shall be concerned with it in the ethnography of Chiapas.[8] Even within this relatively homogeneous area it is subject to variations, but they all contain the essential notion of an animal which shares a common destiny with a man and whose life is coterminous with his. Esther Hermitte uses the apt designation 'co-essence'.[9]

II

The nagual must be classed first of all as one type of relationship between a man and an animal, comparable in some ways to the guardian animal spirit of North America and less exactly to the European witch's familiar or the animal form adopted by the European witch, but it is unlike what has been called 'totemism', where a collectivity bears a special relationship to an animal species. Neither should it be likened to a 'totemistic' relationship (also called 'personal totemism') in which an individual 'respects', in Evans-Pritchard's admirable usage, a particular species of animal, for it is a relationship between an *individual* man and an *individual* animal. A man has no tie with the other members of the species of his nagual, nor does possession of a nagual of the same species create any bond between two men or any connection between them in the eyes of others, save for the implication that their spirits are of a similar nature and strength. Moreover, the nagual conveys nothing about the social allegiance of its 'owner' (who is often uncertain as to the species to which his nagual belongs); it concerns only his spiritual power, his individual moral character and destiny. In short, it defines him as an individual – like a nickname – and not as the occupant of a particular place in the social structure – like a surname. It involves no prohibition and no ritual performances, if one excepts certain techniques for divining the nagual of a new-born babe in certain towns of Chiapas[10] and techniques in connection with curing in Chichicastenango (Bunzel, 1952, p. 318).

Yet if the difference between animals serves to provide the model for defining the relationship between groups in totemism – because they are 'good to think' rather than 'good to eat', in Lévi-Strauss's phrase – it is still the difference between species that, in the case of the nagual, enables animals to represent the spiritual hierarchy of individual men: the eagle flies higher than the sparrow-hawk; the thunderbolt has more burning power than the whirlwind; the tiger is more dangerous than the horse; the dog more cunning than the raccoon. All other naguals have more height, heat, understanding, and power than the *pollito* (chick), who is generally produced as the frailest of all manifestations of spiritual force, the very image of vulnerability. The relations observed between natural entities provide the model for representing the relationships between men.

The nagual has, then, a metaphorical function in making explicit the relative spiritual power of individuals. Yet it has also a metonymical function in defining the moral character of its owner. The horse and the raccoon are peaceful beasts and it is therefore unlikely that those who have such naguals will be accused of witchcraft, but the tiger and the eagle are predatory and in accordance with this criterion their owners are credited with potentially maleficent intentions. Vegetarian animals are not. The attribution of a nagual defines therefore not only the

H   187

power of the man in relation to other men, but the way he is likely to use that power. There is even a distinction made among the naguals that are thunderbolt (*rayo*) according to their colour: the black is generally regarded as more dangerous than the green, but the colours and their significance vary from place to place.

The range of phenomena that may be naguals varies from one community to another. At one extreme one might place Chichicastenango where, according to Bunzel (1952, pp. 274, 318), the list includes reptiles, mammals, birds, stone idols, and any one of a number of divinities.

At the other extreme is San Andrés Larraínzar where, Holland tells us, the list is limited to five-toed animals. (1963, p. 102), and, it appears later, to climatic phenomena. He also mentions what he calls 'dioses del linaje' (lineage gods) which are the jaguar, ocelot, etc.

The flexibility of the system is evident and, given its metaphorical function, this is to be expected. It would demand more space than we have at our disposal here to examine the distribution of forms of the nagual in Central America, but it should be noted that the ranking *order* is always in accordance with the same principles: climatic phenomena are always superior to animals, birds are ranked according to the height at which they fly, mammals according to their relative strength. There is a notable exception in the case of the humming-bird, whose overall precedence is denoted not by height or strength, but by the divine associations of the bird. It is the Ancestor, the protector, a supremely beneficent divinity who is also represented as a small boy with a wide hat. It is therefore confused with pictures of the Niño de Atocha, who is portrayed as a child with an elaborate head-dress. The popularity of this image in Chiapas is perhaps due to this fact.[11]

The attribution of the nagual is in continual doubt. It is never known for certain, a matter of common knowledge like the totemic affiliation of a clansman. It is rather something to be verified and re-verified by various means: prayer, astrological calculation, augurial tests, or oneiromancy.

In some towns of Chiapas a test is used which consists of scattering ash around the house where a baby has been born in order that the footprints of its nagual may be identified after the first night. The test assumes that the nagual will mark its relationship to its newborn owner by approaching as close as possible. (This test appears to be logically contradictory to the belief, firmly asserted on other occasions, that the nagual and the man are born at the same moment just as they die at the same moment, but such logical implications are misplaced where only the identification of the nagual is at issue.) It is significant, however, that, effectively and not conceptually, such a test eliminates the higher ranks of the spiritual hierarchy as candidates for the baby's nagual, since they are all phenomena unable or unlikely to leave a trace around the house.

The nagual is in fact attributed by public opinion in accordance with the performance and reputation of the individual and it gets revised as often as the public image of the person changes. This revision is facilitated by the provision that a person of superior spiritual strength may have more than one nagual and the additional naguals come to be revealed later in life when the owner has made his mark as a person of influence. They belong, it goes almost without saying, to the higher ranks of the hierarchy. The different naguals of an individual are never discussed as if to make an inventory of them and only the most powerful or the most recent is mentioned, though the simple fact of having plural naguals implies superior spiritual strength.

The common identity between man and nagual implies common qualities. Hence the metonymical equation finds support and illustration in the man's personal idiosyncrasies: the man who is whirlwind has a twisting forelock rising from his brow; the man who likes green food is a horse; the greedy timid woman is a raccoon; the weakling child is a chick. An elder of Pinola exploited to good use the metonymical equivalence involved when, as was his custom when drunk (and indians boast only when drunk), he used to put live coals into his mouth. He was an ambitious man and this eccentric and spectacular conduct earned him a hesitant designation as thunderbolt.

The system of attributions leans haphazardly upon the principles of magical association, but it quite ignores the logic of practical knowledge. Contradictions at this level abound: the nagual whose life-span is coterminous with that of its owner may well belong to a species that is known to live for only a few years; the chick grows up in a few months. Later, a supplementary nagual may be attributed and it is thought that the man dies only when his last nagual dies. It is only then that his vital force is exhausted.

The nagual sets a seal upon the social personality of its owner, like a sobriquet; hence, logically in terms of social relations, but not in terms of the system as it is described ideally, small children tend to have innocuous animals for naguals, while the dangerous animals and high-flyers are usually reserved for the mature and especially for the curers. There are, however, babies born with a nagual implying a strong spirit and this places them in particular danger on account of the jealousy they inspire. The recruitment of the curer is effected through the interpretation of his dreams which reveal the strength of his spirit and the nature of his nagual. It is not then recalled, for it is not relevant, that thirty years earlier he was divined to have been a much humbler animal. Spiritual identity relates to the man as he is in the present, not as he was in the past. It would be patently absurd to think that a timid and incompetent man was a tiger or still less a thunderbolt, nor could a man of years who had held high office in the sodalities be a harmless lizard, for the nagual and the person are the same being. The indians themselves make this clear in their speech; they do not say 'X has such-and-such a nagual' or 'X's nagual is a tiger', but 'X is a tiger'. It is not a separate entity, but the same at the celestial level, and its appearance at the terrestrial level is the point of contact between the two levels. Its appearance is therefore rare and constitutes an event of 'extra-ordinary' significance. It is a portent when a man sees his own nagual and many deny that he can ever do so. Moreover, when a man sees the nagual of another, he is rarely aware of it at the time, but only afterwards when it is discovered that in killing or wounding the animal he has done the same thing to the man. It is an interpretation after the facts, like all conclusions regarding witchcraft.

It is not surprising that the chief source of information regarding naguals should be dreams, which are thought to be glimpses of events at the spiritual level. However, dreams are not easily interpreted and it is even believed that false dreams may be given to a person in order to deceive him or to 'test his spirit'.

The capacity to understand the significance of dreams is credited to those with strong spirits (who see how the world is). Hence the task of forming public opinion regarding the nebulous relations at the celestial level falls to the oneiromancy of the elders – a fact that greatly reinforces their power at the terrestrial level. The other source of information is provided by the diagnostic techniques of the curers. Witchcraft is, of course, one of the major aetiological categories and the identification of the witch is often a necessary part of the curing process. A full case-history would include the identification of the naguals of both the aggressor and the victim, since disease on earth is the result of a defeat on the spiritual level, but since the curer is generally forbidden to reveal the identity of the witch, this source of information is not directly available to public opinion.

It is characteristic of this mode of thought that parallel explanations are not excluded. Hence while, according to the system as it has been expounded so far, disease and misfortune are the outcome of a combat between naguals, they can be simultaneously the result of sorcery at the terrestrial level: a witch can inject a foreign substance into the body of his victim or he can place outside his door a *palito*, a twig that has been treated magically so that the evil implanted in it will penetrate the foot of the person who steps on it. Thus the curer is not only concerned to combat at the celestial level the nagual of the witch responsible for the disease; he may also effect his cure by extracting the 'witchcraft' from the body of the patient and stories are told of how this has been done. The man bewitched for meanness had a five-peso note injected into his throat, which caused him great discomfort; his curer successfully extracted it. The man who associated too much with ladinos had horse-hair introjected into his belly.[12] Spiritual strength still remains the effective determinant of these mundane events, but it is of interest that sorcery and witchcraft are distinguished here, not as alternative techniques operated by distinct practitioners, but only as the terrestrial and celestial aspects of the same events of a unique spiritual struggle.

Minor ailments are without celestial antecedence and can be cured by herbs or chemists' remedies. These are called in Spanish *mal de Dios* or *mal bueno* (God's evil or good evil) in contrast to *mal echado* (projected evil). Disease is also caused by loss of or damage to the soul, *ch'ulel* (Tzeltal and Tzotzil). The ch'ulel, unlike the nagual, resides in the body of its owner from which it escapes at death, for it is immortal. Nevertheless it is also confused with the nagual, being equally co-essential with the physical person. Hence it is said that it may be attacked and devoured by a hostile nagual. The two types of soul are not distinguished with conceptual clarity but only by context. As manifestations of the person they are identical, but they are opposed as the active and passive aspects of the person at the celestial level. Sometimes the nagual is said to be the ch'ulel (Guiteras-Holmes, 1961, p. 177) and in Chamula the distinction cannot be made linguistically since the word ch'ulel is used for any conceptualization of the person at the celestial level. The logical contradiction between the immortality of the ch'ulel and the fact that it can be eaten by a hostile nagual and thereby cause the death of its owner was resolved by Manuel Arias (Guiteras-Holmes, 1961, p. 227) by positing the existence of two ch'uleles, one of which will be eaten by the Pukuh (Evil, the Devil, Witchcraft) and the other will go to heaven. This belief is not recorded anywhere else and indians are normally unaware of the necessity to make such a distinction. The idea appears to represent no more than the solution to a logical contradiction of which a thoughtful and intelligent man became aware only through his attempt to instruct his friend, the ethnographer. Have not many of us become aware of the logical implications of what we believe only at the moment when we attempt to impart our beliefs to others and realize that they are contradictory? Have we not also then had recourse to our imagination in order to overcome the contradiction?

The saints are sometimes thought to have naguals, though these do not figure in the case-histories of disease. St Michael, patron saint of Pinola, and St Andrew, patron of Larraínzar, are both said by their parishioners to have the maximum number of naguals, thirteen. Little more significance attaches to such statements than that these saints are spiritually the most powerful and that they are prompt to castigate those who offend them. But the patron saint is said further to be the keeper of all the naguals of the community and sometimes to keep them shut up in a cave in one of the sacred mountains. This role is also fulfilled by the *Anhel* or by the *Me'iltotil* in certain statements.

These divinities are to some extent interchangeable with the patron saint.

The distinction between castigation and witchcraft depends upon the *right* to castigate, which is possessed not only by all the divine personalities and the ancestors, but by living elders who, as guardians and prefects, are entitled to correct their erring or disrespectful charges. Indeed, any elder is within his rights in resenting an affront upon the terrestrial level by meting out a punishment through his spirit which will bring sickness or misfortune to the offender. (It is understandable, therefore, that threats to bewitch should be proffered at the end of a dispute: the threatener is not saying 'I am a witch' but 'I will punish you' – whether the punishment is legitimate or not is another matter.)

Divine permission is required before anyone can be punished and this must be given by *Diosh* (God), it is said, but the notion of God includes all Divinity and hence the saints, the Ancestor, and the guardians. The distinction between the one and the many, which poses a problem to theologians who feel the need to be logical, concerns the indians of Chiapas not at all. Hence the anomaly that divine sanction is necessary for anyone to be punished, yet punishment can still be given illicitly, is not an anomaly to those who have not felt it necessary to define the limits of the jurisdictions of the divine personalities and to construct a universal abstract principle with regard to the exercise of divine authority. The problem of the omnipotence of God and the existence of Evil is resolved at the level of action by positing the malfeasance of a witch, identified by the consensus of the community.[13] The witch is not thought to have made a pact with the Devil and the nagual is not the Devil's servant, but the person himself, whose evil disposition is confirmed, like his spiritual power, only with the years. Thus the adolescent witch, frequent in the annals of European witchcraft, is unthinkable in Chiapas. For the same reason, women are rarely accused of witchcraft; they do not possess sufficient spiritual power.

Such a résumé of the role of the nagual in the conceptualization of the spiritual realm is far too brief to offer a complete understanding, but it suffices to show that this belief is an integral feature both of religion and of witchcraft, which are much less simply opposed than in the Christianity of Europe.

193

The nagual is a means of representing individuals in the spiritual realm and of relating their fortunes to the power structure of the community; the notion of hazard is effectively eliminated and the moral cohesion of the world is maintained. The accusation of witchcraft appears precisely at the point where this moral cohesion comes under stress: where the sufferer has confessed and made amends for all possible offences, yet still suffers. It is levelled at those whose personal ambition threatens the moral ideal of the community. The personification of the nagual in terms of strength of spirit on the one hand and disposition on the other takes account of both the factual and the moral aspects of the system of punishment which is the basis of moral authority in the traditional communities of Chiapas.

The flexibility of the system is such that, while consensus is constantly pending in the discussions of naguals, dreams, curing, witchcraft, and the causes of death and misfortune, it never receives formal recognition in a public act short of the assassination and subsequent trial of the witch (M. Nash, 1961). The conceptual system, by virtue of the fact that it contains so many contradictions in the abstract, provides the possibility of finding a solution to any eventuality in accordance with the *ex post facto* logic of magical reasoning. In a word, the conceptual system becomes as a whole 'systematic' only in the context of action, as a means of integrating events into the history of the community.

III

The description I have given overlooks the considerable variations between one community and another in Chiapas. Yet these variations are matters of detail: they do not affect the general principles of the system. Whatever the list of potential naguals, they are ordered in the same way and their social function is similar. As we go further afield, however, the nature of the nagual appears to change and the system in which it is incorporated differs. In many places in Mexico and Guatemala the nagual appears, not as a co-essence possessed by every individual, but as the name for those members of the community who are thought to be witches and are credited with the power to transform themselves into the shape of a given animal for the purpose of carrying out their nefarious designs. They may be the same animals, but their social function is no longer quite the same.

Foster, in a justly well-known essay (1944), attempted to sort out the cultural history of the different phenomena to which the word nagual has been applied. He found two basic types of relationship between an animal and a man:

1. There is, first, the animal into which a man can change himself, the 'transforming witch'. He claims this as the original sense of the word in Nahuatl.
2. There is, however, another type of relationship with an animal, referred to as the *tona*, a word meaning 'fate' in Nahuatl, from which the *tonalamatl* gets its name. The tona-lamatl was the calendar used by the Mexicans and also by the Maya for augury, divining, and determining the fate of individuals. The days of the calendar were associated with animals, and the individual received his name and his guardian animal from the day of his birth or baptism.

These two conceptions, which are found independent of one another north of the Isthmus of Tehuatepec, become confused as we go south, and the word nagual, where it is used, denotes a relationship with an animal which represents the individual's destiny. The naguals of Chiapas, described above, are an example of this type of relationship. Foster maintains that there is no evidence to support the speculations of the Abbé Brasseur de Bourbourg, and later of Brinton, who reinterpreted the accounts of the Spanish chroniclers to hypothesize the existence of a witch-cult aiming to keep alive the ancient religion – rather as Margaret Murray maintained that the witch-cult in Europe was an underground political movement based upon the survival of ancient paganism – and to organize rebellion against the Span-iards. Foster submits that the elements which enter into the conceptions of the nagual are traditional traits of aboriginal culture, that there was therefore no 'religion of nagualism', and that the problem of nagualism was no more than the problem of the dissemination of a word. He suggests that if the word nagual be used at all to define a general phenomenon it should be returned to its original meaning as the transforming witch, and that the word tona should be used to define the conception of the destiny-animal.

It is questionable whether it is ever wise to borrow from the ethnography the words for our technical vocabulary of anthropology,[14] though it is sometimes hard to avoid, but in this case Foster comes up against the problem that the word nagual is used by the people of Chiapas and Guatemala in the sense that is contrary to that which he recommends for anthropologists, and this can but lead to confusion.

The distinction between the two conceptions is essential but the reconstruction of their ancient history faces the difficulty that we possess no account written independently of the Spaniards, and our sources are limited to:

1. Pre-columbian codices and frescoes: independent pictorial evidence in which the usage of animal disguises is patent and humans are figured in the process of transformation into monkeys, as in the mythology which persists to this day. Indeed, transformation into animals is part and parcel of the common idiom of all mythologies.

2. Accounts recorded by the ethnographers of the day, who, admirable as they were, were none the less sixteenth-century Spanish churchmen.

3. Accounts left by indians who had learned to write under the direction of the missionaries.

We must admit, then, that our knowledge of the beliefs of the indians prior to the conquest is highly speculative. Nevertheless, the previous existence of the two types of relationship to animals of which Foster speaks is generally accepted. There is nothing unlikely in the idea that the officiants who served an animal deity were thought capable of adopting the guise of the animal to which their cult was dedicated: they appear to have represented such a transformation in their vestments. On the other hand, the connection between men and animals through the calendar is firmly established. It is not hard to think of speculative explanations on the basis of the difference between Aztec and Mayan culture to account for the greater importance today of the transformer north of the Isthmus and of the destiny-animal south of it. But we must also speculate about the value of our Spanish sources, for their reports of the indians' beliefs cannot but be influenced by their own beliefs regarding the supernatural.

196

The Spaniards, too, possessed a conception of the transforming witch, but, as I shall show, it was a very different kind of
transformation. On the other hand, the animal co-essence is a
construction that, despite the animal figures of the Zodiac,
remains foreign to the tradition of European thought; even if
we say we are *pisces* or *leo* we do not believe that we are a particular fish or lion. The Spaniards could understand the nagual
only as a transforming witch whose powers were bequeathed by
the Devil and who used them against Christianity. They could
not understand the animal co-essence at all. Even that talented
observer, Thomas Gage, who has left us an account so ably
reported that we can perceive a system very similar to that
which we know from contemporary Chiapas, has himself quite
misinterpreted it.[15] Indeed, we may wonder to what extent the
belief in the transforming witch south of the Isthmus may not
be due to the influence of the missionaries. As long as witchcraft
was a reality for them, the Spaniards, especially churchmen,
concluded that any association between a man and an animal
was the outcome of a pact with the Devil and that such associations were limited to those who had made such a pact. Bishop
Nuñez de la Vega's campaign against the witches of Chiapas at
the beginning of the eighteenth century was based upon the
same misapprehension as Gage's against those of Pinola and
Mixco nearly a century earlier: that the possession of an animal
counterpart was restricted to witches, that witches transformed
themselves into their naguals, and that no particular significance
attached to the species of the nagual. Whatever their understanding of the detail of indian belief, the Spaniards failed to
grasp the principles of the system of thought into which it fitted,
since these were contrary to their assumptions about the nature
of God, Good and Evil, and the natural and supernatural.

None the less, indian and Spanish beliefs were sufficiently
close to one another to allow the detail of one to be reinterpreted
by the other. Hence, if the high-flying archangels were easily
able to take their place in the indian pantheon, and 'Señor
Santa Cruz' could become the guardian against the Evil which
comes from abroad, the protector of springs and water-holes,
and the rain-maker, it is equally true that the indian belief in
the destiny-animal could, without much difficulty, be incorporated into a system which recognized only animal familiars and

the ability of witches to change their shape and the shape of others through spells. Thus in Fuentes y Guzman's account of the battle of Quetzaltenango, the nagual of the king of the Quiché figures prominently. It attacked Alvarado during the battle in the form of an eagle and was killed by him with the thrust of a lance.[16] The king died simultaneously from an exactly similar wound. But it is to be noted that the *real* Alvarado (not his nagual) was attacked by the eagle at the terrestrial level and that the transformation of the king was the work of a fat female indian sorceress. Fuentes, writing in 1690, has incorporated an indian story into a European framework of belief. The failure of his great-great-grandfather, Bernal Diaz, to explain adequately what happened he attributes to the great chronicler's inadequate understanding of *estos encantos de Naguales*. Admitting that we can only speculate regarding the indians' belief system at the time of their first contact with the Spaniards, in this case the battle of Quetzaltenango, it is plausible to suppose that the specifically Christian elements in such stories were the contributions of the Spaniards. The Spanish interpretation of 'nagualism' hinges on the Devil, who clearly had no place in the pre-Spanish conception.[17]

Let us now examine briefly the structure of the notion of the witch in sixteenth-century Spain: he, or more usually she,[18] is one who by an act of will has turned against Christ and become the disciple of the Devil. In the terms of this pact whereby she loses her eternal soul the Devil provides her with the powers to do evil, which include the power of transformation, the power to command devils in the guise of animals, and the power to enjoy sexual relationship with demons in animal, and sometimes in human, form. Indian witchcraft, on the other hand, is simply not concerned with sex. The decorum of indian belief, in contrast to European, is quite striking. Mention of the subject includes little more than the notion that, during intercourse, the ch'uleles of the participants leave the bodies of their owners and embrace. The portals of the Gothic churches depict a relationship between humans and animals that is very different from that between indians and their naguals.[19]

The specific animal into which European witches transform is not important. In the missionaries' accounts we find mention of indians who had the power to transform themselves into a jaguar, a tiger, or an eagle, etc., but the species is not regarded as significant. In Europe the power to transform is unspecific and the fairy-tale witch transforms herself from one animal into another in a whole series which ends sometimes by her turning herself into water and thereby trickling away from her pursuers. The relationship between witch and animal transformation is not one between a specific human and a specific animal or even species of animal, but simply *the power to transform* into more or less any *false apparition*. Consequently, the animal transformation of the European witch has no metaphorical function whatsoever, and in so far as it has a metonymical function this is restricted to signifying a relationship with any member of that class of animal thought to be associated with the Devil, usually through a sexual connotation: cats, goats, reptiles, bats, and toads.

The indians believe that their animal counterparts represent ultimate reality; the Europeans condemn them as deceptions. One might do well, then, to distinguish between 'transformation' and 'incarnation' and reserve the latter term for the indian nagual, whether represented as transformer or co-essence. In both, the man is portrayed in the semblance of an animal, but in the first the intention is to change the visible appearance for the purpose of deceiving in the Devil's cause or to adopt an unnatural' form in order to attend a sabbath in which prohibited pleasures are enjoyed. In adopting 'unnatural' guise the witch demonstrates that he has ceased to be a natural human being. Having sold his soul he has become non-human. In the second case the man incarnates a specific animal and demonstrates thereby, not his loss of humanity, but his possession of a particularly powerful human nature represented by this animal, in contrast to other types of human nature indicated by other inferior animals or by the absence of any animal equivalence. It is not a question of appearance, but of being. The distinction between European transforming witch and American transformer relates to the system in which each finds its significance; that between nagual and transformer and nagual as co-essence relates only to the form in which the animal equivalence is expressed.

In considering the European beliefs with regard to transformation and animal equivalence it is worth taking into account the various forms of peasant belief which never became part of the doctrine regarding witchcraft: the vampire, the werewolf, the *lamia* or *lutin*, and the child-stealer (*roba-niños, sacamantecas*, or *mantequero*). These are all persons whose essential nature is non-human and maleficent. Only the first two are transformers and they change their appearance on defined occasions: at night (the vampire) and when the moon is full (the werewolf), the former into a human with bat-like attributes, the latter into an animal; the lamia is permanently half-human and half-animal (top half human, bottom half fish); only the child-stealer is never represented as an animal or with animal attributes. The forms of these different representations are fixed and invariable: all vampires have the same attributes, all werewolves the same form, etc. Yet the ease with which the form can be changed is illustrated by the curious history of the mantequero (literally fat-stealer, from *manteca*). The word was translated into English as mantigger or man-tiger and was pictured thereafter as a tiger with a human head.

The forms of the European maleficent agents vary: they may transform or not, and their transformations may be multiple and serial, as in the case of the witch, or unique, as in the case of the vampire; but whatever the form of their association with an animal it always denotes maleficence and opposes them to natural human beings. This is not, however, the case with the nagual, and if in some places naguals are possessed only by maleficent witches today, they can hardly have been maleficent when associated with an ancient deity, rather than the Devil. In so far as they resemble the witches of Europe this is surely due to the monks, who ended by imposing their interpretation.

It is not my intention to denigrate the importance of the distinction made by Foster and those who have followed him between the transforming witch and the destiny-animal. For purposes of historical reconstruction it is full of significance, but I would point out that it is a matter of alternative forms within a general system which appears in most places to have retained its main lines, in spite of the confusing interpretations to which it has been subjected and the imposition of ideas of Spanish origin.

As long as the nagual is part of a metaphorical system – that is to say, the specific animal defines the social personality of the

200

man in relation to other members of his community – the distinction between transformer and co-essence is a mere matter of form. If the man *is* the animal he can only be so logically either in time or in space, but not in both. If he is the same being as his nagual at the same time, then it must be elsewhere: in the jungle, in the cave, in the skies, but not beside him in the village or there would be two persons at the terrestrial level. On the other hand, if he transforms himself into an animal, he is the same being in the same place, but differentiated temporally. If he and his nagual were in the same place at the same time they would be differentiable and therefore not the same being, but associated alters such as the witch and her familiar.

Within this logic of form the European and indian systems make different selections. The European excludes the co-essences, for it has no simultaneous celestial realm in which to locate them; heaven is reserved for the deceased. But it can logically have and has both transforming witches and animal familiars. The indian systems provide examples of both transformers and co-essences who demonstrate the strength of spirit of their owners, but the nature of witchcraft (and in particular its relation to spiritual authority) is such that the familiar would be anomalous. There is no role for an associated alter at the terrestrial level.

The ethnography of Chiapas shows how frail and malleable the distinctions with regard to form are and how different forms can be accommodated within the same system. For if the transformer and the co-essence appear to be logically incompatible, one nevertheless finds evidence of both within the same community. Of San Andrés Larraínzar, Holland tells us (1963, p. 113), after giving a typical account of the *wayihel* as co-essence, that bad elders are capable of transforming themselves, and his texts contain references to transformations (e.g. pp. 256, 257, etc.). Moreover, Hermitte, to whom we owe the most sensitive and coherent account of such a system, tells at one point the story of a famous witch who is remembered as having been shot in the act of transforming himself into a tiger so that he died half-man, half-beast, like a figure from Goya's drawings. June Nash mentions the possibility of transformation in Amatenango; but this occurs only at night. Nevertheless, the same animal co-essences are also active during the daytime, for example during a curing treatment, when that of the curer combats that of the witch, but out of the sight of men, at the celestial level. The distinction between what I have called the terrestrial and celestial levels appears, then, to be made according to whether events take place in the visible or invisible realms; at night the naguals are active on the earth's surface or they may be heard flying overhead – but under cover of darkness.

Both forms of belief carry the same meaning: the man and the animal are one and it is the type of animal that is significant, not whether (as in the European system) transformation occurs or not. Indeed, incompatible as they appear to *us* in terms of their conceptualization, the only difference between the transformer and the co-essential nagual at the level of action is that while the latter is active its owner still lies in his bed, whereas in the case of the former he is missing from it. This is something that nobody thinks of verifying, since the distinction is in no context relevant. On the other hand, in a community where only witches have any animal association, the act of transformation is full of significance. In those communities of Chiapas where mention is made of transformation it is not an essential pivot of the system of belief but merely an adjunct, a way of stressing the evil nature of those accused of witchcraft. In other communities it is the mark of a particular kind of witch who is distinguished from magical practitioners of other sorts and from possessors of a co-essence. Such is the case in Santiago el Palmar, where the ability to transform is, as in Europe, dependent upon a pact with the Devil (Saler, 1964).

The possibilities of combining different elements of belief are numberless since the significance of an element depends upon its function within the total system, upon the distinctions it renders possible. Hence it is no wonder if items of belief have been transmitted from the Hispanic to the indian system. They have equally travelled in the other direction. Thus the ladinos of Chiapas frequently believe that they have a destiny-animal in the jungle on whom their life depends, yet they have no concept of a spiritual hierarchy, and when they speak of permission to bewitch they refer to the belief that this is given only by the chief witch of the village, who has authority over the others. Thus, in adopting an element of belief from the indians, the ladinos move it from a unified cosmology which integrates Good and Evil within a single system of thought to a dualistic universe where they are opposed, no longer simply at the level of action, but dogmatically: the powers of Good are distinct from the powers of Evil and they stem from different sources. The witch is not someone who has abused his spiritual strength but one who owes it only to his renunciation of salvation, his attachment to a source alien to the order of Right. Permission to bewitch passes uniquely down the hierarchy of the Devil. Nor is it surprising that indian beliefs should be associated with the powers of Darkness and that indians should be credited with the most powerful witchcraft, since they are opposed by the ladinos to the religious orthodoxy they themselves represent, however inadequately in the eyes of the Church.

It is not, therefore, just by tracing the diffusion of such items that we shall achieve the aim of historical reconstruction, but by attempting to grasp the total systems into which they have been incorporated and to see the significance of these within the society of their day.

NOTES

1. The main sources used in this analysis, which necessarily abridges the data and offers generalizations which are open to qualifications, are Guiteras-Holmes (1961), Hermitte (1964), and Holland (1963). Recognition is also due to the writings of those who participated in the University of Chicago's project: 'Social, Cultural, and Linguistic Change in the Highlands of Chiapas', whose definite publication, superseding Vol. I of the Report, is expected in 1971. I owe a special debt of recognition to Professor June Nash who was kind enough to read this paper in draft and offer valuable comments based upon her own fieldwork in Chiapas. Her paper (1967) gives the following figures for assassinations per annum per 100,000: USA, 4·8; Mexico, 31·9; a 'peaceful' indian village of Chiapas, 36·2; and that which she studied herself, 251·2. When it is reckoned that only adult males are here eligible for accusations of witchcraft, the figures are yet more impressive.

2. 'Reputation of power is power, because it draweth with it the adherence of those that need protection' (*Leviathan*, Chapter X).

3. The instance is far from unique: cf. 'Witches . . . are men who pervert their powers to their own selfish ends' (Middleton, 1960, p. 32). A similar ambivalence attaches to such power among the Tiv, according to Bohannan (1958).

4. The distinction between the 'terrestrial' and the 'celestial' level does not exactly correspond in this analysis to that which is commonly made between the scientific and the magical or the natural and the supernatural. The indians relate their conceptualization of events that take place in the world of dreams, or at night in the skies, to events that anyone can witness on earth. The latter are believed to be caused by the former.

5. The witch may in fact send an evil apparition to alienate the soul of his victim through fright (*susto*), a disease of quite common occurrence not necessarily caused by a witch. A spiritual guardian does not punish in this way. Moreover, a witch may be employed to 'punish' the victim by someone who does not possess sufficient spiritual power to do so directly himself. To conclude that indirect means of causing misfortune are confined to practices recognized as by nature illegitimate would be going too far, however, for an offended guardian may bring misfortune indirectly simply by neglecting to afford protection. He throws to the wolves those who do not merit his spiritual exertions on their behalf. The system of guardianship varies. In the traditional villages of the north the *principal* of the lineage is the guardian of his kinsmen, but in Pinola where the lineage no longer has much importance it is an individual relationship. Typically, however, in this case nobody knows for sure which elder is his guardian.

6. This conception of heat must not be confused with the distinction between 'hot' and 'cold' foods, which is general to the ladinos (and some indians) of Central America, nor with heat as female sexuality, which is important in Spanish culture but normally unknown to the indians.

7. Villa Rojas (1947) gives the earliest description of the nagual in Chiapas and one of the best.

8. The occasional references to the ethnography of Guatemala make no attempt to bring it into the theoretical framework presented here, save with regard to the general thesis that each system of belief can include details borrowed from other systems. Each must be treated as a system in its own right, and once this is admitted there is nothing anomalous in the fact that we find so much variation in other parts of the Mayan Highlands. To take only the area of Lake Atitlán: we find places where the *characoteles* (witches) are quite distinct from the *zahorines* (curers), others where both are distinguished by the way they come into the world, or where the animal form of the characotel, called *tonica*, can be whatever animal he chooses, or where sorcery can be performed by the use of a magical book, as in Europe. DeVore (1968) has made a comparative study of this region, examining the question of variations.

Quite apart from the influence of the Spaniards, it must be remembered that this area had frequent and significant contact with people from north of the Isthmus before the conquest and that the Spaniards brought in a great many more in their retinue.

9. Hubert & Mauss (1902, p. 30) had already long ago perceived the need to distinguish between the magician's auxiliary *être complètement distinct* and his *âme extérieure*. As they explained it: in form there are two beings, in essence only one.

10. E.g. Tenejapa (Medina, n.d.); San Andrés Larraínzar (Holland, 1963, p. 101).

11. It is also due, no doubt, to the activities of the Dominican monks who favoured the reproduction of the pictures. There was a Dominican convent at Atocha just outside Madrid.

12. For rather obvious historical reasons, the horse is an animal associated symbolically with ladinos. Hence in many indian villages indians who own horses refuse to ride them.

13. M. Nash (1961) describes how this is established in Amatenango.

14. I have discussed the question in detail in a recent article, 'On the Word Caste' (Pitt-Rivers, in press).

15. Thompson (1958). An analysis of Gage's account of witchcraft will be published elsewhere.

16. '. . . procuraron (los indios) valerse contra (los españoles) de mayores fuerzas que las humanas . . . trataron de valerse del arte de los encantos y Naguales; tomando en esta ocasión el demonio, por el rey de el Quiché, la forma de águila, sumamente crecida, y por otros de aquellos *Ahaus*, varias formas de serpientes y otras sabadijas' ('. . . the indians managed to take advantage against the Spaniards of more than human forces . . . they attempted to use the magic of spells and Naguals, the devil, as the king of the Quiché, taking on this occasion the form of an extremely large eagle and, as others of those lords, various forms of serpent and other reptiles') Fuentes y Guzman (1882, p. 50).

17. Correa's essay (1960), so rich and so useful from the point of view of research, which rightly insists upon the main point of the importance of the Devil in the conceptual framework of the missionary, is, alas, quite unreliable with regard to the detail of its interpretations and fails to deal with beliefs systematically.

18. The significance of the sex of the witch provides yet another dimension on which the European system differs from the indian, but, fascinating as this is, the problem must be left on one side in this paper. One might nevertheless add that the witches among ladinos are usually female – a fact to be explained by the difference in the moral division of labour between the two cultures.

19. See, especially, Moissac and Beaulieu-en-Dordogne.

REFERENCES

BOHANNAN, PAUL. 1958. Extra-processual Events in Tiv Political Institutions. *American Anthropologist* **60**: 1-12.

BUNZEL, RUTH. 1952. *Chichicastenango, a Guatemalan Village.* Locust Valley, N.Y.: J. J. Augustin.

CORREA, GUSTAVO. 1960. El Espíritu del Mal en Guatemala. In Donald E. Thompson (ed.), *Nativism and Syncretism*. New Orleans: Middle American Research Institute, Publication 19, Tulane University.

DEVORE, PAUL. 1968. Conceptions of Sorcery and Witchcraft in the Region of Lake Atitlán, Department of Sololá, Guatemala. M.A. Thesis, University of Chicago.

FOSTER, GEORGE M. 1944. Nagualism in Mexico and Guatemala. *Acta Americana* **2** (1, 2): 85-103.

FUENTES Y GUZMAN, F. A. 1882. *Historia de Guatemala o Recordación Florida*. Madrid: L. Navarro.

GUITERAS-HOLMES, CALIXTA. 1961. *The Perils of the Soul*. New York: The Free Press.

HERMITTE, M. ESTHER. 1964. Supernatural Power and Social Control in a Modern Mayan Village. Ph.D. Thesis, University of Chicago.

HOLLAND, WILLIAM. 1963. *Medicina maya en los altos de Chiapas.* Mexico: Instituto Nacional Indigenista.

HUBERT, HENRI & MAUSS, MARCEL. 1902-3. Théorie générale de de la magie. *Année Sociologique.* Paris.

MEDINA, ANDRÉS. No date. Unpublished monograph of Tenejapa.

MIDDLETON, JOHN. 1960. *Lugbara Religion.* London: Oxford University Press (for the International African Institute).

NASH, JUNE. 1967. Death as a Way of Life. *American Anthropologist* **69**: 455-470.

NASH, MANNING. 1961. Witchcraft as a Social Process in a Tzeltal Community. *America Indígena* **20**. Republished in J. Middleton, *Magic, Witchcraft, and Curing.* New York: Natural History Press, for the American Museum of Natural History, 1967.

PITT-RIVERS, JULIAN. In press. On the Word Caste.

SALER, BENSON. 1964. Nagual, Witch and Sorcerer in a Quiché Village. *Ethnology* **3**: 305-328.

THOMPSON, J. ERIC S. (ed.). 1958. *Thomas Gage's Travels in the New World.* Norman: University of Oklahoma Press.

VILLA ROJAS, ALFONSO. 1947. Kinship and Nagualism in a Tzeltal Community. *American Anthropologist* **49**: 578-587.

© Julian Pitt-Rivers 1970

10

Esther Goody

Legitimate and Illegitimate Aggression
in a West African State

This paper is an attempt to work out a problem that puzzled me in the field and has continued to intrigue me since: why do the Gonja make a dichotomy between male witches, whose standing in the community seems to be enhanced rather than injured by suspicions of witchcraft, and female witches, who are feared and abhorred, and not infrequently severely punished? On the one hand this is a problem of the definition of male and female roles. But it also raises the question of why mystical aggression should be permitted under some conditions and treated as illegitimate under others. The two problems are analytically separate, but, in the Gonja context, empirically fused. In pursuing them I have concentrated largely on male witchcraft since beliefs concerning this are more complex, and it is the male witches who confound our preconceptions in not being considered evil.

Conceptually, it is most useful to define witchcraft as the covert use of mystical forms of aggression by human agents. There is wide agreement that covert aggression is attributed to those who are not able, for whatever reason, to use direct, overt forms. While this is an over-simplification, it is substantially correct. However, the character of aggression itself needs to be examined in greater detail. Accounts of witchcraft commonly consider the sources of aggressive motivation. This is not of immediate concern here, but it is surely of interest to us as sociologists to consider the function within one society of the attribution of aggressive behaviour to the occupants of various roles. It is in this way that I have chosen to pursue the question of why some forms of covert mystical aggression are 'good', others are 'neutral', and others again are 'bad'.

Apart from the actual injury that may result, there are four major functions of aggressive behaviour that seem relevant to the present discussion. These are: (1) defence or protection, (2) the establishment or preservation of dominance, (3) punishment, and (4) the securing of animal food. It is certainly arguable that the first three are interdependent. Defence of one's home establishes the defender as dominant over the attacker, at least on his home territory; an incursion successfully repulsed may have punishment value (in the sense used by behavioural psychologists) for the loser, and result in his deciding not to try again. And so on. But these different functions are analytically separable, and, as I believe the Gonja material shows, the consequent distinctions are useful in considering both beliefs concerning mystical aggression, and the community's reaction to these.

The Gonja state is a loose federation of divisions lying just north of Ashanti, across the River Volta. Stretching as it does across the whole breadth of modern Ghana, it covers some 14,500 square miles, encompassing within its borders a number of ethnic and linguistic groups, for the most part autochthones who now occupy the role of commoners under the government of the ruling Ngbanya estate. Most divisional chiefs have among their advisers Muslim officials, and there are concentrations of Muslims, some long established and some of recent origin, in the larger towns. For the majority of rulers and commoners, however, Islam is the religion of specialists, the *karamo*, to be resorted to when it is useful, but constituting only a part of the moral order on which their lives are based.

GONJA CONCEPTS AND BELIEFS
CONCERNING WITCHCRAFT

In Gonja, the central concept among beliefs concerning mystical forces, means of aggression through mystical forces, and the control of mystical power by human agents, is *kegbe*. This is best translated as the power that enables a human being to harm others through mystical[1] means. One who possesses this power is *egbe* (pl. *begbe*). There are two sets of beliefs surrounding *begbe*: those concerning the ability to move about apart from the body at night, to change into various animals, to appear as a ball of fire, and to consume the souls of victims; and those about the kinds of medicine (*aduru*) possessed by *begbe*. However, these sets of beliefs represent polarities, not exclusive categories. That is, an *egbe* is held to be able to fly, to consume people's souls while they sleep, to belong to a coven, to incur flesh debts, and so on, *because* he or she has washed his or her eyes in (*fur aniʃi*) or drunk (*nu aduru*) the appropriate medicine and eaten of human flesh. If a person is thought to be *egbe* but not a particularly dangerous one, it is said that he has the minor medicines, but not the strong kind.

The converse of this situation is that anyone may become *egbe*: it is not inherited – on this there is agreement in all parts of Gonja. A man or woman who wishes to have *kegbe* powers may get them from a relative. A woman is particularly likely to offer to teach her last-born (indeed, it is said she can deny him nothing); but if the child does not agree he or she may refuse to learn. The child who is taught may or may not agree to teach the other siblings. *Kegbe* is a thing of the room (i.e. secret) and if his siblings are the sort who spread everything they hear all over the village he keeps the knowledge to himself. But if they do not gossip, he may decide to tell them. A man or woman who has no kinsman and wishes to possess *kegbe* finds it difficult to learn. If you ask anyone outside the close family circle he is likely to deny all knowledge for fear that he will become identified as *egbe*. So you must become acquainted with the chosen *egbe* over a long period of time, and greet him, bringing small gifts, thus showing respect. When the expert sees that you are in earnest, and a person to be trusted, he may agree to teach you how to wash so that you can control the *kegbe* medicines. A part of the initiation is the bringing by the novice of one of his or her own kin to serve as the first meal of human flesh and the admission price to the coven. It is stressed that such an offering must be a valued member of one's kin; one who is beautiful and fat; preferably the child that a parent loves most in his heart. And it is useless to try to deceive one's fellow *begbe* over this; for if the favourite is not killed the medicines will not be strong enough to work.

In this very condensed account of the acquiring of *kegbe*, two themes are clear. Even when *kegbe* appears in both parental and filial generations, it is not inherited in any biological sense, but learnt, consciously. Those who have *kegbe* must have apprenticed themselves to one who already possessed the necessary medicines.[2] However, in discussion it is often stressed that to possess *egbe* is not necessarily to use it. For some want it in order to protect their families. To this point I will return. Here it is sufficient to say that there are believed to be both active and inactive *egbe*, but that all are thought to have purposely taken possession of the medicines.

The other theme is the interdependence of medicines and the immaterial aspects of *kegbe*. A story about an imagined witch describes how 'her *kegbe* got up and refused (to lie quiet) and she had to take her grandchild and put him in the cooking pot'. Here the witchcraft (*kegbe*) is endowed with a will that can force its host to do as it wishes. Several other stories, however, refer to a woman preparing food and putting witchcraft (*kegbe*) into it so that she can poison someone. Here witchcraft is conceived of as strictly similar to a physical substance which might be put into food. It is typical of accounts of witchcraft in Gonja that it is unclear in which sense, the immanent or the material, the concept is being used. Indeed, I would argue that this is not of great importance in Gonja thought. One may hear, as I did, of the chief of one of the divisions: 'He is a very powerful *egbe*, has many medicines, can turn into a lion and even disappear.'

The main reason given to explain why an inactive *egbe* seeks *kegbe* powers is so that he may see other *begbe* and thus be able to ward off their attacks. Only *begbe* who are themselves capable of materializing and dematerializing can see other *begbe* as they 'go about at night seeking meat'.

Thus for the Gonja it is not possible effectively to distinguish between sorcerers (who manipulate a *materia mystica*, and perform acts which might actually be done, although we might doubt their efficacy) and witches (who possess innate powers to change shape, appear and disappear, leave their bodies and, as pure soul-stuff, seek out and destroy the souls of others, i.e. perform acts impossible by their very nature). *Begbe* are those who, by using medicines and the powers these give them – to travel through the air and to act in the form of disembodied soul (*kiyayu*) – are able to recognize others of their kind and to employ a wide repertoire of aggressive forces. The power to use all these mystical forms of aggression is called *kegbe*, which is best translated by 'witchcraft'. I shall therefore use the term 'witch' for *egbe*.

There is a further point on which the people of eastern, central, and western Gonja, members of ruling, commoner, and Muslim estates, all agree. This is that both men and women may seek and obtain witchcraft powers. But (people usually go on to say) it is women, mostly old women (*betʃe numu*), who are the witches who kill; who are the evil witches (*begbe libi*). The emphasis on old women is consistent with the belief that one acquires knowledge of all sorts, and particularly of medicines, cumulatively as one grows older. Thus I have heard the general statement that all old men and old women are witches. And again, in the context of the ritualized singing of the *awoba* dirges during the all-night vigils at the funerals of elderly or important people, it is said that only old men and women dare to go there, only those who, because they are witches, do not fear to be killed. Even those in the prime of manly strength (*mberantia*) are afraid to attend because they do not yet have the medicines necessary to guard them against the witches believed to gather at funerals.

The Gonja, then, believe that witches are people, usually old people, either men or women, who have sought the power they possess; that this power enables them to recognize other witches and to harm people if they wish to, by a wide range of mystical aggressive techniques. These are the core beliefs of Gonja witchcraft. These beliefs also specify how male and female witches are expected to behave.

MALE WITCHCRAFT

Protective function of witchcraft powers

Male witches are expected to use their powers in two main ways. First, they are thought to have sought witchcraft powers in order to be able to protect their dependants against the attacks of evil witches. By virtue of his powers a male witch who is head of a compound will be able to see witches as they congregate at night, in trees near the compound, in the form of balls of fire. Furthermore, he is able to recognize the women who have assumed this form. In the daytime he is said to go and warn them that their activities are known, and that if they do not stop he will report them to the village chief. A wise witch will then cease trying to injure her intended victim. If she does not, the compound head goes to the village chief with his information and the woman is challenged, and, if serious harm is feared, she is made to drink the water of a shrine (*jo kagbir ba nchu*). This ordeal takes various forms but depends on drinking water which has been consecrated to the shrine. If after this the witch again thinks about killing someone, she herself will die. None of the ordeals on which I have information entails the drinking of poison. Rather, it is pure water, dedicated by contact with a sacrificial knife, or with a kola nut, which has the power to bind the woman to the shrine and to kill her if she reverts to her evil ways. That the compound head is himself a witch means, not only that he is able to identify witches seeking to injure his dependants, but also that he dares to denounce them, pitting his powers against theirs. 'And if a man is a witch he is ten times stronger than a woman.'

The protective aspect of witchcraft is most clearly seen in the role of the chief. For reasons that will become apparent, chiefs are *known* to be witches, whereas a compound head ought to have this power but may or may not have been able to find another witch willing to teach him. Although it is possible to be a compound head without being a witch, the Gonja believe that to be a chief a man almost certainly must be one. It is to the village chief that a witch suspected of causing illness or death is reported, and it is the chief who is responsible for controlling her aggressive powers. He will first try to deal with her by warnings. When Dari, a child of five or six, was suddenly taken ill, a man was sent to beat the chief's gong-gong through the lanes of the town. This, we were told, was to warn the attacking witch to leave the boy alone, because the chief had taken him under his protection.

If the witch persists in her attacks despite such warnings, the chief can insist that she drink shrine water. She is given the alternative of doing so or leaving his village. The choice is hers. The child Dari died the day after we heard the gong-gong beaten, and the witch responsible was identified by the traditional means of carrying the 'corpse'. It is not the actual corpse that is carried, but articles intimately associated with it: undergarments, nail-pairings, and hair. These are wrapped in a mat which is slung from a pole, the ends of which are shouldered by two men. So closely is this bundle (*kidi*) identified with the dead person that it is personified: it is said to *be* the dead person and to know who has caused its death, and to seek out the witch responsible by striking against her. In this case the witch was subsequently sent to drink the water of the Wenchi shrine.

If these measures do not end her evil activities, the village chief takes the witch to his divisional chief, who hears the case in his council hall in the presence of all the interested parties, both the accusers and the kin of the accused. In pre-European times the divisional chief had the power of disposal over the witch in serious cases, that is, where the woman had been accused by the victim either before he died, or during the carrying of the 'corpse', that is after his death. Indeed, it appears that the victim's accusations were usually tested and ratified by the subsequent carrying of the 'corpse'.

Once the witch's guilt was established, the chief had three possible courses of action. The first resulted in her death. He might give the witch to his executioner, with the words 'Take her on the path'. This was the death sentence, and the witch was taken outside the town and killed; she was either beheaded or stabbed with a wooden stake especially made for such executions, a stake made without iron. The dead body was then dragged into the bush with a rope around the feet, and left for the vultures.[3]

Other forms of execution are also mentioned. One was the placing of a red-hot iron cooking-pot over the witch's head. (Female witches are commonly believed to get at their victims by placing witchcraft medicines in food they are cooking.) In Daboya a convicted witch used to be thrown into a tributary of the White Volta with a large pot tied around her waist. As the pot filled with water the witch was dragged below the surface. Another method was the entombment alive of a witch in a room containing burning red peppers (the smoke of these has a violently irritant effect on the mucous membranes). Yet another sentence was effective execution. The witch was given a calabash (some say filled with millet) and driven into the bush to find food and water as best she could. One divisional chief is reported to have dug a pit and filled it with firewood, leaving a hole in the centre into which the witch was put, and the wood was then set alight. 'If you are really a witch, fly out of there', he is supposed to have said. Since innocence meant certain

213

death, it would seem that the element of ordeal here is illusory. Rather, a woman whose guilt has been established to the satisfaction of the community is taunted, and proved to be powerless either to do any further harm to others or even to free herself.

The viciousness of these forms of execution is striking. They go far beyond what is required for the removal of a threat to community safety. Indeed, they seem designed to exact the maximum amount of suffering from the witch and have much in common with public executions elsewhere of traitors to state and church. Such viciousness contrasts all the more strongly with the virtual absence of counteraction against male witches.

After presiding over the witch's death, the executioner took possession of all her property, keeping half for himself and bringing half to the chief who could do with it as he liked. Ghosts (*bubuni*) are much feared immediately after death, but the ghost of a witch is particularly dangerous. For this reason, only those with a particularly strong variety of ghost medicine called *jobuni* (literally: to drive away, *jo*, the ghost, *bubuni*) dare take possession of her property. An executioner has need of the strongest medicine of all, for, as the instrument of death, he is particularly likely to be attacked by the ghosts of his victims. And for similar reasons a chief is always assumed to count ghost medicine among his medicines.

Even in pre-European times witches were not necessarily killed. A second alternative was for the chief to sell the witch, and her children if he wished, to itinerant slave-traders, or send her to be sold at Salaga market. This served the same function of ridding the community of the menace of witchcraft, but was far more lucrative than the mere confiscation of her property, which would happen in any case.

A final possibility was for the chief himself to take charge of the witch. On being convicted of witchcraft a woman and her children automatically became witch-slaves, *bagbenye*. The father could collect money and redeem his children, though the chief might decide that one daughter should stay with the mother to help her. But the woman herself could not be redeemed; she became the wife of the chief. That this is still seen as a viable solution came out very clearly in the course of the trial of a witch that I attended in a sub-divisional capital. The woman's guilt was not in doubt. The 'corpse' of her husband had been carried before burial and had gone straight to her room and knocked against the wall repeatedly. The question to be settled was what to do with the witch. After considerable discussion, the aged chief declared: 'The woman is now my wife. No one can hurt me, or do anything to me. I have many medicines. I do not fear.' However, he went on to say that there was no room free in his compound, so she should stay with her brother until the dry season, when a room could be built for her. A brother of her dead husband refused to accept this solution, saying:

'No, her children must come and build a room for her now. They will farm for her. And if the chief sleeps outside, she must sleep outside. And if the chief sleeps inside, she must sleep inside. He must watch her all the time.'

In other words, only a husband, someone who is with the witch both day and night, can be in a position to control her, especially to control her nocturnal activities. And a chief with his powerful witchcraft medicines is in the best position to do this if he is also the husband.

Another account, from the court of the paramount chief at Nyanga, refers to the paramount taking a witch to stay in his compound and to sweep his doorway on Mondays and Fridays, the days on which his chiefs and elders must come to greet him. As this suggests, a witch who joins the chief's establishment is an important addition to the labour force. A chief without wives is nothing, for he must have women to cook for his guests, to carry wood and heat water for all those who come to court. Even if such a woman was only nominally a wife, she provided valuable labour. But, as is evident in the case quoted above, to the other people concerned, the most important reason for sending a convicted witch to become the wife of the chief is so that he may control her aggressive tendencies and prevent her from causing any more deaths. As the compound head protects his dependants, so a chief is expected to protect his subjects. 'People are afraid to live with a witch, that is why the chief must take her.'

This protective aspect of the chief's role becomes especially clear when for some reason it is removed. At one time we lived in a village which was in the early stages of moving several miles to a new site. The divisional chief had gone, with his immediate household, but so far few others had joined them. When I commented on how quiet the old town seemed, one of the young men explained that several years before there had been many deaths among youths as a result of witchcraft directed at them while they danced. Since that time, they had dared to dance only when under the protection of the chief, who was acknowledged to be a very powerful witch. Now that he had moved to the new site only the young girls danced, unless the chief was in the old town on a visit and told them that he would guard their revels. A number of similar references to this situation attest that this was not a private view, but one that in fact shaped the behaviour of the community.

Aggressive uses of mystical powers

There is probably no skill or profession in Gonja without its set of mystical beliefs and practices that are considered necessary to success. There are, however, three occupations in which the possession of medicines has a curiously dual aspect, at once protective and aggressive. These are hunting, warfare, and chiefship. The first two are concerned with the taking of life: an act that requires both superior aggressive powers and protection against the vengeance of the victim's ghost.

Use of mystical powers by hunters and warriors

The central fact about hunting is its inseparability from the control of medicines. No hunter dares to enter the bush without the security these give. The chief protective medicine is probably that which enables a man to become invisible at will. This renders harmless even a charging wounded buffalo, the most dreaded of the threats a hunter faces. Other medicines perfect his aim, lead him to game, and so on.

As characteristic as the ownership of medicines is the hunter's bondage to the taboos with which these are surrounded. Each medicine has a set of prohibitions specific to it: prohibitions on eating certain food, washing in cold water, replying to certain forms of address, or using certain words rather than circumlocutions. But the universal prohibition is that on contact with a menstruating woman. If such a woman enters the room in which a hunting shrine is kept she endangers the effectiveness of its power, and if she should wish to kill her husband this is one way open to her. However, it is unlikely to be used often, for it is firmly believed by the women that if, while menstruating, they enter the room where a hunting shrine is kept, their period will not stop until they have made ritual restitution to the shrine-owner. Contact with an adulterous wife will also spoil the power of hunting medicines, and hunters say they avoid having many wives in order to reduce the incentives to adultery and thus preserve the strength of their medicines.

In addition to protection from the hazards of the chase, and mystical assistance in securing their prey, hunters must have protection from the ghosts of their victims. For this they use ghost medicine. Concern over ghostly vengeance is given explicit form in the requirement that when one of the three major game animals is killed (lion, elephant, buffalo) it must be given a funeral, the main feature of which is the performing of *kpana* songs and dances. These mime and celebrate feats of hunters and warriors, and the power and reputation of both the dead animal and those who are celebrating its funeral.[4]

As befits a conquest state, warfare is the business of the rulers. All men of the ruling estate were expected to know the use of the spear, and later the gun, and horses and horsemanship remain major symbols of chiefly power. But, as the office of war captain (*mbongwura*), and whole sections of towns and even separate villages, attest, the ruling estate sought from time to time assistance from groups of commoners or strangers. Each set of warriors has its medicines for turning aside the spears and bullets of the enemy, for becoming invisible to allow escape if the worst comes to the worst, and for giving added strength and aim to its own weapons and getting through the mystical defences of its adversaries.

While specific medicines appear to differ from one group to another, and indeed new ones are still eagerly sought as additions to the armoury, all men of the Ngbanya ruling estate should partake annually of the major war medicine (*gbandau*). The one essential ingredient of this war medicine is human liver (although nowadays this is hard to get, and some say substitutions are made). Traditionally this liver was secured by secretly directing a ritual at one of the young men before they set out to go to war. This meant that he would be placed in the front line of combatants and would be the first to die; his body was brought back home and the liver preserved for subsequent use. It was believed that if a sacrifice of this kind was not made, the war would be lost and the enemy would prevail.

Warriors also have need of ghost medicine, for a ghost seeks above all to avenge his own death. It is said that human flesh should be used in the preparation of ghost medicine, too, but this appears to be less mandatory. Some say that the flesh of the vulture may be used instead. The important point about ghost medicine in this complex of beliefs about aggressive and protective medicines is that it is one that many men openly possess. In this respect it is in direct contrast to war medicine, which is held only by its custodians among the ruling group, to hunting medicines, which are known only to hunters, and of course to witchcraft medicines, which are highly secret. Ghost medicine is used at every funeral, and by every man who marries a widow, quite apart from its use in hunting and war. Indeed, its container was once pointed out to me spontaneously. It seems likely that consensual validation of this element in the belief complex renders more credible those others that remain unknown to almost everyone – perhaps to all.

Attendance at, and above all participation in, the hunters' and warriors' funeral dance (*kpana*) are limited to those who have faith in their medicines. For while dancing is greatly enjoyed for the rhythm and expression it allows, it is also an idiom of competition. Here, as we shall see again in the Damba dance, competition is on two levels. Men strive to out-sing and out-dance one another, but they also pit their medicines against those of their rivals:

> 'For by singing *kpana* songs men challenge each other to be acclaimed the best singer. They do this through songs that declare [for instance] "The animals I can kill, you cannot kill". But if a man possesses [a type of medicine called] *k'kparangbi*, he can throw it at the singer, calling out his name so that his voice will break and he can sing no longer.'

This may sound like a bit of harmless joshing, but on another occasion the same medicine was described to me in the following words:

'*K'kparangbi* is an instrument which they use to shoot at people so they die at a distance. If you have been boasting to people they shoot you at once. It is a thing which they use to kill people quickly; it is a thing on a tail. Before you get *k'kparangbi* you will give your child to it [i.e. sacrifice]. You must give your child before it will stay with you.'

Thus if men die following such a dance there is a ready explanation in medicines, which, although they may be used simply to render a man mute, are believed capable of killing if employed carelessly or in anger. This is easily believed of warriors and hunters, because both are known to use these or similar medicines in their chosen occupations. Despite the recognition of these dangers, the hunters' and warriors' funeral dance is a famous and favoured performance, for it offers an opportunity for both display and challenge, and if a man's medicines are powerful he has nothing to fear. Interestingly enough, although I attended several performances of this dance and often heard it discussed, no specific death was ever attributed to the participants' use of medicines in my hearing. It may be that, as with the deaths associated with the less serious dancing of the young men referred to above, if deaths do follow *kpana* they are attributed to evil witches made envious by the display. In any event, so far as I am aware, deaths following the hunters' and warriors' funeral dance do not lead to counteraction against the killer by the community.

There are, then, a number of common elements in the mystical aspects of hunting, warfare, and witchcraft, which are outlined in summary form below:

1. Use of human flesh in medicine
(war medicine; ghost medicine; witches eat victims)
2. Sacrifice of valued kinsman to secure the efficacy of medicines
(war medicine; *k'kparangbi*; witchcraft)
3. Association with vultures
(ghost medicine; hunting – vultures crowd round a kill; witchcraft – numerous references, including vultures as familiars)
4. Use of medicines to become invisible and to change shape
(hunters; warriors; witches)

5. Mystical techniques of killing
(hunters; warriors; witches)

6. Killing for meat
(hunters; witches)

7. Possession of ghost medicine as defence against victims'
ghosts
(warriors; hunters; witches).

Warfare has not been an active focus for behaviour or attitudes in Gonja for fifty years, but every community still has its
hunters. The possession of hunting medicines (made obvious to
all by the punctilious observance of the associated taboos), and
the mastery over death that their owners are felt to enjoy, mean
that hunters are greatly respected and not a little feared. Our
friend Samuel was touchingly proud of his father's reputation
as a skilled hunter, but he said on more than one occasion that
he would never go into the bush with him because he had too
many medicines. A man with many medicines is potentially
dangerous, even to close kin. The similarities between the ways
of hunters and the ways of witches do not go unremarked by
the Gonja themselves. It is said that 'As long as there are hunters,
there will be witches; they are both alike; both have powerful
medicines, both kill for meat.'

The two may be similar, but they are not the same: for the
aggression of witches is directed towards people, and their
meat is human; whereas hunters kill animals in order to be able
to feed people. There is a sense in which all taking of life is
dangerous and even wrong; and mystical techniques of aggression are especially feared because, even if fairly readily obtain-
able and openly used, they are mysterious and not easily subject to control. *K'kparangbi* is basically a warrior's weapon.
However, it is also used in contests of singing and dancing skill,
and is feared as a possible cause of death within the group. Once
a man possesses it, who can know how he will use it?

This raises in acute form the question of when mystical aggression is legitimate, and, indeed, how the legitimacy of aggression
can be measured. I suggest, as an admittedly crude index, that
legitimate aggression is that which goes unpunished within the
moral community. There are, I realize, many difficulties with
such a definition, centring, ultimately, on the relation between

force and legitimacy, and of course on the definition of the boundaries of the moral community. However, as a working definition, it has the advantage of being open to observation: a given (alleged) act either is or is not followed by publicly sanctioned counteraction.

At the end of this discussion of male witchcraft I shall consider very briefly a number of cases in which men are alleged to have killed someone by mystical means. In this context the relationship between legitimate aggression and witchcraft will be reconsidered, using publicly sanctioned counteraction as an index of legitimacy. But first let us turn to the material on the use of male witchcraft in establishing and maintaining dominance.

Aggressive witchcraft in the struggle for chiefship: dominance

There is a tendency to assume that a man who is known to have some dangerous medicines will also have others; that he must be a witch. This was clearly expressed in the exclamation with which Fatima responded to my query about a certain chief. 'He has a lot of medicines! It is witchcraft!' (*E kɔ aduru ga na! Kegbe na!*) And she went on to say that on one occasion when he was threatened by a rival's power he simply disappeared, and, on another, turned himself into a cock. As this suggests, it is not only an altruistic desire to be able to protect his subjects from evil witches that leads a would-be chief to seek witchcraft medicines. As one man said:

'Actually, male witches don't kill unless for chiefship, where one might like to seize it from his fellow. Some male witches may be evil, but where male witches just sit in their compound with no chiefship interfering, the witchcraft is only used to look after their families.'

A senior Gonja chief put it even more strongly:

'Since there is fighting for chiefship, we say that one who has chiefship would not have survived the struggle without medicines.'

Fighting for chiefship takes a variety of forms, overt and covert. Candidates for a vacant office are expected to canvass support both from their own kin and from those around the chief in whose gift the office lies. Most chiefs are placed on the skin of chiefship (*kowura ba kawul*) during the annual Damba celebrations. In the period just before these take place I used to find my friends among the important men plentifully supplied with kola nuts. Would-be candidates seek to win support by open-handed distribution of such luxuries. They also make monetary presents to the divisional chief, although they have no assurance that they will be given preference over the other contenders, and none that the presents will be returned if they are unsuccessful. Such gifts were traditionally small and not thought of as bribery, but rather as a common-sense precaution to ensure that the divisional chief 'knew that you respected him'. In effect, they served as a form of tribute and a recognition of the divisional chief's power of decision.

Where gifts and persuasion fail, an ambitious man may turn to coercion. There is a complex but clear relationship between the proximity – both in spatial and in kin terms – of political rivals and the assumed likelihood of covert as opposed to overt aggression in securing office. The basis of succession in Gonja is the circulation of office among dynastic segments of patrikin. Thus a given office never passes directly from father to son, nor between full brothers. This is most clearly seen in succession to higher offices, such as the paramountcy and the divisional chiefships, where occupants must come from the different named segments in turn. But even at the lower levels it is rare for first cousins to be direct competitors for the same chiefship. It is thus a system in which distant rather than close kin succeed to, and compete for, chiefship, and the more generalized succession tensions occur between distant kin: between men who are remote agnates, or who know only that they share descent from one of the 'sons' of the founder of the Gonja state, Ndewura Jakpa. To put this in a slightly different way, competition for office, with its attendant conflicts, occurs in the political, and not within the domestic, domain.

Each division has its own hierarchy of offices. The only chiefship a man can hold outside his natal division is the paramountcy. This is filled by the divisional chief of each of five divisions in turn. Within a division, if the incumbent is of one segment (*kabuna*, literally: gate) his successor ought to be from a different one. Thus where witchcraft is thought to be employed in killing an incumbent so that the office becomes vacant and available to the next in line, it is the killing of a member of one segment by a member of another that is involved.

Once an office falls vacant, however, there is still the problem of selecting among the eligible candidates. These may be from the remaining two out of three gates, or they may, in a two-segment division, be from the same segment. Close kin present a solid front, putting up as their candidate the eldest of their number as yet without office. But there may be in a single gate several groups of agnates, among whom are two or three candidates. It is among these that the elders choose. Members of the same dynastic segment must publicly support the candidate selected by the elders if they wish to receive backing in turn. And the system is such that, without the backing of the office-holders of his own dynastic segment, no man can secure office. Hence competition between men of the same segment is covert, and aggression takes mystical forms, i.e. witchcraft. When men of different segments are seeking the same minor chiefship, antagonisms between them may be more overt, but the use of physical force is not permitted by the senior chiefs. Hence, again, covert mystical aggression is believed to be resorted to.

In the competition for divisional chiefship, open warfare, i.e. civil war, has sometimes occurred. This appears to have happened in Busunu and Daboya in the late nineteenth century, and a major civil war was initiated in 1892 by the Kanyase gate of Kpembe division when all other attempts at securing a turn in the rota for divisional office had failed (for a full account, see J. A. Braimah & J. R. Goody, 1967). Warfare between divisions with the paramountcy as the prize is also well attested. Even vaguely reliable accounts are restricted to the nineteenth century, but for this period there were two wars in which Kung division sought to secure the paramountcy, and another in which the newly appointed paramount from Kusawgu division was prevented from establishing his court at Nyanga. In this last case the unfortunate man ended his life in exile, because his divisional chiefship had already been assumed by his successor.

Mystical aggression is also believed to be employed in contesting divisional chiefships and the paramountcy. Indeed, traditional reluctance to accept the latter office is certainly due in part to the mystical dangers to which the incumbent is subject. For instance, following the second attempt by the chief of Kung division to seize the paramountcy by force, the heads of the other divisions jointly invoked a curse on whoever should next occupy the office. This was resorted to as the ultimate deterrent to Kung's ambitions.

Discussions of the history of the paramountcy usually include references to candidates who never reached the capital at Nyanga, supposedly succumbing on the way to the plots of their rivals. It is significant that it is often left vague whether their death was due to defeat in battle, to medicine placed in their food, or to other forms of witchcraft. Indeed, I had heard the death of the paramount from Kusawgu attributed to the mystical power of his enemies before I heard the highly circumstantial account of the battles connected with his defeat and exile. (Here, attribution of a chief's death to a rival's witchcraft allows the denial of the open schism of civil war within the kingdom.)

The higher the office, the greater the mystical danger, but also the greater the likelihood of open civil war. With the far less powerful chiefships, below the divisional level, the scope of competition is restricted to those readily acknowledged as agnates (though distant ones), and civil war is not a possibility. Here, and usually with competition over divisional chiefships, aggression between rivals for office is restricted to covert mystical attack, but is so widely anticipated that it has come to be treated as a necessary risk in seeking and holding office.

The Damba ceremony is the single occasion in the year when all the minor chiefs must come to the divisional capital and publicly render homage to the divisional chief. The significance of this aspect of Damba (as distinct from the ceremonies honouring the prophet and seeking good fortune for the coming year) is indicated by the fact that the first paramount appointed under the British sought to make it compulsory for the divisional chiefs to come and render homage to him at this time. This had never been part of the ceremony at the national capital; indeed, each divisional chief was occupied with receiving the homage of his sub-divisional chiefs at the time. But it was one of the few ways open to the paramount to assert the greater measure of authority over the divisional chiefs that the British were eager to support.

Since it is the one time that all the chiefs forgather, and is, in addition, an auspicious month (Rabi 'al Awwal in the Muslim calendar), most new chiefs are enrobed directly following Damba. It is thus also a period when there is a convergence of political rivals and a renewing of the intrigues and antagonisms that are associated with struggles for office. Even those who are not themselves candidates for vacant skins (men as yet without office, and minor chiefs) seek to augment their stature and authority. They can do this in a variety of ways. One, to which Damba particularly lends itself, is by a display of fine robes and skilful dancing.[5] Such a display not only shows that a man is a fine fellow, but also constitutes a public statement that he is not afraid of the worst his enemies can do, by overt means or covert, to injure him. For in making such a display, a man is publicly seeking support for his ambitions, and he is doing so in a way that is known to court the attentions of witches motivated by jealousy as well as of his rivals. He is challenging both the good witches (the chiefs) and the bad witches (*begbe libi*).

That courage and confidence in one's own medicines are required in order to make such a challenge is underlined by the fact that even a member of the ruling group who is not intending to enter the competition for office may fear the attacks of witches at this time. Seidu, son of an important minor chief, has for many years remained behind in his father's village when the others of his family have journeyed to the capital for Damba. His nephew explained that this was due to his fear that, although he himself was not interested in office, he might be attacked by witches 'who are everywhere at Damba'.

For minor chiefs, however, there is an *obligation* to dance, in that dancing is a form of greeting, expressing allegiance and subordination to the divisional chief. The obligation is openly stated by the chief's spokesman (*dogte*) offering a horse's tail to a minor chief, who grasps it, dances with it, and finally crouches in greeting before the divisional chief, who releases him with a nod of his head.

225

It is necessary at this point to say something of the significance of the tail in this context. Horses' tails are valued for their association with the animals that symbolize the superiority of the ruling estate over the autochthones, and were no doubt at least partly responsible for the military success that left the former in control. Despite the fact that no horses are bred in Gonja, that the price of one has steadily risen over the past fifty years from a few pounds to thirty or forty, and that there are enough tse-tse flies about to reduce the life of a purchased horse to a few years, every divisional chief who lives far enough away from the centres of infection will somehow manage to keep a horse. Horses have a prominent place in the enrobing and burying of chiefs, and the stylized movements of head and shoulders in the Damba dance are modelled on the carriage of a man on horseback.

But, associations apart, the horse's tail as it is used in the Damba dance, by chiefs sitting in state, and by men riding to war, is a vehicle for both protective and aggressive medicines. To hold a tail is to be elegant, princely, powerful, and safe. Not all chiefs are invited to dance by being presented with the tail by the spokesman. It is a mark of the divisional chief's favour, or it may be a way of forcing a dissident chief publicly to acknowledge fealty. These dances by invitation occur directly after the main feature of the ceremony (which varies from day to day). After this formal phase, any older person – chief, elder, or untitled man or woman – may dance, and many have their own tails. If a man is descended from the ruling estate on his father's side, he may dance with the tail in his left hand; if on his mother's side, he dances with it in his right hand; and if both his parents were members of the ruling estate he has the right to dance with a tail in each hand.

The close association between the Damba dance, witchcraft medicines, and political rivalry is shown in a description of one chief dancing Damba at the time he was a candidate for a vacant divisional chiefship. He danced, my informant said, with his left hand inside his smock the whole time. From this, everyone knew that he had medicines to get his rivals. And it was to the strength of these medicines that his ultimate success was widely attributed. Again, during my stay in another division, there was open canvassing for the chiefship, because the incumbent was very elderly and unwell. At Damba that year the senior man in the segment next in line wore a pair of spectacles in addition to a smock and a hat (always associated with both protective and aggressive medicines), and of course he carried a tail. The spectacles were worn in order to increase his vision; not his mundane vision, but his ability to 'see' the unknown.[6] In other words, they were a direct statement of his occult powers, and hence showed his suitability for office and his superiority over alternative candidates.

But perhaps the most vivid expression of the power and danger surrounding chiefship is the appearance of the divisional chief himself. When he emerges from his inner hall into the arena where the ceremony is to occur, he is covered from head to toe by an immense gown (*burumusu*; from Arabic *burnus*), which has also a hood so deep that, falling forward, it completely obscures his face. At no time during the ceremony is the hood thrown back, and he reclines, a shrouded figure, amidst the colour and movement of the crowded scene. Various stories of mystical efficacy attach to the gown itself, but its main value appears to lie in the dual function it fulfils of protecting those around the chief from his power, which is heightened at this time by the performance of private ritual, and of protecting the chief from the attacks of his enemies (for he is the most vulnerable of all the chiefs to rivals' attacks, occupying as he does the most desirable office).

The divisional chief does not dance at the time when the minor chiefs are summoned by the spokesman's presentation of the tail, or later when there is more informal dancing by those who wish to display their skill and finery. But dance he must during the all-night vigil that precedes the final ceremony of the Damba cluster. No one knows when he will choose to emerge from his room, but it is always in the small hours of the morning, and surrounded by trusted elders, that the hooded figure appears. Still surrounded by the retainers, some holding his gown, others shielding him with theirs, he dances a few steps and withdraws again to the shadows.

Circumstantial support is provided for the belief that chiefs are always in danger of mystical attack by their rivals by the oft-repeated statement that, of all deaths, only those of chiefs are not subject to divination or other form of inquiry as to the cause. This is said to be because a chief has so many enemies trying to kill him with witchcraft that it is only a matter of time before one of them succeeds. Thus the cause of a chief's death is assumed to be the witchcraft of a rival. Sickness is a form of weakness similar to that brought about by quarrels among kin, the breaking of certain prohibitions, or the failure of protective medicines. Witches are known to be on guard for a lowering of any of their victim's defences, and hence the death of a man known to be suffering from a serious illness is still attributed to witchcraft.

Although I have never heard it suggested, it is possible that there is a private attribution of the cause of a chief's death. Whatever actually happens, people *believe* that the cause of a chief's death is not divined. Reliable information on the circumstances surrounding the deaths of divisional chiefs and the paramounts themselves is difficult to obtain. Of the three I have heard discussed seriously by close kin, all are attributed to rivals' medicines. In one case a paramount elect died on the way to the capital for his installation; his dynastic segment is sure that medicine was put in his food. In the other two cases, both chiefs had said before they died that they believed they had (for different reasons) jeopardized the strength of their protective medicines, thus allowing a known enemy to catch them with their guard down and to kill them with his, temporarily, stronger medicines.

Conditions for legitimate aggression

I have suggested that men seek to possess witchcraft, and seek to be believed to possess witchcraft, for two reasons. First, they want it so that they can protect their dependants, and in the case of chiefs their subjects, against witches who may try to harm or kill them; second, they need it as a weapon in the struggle for chiefship itself. Aspiring candidates are expected to use all means at their disposal to secure office, and once in office men must maintain the strength and reputation of their medicines as a defence against would-be successors. The first justification for possessing witchcraft is openly discussed; the second only gradually becomes clear to the observer. But both are recognized and accepted by the Gonja themselves.

Given the assumption that chiefs' deaths are caused by rivals' witchcraft, it is at first surprising that, although there is gossip about the deaths caused in the course of political rivalry, and allegations are made in which reputed assailants are named, there are no public accusations arising out of such deaths, followed by counteraction against the witch. Male witchcraft in Gonja is recognized as potentially deadly in the context of competition for chiefship and is assumed to be the cause of virtually all chiefs' deaths; but the killing of a political rival by mystical means is not actionable. In contrast, women accused of killing by witchcraft were, if conclusively identified and felt to be dangerous to the community, put to death, sold into slavery, or placed under the permanent and personal protection of the chief. Today, with the first two of these methods of control prohibited, the female witch is usually driven out of the village. Counteraction against women witches thought to have killed or injured by mystical means not only is possible but is demanded by a terrified community. Counteraction against male witches has probably always been as rare as it is today (see *Table 1*, p. 231 below).

While working through our Gonja notebooks in preparing this paper, I listed all reasonably well-documented instances of believed witchcraft attack.[7] In classifying these, I found it useful to make a threefold distinction between: (1) gossip – where an attack or misfortune is attributed to witchcraft, but the identity of the witch is not specified; this would include cases where witches are said to belong to a category of people outside the community, for example, the Navaho who live 'over the mountain' (Kluckhohn, 1944, pp. 58, 96); (2) allegation – where both victim and witch are named, but no publicly sanctioned counteraction occurs; and (3) accusation – where a witch is named as responsible for a given attack, and some form of publicly sanctioned counteraction follows.

There are two reasons for making this distinction. On the one hand, it makes it possible to differentiate between reported instances about which there was a measure of consensus (those considered both serious enough and certain enough to justify counter-measures) and other instances that may reflect private grudges and perspectives. Obviously there are degrees of consensus short of that which results in counteraction. And the

Gonja material makes it quite clear that there can be consensus without counteraction. But to treat as equivalent the allegations of individuals and accusations that are ratified by community-approved action is to overlook the element of legal process which inheres in the operation of witchcraft beliefs. This is not to deny the significance of allegations of witchcraft attacks. However, they cannot be fully understood apart from a knowledge over time of the triad: alleged witch – bringer of allegation – victim. And it must be recognized that, especially when informants know that instances of witchcraft attack are being collected by a fieldworker, allegations may in fact be little more than the voicing of personal suspicions and antipathies.

This leads to the second reason for distinguishing between gossip, allegations, and accusations. It appears likely that each serves a different function. Without going into the problem in detail (which would be more appropriately reserved for a methodological study) the following observations can be made.

Gossip can be seen to serve, under certain conditions, to distance the threat of attack; to attribute it to outsiders, or at least to refrain from attributing the cause of misfortune to a particular group member. Second, gossip serves to formulate the norms of both dangerous and desired behaviour, and to state them the more clearly because it does so in a generalized form. Where this is done through gossip, no threat to the group from within is made to appear imminent; no individual is put in jeopardy.

Allegations, on the other hand, *do* affect an individual by undermining his reputation, or, in the case of Gonja and Tiv men, by enhancing it. Allegations constitute an imputation of mystical power: the effect of such an imputation will vary as do the beliefs about the legitimacy and use of such power.

But accusations followed by counteraction have, in at least one respect, radically different implications. For while publicly sanctioned counteraction affirms the possession by the accused of mystical power, it goes further and defines a given attack as illegitimate and beyond the bounds of tolerance. Through accusations, private grievances receive public validation, and the exercise of mystical power by the individual concerned is identified as evil. Where mystical power is an important component of secular power, there must be ways of laying claim to its possession. Action against a reputed witch by the community constitutes a repudiation of such claims. It is for this reason that I have used publicly sanctioned counteraction as an operational definition of the illegitimate use of mystical aggression.

TABLE 1   *Sex of witch and incidence of counteraction following believed witchcraft attacks*

	Men	Women	Total
Accusations followed by counteraction	1	22	23
Allegations– no counteraction	9	19	28
No information re counteraction	0	3	3
Total	10	44	$N=54$

Of the cases in *Table 1*, only one of the ten men thought to have killed or injured by witchcraft was subject to counteraction, whereas twenty-two of the forty-four women, or 50 per cent, were accused and punished in some way. In seeking to understand why there should be such a marked difference in the reaction to male and female witchcraft, we must distinguish between the functions of aggression in the male and the female roles, and, within the male role, between the protective and aggressive aspects of witchcraft powers. As we have seen, the Gonja cite two major reasons as to why men seek witchcraft powers: to enable them to protect dependants against witches' attacks, and to fight for chiefship. In addition, men who possess such powers are believed to use them sometimes to punish infringements of morality. Six of the ten men reputed to be witches were chiefs, and it is chiefly witchcraft, combining as it does all these functions – protective, morality-enforcing, and competitive – that is most fully elaborated in Gonja thought, and best represented in our cases.

In so far as male witchcraft occurs in the course of political competition, it will involve men who are either distant agnates or unrelated. As has been noted above, in the Gonja system of rotational succession, the tensions arising in the political sphere are kept almost completely separate from those of the domestic sphere, and conflicts arising from competition for office fall outside the realm of close kinship relations. It would seem, then, that mystical aggression used against a competitor who is not a close kinsman is, in Gonja, perceived in terms of the idiom of competition rather than as an infringement of community morality.

However, in order to perform his expected role of defending his subjects against dangerous witches, a chief must maintain his own powers. This he may at times do by killing his children, as instanced in a case discussed below (p. 234). Thus chiefly witchcraft is not employed solely against non-relatives and distant kin. But whether a chief kills a kinsman or an unrelated rival, he appears immune to retaliation by the community. For who is there who can challenge a chief? This brings us again to the dominance-maintaining function of aggression, including mystical aggression. The Gonja belief that rivals for office will use mystical aggression against one another, and that the successful survivor will be the stronger and hence entitled to hold chiefship, is an expression of this dominance function. And as one watches the chiefs display their elegant gowns and elaborate steps in the Damba dance (while always flourishing the horse's tail), one is reminded of the posturing by which a robin warns another to keep out of his territory. For to participate in the Damba dance is to proclaim one's dominance, to challenge would-be rivals, publicly, to do their worst.

I would suggest that the fact that accusations of killing by witchcraft are not made against political rivals is directly related to the function of mystical power in maintaining political power, i.e. dominance. For if a man were to accuse another of trying to kill him with medicines in order to gain his vacant chiefship, this would be tantamount, in Gonja eyes, to admitting that his own medicines were not strong enough to protect him, or, by extension, his kin and dependants. Such an admission of weakness would seriously undermine his present position and probably put an end to any hopes of his future advancement. And of course it would, in Gonja thought, be an open invitation to all witches to attack a weakened opponent.

A chief must, above all, guard the reputation of his mystical powers. But this does not explain why a suspected witch should not be accused after the death of an acknowledged rival. There are, I believe, two sorts of reason why this does not happen, neither independent of the other. In the first place, rivalry in chiefship is seen as similar to rivalry in love, wrestling, or war. It is a struggle between two declared opponents and the stronger one is entitled to the spoils of victory. The struggle is expected to be in earnest and both contestants must accept the risks involved. Death in a contest is not murder, even when the contest uses mystical rather than visible weapons. Mystical aggression is the expected mode of political activity between political rivals, and to kill in the course of such a contest is similar to killing in the hunt or in war. It is dangerous, for the spirit of one's victim is sure to seek revenge. But it is not immoral. This is further supported by the regular affirmation that men, and even chiefs, who are renowned witches are not evil witches.

The second reason why a chief's death is not followed by open accusation is more prosaic. As I have indicated, the available methods for controlling a dangerous witch are of two sorts. In the first instance, she will be made to drink a shrine, which places her own life in jeopardy if she even thinks of killing again. But how could a chief be asked to do this? He is *expected* to use his powers to protect his people, and these are thought to operate in part by the threat of out-aggressing other witches. Again, he is expected to try to attack his rivals for higher office, and to seek to injure those trying to attack him and to take his place. For a chief to promise a shrine to refrain from using his witchcraft powers would be the equivalent of promising never again to assume a dominant role. The second sort of counter-action available for the control of dangerous witches is their removal from the community or their neutralization by placing them under the control of the divisional chief. Either form of counteraction would mean the removal from office of the chief, or the barring from office of the aspiring chief.

Within the system of beliefs that the Gonja hold, mystical homicide by men in authority positions cannot be punished, and this is true primarily because mystical aggression is itself

233

a major source of legitimate power. It is legitimate for the hunter, it is legitimate for the warrior, and it is legitimate for the chief. Although it is legitimate, it is nevertheless very much feared. It was said that only two other chiefs in the town dared drink with one of the senior sub-divisional chiefs of Kpembe. He was such a powerful witch that the others feared what he might do when he had drunk too much. There are many such statements. Indeed, it would seem that one of the functions of gossip about the witchcraft powers of men in authority roles is to enhance the very authority that legitimates the mystical powers.

The close link between the legitimacy of mystical aggression and the role of the supposed attacker in the community is clearly seen from an analysis of all the cases in our notes of alleged mystical aggression by men (see *Table 2*).

TABLE 2   *Cases of mystical attack by men, classified by role of witch and incidence of counteraction*

	Counter-action	No counter-action
Chief	0	6
Holder of ritual office or of status ritually defined	0	3
Hunter	1	0

Chiefly witchcraft is not, as the Gonja affirm, subject to punishment. It is particularly significant that, among the six instances recorded above, there is one allegation against a divisional chief of killing his own son in order to enhance his power, so that he would be strong enough to dance Damba. Here we have a clear case of killing a kinsman in precisely the way in which evil witches are said to act. Yet no counteraction was attempted by either kin or community, and although this chief was spoken of as very *strong* he was not described to me as *evil.* Mystical aggression by chiefs appears to be interpreted in terms of the dominance function, even when used against kin.

The ritual specialists (in *Table 2*) include a shrine priest, a learned Muslim, and an elder, famous for his mystical powers. The point of interest here is that in all three cases the believed motivation for the attack was what might best be described as preservation of the moral order. In one case a youth had behaved boastfully to the shrine priest, who punished him by 'throwing' *k'kparangbi* at him; in another the victim was a female witch who had reputedly challenged the Muslim to a duel of mystical strength; and in the third case the elder's (mystically potent) hat was snatched off by a mischievous boy, who since that incident has been both deaf and dumb. All these were seen by those concerned as instances of what I have suggested is the punishment function of aggression: aggression used in defence of the moral order. And each of the agents – the shrine priest, the Muslim, and the elder – occupies a role in the external system that allows aggressive actions attributed to him to be interpreted as morality-sustaining punishment.

As the instance cited above suggests, Muslims are feared as well as respected for their ability to communicate with and control supernatural forces. Just as chiefs are assumed to have witchcraft powers, so I have heard it said that all really learned Muslims are witches. That they are believed to know about, and have at their disposal, very powerful means of mystical aggression is attested by the eagerness of the Ashanti to employ Muslims to provide talismans for success in battle (J. R. Goody, 1968). However, as the low incidence of allegations and accusations against Muslims indicates, in Gonja they are infrequently thought of as employing their occult skills aggressively against others.

Finally, there is the sole example of male witchcraft in which the believed attack led to publicly sanctioned counteraction, that of the hunter. There are several features of this case which might have been instrumental in precipitating counteraction. I have already noted the close resemblance the Gonja consider to exist between hunters and witches. In this case the accused witch was actually seen putting something into the beer drunk by his fellow-hunter just before the latter fell ill (in fact, of tuberculosis). The victim was known to have recently had several

235

large kills, while the witch had been down on his luck. Moreover, the counteraction was initiated by the full brother of the victim who was at that time clerk of the local council and thus able to send a squad of policemen to arrest the witch.

No doubt all these factors, and especially the last, played a part. But crucial here is the fact that the hunter held no office, occupied no status that permitted the definition of his aggression as legitimate. It could not be seen as serving either protective or morality-sustaining functions, and fighting with witchcraft (dominance function) is legitimate only in the context of political rivalry. Since he was a hunter, he must, it was said, have been seeking meat.

In general terms, aggression serves a number of functions, and where these functions are seen as desirable, and as falling within the proper sphere of a given role, aggression in that role may be permitted. Where the functions associated with aggression are not felt to be appropriate to a role, then aggressive behaviour in this role is illegitimate. All killing is dangerous; only illegitimate killing is evil.

FEMALE WITCHCRAFT

Evil purposes of witchcraft powers

Although I believe that the Gonja would agree with what I have been saying about the possession and use of witchcraft by men, I am sure they would feel that to concentrate on male witchcraft gives an unfair picture; for there is virtually complete agreement that while men possess, indeed need to possess, witchcraft powers, it is women who are believed to make the most use of them – especially old women. It is old women who are bad witches, who kill for meat, and who kill for spite or caprice. It is women in general to whom misfortunes are attributed in gossip, and it is women who are openly accused of and punished for killing and injuring with witchcraft medicines.

So far as I am aware, Nadel's treatment of Nupe witchcraft (1952) was the first to suggest that male-female role antagonisms might underlie the tensions expressed in witchcraft accusations. He saw the Nupe situation as a response to the women's failure to accept the limitation of their activities to the domestic sphere, and to the affluence and independence which many enjoyed in consequence. Only a few Gonja women are itinerant traders; their potential insubordination lies in their ability to break off a marriage, virtually at will. I have tried in what follows to suggest a formulation that would account for both the Gonja and the Nupe type of case, and that would at the same time squarely face the fact that it is malevolent *aggression* that is attributed to women in both societies.

Considerations of space make it impossible to pursue here a full comparison of male and female witchcraft. Instead, I shall have to summarize radically those aspects of female witchcraft that are most relevant to the attempt to see it in terms of the functions of aggression. This means setting aside for the moment the customary analysis of the role tensions of which witchcraft accusations are an index. As is apparent from *Table 3*, affines make up the largest single category of those suspected. The role tensions that give rise to this situation have been discussed elsewhere in a quite different context (E. N. Goody, 1962). But consideration of each of the other categories, while of intrinsic interest, is out of the question here. I would, however, point out that it is not only women in kinship or affinal roles, but apparently women in general, who are feared likely to kill by mystical means.

That women in general are dangerous is further suggested by the threat that they present to the power of men's shrines (see pp. 216-17 above). It also emerges from a consideration of the single most feared medium of witchcraft in Gonja, a medicine called *korte*. It is always translated as 'poison' by English speakers and this renders old court records even more than usually tantalizing, for cases of 'poisoning' almost certainly refer to the use of *korte*.

There is no agreement as to how *korte* is prepared. Some say that it is made from roots, some that it is made by dipping a towel in the saliva of a dead man; others maintain that it is immaterial and can be 'thrown' across long distances. The powers of *korte* are equally subject to differing beliefs. It may be put on a knife, and will render lethal an innocuous cut; it may be put on the deadly kernel of an *achee* apple and transform it so as to resemble a kola nut; it may be 'thrown' at a victim, who then contracts virtually incurable yaws. But the most dangerous and most feared form of *korte* is stomach *korte* (*epunto ba korte*).

This is put into food, usually by the woman cooking it, and unless the danger is recognized immediately and medicine taken to make the victim vomit the entire contents of the stomach, it is invariably deadly. The moral that the Gonja draw from this belief is 'never eat food prepared by a stranger'. This places a

TABLE 3   *Relationship between witch and victim in 52 cases of believed attack by female witches*

Victim	No. of cases	% of cases
Affine		
Husband or husband's brother	8	
Co-wife, classificatory co-wife, child of co-wife, or daughter's co-wife	10	
Classificatory affine	3	
	— 21	40
Kin		
Own child or grandchild	7	
Sibling or sibling's child	3	
Distant kin or reputed kin where relationship not known	7	
	— 17	33
Not related	12	23
Not clear if related or not	2	4
	— 52[a]	— 100

[a] The difference between the totals in *Table 1* and *Table 3* is due to several cases of multiple alleged killings. Although, for the analysis of counteraction, multiple killings have been counted only once, for the analysis of relationships between witch and victim each victim has been considered separately.

great strain on travellers, who have, however, found ways of testing food so that they need not starve. But I have several references to food, meat particularly, being given away for fear that it was not safe to eat. More ironic is the fact that, although virtually every ceremonial occasion in Gonja is marked by the sending of cooked food to the other compounds of the village, adults dare not eat this lest one of the women who helped in its preparation should be a witch. The preoccupation with women poisoning food is evident not only on this overt level; of fifty-one stories told by girls about a picture of a Gonja woman cooking, seventeen, or about a third, described her as a witch or referred to the eating of human flesh.

TABLE 4 *Believed mode of attack by male and female witches*

Mode of attack	Men	Women
Korte	2	18
Other named or unnamed medicines	6	4
Shrine[a]	0	1
Eating souls	1	3[b]
Not known	1	26
Total	10	52

[a] Witches are believed to be able to 'tie' a shrine so that it kills for them.
[b] This was a case of multiple killing by a single woman. My informant, paternal half-brother of the three victims, said that the witch must have eaten their souls, since she was living in another town at the time.

That *korte* is associated with women witches is borne out by the data on believed mode of attack from the cases in our records (see *Table 4*). Women are very much more likely to resort to *korte* than are men. However, if all medicines are considered together, there is no difference in the relative frequency with which men and women use medicines rather than other means of mystical aggression. Gonja witches are believed to attack primarily through their control of medicines, whether they are male or female. Of the three women I know to have been executed for killing by witchcraft, two are believed to have used *korte*; about the mode of attack used by the third I have no information. But clearly it is not the mode of attack that distinguishes good from bad witches.

Proscription on female aggression

When I was in the field it puzzled me that not only men but women as well should assert that it was women who were evil witches. Now that I have had the opportunity to consider the pattern of accusations, it is clear that on one level women are simply reacting to the evidence of their senses. For while gossip about witchcraft, and even allegations, concern both men and women, it is *women* against whom counteraction is taken (in 95 per cent of the cases in our sample where some form of counteraction occurred, *Table 1*). At the time, however, I had not recognized this pattern, so I asked women, 'Why are women witches?' Most responded with specific motives which might lead a witch to kill. But one woman whom I knew well replied, 'because we are evil'. And she then went on to explain how the children of co-wives quarrel and their mothers become involved, and set up a pattern of hostility; she described the desperation of barren women, and the resentment among the poorer women when another woman had many fine things in her room. The particular motives she mentioned are not different from those put forward by other women, but her spontaneous exclamation 'because we are evil' puts them in a new light; for whereas there are a number of contexts in which men may kill, and a few in which they *must* kill, there is only one situation in which women may legitimately use aggression. The one exception is where a woman is forced to defend herself and her children against violent attack; physical defensive aggression is permitted in extreme cases, but not mystical.

The reason for the general proscription on aggression by women is twofold. On the one hand, women function within the domestic sphere, or, when operating between domestic groups, do so on the basis of kinship or friendship. Political roles in the external system, roles that engage the dominance function of aggression, are regularly assigned to men. In other words, women do not need to be aggressive in the pursuit of their assigned roles, whereas men often do.

But the second reason is I believe the more basic. This is again derived from the fact that women operate within the domestic sphere. For the characteristic relationships here are primary relationships, or mediated primary relationships, like that of co-wife. And the prescribed mode of such relations is intimate dependence in daily affairs. There are two regular characteristics of the female domestic role. First, in the role of mother, a woman is a focus of emotional ties, undoubtedly complex, but heavily affectively loaded. Then, as wife, a woman is defined as subordinate to her husband, and probably to all other adult men as well. Aggression, if permitted, would threaten both these core characteristics. For aggression is a distancing mechanism which conflicts with the bonding effects of emotional ties. Another of the recognized effects of aggression is its function in establishing, and challenging, dominance hierarchies. Open aggression from a wife is not permissible because it threatens her husband's dominant position. The Gonja are quite explicit about this. A man may beat his wife for various established reasons, or even because he is irritable. If he does it too often or too hard, she will leave. But she will go not because her husband has beaten her, but because he has beaten her too hard, or too often, or because she has a lover with whom she wishes to live (which may be why her husband beat her in the first place). Nevertheless, a woman may not lift her hand against her husband. While neighbours will try to soothe a husband who is beating his wife, if she had tried to strike him, it is said, they would not interfere. And if a wife strikes her husband with her stirring stick (*kadumwule*), he will become impotent; aggression in a woman's role renders a man powerless – it cannot be permitted. Therefore, as my friend said, women who are given to aggressive impulses are evil.

I have argued in connection with male witchcraft that the occupants of certain select roles *are* permitted to use mystical aggression with impunity. When those of high political or ritual status are thought to have killed by witchcraft no public counteraction is taken, and in the cases cited of the ritual leaders, the act was endowed with a morality-sustaining significance. The crucial case for my argument lies, then, in the treatment of women who are either office-holders or ritual specialists. There is, unfortunately, not space here to go into the material in detail. Briefly, though, female chiefs are gossiped about as witches, and they are not infrequently alleged to have been responsible for deaths. There are many fewer female chiefs than male office-holders. During fieldwork in central and eastern

Gonja, over a period of twenty-one months, I knew of only six. One of these was openly accused of killing by witchcraft (she was knocked by the 'corpse' of her victim) and was saved from exile only by the fact that her father was chief of the town and refused to agree with the public demand that she must go.

Although the Gonja say that women do not make medicines, apart from witchcraft medicines, there are a few women who are diviners or medical practitioners. One such woman, whom I knew well, was terrified of being accused of responsibility in the recent deaths of several children. The fear quite transformed her usual lively disposition.[8] Another woman gave up treating sprains, for which she had been well known, and refused to teach even her daughters the technique, for fear, her son said, that she would be thought to know witchcraft medicines as well. Now that her husband was dead there would be no one strong enough to defend her if this should happen.

Thus neither political nor ritual status provides a legitimate basis for the use of mystical aggression on the part of women. Indeed, if it were possible to go into these and similar cases in more detail, it would appear that, if anything, special statuses of this kind are a liability; that they place the occupant in greater, rather than less, danger of public accusation. Whether or not counteraction then follows is mainly a function of whether the accused witch has friends who are powerful enough to intervene on her behalf. Women, even when they hold political or ritual roles, are above all women. And as such they cannot be permitted to act aggressively without endangering the dominance of men, and throwing into doubt the benevolence of the affective relationships on which the domestic group centres.

It is because aggression is not permissible in women that Gonja women who are thought to have witchcraft powers are always condemned as evil. For, unlike their male counterparts, there is no legitimate purpose for which they might use techniques of mystical aggression. None of the functions of aggression that have been mentioned fall within their legitimate sphere of concern (with the partial exception of punishment, and this is clearly restricted to the children and junior women within the domestic group). How a society defines the legitimate use of aggression will vary with other features of its organization. It seems likely that because of their basic identification with domestic and kinship roles, women will usually be denied the legitimate expression of aggressive impulses. But in whichever roles aggression is not legitimate, it is in these that we can expect to find that imputations of covert mystical aggression are made, and, further, that they evoke publicly sanctioned counteraction; that they are considered evil.

NOTES

1. 'Witchcraft is the power to harm others through *mystical* means.' 'Mystical' as used here is not an entirely satisfactory term, but it best covers the collection of modes of attack which the Gonja treat as belonging to the single class, *kegbe*. This includes transvection, the eating of souls, the 'throwing' of immaterial weapons across long distances, the control (by 'tying') of shrines, and the use of substances such as *korte* which act as poisons and may or may not actually be concocted and administered. To the Gonja, of course, they are both real and effective.

2. Even this statement is deceptively categorical, although I believe it is one with which the Gonja would agree. However, I was told of one unfortunate woman who was a witch because her *egbe* sister forced her to share in a feast of human flesh. She wept and struggled, but the other witches compelled her to join in, and once she had eaten there was no help for it; she had become *egbe*. The contradictions that this case implies are typical of many in Gonja witchcraft beliefs. The lack of discussion attendant on secrecy no doubt contributes to such inconsistencies.

3. Vultures are often mentioned as witches' familiars, and as the creatures witches change into. Thus there is something appropriate about witches being, finally, devoured by vultures, as they are believed to devour their own kind,

4. In Ashanti, the hunters' dance, *obofuo agoro*, is performed after the killing of an animal believed to have a dangerous spirit (*sasa*) (Rattray, 1927, pp. 184-185). It is not clear in Rattray's account whether in Ashanti this dance also forms part of a hunter's funeral, as in Gonja. Nor does he indicate whether hunters challenge one another in song in the course of the performance.

5. Arguments over the use-rights in family property often come to a head at Damba, for one of the main forms of wealth is the fine embroidered gowns in which members of the ruling estate dance Damba. While there is virtually no rivalry among brothers for political office itself, there is keen competition over access to the finery in which to state claims against outsiders.

6. At first I was puzzled by the requests of several elders for spectacles. They were not associated with any failure of vision, but related, I finally realized, to the belief that somehow spectacles enabled one to see things that others could not see. In the context of the belief that chiefs and compound heads must find medicine to enable them to *fer anishi* (literally: wash their eyes) in order to see witches who may try to attack their people, this is a perfectly logical assumption.

7. Witchcraft was never of special concern to me in the field, and no systematic attempt was made to collect cases of believed attack. The data referred to in this paper are simply the sum total of all instances that came either to my

notice or to my husband's in the course of our time in Gonja. I spent a total of twenty-six months there, and J. R. Goody somewhat less. I wish to express here my gratitude for the use of J. R. Goody's notes. As these data are not based on a representative sample, and as they combine allegations and accusations which have very different empirical referents, no statistical tests have been employed.

8. After writing this, I learnt that my friend later died 'an evil death'. She was so widely believed to have killed her companion that, when she herself died soon after, she was dragged outside the town and left unburied as a witch.

REFERENCES

Any writer on the subject of witchcraft is indebted to scholars too numerous to mention. And these in turn are, almost without exception, beholden to Professor Evans-Pritchard for his recognition of the central importance of beliefs concerning witchcraft. As a full bibliography would be very long, and would undoubtedly duplicate items included by other contributors, I have listed here only those sources actually referred to in the text, together with three references relating to the concept of aggression.

BERKOWITZ, L. 1962. *Aggression: A Social Psychological Analysis.* New York: McGraw-Hill.

BRAIMAH, J. A. & GOODY, J. R. 1967. *Salaga: The Struggle for Power.* London: Longmans.

GOODY, E. N. 1962. Terminal Separation and Divorce among the Gonja of Northern Ghana. In M. Fortes (ed.), *Marriage in Tribal Societies.* Cambridge Papers in Social Anthropology 3. Cambridge: Cambridge University Press.

GOODY, J. R. 1966. Circulating Succession among the Gonja. In J. R. Goody (ed.), *Succession to High Office.* Cambridge Papers in Social Anthropology 4. Cambridge: Cambridge University Press.

— 1968. Restricted Literacy in Northern Ghana. In J. R. Goody (ed.), *Literacy in Traditional Societies.* Cambridge: Cambridge University Press.

HINDE, R. A. 1967. The Nature of Aggression. *New Society*, 2 March.

KLUCKHOHN, C. 1944. *Navaho Witchcraft.* Peabody Museum Papers, Harvard University, 22 (no. 2).

LORENZ, K. 1966. *On Aggression.* London: Methuen.

NADEL, S. F. 1952. Witchcraft in Four African Societies. *American Anthropologist* **54** (1): 18-29.

RATTRAY, R. S. 1927. *Religion and Art in Ashanti.* London: Oxford University Press.

© Esther Goody 1970

11

Peter Rivière

Factions and Exclusions in Two South American Village Systems

In this essay, which deals with the Carib-speaking Trio Indians and the Gê-speaking Akŵe-Shavante, the intention is to examine how, although in both societies the village is the autonomous unit, in one case sorcery is understandable only if a number of such units are taken into account, whereas in the other the workings of sorcery are fully explicable in the sphere of a single unit. Each tribe will be examined in turn, with emphasis placed on the variables of socio-political structure relevant to the understanding of the operation of mystical sanctions, and the main contrasts are summarized in conclusion.

THE TRIO[1]

The Trio, who number about 650, live close to and on either side of the Brazilian/Surinam frontier, a thickly forested headwater region which escaped any permanent non-indigenous settlement until ten years ago. In its main features, Trio culture is typical of the Guiana Tropical Forest area; subsistence is based on slash-and-burn cultivation of manioc, and on hunting, fishing, and gathering. The density of population is low (about one person to fifteen square miles) and there is no apparent pressure on natural resources although these are not evenly distributed across the whole territory and their presence or absence does exert some influence on the location of settlements and population movements. These points, the settlement pattern and the mobility of population, must be considered in greater detail.[2]

The residential unit is the village, whose average population size is thirty people; the number of inhabitants rarely exceeds fifty. Village sites are moved frequently (about every five years), and for a variety of reasons, including death of an inhabitant or infestation by weeds and vermin. The exhaustion of cultivable land is not one of the important reasons for moving a village and frequently the new village is built in close proximity to the old. However, not only are village sites moved, but their populations are also mobile; to understand this movement, in spatial, social, and political terms, it is necessary to describe the settlement pattern.

A Trio village is an autonomous unit, and the Trio language lacks terms for units larger than the single village. However, it is possible to demonstrate the existence of larger units, and furthermore to show that in statistical and behavioural terms these larger units have importance in the socio-political structure and reality in Trio awareness. The existence of the settlement pattern was first identified by plotting the distribution of Trio villages in terms of days' walk apart. The following pattern emerged: the smallest unit is the *village*; then there is a cluster of three to five villages which I shall refer to as an *agglomeration*. The villages in an agglomeration are half a day to a whole day's march apart. The nearest villages of different agglomerations are two days' march apart. All the agglomerations fall into three *groups*, the nearest villages of different groups being four days' walk apart. These three groups coincide with the three main river basins of the Trio territory[3] and are separated both by watersheds and by stretches of savannah. The social reality of this pattern is revealed by the fact that statistically an individual is likely to find 70 per cent of his kin and affines within his own village, about 80 per cent in his own agglomeration, and 98 per cent in his group. Further supporting evidence for this pattern can be seen in the use of ceremonial dialogue. This is a political institution for mediating situations which are potentially conflictive. The talk, of which this dialogue consists, has three grades of intensity, and information collected on this topic shows a clear correlation between residence and intensity of the talk: those of different groups use the strongest grade, and those of different villages of the same agglomeration the weakest.[4]

This description presents a rather static and synchronic picture of a situation which in fact is highly fluid. However, the misrepresentation is not too bad because the Trio themselves take a rather narrow and short-term view in assessing a situation; friendliness tends to be a contextual and not an absolute quality.

In view of the impermanency of the village site and the mobility of its inhabitants, one may well ask if there is any feature of the Trio village that is stable enough to allow the term autonomous to have any meaning. The answer lies in chiefship, although because of its unformalized nature I prefer to use the word leader rather than chief. The leader of any village is the symbol of that village's existence,[5] and it is on his ability that its duration depends. The Trio leader has neither authority nor power; he is leader as a result of his position in the village's network of kinship ties (there are no political ties which are not social ties) and by virtue of his ability to organize everyday tasks, to attain and maintain cooperation among his villagers, to settle disputes among them, and to represent them against strange visitors. There is no competition for leadership because there are no limitations on the politically ambitious. The founder of a village is automatically its leader and anyone can found a village. Thus, while there is opportunity for anyone to become a village leader, proven ability is necessary to be a successful one. The village of an able leader will be large and its population stable, but that of an ineffectual man will dwindle away until it consists of only his closest kin. The village leader has no power to prevent anyone or any group of people leaving his village.

Population movement, which mainly occurs within an agglomeration, takes place in response to a variety of factors – demographic, economic, or social. Although the Trio express a preference for marriage with someone of their own village this is frequently demographically impossible, and statistically one can show a tendency towards matrilocal residence. People also move from one village to another because they want to visit relatives, or to exploit some natural resource not available at their present village. Such movements can take place in an atmosphere of amity or animosity and it is the latter cases that are important in the understanding of sorcery. Conflict within a village may result from one of a number of causes: misdemeanours (theft or adultery), failure to honour kinship obligations, and lack of cooperation. It is frequently difficult to distinguish between social and economic causes because, for example, scarcity of game will give rise to accusations of meanness and of failure to fulfil social commitments. Thus an economic cause takes on a social manifestation.

A good leader will be able to settle such disputes, but when no settlement is possible the only means of resolving the conflict is for one party to leave the village. Mobility of population acts as a mechanism for reducing tension, but it can work in this way only because the villages of an agglomeration form a catchment area in which mobility is easy. Relationships between the villages of an agglomeration are as unstable as the population of a single village and present a picture of constantly shifting alliances. Inter-village relationships are regulated in the first place in the same manner as intra-village relationships, in terms of kinship, but when such ties are weak or strained ceremonial dialogue may be used. However, the main political institution regulating the relationship between villages is the dance festival which, under ritual conditions, permits a resolution of old disputes.[6]

A feature of Trio political institutions, in so far as they can be described as that, is that they are mainly concerned with mediation and conciliation, a reduction in tension. The question that must be taken up next is the source of this tension. The answer is sorcery.

Any misfortune or sickness may be regarded as being the result of sorcery, and almost all deaths are. For the Trio, death is neither a natural nor an inevitable event, and they say that no one would die unless he had been cursed. Accusations of sorcery are directed against members of other villages, particularly unknown shamans and strange visitors. Fear of sorcery is the reason the Trio give for having their villages so far apart and for not visiting each other more often than they do. This fear has a rational basis, since sickness and disease frequently and observably follow in a traveller's footsteps. At the same time, fear of sorcery maintains the code of hospitality without which travel in the area would cease: any stranger is potentially a sorcerer and the only prophylaxis against sorcery is being open and generous. On the other hand, the visitor fears the sorcery of his hosts, and the formal greeting in ceremonial dialogue on arrival at a strange village always contains, on both sides, assurances of goodwill and specific denial of being a sorcerer.

As described, Trio ideas of sorcery are simple and coherent, but the Trio also express their claim that sorcerers are non-residents in the reverse way, saying that people do not curse those of their own village. Put in this way, it brings one straight back to the problem of defining the member of a village. The resolution to this problem would appear to be that, since it is impossible to define membership of a village except at a particular instance in time, any incident of sorcery has to be judged against the existing situation. With this understood, it is possible to reassess the claim that no one curses a member of his own village, although, because I remain uncertain whether anyone actually commits sorcery other than revenge sorcery – of which I treat below – it is safer to pursue this discussion in terms of accusations. Expressed thus, i.e. that accusations of sorcery are not made against members of the same village, the claim is very close to the truth. Accusers and accused will certainly not remain in the same village after the accusation is made, and, since gossip always precedes open accusation, one party (presumably the weaker) is likely to have left before this stage is reached and violent retribution is taken. When the Trio say, then, that only outsiders are sorcerers, they are stating something that is very close to the truth and expressing the ideal conception they have of the community. One should also note that suspicions of sorcery directed against another member of the village will occur only if some discontent already exists within the village. In a village free from conflict, misfortune will result in accusations against outsiders, even unknown ones. Within the village setting there is no structural position that seems particularly prone to suspicion. Certainly accusations are made against in-marrying males, as one might expect, but not exclusively so, and they do appear among brothers; in one case a village split along the generation gap, with all the younger married men leaving the village.

There is one further feature of Trio sorcery which, for comparison with the Shavante situation, it is important to describe. The Trio response to sorcery, especially sorcery that results in death, is sorcery.[7] This is well displayed in the institution of revenge sorcery. If a member of Village A dies (which must be the result of sorcery) the other members of the village perform revenge sorcery, a curse that does not require a specific victim.

In due course they hear that someone in Village B has died and they conclude that he was the sorcerer who was responsible for their co-villager's death and that he has died from their revenge sorcery. Meanwhile, their co-villager's death may have been seen by members of Village C as the result of their revenge of an earlier death. However, members of Village B do not see the death in their village as the result of revenge sorcery but as an initial act of sorcery and thus the start of a new series. Because there are always people dying there is no way of breaking out of this cycle unless the assumption that all death is the result of sorcery is dropped.

Finally, one should note that, for the Trio, sorcery redefines the physical and conceptual boundaries of the village, and it does this whether the accusation is directed against a stranger or a (recent) member of the community. In the first case the boundary is reaffirmed by stressing the external danger, in the second by excluding the dangerous elements from within.

THE AKW̃E-SHAVANTE[8]

The Shavante live on the central Brazilian plateau, mainly concentrated in the basins of the Rio das Mortes and the Araguaia. This is savannah country, covered with high scattered shrub and bush, but not entirely lacking in forest which is to be found as galleries along the water courses. The important subsistence activities are gathering and hunting (in that order) but a little agriculture is also practised. The Shavante lead a semi-nomadic life and the needs of their subsistence economy mean that they spend many months each year travelling, but these treks are centred on semi-permanent villages.

There are about 2,000 Shavante (Maybury-Lewis, 1967, p. 6), divided among eight villages; between 1958 and 1964 the villages varied in size between 80 and 350 inhabitants (ibid., p. 333), and were 'rarely less than a full day's journey apart' (p. 13). Shavante villages, therefore, are both bigger and slightly more widely dispersed than those of the Trio. Like the Trio, Shavante villages are autonomous units, but unlike the Trio ones they appear to be more or less demographically and economically self-supporting as well. Communication between Shavante villages is poor. They do not combine for ritual and there is little inter-village trading. Relationships between settlements are mainly of a political nature and may take the form of alliance or hostility. Movement of population between villages is a response to political pressures, and, as among the Trio, if an individual or segment of the village population finds life dangerous or difficult, he or it can secede and go to live elsewhere. Asylum is never refused to refugees, although their arrival might upset the delicate balance of power not simply within the village but between villages (pp. 205-213). The role of Shavante sorcery can be understood only in the context of this power balance.

The structure of Shavante society is far easier to describe than is that of the Trio because there is a set of clearly defined social institutions. Shavante society is divided into three exogamous patriclans; a Shavante thinks of his fellow-clansmen (wherever they live) as potential allies and of non-clansmen as potential enemies. This, however, is an ideal representation which is rarely adhered to in practice. For practical purposes it is the lineage that has social and political importance (pp. 167-169). Factions are the units of Shavante politics and 'A faction consists of a lineage and its supporters, who may be other lineages of the same clan, other individuals, or even lineages of another clan' (p. 169). Ideally, factional loyalties are lineage loyalties but in practice this does not always work out, although fictive lineage ties may result from loyalty to a faction not based in one's own lineage.

Factions contend for 'the ultimate prize of the chieftaincy' (p. 190) but, paradoxically, there is no such office, and the chief is simply the head of the dominant faction in the village. The strength of the chief's position depends on how powerful his faction is. However, for reasons outlined below, power is used only as a last resort, and it is the insecure chief, i.e. the one whose faction is not overridingly dominant, who is most likely to use force. The strong chief is able to maintain control by his ability to influence public opinion and to ensure that disputes are talked out in the men's council. There are no tribal or inter-community organizations, and the chief is a chief only in his own village because it is only there that his power, i.e. the coercive force of his faction, exists.

Sorcery enters into most serious inter-factional disputes, and 'A sorcery case is therefore a political matter' (p. 188). Accusations of sorcery are made by the more powerful against the less powerful, while sorcery itself is made by the weaker against the stronger. In villages where no faction has clear-cut dominance, accusations appear to pass in both directions (pp. 185-186). In this matrilocal society sons-in-law are always suspected of sorcery since they are in a subordinate position to their wife's kin. This scheme of ideas, whereby accusations of sorcery are directed against the weaker and acts of sorcery against the stronger, is not limited to the relationship between factions within a single village but also emerges in the relationship between Shavante villages and even between the Shavante and neighbouring tribes. Other villages and other tribes are feared because of their sorcery; this carries the assumption that they are, therefore, physically weaker and inferior. For the Shavante, physical force is associated with superiority, mystical sanctions with inferiority.

An accusation of sorcery is the most serious charge that a Shavante can make, and a man of subordinate faction who makes such an accusation against a member of the dominant faction and fails to receive the support of his faction will be killed if he does not leave the village first. If a man is supported in his accusation by his faction, it will mean disruption of the community since it amounts to challenging the superiority of the dominant faction. On the other hand, accusations made by the dominant faction are excuses for political action and the eradication of rivals. This, as has been mentioned above, is more likely to happen in villages where the chief is not secure, i.e. where there are rivals. It is in the interest of a chief to stop accusations becoming open, for they must lead to violence and the flight of the minor faction. While this will strengthen the position of the dominant lineage internally, it will weaken the village's position against other villages because this is assessed in terms of numerical strength. Indeed, if the reduction in population is too great, the village may not be able to survive as an autonomous unit and will have to join another village in which the once-dominant faction will find itself a minor one. Thus it is possible for power, when it is misused, to result in the opposite of that which it is intended to achieve. For the Shavante, sorcery is a tool of political action, but it is a double-edged one which must be applied with care.

Finally, suspicion of sorcery surrounds death or sickness unless there is good reason to suppose otherwise, as for example in a case of violent death. The Shavante also have some awareness of contagion, so sickness following contact with such a complaint is not necessarily attributable to sorcery. In other cases the death of a man is seen as the political manoeuvrings of his factional opponents. A death, therefore, may spark off an accusation if the political situation is already critical, but it does not appear that all deaths result in accusations, although any death in which sorcery is suspected must necessarily have political consequences even if it merely reinforces the existing political differences (pp. 274-275).

CONCLUSIONS

The variations that exist in the operation and incidence of sorcery in these two societies seem to spring from two vital differences between them, one in their socio-political structure and one in their cosmological and sociological ideas. In each society these two factors are necessarily interlinked.

Both Shavante and Trio villages are autonomous units, but the Shavante village, which contains factions, is, in a political sense, a multi-cell unit. The Trio village is a single-cell unit and, furthermore, among the Trio there is no equivalent of the Shavante multi-cell unit. The villages forming an agglomeration fulfil some of these functions: the total number of an agglomeration's inhabitants is roughly similar to the total of a Shavante village, and it is more or less an economic and demographic self-supporting unit. However, its function in the field of politics and sorcery is very different from that of the Shavante village, in so far as each of its constituent villages is an autonomous and sorcery-free unit. The Trio village, being a single-cell unit, cannot support divisions within itself, and the appearance of tensions can be resolved only by fission – either by the migration of population into another village or by the formation of a new single-cell unit. The absence of any regulative device for conflict within the village other than dispersion, and the nature of the agglomeration – a cluster of relatively closely located villages joined by economic, social, and ritual ties – without which dispersion would be far more difficult, are, without implying any cause or effect, clearly interlinked. Furthermore, there are closely associated with these factors the Trio ideas about the purity of their community and its freedom from malevolence, which is associated with the world outside the village. The basic dichotomy in Trio thought is inside versus outside, and many Trio social institutions can be interpreted as means of resolving or reinforcing it. Sorcery acts to confirm the distinction.

As we have seen, for the Shavante, sorcery can enter into the relationships between villages, but it is only within the village that it has true meaning. The dichotomy of 'us' and 'them' exists within a single community since this is the sphere of political action of which sorcery is an adjunct. The opposite to mystical sanction is physical force, and the path to the chieftaincy, a political ambition only realizable in the sphere of the village, lies through the latter. Thus, while for both the Shavante and the Trio accusations of sorcery within the village are disruptive, and result in both cases in a reduction in the community's numbers, the overall outcome is very different. In a Shavante village an accusation of sorcery will strengthen the dominant faction's position and thus the internal unity of the village, but the village will be weakened in respect of other villages, for in the wider tribal sphere a village is judged by its numerical strength. Because, for the Shavante, might is right, they are concerned with the physical realities of their world.

The numerical weakening of a Trio village results in the reinforcement of its boundaries and reassurance concerning its internal purity. The concepts of domination and subordination are alien to the Trio, and their response to sorcery is sorcery; indeed, given the reliance that every village has on its neighbours, this seems almost essential. Violence is particular and manifest; sorcery, and particularly revenge sorcery, is not specific (although inevitably fatal) and can be denied. Acts of violence are irrevocable but accusations of sorcery can be rectified.

Finally, one might perhaps note that, for the Shavante, sorcery is evidence of hidden political ambitions; for the Trio, it is a manifestation of the innate malevolence of the unknown. For both tribes their ideas of sorcery are a clear reflection of the world as they have made it.

NOTES

1. The detailed evidence for my remarks on the Trio will be found in Rivière (1969), a monograph based partly on written sources and partly on my own researches among these people. My fieldwork in Surinam in 1963-64 was sponsored by the Research Institute for the Study of Man, New York.

2. By the time I reached the Trio in 1963 the traditional settlement pattern had largely disappeared as a result of missionary influence. The followng description of the settlement pattern is mainly a reconstruction, using information provided by Schmidt (1942).

3. That is to say, as it was in 1940-42 when Schmidt travelled through the region. At that time the Trio were living in the basins of the Sipaliwini, of the Marapi/West Paru, and of the Citaré/East Paru. Today they are living in the basins of the Sipaliwini, of the Paloemeu/Tapanahoni, and of the West Paru.

4. A detailed study of Trio ceremonial dialogue is in preparation (Rivière, in press).

5. The word for village is *pata*, which really means a place. A village is known by its leader's name – so-and-so's place.

6. It is also the source of new disputes. There is unfortunately no space in which to examine the political functions of the Trio dance festival.

7. This is not to say that violence does not exist among the Trio, and there are examples of killings. However, the Trio seem to be aware that violence leads to irresolvable disruption.

8. All my information on the Shavante is taken from Maybury-Lewis (1967), and all page references refer to this work. I am grateful to Dr Maybury-Lewis for reading and commenting on an early draft of this paper but I am responsible for any distortion of his excellent ethnography. For a summary but more extensive description of the Shavante than that offered here, the reader is advised to consult Neel *et al.* (1954, pp. 54-64).

REFERENCES

MAYBURY-LEWIS, D. 1967. *AktWe-Shavante Society.* Oxford: Clarendon Press.

NEEL, J. V., SALZANO, F. M., JUNQUEIRA, P. C., KEITER, F. & MAYBURY-LEWIS, D. 1964. Studies on the Xavante Indians of the Brazilian Mato Grosso. *American Journal of Human Genetics* 16 (1): 52-140.

RIVIÈRE, P. G. 1969. *Marriage among the Trio.* Oxford: Clarendon Press.

—— (In press.) The Political Structure of the Trio Indians as manifest in a System of Ceremonial Dialogue.

SCHMIDT, L. 1942. Verslag van drie Reizen naar de Bovenlandsche Indianen. Edited by G. Stahel. *Departement Landbouwproefstation in Suriname*, Bulletin 58.

© Peter Rivière 1970

12

Anthony Forge

Prestige, Influence, and Sorcery
A New Guinea Example

Since the publication of Evans-Pritchard's study in 1937, the
bulk of writing concerned with witchcraft and sorcery has related
to African societies. Despite the similarity of the basic beliefs in
Africa and New Guinea, the operational working-out of these
beliefs in accusation and action takes a different form in the
aggressively egalitarian societies of New Guinea from the forms
reported from Africa.

In New Guinea societies, the political systems usually have a
formal structure based on descent groups, within which operates
a series of factions centred on influential men, referred to usually
as big-men. In some areas, particularly in the Highlands, there
are superior big-men who exercise considerable influence over
quite large groups including lesser big-men. In other areas,
villages contain several big-men of roughly equal importance,
who are in that state of continuous rivalry and cooperation
typical of relationships between men of similar prestige in New
Guinea and involving ceremonial exchange. Indeed, it is by con-
centrating the external exchanges in their hands that men
become big-men inside their group. In this type of society, the
struggle for prestige, and for the influence over one's fellows that
it brings, is endless; no one has secure authority. In the political
sphere the concept of legitimacy is inapplicable and hence there
can be no concept of subversion. It is not surprising, therefore,
that supernatural aggression of one type or another is commonly
found as an integral and expected part of the political process

This is not to suggest that sorcery and witchcraft are considered good of themselves – indeed, their existence is universally deplored – but, given that they exist, it is vital for every
group to have access to both protective measures against, and
active means of, supernatural aggression, with which it can
redress the balance and maintain its position relative to other

257

groups. Since there is no authority that can punish evil, the agreement that sorcery is bad is irrelevant to political life. Self-help is the only recourse, and the context determines whether an act of sorcery is good, being just revenge, or bad, being malicious killing. It follows that a man aspiring to influence his fellows into accepting his leadership must at least implicitly offer them access to either protection from, or revenge for, supernatural aggression, or both.

This association between political eminence and the aura of sorcery is very widespread in New Guinea. Even where some form of inherited status exists, and hence some form of authority in political life, sorcery is far from being considered as wholly evil. For instance, virtually the only punitive sanction available to the Trobriand chiefs was the employment of the best sorcerers (Malinowski, 1922, p. 64). In most societies that lack inherited status the association is less public but none the less present. A correlate of this association is that those who are suspected of being active sorcerers are strong, active, and ambitious men, using sorcery as one of a number of means to further their political ends. Also, where there are no universally acceptable standards of proof, there can be no convictions for sorcery and no punishment except counter-sorcery. Sorcery in the abstract is bad, but in actual life it is morally neutral. Far from carrying a stigma, a reputation for being concerned in sorcery marks a man as one to be treated with caution, even respect, and it is an aid in the competition for influence and prestige that is the essence of the political system in the highly egalitarian New Guinea societies. In the struggle of equal with equal, all means are legitimate; the restraints are only those of equality, the right to return whatever was given, be it a valuable, garden produce, or a death.

Another distinctive characteristic of New Guinea societies is the very small size of the political units: the villages (or clan parishes in parts of the Highlands) are the war-making units. Enemies, with whom one actually fights, live within a few miles and often much closer, and it is such close enemies that are usually considered responsible for sorcery deaths – thus at least the overt accusations are directed outside the group. Yet because of the very small scale of the warring groups this is not just a simple externalization of aggression. The enemy groups are an essential part of the moral universe. In many societies they are the prime source of wives; in others, their participation at ceremonies is essential. In all, active warfare alternates with vital social contact and especially exchange relationships. The political process, with its unremitting struggle for prestige, transcends the boundaries of the war-making units. The direction of accusations outside the group is therefore usually a move in the struggle for influence within the group as well as an expression of inter-group hostility.

THE TECHNIQUES OF ABELAM SORCERY

The Abelam, a tribe of some 30,000 living in the Sepik District of the Trust Territory of New Guinea, despite the mutual intelligibility of their various dialects, display considerable variation in social structure and culture within their area. The basic structural principles are the same: it is rather that certain aspects are emphasized in some parts of the area, while others are prominent elsewhere.[1] The material presented in this paper will be mainly from the Eastern Abelam, whom for convenience I shall refer to simply as the Abelam, except where other parts of the tribe are specifically mentioned.[2] The Abelam make a clear distinction between sorcery and witchcraft, a distinction that corresponds in its essentials to that of the Azande (Evans-Pritchard, 1937). That is, sorcery is a technique requiring no innate qualities, able to be learnt by any man, and involving the treatment of some 'leavings' of the victim with intrinsically powerful substances, inevitably resulting in the illness or death of the victim. Witchcraft is innate and may operate without the conscious intention of the witch. For most of the Abelam, this dichotomy is reinforced by a sexual division, sorcery being exclusively the province of men and witchcraft of women.[3]

For the Abelam, all death, except that of infants, is due to either 'the spear by day' or 'the spear by night'. The first is direct physical violence producing death at once or within about twelve hours, and the second is sorcery. Sorcery can also produce other harmful effects, for instance epilepsy, severe or debilitating illness, and, according to some authorities, running amuck. The name for a sorcerer is *Kwis'ndu*, literally paint-man. It is a form of paint that is believed to be the active

K*   259

substance in all sorcery. All intrinsically powerful materials are classified as paint, and even the paint used on carvings and on the flat, although not in itself active, becomes, after its use in ceremony, a carrier of the benefit of that ceremony and the means by which the benefit is distributed (see Forge, 1962, 1970).

One outstanding feature of Abelam beliefs about the techniques of sorcery is the openness of the proceedings at every stage. The paint used in sorcery is believed to be prepared by the Plains Arapesh to the north, and secretly traded in small quantities to the sorcerers in Abelam territory.[4] When collected and refined it has to be tested to see whether it is 'hot'. This is believed to be done by the Arapesh and requires a party of men. They place the tightly corked bamboo section containing the paint in a house, which is then burnt down. If the paint is active, after the blazing house has collapsed there will be a large explosion and the bamboo container will fly out, soar up into the sky, and fall undamaged a good distance away. Abelam accounts always emphasize that many men are needed to be sure of tracing and recovering the 'hot' paint. Similarly, the actual 'cooking' of the victim's leavings, wrapped in a bundle of specified leaves with some of the paint and supplementary noxious substances, requires a large fire into which the bundle is thrust.[5] As it burns, small insects emerge and the fire must be surrounded by plenty of men who carefully collect every one and return it to the fire. Should one insect escape, the victim will only be ill and will eventually recover.

This procedure, like that of testing the paint, must take place at night, and both require fires with flames, in contrast to normal Abelam fires, which smoulder. Occasional night blazes in other villages are unhesitatingly identified as sorcery activity. The importance of these beliefs about sorcery techniques is that they provide empirical justification for the Abelam when they assert, as they always do, that there are no sorcerers in their village. It would be impossible to cook a victim's leavings within the village and keep it secret; a blazing fire at night within the village alarms everyone unless it is for some public ritual occasion, because Abelam hamlets burn down easily and leaping flames bring everyone to investigate and, if necessary, help.

Moreover, the beliefs are not just fantasy. Green bamboo does explode and jump in a fierce fire, and, since all fires are made with old or rotten wood, termites and other insects are to be seen frantically trying to escape. The point of interest to us is that the universal assertion that 'we have no sorcerers in our village' can be taken as true, and so can the implication of the totality of these assertions, that no one in fact practises sorcery, at least according to the techniques believed in by the Abelam. The latter step in the reasoning is not taken by the Abelam, since knowing themselves to be innocent proves to them that everyone else must be guilty.

All Abelam believe that the actual 'cooking' is done in other, principally enemy, villages, and is part of the continual killings and counter-killings that take place between hostile villages, sometimes openly in battle, more frequently in ambushes and betrayals, but most of all through sorcery. Nevertheless, given that the operators who actually kill are in enemy villages, they cannot operate without access to leavings of their intended victim. Further, although in discussing sorcery Abelam talk as if the enmity between villages was sufficient reason for killing anybody whose leavings the sorcerer had in his possession, when a death occurs such generalized hostility is never of interest; it is always the specific dispute that caused the victim to be killed now that is the main subject of divination. Abelam are very careful about the danger of their leavings falling into the wrong hands when they visit other villages, whether friendly or enemy. They take pains to ensure that any fragments of food, tobacco, or betelnut that have been in contact with their mouths are thrown into dense bush or even carried home for safe disposal. Young men, even at ceremonial held in friendly villages, will refuse food or drink unless it is offered to them by a kinsman or someone with whom they have a relationship of classificatory or quasi brotherhood.

The most dangerous forms of leavings are semen, in the case of men, and sexual secretions, in the case of women. Young men are constantly being told that they are giving away their lives when they succumb to the charms of strange women. These admonitions have little effect, since women tend to be sexually aggressive and the men regard it as almost impossible to resist a woman who indicates desire. Copulation, both marital and adulterous, usually takes place in the bush and great care is taken to avoid detection and leave no traces, not so much to elude observation as such, or for fear of an adultery being reported,[6] as because of the danger that a leaf with a drop of secretion or semen might be taken by an observer. Fear of putting one's life in the hands of sorcerers is acute, especially among the young, as is well illustrated by a story told me by a young man. As a boy, he once woke up in the middle of the night with a cry, and, sitting up, saw a man rush from the house while his pubescent unmarried sister was lying with her legs wide apart. The sister claimed that she had just woken up and the boy was convinced that the man had merely been after sorcery material which he had taken from the sleeping girl. When I suggested that she might have been entertaining a clandestine lover he clinched his argument to his own satisfaction by saying that she had died some years later after bearing two children.

It is obvious to the Abelam that only a small proportion of them will have allowed known enemies to acquire directly some of their leavings, and yet everyone dies and sorcery is everywhere. It follows that the material on which the enemy sorcerer works must in many cases have been supplied from within the village where opportunities for securing leavings abound, and where even the greatest care cannot adequately protect. It is relevant to the Abelam's view of his fellow-villagers that in the spirit-villages of the after-life sorcery is absent, not just because there are no enemy villages to harbour sorcery technicians, but because the after-life villages are one-clan villages, instead of multi-clan villages as are those of the living. In the after-life, surrounded by no one but one's own clansmen, one's leavings are safe from the danger of sorcery, at least in theory; in practice, as we shall see, it is unwise to trust all one's clansmen.

Sorcery occurs, then, through a combination of a technician in an enemy village and an evilly disposed person in one's own. The supplier of the leavings is believed to have laid his plans well in advance. In fact an ambitious man should neglect no opportunity of obtaining some leavings of virtually everyone in his own village, and these are believed to be transferred to known sorcerers to be kept in readiness. When the moment comes, the supplier sends a shell ring of high value to the sorcerer, with instructions to kill; the victim must be named since the name is needed for the incantations that form part of the process. However, transactions are rarely as straightforward as that. First, no one ever admits to knowing a sorcerer; occasionally men say that they know another man who knows a sorcerer, but they deny knowing one themselves. Men accused of trafficking in leavings in a specific case always deny it vigorously; men accused of trafficking in general either deny it or remain silent, sometimes with a slight smile, since it does the ambitious man no harm to be thought able to kill if he wishes. Second, it may become known that sorcerers in a certain village have leavings of someone. In such circumstances anyone with a quarrel with that person may send a ring through his contacts in that direction to try to find the right sorcerer and persuade him to kill. There are thus three persons or groups involved in any sorcery case:

A. The sorcerer and his assistants in an enemy village.

B. The supplier of the leavings, usually a member of the victim's village.

C. The man who pays A to kill, who is always someone in close relationship with the victim, if not actually in his village.

B and C may be the same person. In theory, A could perform all the roles, but I have never heard of a case where this was alleged.

Whatever the pattern of events in any particular case, all sorcery must involve intimate and secret contact between individuals in different villages, often enemy villages. It is in this field that the role of the big-man becomes important. Young men and unimportant men may have affines and matrilateral kin in other villages, including enemy villages, but on the whole they make only carefully arranged visits or meet at yam displays or important ceremonial with plenty of people present; they would be reluctant to visit unannounced lest they find themselves in the strange or hostile village without their kin to protect them.

Big-men owe their pre-eminence to their skill in growing long yams, a process in which, apart from technical gardening ability and inherited or acquired spells and incantations, a most important part is played by their access to supplies of magical paint. (The same word *kwus* is used for both yam and sorcery paint, the one being *wapi kwus*, literally long-yam paint, and the other *kabrei kwus*, literally bad paint.) This paint likewise is not a local product and must be obtained from a distance; it travels down 'roads' from its origin, linking at most one or two big-men in each village through which the road passes. These men will be vying in the excellence of their yam production with other big-men in their own villages who obtain paint from different roads. The immediate source of the paint must therefore be kept secret from rivals within the village, who might try to suborn the supplier or interrupt the supply in some way. Thus, growing fine long yams, which is the precondition of prestige and influence within the village and the highest and best point of male aspirations, involves the same secret trafficking in paint, payment for which is also made in shell rings, as does the antisocial death-dealing sorcery. It is the big-men of different villages who exchange long yams with each other, drawing on the best of their group's production to maintain the prestige of their village in exchanges with both enemy and allied villages. Big-men also organize the ceremonial and the assistance that both friendly and hostile villages give; they are the only ones whose interests and contacts transcend, to any considerable extent, the boundaries of the miniscule warring republics that are the individual villages.

DIVINATION

The Abelam have many means of divination, each designed to determine either the sorcerer or the dispute that caused the present action to be taken. They have little confidence in any of them, and even if they all give the same result, which they sometimes do with a little manipulation, it amounts to no more than a strong suspicion. The only form at all commonly used before death has occurred involves half-coconut shells filled with water. Each shell has in it the leaf or grass emblem of one of the clans that is thought likely to have a grudge against the victim or his close kin; hot stones are added until the water boils, and if the water turns red in a shell the clan whose emblem it contains is held responsible.

But on the whole, while the victim is still alive, there is little search for the villain within the village, although general appeals are made. Rather, attention is directed towards finding and buying off the sorcerer himself. Close kin of the afflicted

approach every big-man within the village and important contacts outside it, trying to find one who will accept a large ring,
acceptance implying that the man concerned believes that he
may know others who may know the sorcerer. Should the victim
die, the ring is returned; should he recover, it is retained – but
by whom it is impossible to find out. These sorcery payments,
like the yam paint roads, vanish into mild denials and smiling
silence.

There are, as well, more generalized attempts to persuade the
sorcerer to relent. Symbolic messages are sent, consisting of a
sharpened bamboo to which are attached as many as ten or
twelve pieces of leaf, grass, and such-like. These specify the
clan of the victim and that of his mother, and sometimes give
an indication of the clan of the believed sorcerer; they may include reminders of common phratry membership, or of other
ties between clans and individuals of the two villages, and
symbols of aggression and death as warnings of the consequences
of persisting in the present case of sorcery. A man from the
victim's village with close ties in the accused village will carry
one or more of these, and, walking straight to the centre of the
principal ceremonial ground, will drive the bamboo into the
ground and leave its message there for all to read. The carrier
may make a speech, in which case argument follows, but usually
he walks on and off without a word to or a glance at anybody,
ignoring the inevitable shouted denials that his mission evokes.

After death there is no longer much concern with the identity
of the sorcerer. Attention now focuses on the man who paid to
have the victim killed, or rather, to use the Abelam way of
phrasing it, on the dispute (*pau*) that killed him. While dying,
the victim is eagerly consulted about his last visions or dreams,
but it is at the funeral and afterwards that the truth should be
revealed. I give below a brief summary of some of the most
frequently used methods of divination. There are others, and
not all those listed are always performed. They are described as
for a dead man; if a woman dies, the roles played by the mother's
brothers are played by her real and classificatory brothers.

1. At the first sunset after the death, the victim's mother's
brother's daughter's son calls to the soul, using both personal
names and the kinship term. Some reply, usually a cry, is

listened for; the direction from which it comes indicates the village of the sorcerer.[7]

2. The body is placed in the grave, lying on banana leaves, by the mother's brother and his sub-clan, the mother's brother holding the head. Sections of banana-plant stem are placed between the arms and the body, each standing for one of the disputes considered likely to have been responsible for the death. The grave is covered with a large banana leaf and the mother's brother taps on this leaf asking the dead man to identify the cause of his death. The leaf is removed and the stem sections are examined; if one has moved, that dispute was the cause of death.

3. As the burial party return to the ceremonial ground they are subjected to various cleansing procedures. The last of these is a symbolic washing: a small quantity of water is poured over their hands at the ancestral stones of the victim's clan. The small area of earth wetted by the falling water is marked out, and the first seedling to appear there will be of the species emblematic of the clan of the man who paid for the killing.

4. The man who held the head of the corpse as it was buried observes very strict taboos for three days. His skin is particularly dangerous to himself and others. During this period he has to be fed by others, may not smoke without using a cigarette holder, and so on. At the end of three days he throws away the forked twig he has been carrying, which represents the soul of the deceased, and washes. He is then served a bowl of the finest soup made from the victim's yams by the victim's wife, using all her normal utensils. As he eats he carefully puts on one side any impurities that he finds. These are then examined and interpreted. For example, a sharp splinter is a sago thorn and indicates a dispute over sago; a piece of grit means a dispute over land; yam skin a dispute over yams; a morsel of white substance is pig fat and signifies a dispute over pigs; red or purple paint means a sorcery accusation; and so on. All possible disputes are covered with the sole exception of those over women, which are not considered to be sufficiently serious to involve death.

5. Burial previously took place under the victim's house, but one of the few government innovations that has been whole-heartedly accepted is the graveyard, situated just beyond the houses. The body is placed at the bottom of the grave, three feet or so deep. It is not covered with earth, but split palm planks are put over the grave and the earth is piled on top. When the planks rot the earth drops down and the grave gradually disappears. The new grave is watched until, the Abelam say, a host of flies crawl out of the earth and fly off in a swarm; the direction they take again indicates the village of the sorcerer.

Close kin of the deceased sometimes claim that he has appeared to them in dreams and made veiled or occasionally direct accusations, but there is no form of spirit-mediumship among the Abelam although a recently introduced method of divination had some vogue for a time. This involves asking questions of a ten-foot piece of bamboo which, held by several men, appears to move by itself and is addressed as if it were in some way possessed by the deceased.

It is obvious that all these methods are very susceptible to manipulation, and in the ones intended to discover the dispute that caused the death (2, 3, and 4) only a pre-selected range of disputes are offered as possibilities. In theory, method 3 could point to any clan in the village or region, but it takes some time and, in any case, the seedlings of all the relevant plants look much alike. I have never heard of this method doing more than provide confirmation for a decision already reached. Methods 1 and 5 show the village responsible and are of little concern to the kin of the dead man at the time; this aspect of the death is chiefly of interest to the village as a whole, since even if the dead man was killed through the malice of one of his fellow-villagers, the actual killing was done by enemy technicians and as such was an act of inter-village aggression to be added to the balance-sheet of deaths that villages keep with all their neighbours.[8]

WITCHCRAFT

Witches are always women, who have in their vaginas a little creature (*kwu*) from which they derive their name – *ku-tagwa*

267

(*tagwa*=woman). Men claim to have seen *kwu*, although I never managed to obtain a coherent description of one.

Witches leave behind their sleeping bodies and fly in the night on their evil errands, of which the most important is killing infants. In the Eastern Abelam villages for which I have accurate census data, about half of all live births died within a year or fifteen months, which is the period during which deaths are attributed to witches.[9] The *kwu* would appear to be inactive before puberty, but thereafter is activated by participating with a group of witches in the disinterring and eating of a newly buried baby. Other results of *ku-tagwa* activities are the sickness, death, or running away of pigs; the unexplained breakage or failure of pots or other domestic utensils; and, indeed, almost any disaster in the field of wholly female activities, of which the care of infants and the care of pigs are the most important. Once a child can toddle about and is no longer always with his mother, his death is considered to be an attack on his father, that is sorcery. The Abelam believe that it is impossible to discover witches by divination, and accusations are rarely made. Witchcraft beliefs are therefore irrelevant to political life, and will not be considered here.

It is worth noting in passing that the beliefs, by explaining the enormous rate of infant mortality, reduce the number of deaths attributed to sorcery to about half of all deaths; and that, since women with *kwu* express their aggression directly, and not through an intermediary technician, *ku-tagwa* are believed to operate within the village and not outside it. Witchcraft, too, has its positive side. Formerly, old women believed to be *ku-tagwa* were entrusted with the care of wounded warriors, for which they were paid. They were believed to change themselves into rodents and in this guise they extracted spear splinters from the wounds and licked them clean.

SORCERY AND POLITICS

In the context of inter-village relations, accusations of killing each other's members by sorcery are part of the common coin of discourse, as are attacks by such other magical techniques as causing excessive rain; causing high winds; causing drought; and attacking the ground in which the long yams are planted to neutralize the effects of yam magic. The practice of these techniques has no necessary connection with ability as a sorcerer. Indeed, they are all hostile aspects of arts that are beneficial when used as aids to the magician's own village. To some extent there is a similar duality with regard to sorcery; that is, although, as I have argued, the Abelam know that they have no sorcerers in their own village, they hope and believe that their big-men have access to sorcerers well disposed towards them. A death in an enemy village is just cause for pleasure, especially if it is thought that one's own village had some part in it and that it can be set against the never-balanced score of sorcery deaths. Big-men, and those ambitious to become big-men, sometimes indicate by innuendo that they were involved.

In 1959 a new so-called echo virus was sweeping through the district; it produced high fever, collapse, and an incredible headache usually lasting for three days and leaving the sufferer exhausted but alive. As it approached from the West, reports of people dropping in their tracks came in, and it was widely believed that it would prove fatal. In Bengragum village a certain ambitious and important man, who had not yet the undisputed position of big-man, let it be known that this new form of sorcery paint was in the hands of his associates and that they were already mounting a massive attack on enemy villages to the West. He was immediately much courted; many men and groups came quite casually to discuss with him deaths they had suffered over the past years. At no stage did he make any specific claims, nor in any of the discussions was anything said directly; there was in fact nothing 'actionable' in the whole affair, yet it was quite obvious that he was receiving what amounted to offers of reward if certain revenges were carried out. In the end his plans misfired because the majority of the inhabitants of Bengragum and all other villages, both friend and enemy, suffered from the illness; so did I, and Europeans are believed to be immune to sorcery. But most important was the fact that nobody died from it, which proved that it was not sorcery but an introduced disease like gonorrhoea. The man's ambitions were frustrated, at least for the time being, and when I revisited Bengragum in 1963 he had still not recovered his former influence.

The Abelam believe that their own village's big-men have

access to sorcerers, but they believe that most of the big-men of other villages, both friend and enemy, are sorcerers. Men who encourage, however indirectly, these beliefs sometimes indulge in what amounts to extortion, although such behaviour leads to great hatred and in former times would have resulted in betrayal by bribed associates, and assassination. One such man was feared in half a dozen villages. He was not only a big-man in the traditional system, but also the *luluai* (government headman) of his village, and was thought to be in good favour with the government. He had indeed taken to court several alleged sorcerers from nearby villages, all of whom had been convicted and sentenced to terms in gaol.[10] He employed every possible ramification of the kinship, clanship, and phratry systems to solicit loans of shell rings in a perfectly correct traditional manner, but cast his net much wider than was normal. People were reluctant to refuse him and he was always most effusive about the speed with which he would repay and the obligation under which they would place him. When, however, he was approached for repayment, he tended to reply that he was desolated but at that moment he had no rings at all. If the application was repeated he would suddenly start talking about a recent death and speculating on who could be responsible. Usually the hint was taken and the creditor withdrew. Although he did repay many of his debts eventually, he had certainly managed to acquire many more loans over much longer periods than any other Abelam in the whole of the Eastern part of the tribe.

Although this is an exceptional example, probably only made possible by the temporary situation resulting from contact nullifying the traditional restraints in a particular case, I have included it because it carries to its logical conclusion the association between political influence and sorcery that is present in the traditional system. Abelam society is aggressively egalitarian: there is no form of inherited status; even to be the son of a big-man gives virtually no advantage in the unending battle for prestige. Prestige, and the influence over one's fellows that it confers, come from success in the various highly valued male activities, of which the most important is growing yams longer and better than those of ordinary men. Oratory, courage in battle, knowledge of ceremonial, artistic skill, and a cool and calculating disposition are all aids to prestige, but the ability consistently to produce fine long yams is the *sine qua non* of high status.

Differential yam-growing ability is, as we have seen, attributed almost entirely to access to powerful paint, essentially involving secret contacts with big-men in other villages and transactions in which small quantities of magical substances and valuable shell rings are passed from hand to hand. These transactions are wholly good, and essential if the village and its component groups are to maintain their prestige and exchange obligations. That exactly the same sort of operation is involved in sorcery is not lost on the Abelam; when someone is sick, generalized reproaches are sometimes made: 'You important men, you walk about, who knows where you go? Who knows who you see? Who knows what you do? If you stayed in the village we would not die all the time. You should not kill us.' Nevertheless, it is accepted that big-men are essential for the prestige and welfare of the group and that to function they must have widespread and important contacts outside their village.

A full analysis of Abelam political life cannot be undertaken here, but big-men, who usually have a broader vision and a better understanding of the political system than the ordinary villager, use their external contacts to pursue their ambitions and to thwart their rivals within the village. Their interests lie in the promotion of their faction within the village and among its external supporters, against the rival factions and their external supporters. In public, of course, they maintain the necessary façade of total hostility to enemy villages and suspicion of the intentions of friendly ones, constantly harping in their speeches on the importance of that village unity which many of their actions in fact undermine. After a death, the various divinations conducted under the eye of the big-man of the dead man's faction usually indicate, as the cause of death, an internal dispute with another village faction, and, as the sorcerer's village, one of the enemy villages with whom a rival big-man has close contacts. If direct accusations are made they are soon denied, and counter-accusations start a debate in which all the deaths in the two factions for the last few years are reviewed. During such debates it is often implicitly admitted that deaths in the past were due to sorcery instigated from within the village.

271

Reproaches often take the form of asserting that: 'The balance of kills between us was equal. Why then have you started again pursuing your hatred to the extent of letting the enemy's evil power breach the village defences? Further deaths will follow.' Such debates are always inconclusive, but there is an expectation by the aggrieved party that revenge will be taken and that their big-man should see that it is arranged. When a death occurs in the faction previously accused, the situation is reversed, and so the factional struggle proceeds.

Each death results in a double accusation – of the group who instigated the death and of the village that carried out the sorcery techniques; both accusations are made to further the factional rivalries and political ambitions of big-men. The cumulative effect of such accusations may be to split the village. Such splits have occurred in all villages in the past and sorcery is always the first reason offered for them. It is only by probing that one can obtain information about the more material disputes over land or yams that gave rise to the necessary concentration of accusations.

The alliances and enmities between villages are not fixed, although they change only slowly; again, such a change is heralded by sorcery accusations. Allied villages should not kill each other by sorcery but the possibility is always there. The relations between Bengragum and Wingei, a large village five miles to the North, will serve to illustrate this process. Wingei as a whole should have been an ally. It had many times fought with Bengragum against their bitterest enemy in the North. One of Wingei's main ceremonial grounds was associated with the founders of one of Bengragum's main phratries, and was mentioned by name in their invocations and praise songs. Nevertheless, by 1958 many recent divinations had directed suspicion at this Wingei group as the home of active sorcerers; and in a ceremonial held that year the name of the ceremonial ground was removed from the phratry's liturgy and another substituted. This public ceremonial act was a disastrous defeat for one of the Bengragum big-men whose main external contacts were with the Wingei group most under suspicion, and a corresponding victory for his rivals. By 1963 the defeated big-man had completely retired and the core of his faction was now led by a younger man who had long cultivated contacts with another Wingei group, itself a rival of that accused of harbouring sorcerers.

Abelam sorcery beliefs, then, while setting up a stereotype that all deaths (except of infants) are due to the evil practices of enemies external to the village and to that extent directing aggression outside the group, nevertheless permit the use of accusations as an essential part of factional struggle within the village. There is no way in which anyone can be 'convicted' of sorcery and hence no form of punishment or compensation; revenge is possible only through the use of sorcery. Men of prestige and influence must have external contacts and be adept at secret trafficking with men of power beyond the village, to secure powerful yam paint, to try to buy off sorcerers who attack their followers, and to avenge them after their death. Thus although in the abstract sorcery is wholly evil and the Abelam often long for its disappearance,[11] a man who is innocent of any suspicion of complicity in sorcery will have little influence and no chance of becoming a big-man. Such men exist, and, if they also excel in other male activities, are called *yigen-ndu* (good man). They conform to the stated ideals of Abelam society, but they are never *nema ndu* (big-man), and to be a big-man is the practical ideal towards which virtually every Abelam strives, at least in his youth.

As with witchcraft, sorcery too has its positive, even beneficial, side; neither are to Abelam eyes totally evil and to be abhorred. Sorcery in particular plays an essential part in the political system and the institution of big-men. It is worth noting that the network of ties between big-men that cuts across the village boundaries appears to have operated very successfully to control inter-village fighting, thus reducing the number who 'die by the spear by day' and inevitably increasing those who 'die by the spear by night'.

NOTES

1. For excellent accounts of the Northern Abelam, see Kaberry (1941 and 1965-66). Sorcery beliefs are much the same throughout the area, but the importance of witches appears to be less in the North.

2. I spent nineteen months in 1958-59 in the two Eastern Abelam villages of Bengragum and Wingei, supported by an Emslie Horniman Scholarship of the Royal Anthropological Institute. I am also most grateful to the Bollingen

Foundation who generously financed a further field trip in 1962-63, and to the Wenner-Gren Foundation for assistance between the two trips.

3. Unfortunately there is no space here to consider the implications for Abelam cosmology and classification of this division, or to relate it to their conceptions of male and female. In the South-West of the Abelam area, where the division between the sexes is less strongly emphasized – e.g. there are no menstrual huts where menstruating women are secluded – male witches are believed to exist. They have much the same powers as female, but their interests are different; they commonly manifest themselves as dangerous wild boars.

4. It is also the Plains Arapesh who are believed by the Mountain Arapesh to be powerful sorcerers (Mead, 1939 and 1940). Despite their present sophistication, the Mountain Arapesh, who nowadays live on the coast, still trek right across the mountains seeking to recover the leavings of their sick from the Plains sorcerers. Although the Abelam believe the Arapesh to be manufacturers of powerful sorcery paint, they have no special regard for their ability as sorcerers.

5. 'Hot' and 'cook' are exact translations of the normal Abelam terms; they are also the words used in pidgin English. They refer to the basic Abelam association between power and heat, both in substances and in human beings. A man with heat in his belly is a man to be feared, one who is likely to convert his threats into action. The concept of heat is of course linked with that of fire, as one of the prime creating forces of Abelam society and as a human-controlled source of power over nature and each other. Fire, like every other sacred power source, was originally of female creation. 'Leavings' is used here as a technical term but corresponds with Abelam ideas. The various substances associated with the victim that sorcerers use are usually referred to by their ordinary names: semen, betel wad, cigarette end, etc.

6. To report an adultery is to stir up trouble, in itself an offence. A person who reports an adultery without being very closely related to the cuckolded husband is liable to the same fine as the lover, one large shell ring.

7. The relationship between mother's brother's daughter's son and mother's father's sister's son should be one of brotherhood since they share the same mother's brother, or, more accurately, the elder's mother's brother's son is the mother's brother of the younger, but he will have assumed the role of mother's brother to both at the death of his father. Although they should behave like brothers they are at least potentially rivals for their common mother's brother's services, a rivalry that is given expression in the kinship terms used, the elder being called *mama*, literally enemy, and the younger *bang*, literally a small orange fruit used as a symbol of a killed enemy.

8. Each village keeps two balance-sheets with each of its neighbours, one for deaths by sorcery and the other for deaths by physical violence. Deaths cannot be transferred from one to the other. When important ceremonial is due and it is essential to make peace with the surrounding enemies, it is only for the deaths by violence that equivalence must be achieved either by payment of compensation or occasionally by betrayal. The balance of sorcery deaths is of its very nature uncertain and is never agreed by both sides. Furthermore, responsibility for sorcery deaths is sometimes transferred years after they have occurred, ostensibly because of new evidence, but always in accord with the changing political situation.

9. This very heavy infant mortality is mainly due to malaria (see Peters, 1960, and Schofield & Parkinson, 1963). Residual spraying of DDT by Malaria

Control had started to take effect in 1963 but as yet the declining infant mortality had had no influence on *ku-tagwa* beliefs.

10. The Australian Administration sentenced alleged sorcerers if they were convicted of the possession of sorcery working materials. Since every Abelam man has little bundles wrapped in leaves stored in his house thatch and the administrators had to rely exclusively on local evidence as to what was sorcery material, unscrupulous native officials could fairly easily obtain convictions.

11. Although the Northern and Eastern Abelam have on the whole resisted cargo cults, they find the cargo prophets' promise of an end to sorcery at least as attractive as they find the promise of the cargo itself. Many Abelam complained to me that although the Europeans were themselves immune to sorcery they had neither wiped it out nor passed on their immunity.

REFERENCES

EVANS-PRITCHARD, E. E. 1937. *Witchcraft, Oracles and Magic among the Azande*. Oxford: Clarendon Press.

FORGE, A. 1962. Paint – A Magical Substance. *Palette*, No. 9.

—— 1970. Learning to See in New Guinea. In P. Mayer (ed.), *Socialization: The Approach from Social Anthropology*. A.S.A. Monograph 8. London: Tavistock Publications.

KABERRY, P. M. 1941. The Abelam Tribe, Sepik District, New Guinea. A Preliminary Report. *Oceania* **11**.

—— 1965-66. The Political Organization among the Northern Abelam. *Anthropological Forum* **1** (3-4).

MALINOWSKI, B. 1922. *Argonauts of the Western Pacific*. London: Routledge.

MEAD, M. 1939. The Mountain Arapesh – An Importing Culture. *Anthropological Papers of the American Museum of Natural History* **36**.

—— 1940. The Mountain Arapesh – Supernaturalism. *Anthropological Papers of the American Museum of Natural History* **37**.

PETERS, W. 1960. Studies on the Epidemiology of Malaria in New Guinea. *Transactions of the Royal Society of Tropical Medicine and Hygiene* **54**.

SCHOFIELD, F. D. & PARKINSON, A. D. 1963. Social Medicine in New Guinea: Beliefs and Practices affecting Health among the Abelam and Wam Peoples of the Sepik District. *Medical Journal of Australia* **1**.

© Anthony Forge 1970

PART IV

Alternative Interpretations of Misfortune

13

Godfrey Lienhardt

The Situation of Death
An Aspect of Anuak Philosophy

I here record something of what the Anuak[1] told me about the
dying and the dead. In order to bring out more clearly some
characteristics of Anuak thought, I have also referred to two
other closely related Nilotic peoples, the Dinka, whom I had
visited earlier, and the Nuer, known through the writings of Professor Evans-Pritchard, who in addition knew the Anuak well
and gave the first full account of them (1940). But these references to Dinka-Nuer[2] are primarily for descriptive convenience:
a more rewarding analytic comparison would require fuller and
more systematic presentation.

Differences between Anuak on the one hand and Dinka-Nuer
on the other, which bear upon what follows, are three, and they
seem to me to be connected:

1. The Anuak are basically agricultural and sedentary, living
in many distinct, largely self-sufficient and often very crowded
village communities, where they are in constant and intense
individual contact. The Dinka-Nuer are first and foremost
pastoral peoples, necessarily transhumant, with regular dispersal and regrouping of members of local communities. In the
nature of their occupation, the Dinka-Nuer individually live
more solitary lives than do the Anuak.

2. The frequent dispersal of the Dinka-Nuer as compared with
the concentration of the Anuak may be associated with a much
greater interest shown by the Anuak in individuals and personalities. They have an extensive psychological vocabulary, and
their village politics, as I have elsewhere (1958) shown, are
conducted through an interplay of character as well as of
faction. Anuak are interested in people, Dinka-Nuer more interested in cattle. For the Anuak, this lively interest is a
practical necessity in the conduct of their village affairs, with

their frequent plots for the promotion of sectional and individual interests in the headmanship. Dinka-Nuer belong to the uncentralized type of African political society: there are no courts where individuals might seek special favour and support from influential men of rank. Anuak nobles and headmen, though often without any judicial or political control over their people, nevertheless have great prestige and are treated with outward deference. Not that the importance of men of rank prevents Anuak from being individually extremely independent. Rather, it permits any ambitious individual a wider scope for political activity than could be achieved by most Dinka-Nuer, who are dependent on their lineage kin, and for whom large agnatic groups provide the only organizing principle of collective action.[3] An Anuak who feels himself slighted by a particular headman will eventually find those with whom to combine in an attempt to replace him, or can go to seek favour at a noble's court. The Anuak have institutions based on favouritism, and competitiveness for favour, which could not develop among the Dinka-Nuer, who have no individuals of rank that it would be profitable to cultivate.

3. Anuak recognize a transcendent Divinity associated with the sky, and various Powers or spirits connected with particular rocks, trees, stretches of river, etc., but there are no sacrificial cults either of the Supreme Divinity or of the Powers. Compared with the Divinity of Dinka-Nuer, the Anuak Divinity is otiose. Dinka-Nuer have little ceremonial, but considerable religious ritual in sacrificial cults; Anuak have much ceremonial at the courts of headmen and nobles, but little religious ritual. Anuak have produced headmen and nobles, but no significant priests or prophets; Dinka-Nuer have produced priests and prophets, but no secular nobility.

The Dinka, and, according to Professor Evans-Pritchard, the Nuer also, can scarcely be persuaded to talk of death. The Anuak talk freely of the situation and importance of the dead and the dying. Differences between Dinka-Nuer and Anuak in this respect seem to be expressed even in details of behaviour. I never saw a burial in Anuakland, but was told that the mourners there faced the grave while covering the corpse with earth. Dinka-Nuer crouch with their backs to the grave and push in the earth without glancing behind. The Anuaks' interest in death is not so much in what happens to people after death – in supposed 'spirit worlds' or in other eschatological speculation; like most Nilotes I have met, they tend to be sceptical and indifferent about such matters.[4] Their interest is in presentiments of death and in the dispositions of the dying as they affect the survivors after death. This is not accompanied by any developed ancestor cult (nor do the Dinka-Nuer have such a cult) though offerings of beer are made at the graves of the fairly recently dead. Graves (except those of some nobles) are obliterated after a period of two years or so.

There are certain well-known signs (*gawado thou*) by which Anuak think themselves to be reminded and warned of the possibility of death. Those presentiments given to me as common were: consistent failure in hunting and fishing; persistent tiredness or inertia; the appearance of certain birds in the homestead, particularly the owl, which, according to the Anuak, cries *tudo yi bur*, 'draws into the grave'; to find oneself often sitting with one's hands on one's head, which for the Anuak is an attitude of dejection; for lice to leave a man's clothing;[5] and (significant in the light of beliefs about the dog, later discussed) to be avoided by dogs. As is to be expected, presentiments of the deaths of nobles, and their effects, are believed to be more cosmically important than those of others. Extensive floods, plagues of rats or other vermin, torrential rains, shooting stars or comets, and a special kind of thunder (particularly in the afternoon), are omens of nobles' deaths.

With this kind of interest in whether death is approaching, it may be rightly inferred that the Anuak are concerned with anticipating death when it must occur. A preparedness for death is an essential part not only of their philosophy, but also of the system by which inheritance, both of tradition and of material possessions, is assured. More difficulties arise among the Anuak when a man dies without having prepared himself than would arise among the Dinka-Nuer. Anuak possessions include such objects as rifles and strings of beads, which can be held more or less outright by only one individual and cannot be equally shared. A man's testamentary bequests may thus involve choosing particular members of his family to be given particular objects of value. The Dinka-Nuer, with their wealth mostly in cattle, are faced with this problem less often since the herd is a collective responsibility which, for practical reasons alone, could not be split up at a man's death even were he to wish to further the interests of one son at the expense of the others.

The Anuak myth of how death came into the world, and stories ancillary to it, show a marked contrast with Dinka-Nuer attitudes, closely related as all these peoples are both ethnically and linguistically. Dinka-Nuer, in rather different ways, account for the presence of death by myths which represent an original unity of Man and Divinity, earth and sky, severed by an act for which human beings (at least among the Dinka) were morally responsible. Divinity was originally kind to men and near to them. But the Anuak story represents the first man and woman, sometimes said to have been twins, as having been 'born' of Divinity, who when he had borne them disliked them and told Dog to cast them away. (The Anuak may also use the equivalent of the word 'create' in this context, but 'born' (*nyiwol*) is more common. Dinka-Nuer could never use any word except that signifying creation, or making.) Dog instead looked after them, and gave them to Cow to suckle. Divinity saw them again when they had grown up and (in some versions) decided to tolerate them; more usually, he still disliked them, and said that they should be the creatures of Dog and not the creatures of Divinity. Through Anuak animal stories there runs the theme of the preference felt by Divinity for the animals of the wild, and in some cases it is by Dog's cunning that human beings, and not wild animals, as Divinity first intended, get their cultural possessions. So, for example, spears were originally intended for Buffalo, but Dog obtained them for Man by a Jacob-like ruse of imitating Buffalo's voice.

Another connected story is that Divinity planned to throw a stone into the river, so that men should die. Dog, who had a superior instinctive wisdom (hence the point of a dog's turning away from a man as a presentiment of death), urged Man to look after the cattle on that day, and let him listen to Divinity's words. Man refused, so the stone was thrown into the river. Dog tried to persuade Man to pull it out, but Man would not do so. Dog therefore tried by himself, and returned with a small piece of the stone only. This piece represents the small span of life that Dog saved for Man.[6] So the Anuak story implies that Divinity wills the death of men, and with this background of myth it is not surprising that Anuak, unlike Dinka-Nuer, do not conspicuously turn to their Divinity in situations of suffering and misfortune.

Ancillary to the stories summarized is another, unlike anything reported from the Dinka-Nuer, which explains why the white (or red) men are more prosperous than the Anuak. Here is a modified form of a text:

The white men and the black men and all people were all created at one time. Divinity gave the Anuak to a Dog. Divinity became sick, and said to the black people, 'Give me a skin to be laid in when I die.' The black people said, 'But what can we do with a person who is going to die just now?' (that is, what is the use of bothering about a dying person?)

Divinity pleaded with the black men, but they were adamant.

And Divinity said, 'Go from me, for you have refused me this.' And all the people were dressed in skins, both Anuak and white men. Divinity said, 'You ugly, bad white people, give me a skin.' They did so. Divinity said, 'Good my son, you gave me a skin for death that I will die on.' He said to the black people, 'You did not give me a skin for death, so you shall be poor all your lives. And that skin you would not give me, you will buy now from my white son. You belong to the Dog.'

Divinity's dying wish (*gwith*) to white men was that they should travel on the river in boats, and in the air. That is why white people have received everything, because it was Divinity's dying wish. The Anuak were left with the haunting of the dead (*acyeni*).[7]

There are other contexts in which it is clear that the Anuak do not think of Divinity as having died; but that for the purposes of this story they are able to entertain such a notion shows how significant for them the situation of death is. There is nothing in Dinka-Nuer belief, it seems, that compares with the Anuak preparedness here to subordinate the attributes of Divinity to the importance of the situation of death. Divinity is here said to be dying in order to convey the absolute and irrevocable nature of his wishes.

L   283

Anuak, then, attach very great value to the words and intentions of the dying. I was told that at his death 'a man was as he really was',[8] revealing his quintessential character and defining his real wishes. Consequently these wishes are to be scrupulously respected and are thought to act powerfully on the survivors.

What men solemnly desire for others is called in Anuak *gwith*,[9] and what a man wishes when dying is the strongest form of *gwith*. It may have the significance of blessing or cursing, but I think is more usually associated with blessing. Older men among the Anuak often wear considerable numbers of small pieces of wood and objects sewn in little leather pouches, which resemble charms or amulets. They are called *jap dhok*, 'thing of the mouth', and each represents what might be called an intention of some other person, often a dead person. These 'things of the mouth' are worn by nobles and chiefs, especially by nobles, as memorials to friends or relations who are dead, and whose good wishes, which the amulets represent, are regarded as a support in the difficulties of life. To take an example, a man may wear pieces of a particular kind of wood because his father used such wood in a fence for his tobacco garden, and cultivated a very good crop. At his death he wishes that his son should be equally successful. Another example would be the wearing of a bit of bark from a tree under which an older man had sat in the shade and enjoyed good conversation. He hopes that his children will also share and remember this happiness when he asks them to carry with them a bit of this bark.

People, then, will for others the gifts and good fortune they themselves have enjoyed, or would have wished for, in life. Parents wish their children to be successful in the pursuits in which they have been successful, and a *gwith* is often made with reference to some game that a man has killed: 'As I killed that buffalo, so may so-and-so happen for you', for example. The handing on of the *gwith* of the dying is a means of passing on a tradition, and, more important practically, an inheritance, in an atmosphere which is emotionally highly charged.

This interpretation is reinforced by a custom which in this form of elaboration is, as far as I know, confined, among all the Nilotes, to the Anuak.[10] When a man feels himself to be dying or to be in danger of death – if he is setting out on a journey, for example – he calls to him his closest friend of about his own age and speaks a testament to him. This testament is repeated over and over again and rehearsed until, in theory at least, the exact words are remembered. It then remains the secret of the testator and his friend.[11] When the man has died, and some time after the burial, his kinsmen brew beer and they and his friends assemble at his home. Then the spokesman, who has fasted for a day before, solemnly speaks the testament before the assembled company.

I attended two of these ceremonies, the first unfortunately too early in my stay in Anuakland to enable me to get more than the gist of what was being said, and the second by chance in a village I was merely passing through, where many local references escaped me and where I arrived after proceedings had got under way. Nevertheless, I saw and heard enough to confirm what I had been told happened in such circumstances.

For a visitor as, conspicuously, for the Anuak, the ceremony has a deep pathos, and, in those I saw, the sad demeanour of those present contrasted strikingly with the Anuaks' usual jocularity and ebullience at a beer party. The friend of the dead man enters the hut in which he had died as though to speak with him, and, after a period spent in imaginary communication, appears before the assembled people, who are sitting around him, and *in the first person* speaks the testament of the deceased. The effect, then, is as if the dead man were himself speaking from the grave. In the first ceremony I saw, the spokesman trembled with emotion (I was told he was weak from fasting) as he conveyed the hopes of the dead man for the wellbeing of his survivors, and announced the distribution of his property. If any of the potential legatees were disappointed, they did not show it. In the second ceremony, it was a woman who had died, and a woman therefore who spoke her testament. With the help of my great friend Obala wi Nyigwo, I was able to jot down after the speeches a fairly accurate representation of some of what was said. The deceased was a poor woman who had little of significance to bequeath, and such as she had had been distributed before the ceremony. Part of the spokeswoman's address went as follows:

And now I am grieved because my men children all died, and I die now without a living male child left; but you shall all

285

bear children as numerous as the fruits of the *dipok* tree. No one of you shall be barren.

(The gathering was aspersed with water in which leaves of this tree had been infused.)

I started to make pots when I was a very little girl, and my mother broke them (i.e. if they were not satisfactory). When I decorated my pots, I started by using the jawbone of the olwak fish. And there was nothing that I was unable to make. I made winnowing trays, and beer-mats (for covering beer-pots), and the large beer-jar. And now Akonya, my daughter, I tell you my daughter that you should not agree to settle in the land of the nobles. What I say is so.

(Anuakland is divided into the land ruled over by village headmen (*po kweri*) and the land of the nobles (*po nyiye*), which, owing to the fierceness of dynastic rivalries and the inaccessibility of any administrative or medical services, is considered much more dangerous.)

And the one person who is left to us (she refers to her daughter's son, the child of a noble) shall grow in strength, and when he is grown, bring him here to live with his mother's brother's people. I do not agree that he should stay in the land of the nobles. But you must decide, my daughter. It was not my wish that you should be married by a noble. And now, my kinsfolk, I die without a son left outside upon the earth.[12] It is good, for now none of you again shall die without a son. That has been ended with me. And I die poor, but it is well that I should give you something you will remember me by. You will drink *otango* (an infusion of leaves) and water in which the *dipok* fruits have been placed, so you may always be in health. And may people never say that I cursed you, nor did you curse me. I was not killed by you, I was killed by God who made me die without a son.

I hope it will be felt, from the spirit of this text, how it is that a testament is not lightly disregarded. In fact, Anuak families, with the kind of heritable property that cannot easily be shared equally, and the frequent rivalries of children for their parents' regard, would be likely to pass through a most contentious if not destructive period on the death of the father were it not for the incontestability of a man's words spoken from the grave. From there his *gwith* prolongs his influence, as may be seen from a recorded case of refusal to speak a last testament. Mr Grover, at one time District Commissioner in Akobo, thus reported on the background to a dynastic murder in the noble house.

> The reason for the murder appears to be an old case of grievance. When Cam war Akwai died, he left no 'will' or last-minute instructions about the disposal of the emblems[13] and his other property and wives. He was displeased with all his half-brothers so he died intestate to spite them. Normally a dying king will summon two or three trusted old men and give them his dying instructions about the emblems (if he has them) and his property and wives, and will tell them about the various cases he has on his hands. About fifteen days after his death, the old men will read (it should be 'speak') the will before the assembled people. In this case there was no will and Gila and Abula quarrelled and could reach no agreement or compromise over Cam's property. Eventually Abula, not having a big enough following to take over the emblems and property by force, fled away disgruntled.

From this followed a history of murders and eventually banditry, ending when the Abula mentioned above, having given himself up, was judicially hanged in Malakal. And here again, as I am told by my friend Mr Karrar Ahmed Karrar, also once District Commissioner in Akobo, the last testament produced difficulties. Abula's will was dictated and certified in Malakal before he met his death but (unlike such testaments generally) was contested on the grounds that it had not been memorized and declared to the public in the solemn traditional manner.

So far, the force of the beneficent intentions of the dying has on the whole been emphasized; but at least equally important for the Anuak is the strength of their curses. Already in one text (p. 283 above) it has been mentioned that the Anuak were given by Divinity *acyeni*, haunting by the dead, as though the Anuak themselves regarded this ghostly vengeance as specially characteristic of their people, and again in the woman's testament I have quoted she insists that she has not left a curse behind her, nor does she think that her death is the result of curses. To the significance of these beliefs I now turn.

The haunting vengeance of the dead, in Anuak *acyeni*, seems to be known in some form, and by some form of that name, in most Nilotic societies. It certainly occurs among the Dinka-Nuer where, however, it plays a much smaller role proportionately to the total set of religious and philosophical conceptions than among the Anuak. In various ways (including by a brief invasion) Nuer cultural influence has probably increased in Anuakland during the last eighty years. There are now several Nuer sky-spirits in the country, to which, along with *acyeni*, sickness and death may be attributed; but Anuak say that they originally had no such spirits. It was *acyeni* alone that killed them. It may be that the extent to which foreign spirits have been replacing *acyeni* as an explanation of suffering and death is a measure of the extent to which Nuer values have entered into the exclusive Anuak village communities and their hitherto inward-looking world.

The symptoms of *acyeni*, by which a man concludes that he is cursed and haunted by someone who has borne a grudge against him to the grave, are several. A man may wander off into the forest and never return, or his blood may become 'like water', or he may be suddenly struck by acute pains in the head, or, most commonly, sharp pains are felt moving from one part of the body to another. Mr Elliot-Smith has told me that from his experience the accounts of *acyeni* he received from Anuak strongly resemble the effects of rheumatism or arthritis. These physical symptoms are of course indicative of a moral condition. To attribute suffering to the haunting vengeance of the dead is to have a guilty conscience, since *acyeni* is an ultimate retribution for some evil that the victim thinks he must have done. As long as they have a lively memory of the dead, the Anuak are permanently fixed in that relationship to them which their dying intentions define, and the greater the number of people a man knows himself to have offended, the greater his danger of being haunted. The more hatred and malice there are in a community, the more prevalent is *acyeni*. Hence the nobles, rivals who in the nature of Anuak politics must frequently kill one another, or did so in the past, are thought to be more prone to die of *acyeni* than are others, and the land of the nobles has a reputation for the prevalence of this cause of death. It is said also that in the past suspicious village headmen might send observers to the deathbeds of their people in order to discover whether or not they had been cursed.

Though *acyeni* involves a moral assessment of human relations, it is recognized by pronounced physical symptoms, as I have described, and is treated by diviners in a markedly physical way. The Anuak do not sacrifice much, nor have they a sacrificing priesthood, as do the Dinka-Nuer, whose action when sickness overtakes them tends to be to sacrifice and pray for help. The only religious expert among the Anuak is the *ajuaa*, a person – most usually a woman – whose main traditional tasks were to find witches and deal with witchcraft, and to try to remove *acyeni* from its victims. The *ajuaa* combines the role of diviner and doctor, and gives both physical and what we should call psychological treatment. I never saw a full-scale seance for the removal of *acyeni*, but Professor Evans-Pritchard has described one and his account (1953) was confirmed by everything I heard. The doctor appears to pluck the *acyeni* from the victim, transfer it to herself, and rush with it towards a fire into which it is thrown. The Anuak told me that in minor cases of *acyeni* (which in their effects resemble fits or hysteria) the task of the doctor is to hold on to the *acyeni* (which of course has no material form) and try to hold it until she can cast it into a fire. Consequently, a doctor makes all the gestures of wrestling and struggling with the cause of the patient's sickness, and the more convincing the appearance of struggle the more vivid the sense of having the haunting removed. I do not doubt that Divinity could be invoked or referred to in a dying curse as in a dying blessing, but from the direction of Anuak interest it seems that what is significant in the dying curse, as in the blessing, is the direct effect of the dying upon the living.

It will have been apparent that, in contrasting Anuak with Dinka-Nuer beliefs, what we have been examining is a difference of emphasis in the explanation of fortune, good or bad, in the treatment of and approach to suffering and death. To put the contrast somewhat boldly: Dinka-Nuer ideas of moral causation are God-oriented, those of the Anuak man-oriented, and I have suggested some of the ecological, political, mythological, and legal differences congruent with this striking contrast between the philosophies of these related peoples.

Godfrey Lienhardt

NOTES

1. I made two trips to Anuakland, on the southern borders of the Sudan and Ethiopia, and spent altogether something over a year there during the period 1952-54. My work was financed by a Research Fellowship of the International African Institute, created with funds originally made available by UNESCO for the study of African cosmologies. I am grateful to the Institute and its Director Professor C. Daryll Forde, and also to the Warden and Fellows of All Souls College, Oxford, for their generous help.

2. The Dinka and the Nuer differ from each other in many respects, but in the matters here touched on they are similar, and I link their names together for simplicity of expression.

3. With few exceptions of prophets or other outstanding men.

4. The following is an outline of a conversation with a witty, elderly Anuak, Didimo:

> *Didimo:* What do you think happens after you have died?
> (I gave a brief account of Christian belief.)
> *Didimo:* All lies! Nobody knows where the dead are, they have not seen them.
> *I:* But you believe England exists and you have not seen it.
> *Didimo:* No, but I have seen people who come from there, and I have never seen even my dead mother again.

5. Anuak say this, but I never saw lice in their country.

6. Longer versions of these and other stories are given in E. E. Evans-Pritchard & A. C. Beaton, 'Folk Stories of the Sudan', I, 1940.

7. This is explained later.

8. After collecting this information, by coincidence I read, in Anuakland, Wordsworth's 'Prelude', where the following lines seem curiously linked with Anuak thought:

> ... *They whom death has hidden from our sight*
> *Are worthiest of the mind's regard; with these*
> *The future cannot contradict the past:*
> *Mortality's last exercise and proof*
> *Is undergone, the transit made that shows*
> *The very soul revealed as she departs* ...

9. I was told that a *gwith* that someone should eventually return home to Anuakland would 'burrow like an ant-eater into the heart'.

10. There may be some influence of Ethiopian custom here, as there is in other features of Anuak culture. (I have since heard of something similar among the Shilluk and the Luo of Kenya. G. L., 1970.)

11. I do not know if a relation would be acceptable. In the logic of the situation it seems unlikely that a close relation, with a personal interest in the distribution of the inheritance, would be a very suitable person.

12. The dead woman sees herself already in the grave, with the survivors above and outside it. It was a very touching moment and there was a good deal of quiet weeping.

13. The most important royal emblems are old necklaces, with which the sons of nobles are invested to give them the right to pass on nobility to their sons.

ACKNOWLEDGEMENT

Dr Lienhardt's paper, 'The Situation of Death: An Aspect of Anuak Philosophy', is reprinted, by kind permission of the Editors, from the *Anthropological Quarterly*, Vol. 35, No. 2, 1962.

REFERENCES

EVANS-PRITCHARD, E. E. 1940. *The Political System of the Anuak of the Anglo-Egyptian Sudan.* London School of Economics Monographs on Social Anthropology 4. London: Lund.
—— 1953. A Note on Ghostly Vengeance among the Anuak of the Anglo-Egyptian Sudan. *Man* 53.
EVANS-PRITCHARD, E. E. & BEATON, A. C. 1940. Folk Stories of the Sudan I. *Sudan, Notes and Records* **23** (1).
LIENHARDT, G. 1958. Anuak Village Headmen. *Africa* **28** (1): 23-36.

© Godfrey Lienhardt 1970

14

I. M. Lewis

A Structural Approach to Witchcraft and Spirit-possession

INTRODUCTION

It has long been recognized that unsolicited possession by malevolent, capricious spirits may serve as an explanation of illness and affliction in much the same fashion as witchcraft and sorcery. But, whereas a substantial body of anthropological research amply demonstrates how accusations of witchcraft reflect social tensions, recognition that a corresponding nexus also exists in the case of possession by such spirits is still something of a novelty. After certain necessary preliminaries, this paper illustrates by way of a few selected ethnographic examples how what I shall call 'peripheral' spirit-possession does relate to situations of stress and conflict. It then ventures into a wider discussion of the possible structural correlates of witchcraft on the one hand, and of spirit-possession on the other.

I shall argue that the most significant distinction between these two phenomena is not the obvious cultural one, but the manner in which they operate and are utilized. The victim of affliction who attributes his difficulties to witchcraft is employing a direct strategy which assigns responsibility for his troubles to a rival or enemy. On the other hand, the victim who interprets his affliction in terms of possession by malevolent spirits utilizes an oblique strategy in which immediate responsibility is pinned, not on his fellow-men, but upon mysterious forces outside society.[1] Here it is only indirectly that pressure is brought to bear by the victim on the real targets that he seeks to influence. It is in the reaction of other members of his society to an affliction, for which the victim is not himself accountable, that a measure of redress is achieved. From the standpoint of the victim of affliction, the effect may be broadly similar inasmuch as in both strategies he becomes the centre of attention and succour. But the fact that the means of achieving this end differ in the two cases, and have different effects on other members of society, suggests that one strategy might be more appropriate to a given set of social circumstances than the other. This suggests that there should in fact be distinct social correlates of each strategy; and, as I hope to show, I think that this is to a certain extent empirically true.

Let me first explain, however, what I mean by the expression 'peripheral possession'. I have in mind two aspects of peripherality. First, the spirits with which we are here concerned are themselves peripheral in the sense that they are not morally charged powers held to be responsible for upholding public morality by rewarding meritorious acts and punishing sins. On the contrary, they have no direct moral responsibility and are quite separate from other spirits which may be invoked as the guardians of customary morality. Thus they stand apart from the central morality cults of the societies in which they cause such wanton affliction, and, indeed, are regularly believed to be of foreign origin and provenance. Sometimes they are conceived of as the spirits of hostile neighbouring peoples and, perhaps equally frequently, as mischievous nature spirits totally outside society and culture.

Second, contrary to the arbitrary and capricious qualities with which they are credited, these spirits are in fact often mobilized in particular social contexts which can be charted and specified with at least as much clarity and predictability as in the case of witchcraft accusations. One of the most obvious and widespread of these is the marked predilection which such spirits regularly show for women in general, and, on a more restricted front, for certain depressed and despised categories of men, as well as for individuals of either sex in circumstances of unusually severe social disability (cf. Lewis, 1966; Wilson, 1967).

Since, however, particularly when they belong to low-status or low-caste groups, men may also be involved, the high incidence of possession in women cannot very plausibly be ascribed to any inherent biological predisposition on their part. On the contrary, the facts here point to a common denominator of deprivation, frustration, and discontent. This conclusion is moreover fully supported by an examination of the treatment or response given to the victims of these spirit maladies. What clearly emerges is the special consideration, privileges, and unusually exalted status accorded to women who in other circumstances are treated as legal minors, or to men in subordinate positions who are normally subject to strong discrimination.

For those who fall in such 'peripheral' social categories, as well as for abnormally hard-pressed and precariously placed individuals, such possession has much to offer as a response to affliction where its treatment leads to the enhancement, even if only temporarily, of position and status. To demonstrate this function of peripheral possession is not, of course, to offer a total explanation of the existence of the phenomenon. Nor does it rule out the possibility that other functions may also be served concurrently, or separately, by what some writers have called the possession syndrome.

TYPICAL EXAMPLES OF PERIPHERAL POSSESSION

These points can best be documented by reference to a few ethnographic examples. Consider, first, the BaVenda of Southern Africa as described by Stayt (1931). Among the BaVenda there is a central morality cult of patrilineal and matrilateral ancestors. However, Stayt also records that from 1914 onwards there has been an upsurge of new, non-ancestral spirits which are identified as having come from neighbouring Shona tribes. These invasive powers (*tshilombo*) which possess women, causing them to speak in Chi-Karanga, or in a mixture of that language and Venda, provide a clear example of what I mean by peripheral spirits. They are above all mischievous, causing illness, and usually live in the crevices of trees where they make weird, unnatural noises (Stayt, 1931, p. 302). Their presence in sick married women whom they regularly torment is diagnosed by doctors (*nganga*). Following diagnosis, the husband quickly summons help, especially from his wife's kin, and calls in the services of a drummer who knows the spirit-dance beat (*molombo*) and of a rattle-diviner (a female shaman). The patient, who is plied with medicines, eventually responds to the music and dances wildly until she falls on the ground. After repeated periods of dancing and resting, the spirit eventually reveals itself by a deep bull-like grunt from the patient who is now questioned by the rattle-diviner shaman. The spirit usually replies in some such terms as follows: 'I am so and so, and I

295

entered you when I was walking in a certain place; you did not treat me well; I want a present, some clothes or ornaments.' She may, adds Stayt, even demand such symbols of male authority as a spear or axe of her ancestors, or a tail-whisk or kerrie stick, as well as the brightly coloured clothes favoured by the spirits. All the objects demanded are readily promised by the husband and relations of the afflicted woman. Her husband also provides a goat for his wife to feast on, and pays for the diviner's services. All these gifts are offered indirectly to the woman through her invasive familiar, who is exhorted to take them and permit the patient to recover.

Such relief, however, is only temporary. Following her first possession, a married woman regularly succumbs at times of difficulty and distress to further attacks of possession and, when seized by the spirit, dons her special clothes and dances the *molombo* beat. She is in fact now a novitiate member of a coterie of recurrently possessed women and may in time graduate to the position of female rattle-diviner, or shaman, who is a mistress of spirits. Whenever she is possessed, her husband and relatives must treat her with respect and consideration, saluting her 'as if she were a chief'. Her husband, in turn, is addressed as 'grandchild'. And, of course, each new attack of possession involves further outlays of gifts and food by the husband. It is therefore perhaps not surprising to learn that, after the departure of the spirit following such an attack, the woman often becomes very fat (Stayt, 1931, p. 305)!

It is obvious that what is involved here, if not a mystically couched feminist movement, is a culturally accepted procedure whereby down-trodden wives in this male-dominated society press their claims for attention and regard from their menfolk. Individual cases of possession are responses to situations of stress or discontent where more direct methods of ventilating grievances are blocked or not available. The formal ideology of male dominance is maintained in this society where divorce is rare and allowed only in very special circumstances (see below).

This aspect of the situation emerges clearly in a case cited by Stayt (pp. 306-307). Here the victim was not a married woman, but a girl betrothed against her will to a man she did not like, such arranged marriages being the norm. In this instance, after being taken unwillingly to her betrothed's village, she bolted home. There her father beat her soundly and she ran off into the bush and disappeared completely for six days. After this she returned looking very ill and complaining bitterly. Her father sent for a doctor who diagnosed that the reluctant bride was possessed by a spirit. That night the girl rose and commanded her father to follow her. He protested but, since she spoke in a strange Chi-Karanga spirit-voice, he was afraid of her and obeyed. It is hardly necessary to follow this account further here, except to say that this was the beginning of this girl's career as a mistress of spirits. By the time Stayt arrived, he found that this woman had become one of the most famous rattle-diviners and shamans in Vendaland.

I do not need to labour the point I am making about the use made by women of these spirits, but I want now to refer briefly to the Gurage of Ethiopia to show how the locus of spirit-possession may be widened to include men in subordinate social categories. The Gurage have a main morality cult centring on a male God (*waka*) who is worshipped by men as the upholder of social values and general morality. This cult does not involve possession. They also have, however, a cult centring on a female deity (*damwamwit*) who is worshipped by and possesses all free-born women and all men of the despised Fuga carpenter class. Participation by women or Fuga men in the calendrical rites addressed to this spirit, or possession by her in times of particular distress or affliction, enables both to behave and to be treated as though they were noble Gurage males (Shack, 1966). Again, despite its at least initial association with illness and its continuing connection with distress and discontent, the advantages of possession are obvious. And in the case of the Fuga, possession-involvement in the cult evidently represents a sort of mystical neutralization of revolutionary tendencies, much in the same manner as Luc de Heusch has suggested applies with Hutu participation in the *kubandwa* possession-cult in Rwanda (de Heusch, 1966, pp. 158ff.).

A similar content seems to have been present in the nineteenth-century Fijian water-baby cult, which presaged the later cargo cults of the region and which, in its nomenclature at least, is also in some respects a precursor of our contemporary 'flower people'. Here young people and minor chiefs excluded from high positions in the traditional power structure rallied together to join the water-baby cult, being possessed by forest- and water-sprites, and taking new personal names – usually those of flowers (Worsley, 1957, pp. 26-27).

As a final illustration I refer to M. E. Opler's richly documented analysis of spirit-possession in Northern India (Opler, 1958). Here, in Uttar Pradesh, disaffiliated malevolent spirits, or ghosts, haunt the weak and vulnerable and those whose social circumstances are precarious. Thus the young married woman 'beset by homesickness, fearful that she may not be able to present sons to her husband and his family, may label her woes a form of ghost possession'. And, 'if she has been ignored and subordinated, the spirit possession may take an even more dramatic and strident form as a compensation for the obscurity under which she has laboured' (Opler, op. cit., p. 565). Equally, people of low caste express their aggression towards the higher castes to which they are subordinated through possessing spirits which allow them to insult and castigate their superiors. Those of high caste, in turn, tend to be 'persecuted by large, dark, low-caste spirits'. And, most interestingly, in the troubled period following Partition, 'the ghosts of deceased Muslims were exceedingly active in persecuting Hindus' (Opler, op. cit., p. 566).

PERIPHERAL POSSESSION AND WITCHCRAFT

These examples show clearly how the incidence of possession by peripheral spirits relates to social tensions, particularly between subordinate and superior. The parallel with witchcraft and sorcery accusations is obvious. It remains to explore the distinctions that were noted earlier between these phenomena as, respectively, oblique and direct redressive mystical strategies. Perhaps before we attempt this, however, we should dispose of the prior question: If spirit-possession and witchcraft (or sorcery) both reflect tensions, albeit in different ways, are they mutually exclusive? For those who approach the question from the cosmological angle, the answer usually given is: Yes. Thus, in his paper on Nuba shamanism, Nadel says: 'The Nyima have no witchcraft. Shamanism absorbs all that is unpredictable and morally indeterminate and saves the conception of an ordered universe from self-contradiction' (Nadel, 1964, p. 34). Likewise, many would tend to argue that people who suppose that spirits can injure them out of pure malevolence do not require the idea of a witch to fill a gap in their picture of the universe.

The facts are, however, quite the contrary. In many cultures, witchcraft and malevolent spirit-possession of the kind discussed here both occur. This is so for a start among the Venda; and equally among the Kamba, BaThonga, Lenje, Zulu, Pondo, Valley Tonga, Luo, Lugbara, Banyoro, and Taita – to cite merely a few scattered African examples on which data are readily available. Indeed, the very common association of witchcraft with spirit-familiars – often of opposite sex to the person possessed – is a rather obvious indication of the impossibility of regarding these mystical forces as mutually exclusive in any given society or culture. Nor, of course, is it necessary to look very far afield for striking examples of the coexistence of witchcraft and spirit-possession. Our own sixteenth- and seventeenth-century Christian culture is abundantly rich in instances of witches whose malign power was intimately connected with invasive incubi and succubi.

Thus, evidently, in many cultures these two forces coexist and sometimes even blend into a hybrid entity. This evidence provides us with an excellent opportunity for testing our initial deduction that, since they represent different strategies of attack, spirit-possession and witchcraft should have distinct social correlates, or occur in contrasting social situations. *Table 1*, which summarizes the evidence from some of the peoples I have referred to, seems to indicate that this is the case. In the examples listed, involuntary seizure by capricious peripheral spirits appears to be primarily restricted to the domestic domain, where it is used by female dependants against their menfolk; and sometimes, as with the Gurage, it is also applied by male subordinates to bring pressure to bear upon their superiors. Witchcraft and sorcery accusations, by contrast, seem to operate in a wider sphere of interaction and to be utilized in general contexts of hostility, particularly between equals, or between superior and subordinate. Where, moreover, witchcraft accusations are levelled by an inferior against a superior (as in the case of the unpopular Lugbara elder), the intention is to cast the superior down from his pedestal and to assert equality. More specifically, in the polygynous family nexus: rivalry between co-wives characteristically takes the form of accusations of witchcraft (or sorcery); in conflict between husband and wife, the latter tends to resort to spirit-possession, while the former may accuse his wife of witchcraft.

TABLE 1 *Social contexts of peripheral possession and witchcraft*

People	Context of primary peripheral spirit-affliction	Context of witchcraft (and/or sorcery)
Akamba	domestic domain: women versus men	generalized enmity, including that between co-wives
BaThonga	ditto	ditto
Lenje	ditto	ditto
Taita	ditto	ditto
BaVenda	ditto	ditto
Zulu	ditto	ditto
Valley Tonga	ditto	ditto
Luo	ditto	ditto
Lugbara	?	ditto
Banyoro	ditto	ditto
Gurage	ditto, and subordinate Fuga contra free-born Gurage men	?

I do not claim that these distinctions are absolute, but I think that the evidence indicates trends in these two directions. This suggests that the oblique spirit-possession strategy attempts to redress a situation of adversity by making claims for attention and demonstrations of regard from a superior in a relationship of inequality without completely challenging that relationship. It expresses insubordination, but not generally to the point where it is desired to sever the relationship or subvert it entirely. It ventilates aggression and frustration within the *status quo*. Witchcraft and sorcery accusations, on the contrary, representing as they do a much more direct line of attack, express hostility between equal rivals, or between superior and subordinate (here paralleling the operation of spirit-possession in the reverse direction), and often seek to sunder an unbearably tense relationship (cf. Marwick, 1965, pp. 171-191). Thus, where they occur together in the same culture as alternative strategies, generally peripheral spirit-possession offers a milder, less revolutionary line of attack, a conflict strategy which is less disruptive in its effects.

Consistent with these distinctions, possession-afflictions in wives do not normally seem to provide immediate grounds for divorce by the husband, whereas accusations of witchcraft directed against a wife may be used to this effect. Thus, for example, among the Venda, where in Stayt's time at least divorce was rare and not readily obtained, one of the special circumstances in which a wife could be divorced was precisely when she had been designated a witch (Stayt, 1931, p. 152). Again among the Venda, some indication of the relative strengths and severity of the two lines of attack is provided by the fact that, if peripheral spirit-possession actually led to a possessed woman's death, her husband would accuse his wife's mother of being a witch and would demand and receive compensation for the killing (Stayt, op. cit., p. 305).

Finally, at the cosmological level also, I think that we can detect the same regular contrasts between the severity and relative heinousness of the two types of power. Witchcraft and sorcery are regularly identified with incest and subversion, or even inversion of all commonly accepted moral values. In the popular folk view they represent the negation of morality and of normal social relations. The peripheral spirits with which we are concerned here, however, although also evil, are often not painted quite so black. Above all, they are capricious and mischievous, striking without any cause that can be directly referred to social relations or moral assumptions. In fact they seem to epitomize amorality rather than immorality: they stand totally outside society and inhabit a world apart from that of men, yet one that in many ways is modelled on that of men. Typically, they range free in nature and are not subject to human constraints. Characteristically, they roam wild in the bush, are disaffiliated, inhuman, and come from outside any given culture in which they figure as sources of tribulation. All

301

this seems consistent with the distinctions noted previously between these two types of mystical attack.

So far I have been arguing that where spirit-possession and witchcraft both occur in the same culture they tend to function in different social contexts and to have different social effects, although I admit that the differences may be only of degree. However, in many societies the situation is in reality more complex than this, since the two phenomena frequently merge or coalesce into a hybrid force, at least in some contexts.

Thus for example among the Lugbara (Middleton, 1969) there are two separate classes of diviner: the first, who are exclusively men and whom Middleton calls oracles, divine sickness caused by the ancestors in punishment of sins. The second, exclusively women, or homosexual males, divine in cases of sickness ascribed to witchcraft or sorcery. These latter female diviners, unlike their male counterparts, are inspired through possession by peripheral spirits. From Middleton's earlier published data it is not clear to me whether spirit-possession also operates in the conjugal context discussed earlier in this paper, but it is surely highly significant that here we find spirit-possessed women enlisted as diviners in cases of witchcraft and sorcery which often arise in situations of lineage fission and lead to the dissolution of the authority of established leaders (Middleton, 1960). Among the Lugbara, such spiritually inspired divination is reported to be a recent innovation. This suggests that it may perhaps be interpreted as a kind of spiritual suffragette movement having the effect of opening up new and highly significant avenues of social advancement for women.[2]

Whether or not this is a valid interpretation, here we see spirits enlisted in the fight against witches: whether diviners are also sometimes suspected of being themselves witches or sorcerers is not clear at the moment. However, in a number of other cases (*Table 2*) this association is definitely present. In Bunyoro, for instance, where it is evident from some of Beattie's case-material (1961, p. 24) that peripheral spirit-possession may function as a restitutive mechanism in the conjugal situation, the same type of possession is also involved in one kind of sorcery and in divination (Beattie, 1963, pp. 44-54). Here 'professional sorcerers' who sell their services to the public are also spirit-inspired diviners; and sorcery can be employed either through the use of malevolently powerful *mahembe* horns, or through medicines and techniques supplied by mediums possessed by peripheral spirits of foreign origin.[3] The latter spirits, called *mbandwa,* include the Cwezi 'hero-gods' associated with the former legendary rulers of Bunyoro.

TABLE 2   *Peripheral possession linked with divination and witchcraft*

People	Context of primary phase	Context of secondary phase
Luo	conjugal and domestic	anti-witchcraft divination; diviners suspected of witchcraft
Banyoro	ditto	ditto
Lenje	ditto	ditto

Again, among the Luo of Kenya, where a well-defined peripheral spirit-possession cult connected with women has been clearly described by Michael Whisson (1964), diviners may also be inspired by such spirits both to cure and to cause disease. In this case married women regularly succumb to possession-afflictions to bring pressure on their husbands, and in due course graduate to become spirit-possessed diviners. Those who thus come to control these spirits, however, may also use them in witchcraft against others. Much the same appears to be true in the case of the Lenje described by Earthy (1933, pp. 196ff.), where wives are armed by spirit-possession against their husbands and may also graduate in time to become mistresses of spirits operating both as diviners and as sorcerers (or witches). Male diviners, in contrast, operate in the context of the ancestor cult.

In dealing with this and other similar material it seems to me useful to distinguish between what might be called a 'primary' and a 'secondary' phase in the onset and socialization of possession. In the primary stage, women use 'involuntary' and uncontrolled possession in the domestic domain as a recurrent

303

means of coping with the stresses and difficulties of matrimony, for which (with true female logic) they hold their husbands responsible. These are alleviated by gifts and special gestures of conciliation and consideration from the husbands. In the secondary phase, such women have graduated through membership of a regular possession coterie or cult group to become controllers of spirits. They now function as diviners, thus assuming an active role which readily leads them to be accused of being witches or sorcerers. The factors that lead them into the second phase may relate to radical changes in their domestic situation (e.g. divorce or bereavement), or to different stages in the developmental cycle of the family. In any event, I suggest that the hostile reactions that primary-phase possession undoubtedly evokes on the part of men come to focus mainly on the secondary phase, in which possessed women, controlling their spirits, assume authoritarian roles which more directly threaten, or challenge, male authority. Hence the assumption that such diviners may be sorcerers (or witches). Hence also the equation, controlled spirit-possession=divination-sorcery (or witchcraft).

CONCLUSIONS: STRATEGIES OF MYSTICAL ATTACK

So far we have been concerned with possession by peripheral spirits as a response to tension experienced in different social contexts and its institutionalization in divination by women who are liable to be concurrently suspected of being witches. In other cultures a further pattern of association between witchcraft and possession is evident.

Among the Pondo of South Africa, for example, witchcraft is quite unambiguously connected with possession by evil peripheral spirits. Witches are generally women and are inspired by obscene familiars – the *tokoloshe*, with their grotesquely large penises, and through whose malign power they can illegitimately destroy life and property (Hunter, 1936, pp. 275-320). The concept of witchcraft here is very close to that held in Europe between the fifteenth and seventeenth centuries, with witches inspired by possessing incubi. As in European witchcraft, among the Pondo the possession of such familiars is taken as proof of witchcraft. Here, however, it seems that no distinction is made between 'primary' possession in the conjugal sphere and witchcraft at large; that is, there is no specialized female possession which can be distinguished from witchcraft and used against husbands in the marital context. Yet women also figure significantly as diviners, fighting witchcraft; but in this case they are possessed not by peripheral spirits (=witchcraft), but by the ancestors. Thus an unambiguous conceptual distinction is made between those spirits that animate witchcraft and those that inspire anti-witchcraft diviners, although both roles are generally held by women. Antisocial malevolence is ascribed to the invasive peripheral spirits which possess witches; diviners owe their power to the ancestors who uphold customary morality. These female diviners thus act as auxiliary functionaries in the Pondo main morality cult of ancestors.

This clear-cut polarity between the sources of witchcraft and the afflictions ascribed to its influence on the one hand, and of ancestor-inspired diviners on the other, is fairly closely paralleled among the Gusii (LeVine, 1963). Much the same applies in Christian Ethiopia (Levine, 1965, pp. 68ff.), and in those Philippine communities recently described by Lieban (1967) where sorcerers are inspired by malign peripheral spirits, and diviners and healers by good spirits which are part of the main morality cult; in this case the cult is that of Latin Christianity, and it has not only morphological resemblances but also direct historical links with the older European tradition. The essays by Brown (pp. 17-45) and Cohn (pp. 3-16) in this volume discuss European witchcraft in detail. Here I would only reiterate that, in its developed form, European witchcraft involved possession by devils, while power to treat the bewitched and to cast forth their satanic spirits lay with clerical exorcists who were inspired by Christ and the Holy Ghost. In practice, this ideologically rigid polarity was sometimes transcended in those not uncommon cases where exorcising priests themselves fell a prey to the devils they sought to exorcise.

There are thus at least two patterns of connection between witchcraft (or sorcery) and spirit-possession. In the first, possession by peripheral spirits is the source both of witchcraft and of anti-witchcraft divination, of affliction and its remedy. In the second, peripheral spirits animate only witchcraft; divination is inspired by powers which directly uphold social morality. From the material discussed in this paper it seems that, where

305

peripheral possession has an unsolicited, uncontrolled, primary phase (as in the domestic situation), its controlled use in divination automatically associates the latter with witchcraft. Since it can be applied for good (divination) as well as for evil purposes (sorcery) there is no need to enlist the main morality powers as alternative sources of divinatory and curative inspiration. Where, however, the possessed person is not regarded as the helpless victim of the spirits but is believed to have solicited their support, and only a controlled nexus between possession and peripheral spirits is posited, it becomes necessary to enlist the main morality powers in divination and healing. In the first case, peripheral possession-afflictions are ultimately dealt with by taming and domesticating the spirit, by bringing it under control. When this happens, those who can control spirits and treat the afflicted are automatically suspected of being witches. In the second case, evil peripheral spirit-possession is treated by the exorcism of the afflicting spirit, by casting it out, not by taming it; and this requires the enlistment of superior mystical forces.

I do not claim that these conclusions by any means exhaust the problems discussed in this paper. Nor do I maintain that in all circumstances an unequivocal distinction can be made between the operation of peripheral possession and the operation of witchcraft where these two phenomena coexist separately in the same society. But I do suggest that it would be useful to examine other data from the point of view I have put forward here. This approach has at least the merit of shedding some new light on phenomena which are customarily treated as existing in water-tight compartments, subjected to very different styles of analysis, and even mistakenly regarded as being mutually incompatible.

Indeed, in order to understand the strategy employed by the victim of affliction in seeking an advantageous outlet for his distress, either through the medium of spirit-possession or by accusing one of his fellows of bewitching him, it may sometimes be more illuminating to discard the culturally grounded expressions 'spirit-possession' and 'witchcraft' altogether and think rather in terms of oblique and direct mystical attack. It may seem strange to speak of the action of the accuser, rather than of the accused, as mystical attack. But it is after all the accuser, and not the accused witch, who sets the whole process in motion; and it is certainly the 'witch' against whom public opinion is mobilized, and who is ultimately the victim of social action. If we adopt this point of view, it is obvious that witchcraft is not the only mode of direct mystical attack: cursing also belongs here. Thus the ambivalent aspects of the Lugbara elder's role as legitimate invoker of the ancestors' curse and as a suspected witch fall into place, and it becomes easier to understand those cases of 'witchcraft' used legitimately, or in a socially accepted fashion, that loom so large in many of the other contributions to this volume.

NOTES

1. I recognize, of course, that the use of external 'witches' as scapegoats corresponds closely, in its effects, to this oblique use of spirit-possession. As I argue later in the paper, the line between what is usually called 'spirit-possession' and what is usually called 'witchcraft' is by no means absolute.

2. Although very little is generally known of the history of peripheral possession cults in tribal societies, most observers of these cults, at least in Africa, report that they have arisen within this century. Since, almost invariably, they predominantly involve women and clearly operate to some extent as women's protest movements, it seems probable that they reflect changing aspirations and attitudes towards their traditional status on the part of women. Thus, as the character of the spirits themselves suggests, they seem to be responses to social change, and, perhaps, often direct reactions to the diffusion of modern views on the enfranchisement of women. Certainly, contrary to Wilson's unconvincing assertions concerning the alleged complete socialization of women in traditional roles (Wilson, 1967), in many cases there is direct evidence of spirit-possessed women seeking to assume male roles which they specifically covet, and their exclusion from which they explicitly resent. For particularly clear evidence of this, see Harris (1957).

3. The fact that Banyoro diviners are often inspired by peripheral spirits associated with witchcraft, and are frequently women, seems to me to go far to explain why it is that divination is connected with the left-hand – an ethnographic 'puzzle' that Dr Rodney Needham has recently sought to explore by means of an elaborate excursion into symbolic analysis (Needham, 1967).

REFERENCES

BEATTIE, J. 1961. Group Aspects of the Nyoro Spirit Mediumship Cult. *Human Problems in British Central Africa (Rhodes-Livingstone Institute Journal)* **30**: 11-38.
—— 1963. Witchcraft and Sorcery in Bunyoro. Pp. 32-54 in J.

Middleton & E. H. Winter (eds.), *Witchcraft and Sorcery in East Africa*. London: Routledge & Kegan Paul.

COLSON, E. 1969. Spirit Possession among the Tonga of Zambia. In J. Beattie & J. Middleton (eds.,) *Spirit Mediumship and Society in Africa*. London: Routledge & Kegan Paul.

EARTHY, E. 1933. *Valenge Women*. London: Oxford University Press.

GLUCKMAN, M. 1954. *Rituals of Rebellion in South-East Africa*. Manchester: Manchester University Press.

HARRIS, C. 1957. Possession Hysteria in a Kenyan Tribe. *American Anthropologist* **59** (6): 1046-1066.

HEUSCH, L. DE. 1966. *Le Rwanda et la Civilisation interlacustre*. Bruxelles: Institut de Sociologie de l'Université libre.

HUNTER, M. 1936. *Reaction to Conquest*. London: Oxford University Press.

JUNOD, H. A. 1922. *The Life of a South African Tribe*. New York.

LEVINE, D. N. 1965. *Wax and Gold: Tradition and Innovation in Ethiopian Culture*. Chicago: Chicago University Press.

LEVINE, R. 1963. Witchcraft and Sorcery in a Gusii Community. In J. Middleton & E. H. Winter (eds.), *Witchcraft and Sorcery in East Africa*. London: Routledge & Kegan Paul.

LEWIS, I. M. 1966. Spirit Possession and Deprivation Cults. *Man* (n.s.) **1**: 307-329.

LIEBAN, R. 1967. *Cebuano Sorcery*. Berkeley-Los Angeles: University of California Press.

LINDBLOM, G. 1920. *The Akamba in British East Africa*. Uppsala.

MARWICK, M. 1965. Some problems in the Sociology of Sorcery and Witchcraft. In M. Fortes & G. Dieterlen (eds.), *African Systems of Thought*. London: Oxford University Press (for the International African Institute).

MIDDLETON, J. 1960. *Lugbara Religion*. London: Oxford University Press (for the International African Institute).

—— 1969. Oracles and Divination among the Lugbara. In M. Douglas & P. Kaberry (eds.), *Man in Africa*. London: Tavistock Publications.

NADEL, S. F. 1946. A Study of Shamanism in the Nuba Hills. *Journal of the Royal Anthropological Institute* **76**: 25-37.

NEEDHAM, R. 1967. Right and Left in Nyoro Symbolic Classification. *Africa* **37** (4): 425-452.

OPLER, M. E. 1958. Spirit Possession in a Rural Area of Northern India. In W. A. Less & E. Z. Vogt (eds.), *Reader in Comparative Religion*. New York: Row, Peterson.

SHACK, W. 1966. *The Gurage*. London: Oxford University Press.

STAYT, H. 1931. *The BaVenda*. London: Oxford University Press.

WHISSON, M. G. 1964. Some Aspects of Functional Disorders among the Kenya Luo. In A. Kiev (ed.), *Magic, Faith and Healing.* New York: Free Press of Glencoe.

WILSON, P. J. 1967. Status Ambiguity and Spirit Possession. *Man* (n.s.) **2** (3): 366-378.

WORSLEY, P. 1957. *The Trumpet shall Sound: A Study of 'Cargo' Cults in Melanesia.* London: MacGibbon & Kee.

© I. M. Lewis 1970

15

Brian Spooner

The Evil Eye in the Middle East[1]

'In the Name of God, the Merciful, the Compassionate
Say: "I take refuge with the Lord of the Daybreak,
    from the evil of what he has created,
    from the evil of darkness when it gathers,
    from the evil of women who blow on knots,
    from the evil of an envier when he envies."'

Koran cxiii, trans. Arberry, 1956.

The Evil Eye is a phenomenon familiar to all, but apparently as little described by ethnographers as it is discussed by those who fear it. The following notes constitute an attempt to interpret the literature that exists in the light of my own field experience and of discussions with colleagues who have recently worked in Muslim countries. If the attempt should prove abortive (which is the more possible because the scanty material available includes no detailed case-studies) it is nevertheless justified by the present context, for the concept of the Evil Eye is reported throughout Europe, the Middle East, and North Africa, and in so many cultures elsewhere that it may be regarded as a universal phenomenon (cf. e.g. Andrée, 1878, pp. 35-45). Further, it is reported in circumstances which show it to be undoubtedly of the same order of phenomena as witchcraft. Its role in social organization is not as well defined or conspicuous (or as well studied) as that of witchcraft. For instance, there are no public accusations. In many cases it may be dismissed as a superstition. Generally, however, it represents a real fear of evil influence through other people. For instance, in Persia:

'The possessor of an evil eye may or may not know that he has it. He may have been born with it. . . . It exists in various degrees of power in different people. It is said by some, however, that there are few who actually do have it, and that perhaps most of them do not realise that it is in their possession. One Shaikh expressed the opinion that most of the fear of the evil eye has been created by the imaginations of the people, and that the real causes for it are not nearly

311

so numerous as they think, but the fear of it is certainly general, and so many ills and misfortunes are ascribed to it, that most people have been suspected at some time of being the cause of calamities that have come to those with whom they have had contact. . . .' (Donaldson, 1938, pp. 15-16).

The main general characteristics of the Evil Eye are that it relates to the fear of envy in the eye of the beholder, and that its influence is avoided or counteracted by means of devices calculated to distract its attention, and by practices of sympathetic magic. Jealousy can kill via a look:

'Dans une de nos caravanes un mulet de charge, très vigoureux, excita la convoitise d'un bédouin qui le regarda fixement; quelques instants après, le mulet se cassait la jambe. Le propriétaire en reconnut la cause dans le mauvais coup d'oeil du bédouin' (Jaussen, 1908, p. 377).

The most common name for the Evil Eye is simply 'the Eye' (Arabic: *ᶜayn*). Verbal forms 'to eye' or 'to eye-strike' are also used. In Persian it is most often referred to as 'the Salty Eye' (*cašm-e šur*). Variations such as 'the Narrow Eye', 'the Bad Eye', 'the Wounding Eye', 'the Look', are also found. In some accounts it is an independent evil power which acts through certain people and in certain situations; in others there are simply certain people whose look is evil.

The concept existed before Islam, and is found under each of the universalistic religions represented in the area (Islam, Christianity, Judaism, and Zoroastrianism). The evidence suggests that it pre-existed all of them. Particular beliefs and practices concerning the Evil Eye tend to be neither exclusive nor well defined: that is, generally, in any situation there are other evil agents besides the Evil Eye which may be blamed; and some of the rites that are used to counteract it may also be practised for other purposes. The present ethnographic situation is complicated by the fact that the belief operates within the framework of these formal universalistic religions (cf. Hocart, 1938), and the spread of these religions may possibly be responsible for much of the uniformity of practices and attitudes concerning it. It is not actually mentioned anywhere in the Koran, but the quotation at the head of this paper – especially the last two lines – is a text commonly cited in support of the belief in Islamic countries. It is a vague text, which obviously makes room for popular explanations of the problem of evil alongside more formal theological resolutions. Knotting pieces of thread and blowing on objects and patients are common ingredients in black and white magic rituals throughout the area. The formal religion is made use of to ward off the Evil Eye, as it is also to scare away *jinn* and other evil influences. Certain verses of the Koran are particularly effective, spoken or written. On the northern side of the Mediterranean, besides the crucifix, obscenity, in a sense the opposite of religion, is much used to deflect the Evil Eye. However, in Islamic countries there is no reference to its use in this context (unless the origin of the Beja women's coiffure is phallic; cf. Murray, 1935, p. 72). Such a general difference may perhaps be related to other general differences between Islam and Christianity such as the different orientation of each towards sex and marriage, but there are also many minor local variations in ritual which bear no relation to the religious régime.

Variations also occur from place to place in the application of the belief, but in general the evil eye may be posited as the cause of any misfortune from the most trivial to sudden death (cf. for example in Barth, 1961, p. 145), though a gradual wasting sickness seems to be thought of as its most characteristic effect. There are examples of its influence being feared because of the visit of a particular person – invariably a stranger, or someone with some unusual physical trait – and there are ritual practices for its neutralization where a particular misfortune, especially sickness, might be alleviated. In general, it is unusual people – persons who for some reason or other do not fully belong to the closely knit community, either because they are strangers or because they have some physical defect or abnormality, not necessarily of the eye or sight – who are suspected of being vehicles of the Evil Eye. A stranger is thought of as a temporary vehicle. A man with a physical defect is likely to be suspected of having been born with the Evil Eye. A cognate conception of an Evil Tongue is also found in some communities, and a Turkman saying states that the eye alone does no harm unless the agent also speaks envious words (viz. *Wez deghmez, dil degher*).[2] In the east of Persia it is said that 'the loving eye is more dangerous than the Evil Eye' (*cašm-e nāz az cašm šur bad-tar ast*). This warns of the dangers of, for example, the doting glance of a

313

mother. I am inclined to interpret this as an extension of the concept of the Evil Eye. An outsider envies, an insider dotes. Both attitudes are forms of undue attention (cf. Evans-Pritchard, 1956, p. 15).

Finally, it is interesting that observers of nomadic communities devote very little attention to the Evil Eye, and certainly much less in general than do observers of peasant communities. The concept exists among nomads, and their children are often covered with prophylactic charms, but other precautions and the find-the-culprit rituals are seldom if ever seen. This situation could be due to the much greater mobility of nomads both as herding groups and as individuals. Nomadic communities have a better defined and more inclusive role structure than peasant communities. Among nomads there is no private life, and the stranger-guest is an integral feature in the life of the community. Among peasants, where each family jealously guards its privacy, the guest is entertained by similar, perhaps more conspicuous rituals, but is nevertheless in most cases separated by a wall from the private life of the family.

A brief, generalized summary of the facts relating to the belief as far as they are known, and of the relevant sources of ethnography, is given below. Meanwhile, if I may hazard an interpretation at this stage: the concept of the Evil Eye appears to be an institutionalized psychological idiom for the personalization, or simply the personification, of misfortune, in particular in so far as misfortune, or the fear of it, may relate to the fear of outsiders[3] and their envy. The cognate idea of an Evil Tongue has been mentioned. A further cognate idea of an 'Evil Soul', being evil which comes by way of the breath, is also reported (Canaan, 1927, p. 181). Of the possible modes of communication, only actual physical touching is not represented. It is interesting that, of these four modes of communication, the influence of evil is communicated most commonly via a look, whereas the complementary influence of good (from *baraka*) is communicated by touch. Why the Evil Eye (and not the Evil Tongue or the Evil Breath) should be a universal phenomenon is probably a psychological, rather than a sociological, question. However, staring is an act with connotations which vary from inauspiciousness to downright rudeness, according to culture. Marçais (1960) cites 'the naturally injurious power of a strange and staring look'.

Annex I

The Attack

In the case of personalization, the suspected vehicle of the influence of the Evil Eye is invariably a person who is in some measure an outsider in the immediate group and could in some way be tempted to envy. Therefore, persons with obvious physical or economic defects are especially suspect, whereas pregnant women and small children are the most vulnerable. Beauty is always vulnerable, and it has been suggested that the origin of the veil is connected with the fear of the Evil Eye. Similarly, individuals passing through *rites de passage* are particularly vulnerable. The following are some of the more common categories and traits that may attract suspicion:

1. Women are particularly liable to suspicion. Since their social role is more strictly defined than men's, and they are at a physical and social disadvantage to start with, any unusual behaviour, or any trait that prevents them from fulfilling their women's function, may make them suspect: e.g. barrenness, brashness, unexplained visits, etc.
2. Beggars are generally suspect, and owe much of their income to the suspicion. The practice of presenting a guest with any object he admires, similarly, is very probably connected with the Evil Eye in origin.
3. Blue or green eyes are often cited, but this appears to be true only in those parts where these are really rare.[4] Any other peculiarity of the eyes or sight may be equally suspect.
4. The stare of certain animals, in particular, the snake, is thought to carry the Evil Eye.
5. Any form of admiration is feared as a potential vehicle for the Evil Eye.

Annex II

The Defence–Selected Devices

A. Before the fact, as a regular ritual or habitual practice:

1. Fumigation, for which the wild rue in particular is almost universally used.

2. Use of charms, amulets, etc. Young children in particular are often covered with them. They may take many forms, from sheep's eyes to miniscule Korans. Cowry, agate, blue beads, onyx, horn, and mirrors are very widely used, and, as with the veil, the origin of the wearing of jewellery may be connected with fear of the Evil Eye. Tattooing is also cited. Brightly coloured clothing is also used, and pieces of red rag are known as inimical to the Evil Eye (and witchcraft) from Donegal to Japan. Amulets may contain a leopard's claw or strands of wolf's hair, tokens of fierceness.

3. If bright colours distract, dirt disguises. Children are often left filthy and never washed, in order to protect them from the Evil Eye.

4. Avoidance of ambition and perfection (cf. Nemesis). It is usual to avoid round figures, even in trade, and a shepherd will not count his sheep. (The 'Thousand and One Nights' and other similar figures may derive from this, but see *Encyclopaedia of Islam*, 2nd edition, art. 'Alf Layla wa Layla'.)

5. The five fingers of the outstretched hand (which is never identifiable as either right or left). This appears to be restricted to North Africa, perhaps because it has acquired a religious symbolism among Shi'a Muslims further east, among whom it represents the hand of Abbas which was severed at the battle of Kerbala (cf. Donaldson, 1938, p. 208).

B. After the (suspected) fact (for instance, in the case of sickness, or if someone has expressed undue admiration for one's child):

1. Fumigation (as in A.1. above).

2. The burning of alum, which pops like an eye bursting.

3. Recitation of various formulae.

4. Salt is generally regarded as inimical to the Evil Eye, and there are a number of practices which involve its use.

5. The giving away of sweets at joyful events or after particular successes may be explained as an effort to prevent envy and the Evil Eye (Barth, 1961, p. 145), and a general symbolic opposition between sweet and salt has been suggested.[5]

6. Spitting.

C. Divining the culprit: generally, a number of small objects (e.g. eggs, stones) are taken, and each is designated to represent a particular suspect. A simple ritual then exposes the culprit from among them. A common method is for someone to hold an egg lengthwise between his palms, and to press on it as the name of each suspect is spoken. At the name of the guilty person the egg will break. When the cause is thus established a common measure is to obtain a piece of the guilty person's clothing and burn it, either separately, in the fumigation ritual, or with a piece of alum.

NOTES

1. In the preparation of this short survey I have greatly benefited from discussion with the following, who have recently conducted anthropological fieldwork in Islamic communities: Miss Nadia Abu-Zahra, Mr D. H. M. Brooks, Mr & Mrs R. Tapper. Dr Rodney Needham also kindly drew my attention to some items of bibliography.

2. Personal communication from Dr William G. Irons.

3. Barth (1961, p. 145) states that 'since it is the unconscious envy that harms, only friends, acquaintances and relations (khodeman – one's own people) cast the evil eye, while declared enemies are impotent to do so'. In my own experience it is not only unconscious envy that harms. Further, 'one's own people' in Persia is a concept that varies according to context, and, among peasants, would not normally include acquaintances or more distant relatives. It is, however, just these categories (again, in my own experience) that are most open to suspicion. Similarly, in the peasant society of southern Egypt, 'which suffers greatly from the stresses and strains that obtain between relatives', it is especially necessary to guard against the effects of the Evil Eye from relatives (Ammar, 1954, p. 62). Presumably this must mean relatives outside the economic family unit.

4. According to Amin (1953, p. 58), in Egypt the colour green (*akhḍar*) is inauspicious and blue is auspicious, and he actually goes on to say that blue is confused with green.

5. By Mr D. H. M. Brooks in a personal communication.

6. Dr Rodney Needham kindly drew my attention to some of them.

BIBLIOGRAPHY

In addition to giving details of references indicated in the text I have included below a selected bibliography. This is not a comprehensive bibliography of the Evil Eye, but includes all the references which have come to my notice[6] and may be considered to have some analytical value. Few even of these are rewarding. I have not so far been able to consult Einssler (1889), Seligman (1910, 1922), or Koşay (1956).

Of the more noteworthy items: *Hastings's Encyclopaedia* has a good general article, but is mostly concerned with Europe. Elworthy (1895) provides an impressively detailed catalogue of practices, devices, and gestures, mainly from southern Europe but with references to North Africa. The best brief general account for the Islamic world is Marçais (1960). The most detailed account of Islamic practices is in Westermarck (1926, Chapter VIII); most of the practices he catalogues were observed in Morocco, but are found throughout North Africa and the Middle East. The first chapter of Donaldson (1938) is devoted to attitudes and practices observed in the north-east of Iran; and Doutté (1908, pp. 317-327) has ten pages on the Evil Eye in the Maghreb. All these works also contain further bibliography.

AMIN, AHMAD. 1953. *Qāmūs al-'Ādāt wa'l-Taqālid wa'l-Ta'ābīr al-Miṣriyya* (in Arabic). Cairo.

AMMAR, H. 1954. *Growing up in an Egyptian village*. London: Routledge & Kegan Paul.

ANDRÉE, RICHARD. 1878. *Ethnographische Parallelen und Vergleiche*, pp. 35-38. (Includes further bibliography.) Stuttgart.

ARBERRY, A. J. 1956. *The Koran Interpreted*. 2 vols. London: Allen & Unwin.

BARTH, F. 1961. *Nomads of South Persia*, pp. 144ff. London: Allen & Unwin.

BLACKMAN, W. S. 1927. *The Fellahin of Upper Egypt*, pp. 218ff.

CANAAN, T. 1927. The Child in Palestinian Arab Superstition. *Journal of the Palestine Oriental Society* 7.

DONALDSON, B. A. 1938. *The Wild Rue*. London: Luzac.

DOUTTÉ, E. 1908. *Magie et Religion dans l'Afrique du Nord*. Algiers.

EINSSLER, LYDIA. 1889. Das Böse Auge. Z. d. *Deutschen Palästina-vereins*, 10 bd., S. 200ff.

ELWORTHY, F. T. 1895. *The Evil Eye*. London: Murray.

EVANS-PRITCHARD, E. E. 1956. *Nuer Religion*. Oxford: Clarendon Press.

GRANQVIST, H. 1931 & 1935. *Marriage Conditions in a Palestinian Village*. 2 vols. Helsinki.

—— 1947. *Birth and Childhood among the Arabs*. Helsinki and Copenhagen.

—— 1950. *Child Problems among the Arabs*. Helsinki and Copenhagen.

—— 1965. *Muslim Death and Burial*. Helsinki.

HASTINGS, J. 1908. *Encyclopaedia of Religion and Ethics*. Edinburgh: Clark.

HEDAYAT, S. 1956. Cašm-e zakhm. In *Neirangestan* (in Persian). 2nd edition. Tehran.

HOCART, A. M. 1938. The Mechanism of the Evil Eye. In *Folklore* 49: 156-157.

JAUSSEN, A. 1908. *Coutumes arabes au pays de Moab*. Paris.

KOṢAY, HAMIT. 1956. Efnografya müzesindeki nazarlık, muska ve hamiller. *Türk Etnografya Dergisi* 1: 86-90.

KRISS, R. & KRISS-HEINRICH, H. 1960-62. *Volksglaube im Bereich des Islam*. 2 vols.

LANE, E. W. 1966. *The Manners and Customs of the Modern Egyptians,* pp. 58, 59, 148, 256ff., 511, 513. London: Dent (Everyman's Library). (Reprint of the 1836 edition.)

MARÇAIS, PH. 1960. ᶜAyn. In *Encyclopaedia of Islam,* 2nd edition.

MURRAY, G. W. 1935. *Sons of Ishmael.* London: Routledge & Kegan Paul.

SCHLIMMER, J. L. 1874. *Terminologie Medico-Pharmaceutique et Anthropologique* . . .

SELIGMAN, SIEGFRIED. 1910. *Der Böse Blick.* 2 vols. Berlin.

—— 1922. *Die Zauberkraft des Auges und das Berufen.* Hamburg.

SZYLIOWICZ, JOSEPH S. 1966. *Political Change in Rural Turkey: Erdemli,* p. 105. Mouton.

THOMAS, BERTRAM. 1938. *Arabia Felix,* pp. 80-81, 94, 144, and photograph facing p. 14. London: Cape.

THOMPSON, R. C. 1908. *Semitic Magic.* London: Luzac.

WESTERMARCK, E. 1926. *Ritual and Beliefs in Morocco.* London.

© Brian Spooner 1970

16

G. I. Jones

A Boundary to Accusations

Although all Ibo communities share common beliefs in witch-craft and sorcery with their neighbours, most of the Ibo are little troubled by fear of witches.

For the purposes of this paper I distinguish three cultural areas in Eastern Nigeria, namely:

1. Cross River, those tribes speaking Cross River languages in the Ogoja and Calabar provinces, including Efik, but excluding other Ibibio and including the Cross River Ibo.
2. Ibibio.
3. Ibo, including the two culturally marginal groups of Riverain and North-eastern Ibo.

In these regions a clear distinction is made between the two concepts that Evans-Pritchard, in describing the Azande, distinguishes as witchcraft and sorcery. The first implies the use of psychic power to harm; the latter the use, for the same purpose, of the power believed to inhere in magical or medicinal concoctions. People are expected to be on their guard against the possible use of magic against them, and if necessary to resort to counter-magic. But whereas sorcery is normal and expected, there is a general feeling that witchcraft is something horrible and abominable.

These distinctions, which are made readily enough when one is speaking in general terms, become more confused on closer study.

SORCERY

The use of harmful juju (nshi) is part of the wider field of magic and medicine. Its power may come from actual toxic substances in the medicine, or from imagined supernatural force, *juju*, derived either from the magical compound itself or from a

321

Eastern Region of Nigeria: differential concern with witchcraft

Degree of concern with witchcraft
as distinct from sorcery:

Intense

Slight to moderate

Negligible

Boundary of
Eastern Region

Boundaries of
IBO groups

spiritual being associated with it or from both. The use of the word poison as a translation of the Ibo term *nshi* (and of its equivalents in other local languages) has naturally confused both administrators and earlier anthropologists, who have attributed the most remarkable and improbable proficiency in toxicology to local native doctors. Talbot reported that: 'It is possible that the Ibibio are the most expert poisoners on earth, though other semi-Bantu tribes would run them close' (Talbot, 1926, p. 162). *Nshi* is also used to describe the familiars (*agu nshi*) of these native doctors, and the power of these spirits, like the power of the native doctor's magic, is ambivalent.

The crime of 'using harmful juju' may involve the use of medicines which are not normally called *nshi*, for example charms placed on land or other property. These are disapproved only if placed by a person who has no rights over the property. There are also medicines which promote the good fortune of the owner and attack no one directly. But some of these can become 'bad' if it is believed that their power works at the expense of the luck or good fortune of the owner's fellows. There are again, at least among the central Ibo, certain unduly lucky individuals of this type whose luck is held to be innate and not derived from medicines. These people are not thought of as witches, for they have no intention of harming anyone, but it is dangerous to receive anything from them, whether money or other property, livestock, or a daughter in marriage. For this luck is contagious; and the property, livestock, or children transferred will prosper mightily, but at the expense of any other property or wives of the receiver.

Again, it would be an over-simplification to say that whereas witchcraft operates between close kin and neighbours (and typically between people of the same village section and corporate lineage), sorcery occurs between people of different villages and village sections. Sorcery may be feared at close range and witchcraft sometimes at a distance. In villages whose unity is disrupted by excessive or unresolved political rivalry, accusations of sorcery, some genuinely believed in, others deliberately fabricated, are directed against each other by the protagonists and their supporters, often irrespective of their lineage affiliations. Similarly, in crises of public confidence, the fear of the use of supernatural evil power by fellow-villagers becomes intensified and finds an outlet in accusations of witchcraft or sorcery, or in some cases of both; and in Old Calabar and in the middle Cross River area, where the fear of witchcraft could be said to be endemic, witchcraft and sorcery come together and support each other. Many deaths are believed to be caused by witches who may use sorcery to kill their victims.

Wherever witchcraft fears are prevalent there are also fears of sorcery. Sorcery ('poison') provides an explanation for sudden death, and for unexpected occurrences of mental disorder even in areas where the fear of witchcraft is slight. There are, for instance, certain Ibo communities where informants maintain that their communities have not been troubled by witches but they can remember periods when they have suffered from the attacks of sorcerers. The ones that came to my notice were in the Owerri and Ahoada divisions. The alleged sorcerers were from different but neighbouring villages or village sections. Talbot actually quotes an Ozuzu (Ahoada) Native Court case in which the accused was a brother of the deceased (Talbot, 1932, p. 128).

WITCHCRAFT

In this region, witches (who can be people of either sex) are believed to attack their victim on the supernatural, spiritual, plane, sometimes explained in the expression 'the soul of the witch eats the soul of his victim', sometimes as 'the witch sucks the blood of the victim'. Rodent ulcers and other sores that will not heal are held to be proof of this.

At the same time, witchcraft is also thought of as a substance or creature that exists inside the witch's body and that can be discovered by an autopsy. On the Cross River and among many Ibo groups it is held to be a creature that lives in a person's belly, or, in the case of a woman, in her womb. Barren women are believed to be witches, as may be those who die in child-birth (if they are not suspected of unconfessed adultery). The witchcraft creature in the pregnant woman refuses to be expelled with the child and in the resulting struggle the witch dies. In the Ogoja division they will tell you that only ignorant witches die in this way. The witch who knows what to do will retire into hiding when her labour begins, with a large piece of bloody beef. When she kneels to deliver her child she uncovers the beef and puts it on her head. The witch creature cannot resist the lure of blood and rushes out to drink it. In its absence the woman is able to expel her child.

Witchcraft is also associated, particularly on the Cross River, with success in political or economic activities. This success is at the expense of the witch's close relatives, typically his junior agnates and children. These relatives are given by the witch to the society of witches of which he is a member to be killed and eaten by them at a society feast. They are given in repayment of a debt, usually termed a 'flesh debt', which is incurred when the debtor partakes of the human meat provided by another witch at a previous feast. A man may be tricked into eating such meat and so become a witch and an indebted member of the society, or he may eat and join of his own volition. He can, moreover, become so involved in such transactions that he has to continue providing victims until all his children and close relatives have been sacrificed in this manner, and when he eventually fails to produce a victim he himself is taken. Mbembe and Ikom people point out that wealthy men leave no heirs and that their families always decline. Among some Ibibio and Riverain Ibo, female witches are believed to 'sacrifice' their children to repay such 'flesh debts'.

The accepted method of avenging a death imputed to witch-craft was by the poison ordeal, though this was restricted to those areas where the fear of witchcraft was most intense. The person accused was obliged to prove his innocence by drinking a concoction made of sasswood in the savannah area, of esere bean in the forest area. Death from the poison was a proof of guilt; vomiting it in time, of innocence.

There have been many types of witchcraft detection, and anti-witch movements. They have ranged from various forms of spirit-possession to lethal medicines like *Mfam*[1] of the Ogoja division.

ATTITUDES TOWARDS WITCHCRAFT

Although these witchcraft beliefs are found among all the tribal groups in the region, the intensity of feeling aroused by them varies remarkably. I am struck by the fact that though Ibo share these beliefs, most Ibo areas are singularly free from fears of witchcraft and from witchcraft persecutions and purges.

At the opposite extreme are most of the people in the Cross River area from the Efik of Old Calabar to the Mbembe, Ekoi, and Bekworra of Ogoja division. Other areas, for example most Ibibio communities, the Riverain Ibo, or the Yakö of the Cross River, occupy an intermediate position. That these differing responses are not a recent phenomenon but are, as it were, incorporated into the social structure can be seen if we examine the different categories of people who are believed to be witches in the different communities.

Among the Ibibio and the Riverain Ibo, accusations of witchcraft are directed mainly against women married into the group, and accusations between agnates are said to be rare because their ancestor cults enjoin and sanction cooperation between their agnatic descendants.

In the Cross River area, people live crowded together in compact villages and anybody can be said to be in close contact with his fellow-villagers and therefore a potential witch. This proposition is indeed accepted by most Cross River communities, but, whereas some agree that this is the case in their villages, others, while believing that it happens thus in other communities, maintain that the situation is modified in the case of their own people in various ways and for various reasons. Thus the Mbembe and many Ekoi say that any member of their villages can be a witch, though the most dangerous are elderly people and the more powerful and wealthy men. The Efik accept the general proposition, but consider that the people most likely to be guilty of witchcraft are agnates and women married into the lineage. The Yakö, on the other hand, maintain that the patriclan fetish is powerful enough to prevent agnates from bewitching each other (the Yakö have no ancestor cults) and that they do not expect matriclansmen to bewitch each other (Forde, 1958). Thus accusations of witchcraft in this tribe, as with the Ibibio and the Riverain Ibo, are directed mainly against women married into the community. Most Cross River Ibo say that while it is possible for anybody to be a witch, and that this is the situation in adjacent tribes of non-Ibo, they themselves are not troubled by either male or female witches.

This is the case with most other Ibo communities, those who live near the Riverain Ibo giving as the reason that, unlike the Riverain Ibo, their people eat cocoyams, a plant which, they say, witches cannot tolerate. This explanation of their immunity is not given by Ibo bordering the Cross River, where cocoyams are eaten by both witch-fearing and witch-immune communities.

We can thus construct a scale with, at the one extreme, communities where no specific categories of people are accused of witchcraft, and, at the other, communities where no categories of people are exempt from such accusations, and in between these extremes are communities where accusations are said to be directed against a limited category of people (e.g. women), and where other categories are either specifically excluded from such accusations (e.g. agnates in Yakö societies) or are held not to indulge in evil witchcraft or to practise it only in exceptional cases.

THE SOCIAL TENSIONS HYPOTHESIS

In his study of Ceŵa sorcery, M. G. Marwick has argued that 'beliefs in sorcery provide a means by which tense relationships may be formulated and sometimes redressed' (Marwick, 1965, p. 283). Other Central African research has supported the suggestion, originally derived from Evans-Pritchard's Azande study, that witchcraft and sorcery beliefs are used to manipulate situations in which roles are competitive and ambiguously defined. The Niger Cross River material which I have summarized offers itself for a testing of the sociological hypothesis. We should expect to find less tension, less conflict, more overt ways of reducing ambiguity, in the tribal areas where witchcraft by close neighbours is not feared. Most of the Cross River Ibo tribes have no fear of witchcraft – a few of them in Arochuku have a slight fear, mainly of female witches – and no regular methods of detection and punishment of witchcraft. The same is true of the Yakö, who maintain that male agnates cannot bewitch each other and are not greatly worried by female witchcraft. On the other hand, the Mbembe, Ikom, Ekoi, and Boki seem to fear witchcraft as intensely as do the Efik.

If Marwick's hypothesis is to stand, it would imply that in Ibo communities social relations are freer or conflicts more open than in Ibibio and Yakö, and even more so compared with Mbembe and the other witch-fearing tribes.

Such an assessment of the quality of social relations, to be objective, would be extremely difficult to make except by specially planned research. However, the literature and my own experience in the country allow certain impressions which are worth recording in the hope of stimulating further research.

The Ibo are a voluble, individualist, and egalitarian people. They seem to have a self-reliant, uncomplicated attitude to life, particularly the North-eastern and Cross River Ibo and most of the Northern and Southern communities. In the field of interpersonal relationships Ibo societies show a marked absence of roles expressing extreme respect, avoidance, or even institutionalized joking. People of all generations and relationships address each other freely and with familiarity; a man may correct his father, a wife tell her husband what she thinks of his behaviour; respect tends to be reserved for those who have acquired it, typically for successful elders. More striking is the presence of usages which seem designed to promote the release of tension. People are expected to express and not conceal their feelings and opinions. They are encouraged to complain, 'to tell the world' of their wrongs.

A title in Yoruba or Benin is a unique and exclusive rank and office. In the Ibo country, apart from lineage and community headships (offices that pass either to the eldest son or to the oldest male in the lineage), a title can be made by any free-born man who can accumulate sufficient wealth. If there are a number of such men they can all make the same title and at the same time. A title dies with the holder; a son cannot inherit it, but must make it afresh, and if he and his father have the wealth he can even make the title during his father's lifetime, provided the father's title is made before that of the son.

In its territorial layout, Ibo social structure seems to be planned to minimize conflict within the local community. Each local community is a village group (town) and consists of a segmentary lineage system in which the maximal lineages are the villages; each corporate lineage lives on its own residential land but has a right to a portion of the farmland which is collectively owned by the village. The layout of this village group is not merely a physical expression of the social structure: it also provides for its expansion and provides for it in a way that minimizes conflict between the land-owning units, the villages.

This is achieved by grouping these villages reasonably close together in a residential area of compounds, dispersed among shade gardens and palm and other economic trees, and allocating to each village, for its farming needs, the land extending in a specific direction away from the residential area and, more important, from the other villages. Thus as its population increases it continues to clear and farm the land in this direction. Those in need of land find it, not at the expense of their near neighbours, but on their village's section of the village group boundary. When this gets too far distant, those in need of land in the village group move off well beyond this boundary to found a new settlement with a similar structure and layout to the parent community.

Many of the causes of tension are likely to occur only in a static or contracting economy. Ibo men are not expected to depend for their social advancement on the grudging surrender by their fathers and grandfathers of rights over land and of wealth to acquire wives and other scarce resources. While it remains an Ibo father's responsibility to provide his son with a wife and with land to support a family, if he is unable to do so it is up to the son to go out and find the land or accumulate the capital to satisfy his needs. A man is not so likely to become jealous of an elder brother if he has not been brought up to be dependent on him but rather to rely on his own abilities and initiative. Tension between brothers, real or classificatory, is not likely to develop if one or both of them are absent from the village; and should both be working in a foreign place they are more likely to feel the need to join together for mutual support and to extend the concept of 'brotherhood' to cover any other members of their 'town' or neighbourhood who are residing there. The Ibo 'town unions' or 'family unions' that have developed in these places of employment carefully avoid getting involved in commerce, industry, politics, or other divisive activities. So Ibo are able to carry back with them to their home towns a considerable measure of the unity and solidarity they found necessary in their residence abroad.

In the same way, an Ibo woman is not so likely to become jealous of her co-wives if she is vigorously interacting with a large number of other women, trading in the elaborate network of markets all around her, and is actively involved in associations

329

of the types described by Margaret Green in *Ibo Village Affairs* (1947).

The extent to which these factors are general to the region or peculiar to the Ibo is difficult to judge. What is more clear is that the Ibo have experienced a steady territorial expansion outward from a centre in the southern part of Awka division, namely to the east and south. Their expansion has met with no setbacks or opposition except in the west. Nor, except again in the west and in the extreme north, have there been any invasions or other disturbances to upset this original distributive pattern. In the west, that is the Niger Riverain area and beyond, Ibo expansion has encountered and become fused with the expansion of formerly Edo-speaking groups coming from the Benin direction. The descendants of most of these now form the dominant section of the community (e.g. Onitsha). Elsewhere the expansion must have been into unoccupied forest or into the territory of weaker groups, who either withdrew or became absorbed. Such territorial expansion has long since ended in the central area. It was still continuing in the nineteenth century in the marginal areas from new centres of expansion, notably in the Ohuhu-Ngwa and Cross River and North-eastern Ibo areas. In the central area, territorial expansion has been replaced since the eighteenth century, if not before, by specialization in the form of migrant craftsmen, including ritual specialists, market-traders, and, more recently, agricultural and other labourers. This type of expansion has been continuing at an ever-increasing rate up to 1966.

In the Ibibio area one finds exactly the same pattern of territorial expansion, outward from a common centre between Abak and Uyo stations, but the increasing density of population in this centre has not been relieved to the same extent. Although the pattern of migration to work outside the area now extends to the Ibibio, it came much later. Ibibio migrants found themselves in competition with Ibo from the central Ibo area, who by then had a virtual monopoly of the more lucrative commercial and trading occupations.

In this region there may be a more general correlation between expansion and absence of witchcraft fears. Areas of notable expansion (whether territorial or economic), namely most Northern and Southern Ibo, and Cross River and North-eastern

Ibo, are areas where witchcraft fears are low; areas of contraction (e.g. Mbembe, Efik) or stagnation (e.g. Ekoi, Bekworra, and Boki) are areas where such fears are at their greatest intensity; intermediate areas, where expansion has not been so rapid or has been checked or come to a temporary halt, namely Western and Riverain Ibo, Ibibio, and Yakö, are areas where such fears are said to be slight.

This comparative survey has been far too brief and generalized to permit anything more than very tentative conclusions.

It has, I hope, suggested a correlation in Ibo societies between absence of fears about witchcraft and absence of local tension, and has submitted that this absence of tension is reflected, first, in certain social institutions which reduce conflict between their members, and, second, in an expanding economy which offers new opportunities to satisfy social needs.

NOTES

1. The 'witches' in fact died from cerebro-spinal meningitis. *Mfam* medicine was actually harmless. But the people who introduced *Mfam* to the various villages were also without knowing it spreading this infection.

REFERENCES

EVANS-PRITCHARD, E. E. 1937. *Witchcraft, Oracles and Magic among the Azande*. Oxford: Clarendon Press.

FORDE, DARYLL (ed.). 1956. *Efic Traders of Old Calabar*. London: Oxford University Press (for the International African Institute).

—— 1958. Spirits, Witches, and Sorcerers in the Supernatural Economy of the Yakö. *Journal of the Royal Anthropological Society* 88 (2): 165-177.

GREEN, M. M. 1947. *Ibo Village Affairs*. Part III. London: Sidgwick & Jackson.

JONES, G. I. 1956. The Political Organization of Old Calabar. In D. Forde (ed.), *Efik Traders of Old Calabar*. London: Oxford University Press (for the International African Institute).

LEONARD, A. G. 1906. *The Lower Niger and its Tribes*. London: Macmillan.

MARWICK, M. G. 1965. *Sorcery in its Social Setting*. Manchester: Manchester University Press.

TALBOT, D. 1915. *Woman's Mysteries of a Primitive People*. Chapter XI. London: Cassell.

TALBOT, P. AMAURY. 1923. *Life in Southern Nigeria.* Chapter V. London: Macmillan.

—— 1926. *The Peoples of Southern Nigeria.* Vol. II, Chapter XI. London: Oxford University Press.

—— 1932. *Tribes of the Niger Delta.* Chapters VIII, IX, X. London: Sheldon Press.

WADDELL, REV. HOPE MASTERTON. 1863. *Twenty-nine Years in the West Indies and Central Africa.* London: Nelson. Second edition, London: Frank Cass, 1970.

© G. I. Jones 1970

17

Malcolm Ruel

Were-animals and the Introverted Witch

Professor Evans-Pritchard, in discussing whether Azande witches are 'conscious agents', points to the discontinuity in the terms according to which Azande speak of witchcraft as an attribute of other people's actions and their own. In this matter Azande are inconsistent: 'Although they assert the moral guilt of others, nevertheless, when accused of witchcraft themselves they plead innocence, if not of the act – for they cannot well do that in public – at least of intention' (Evans-Pritchard, 1937, p. 119). The point has comparative relevance since so much of the subsequent study of witchcraft has been concerned with these beliefs as projected onto other people: the witch is the aggressor, the other person, the unknown enemy who must be unmasked. So in analysis, the positive facts, the 'social actions' which have been taken as a point of departure, are the accusations made: the identification of the witch from among the hostile, and perhaps otherwise uncontrollable, 'others'.

But there are societies in which explicit, particularized accusations are *not* made, and where the identity of the witch is not pinned so neatly onto others, potentially hostile. One such society is that of the Banyang, who certainly believe that witches can harm others, but who only rarely and in unusual circumstances will ever positively and deliberately accuse another of maleficent witchcraft. Indeed, when Banyang seek to account for misfortune, the pressures of their society operate in quite a different direction: it is one's own actions rather than those of others that must be scrutinized. One of the most frequently repeated proverbial songs, often quoted in a witchcraft context, makes precisely this point: 'If something is lost at home,' the singer chants, 'you yourself should look for it.' Most illnesses and almost all deaths following upon illness are believed to be consequent upon a person's own witchcraft actions. To avert such illnesses or deaths the pressures are not to 'accuse' but to 'confess'. For Banyang, witches stand identified not because of what others say about them but because of what they say about themselves.

This 'introspective' character of Banyang witchcraft can be related to a second feature, which is unusual perhaps less in the principle involved than in the extent to which this principle is developed: this is the belief that people can change into or can send out 'animals' and that it is these animals that carry out the evil (witchcraft) intentions of their owners. I shall return later to the definitional problem that is involved here (for, unlike most 'witchcraft' beliefs, were-animals for Banyang are not necessarily culpable, their actions not necessarily evil), but if we may take the definitional association of the two for granted, the point of interest in the were-beliefs is their very complexity and many-sidedness. Banyang can and do speak simply and directly about the 'were-person' (*mu dɛbu*) as the 'evil person', the 'person of the night', and such statements fit the relatively simple and unelaborated stereotypes of the witch as the anti-social, evil agent of many societies. Yet – and it is this that I would emphasize – this simple stereotype is for Banyang quickly shattered into a great number of different 'images' or 'types' that a person's witchcraft potential (now to beg the question that Banyang so consistently beg) can take. A 'were-person' or 'witch' (*mu dɛbu*) can be referred to in general terms as an evil or deceitful person, but it is also understood that all human beings have in some form 'were-animals' (*babu*), and there is indeed a very great range of named were-animals that people are said to possess. Moreover, this range of were-animals extends from those that are most evil, the most perverted in their abilities, to those that are entirely unreprehensible and appear sometimes as little more than metaphorical descriptions of a person's individual talents. Again, one person may possess a number of were-animals, drawn from different points on the total range, which determine as it were his 'complexion' as a were-owner.

The argument that this paper presents comes from the linking of these two features. The very elaborateness of Banyang were-beliefs stems, I shall claim, from the much more sophisticated set of categories that are necessary to any 'introspective' moral inquiry about a person's *own* activities. If the witch is the 'other' person, one can be content with a simple representation of his moral character and actions; but such a simple stereotype is no longer appropriate to any self-conscious inquiry about one's own implication in potentially evil actions. It is precisely this more elaborate expression of a person's responsibilities for his own actions and his relationship to others that Banyang were-beliefs make possible. Professor Evans-Pritchard has pointed to the uncertainty that Azande express when the possibility of their own witchcraft is mooted. Banyang were-beliefs develop in an extended form just this balance of uncertainty in the expression of a person's own guilt, while still retaining the certainty that 'other' people are witches – for they stand confessed.

I

Banyang (who live in the sparsely settled forest country of the upper Cross River in present-day West Cameroon) hold that in certain circumstances people have the ability to transform themselves into, or to send out as an extension of themselves, 'were-animals' or 'were-types' (*babu*) which in this form are able to act in ways that would not be possible to the person in his ordinary, human body. There are occasional stories of actual physical transformations: someone who has seen a person change into a bush-pig and then back into a person again, or people who are able to turn into a kite or a mole. But for the most part Banyang speak of the were-animal or were-type as having a separate existence, mystically linked to but materially independent of the person who 'owns' it as an attribute. Typically, the person with a were-attribute is said to 'move with it' or, more positively, to 'remove' it or to 'send' it out at night when he himself is sleeping in his own house. There are, however, many variants in the modes of manifestation: from the manipulative conjuring of an (ostensibly real) leopard from leaves, woods, and medicines, to the projection of the person's 'shadow' or 'spirit' which takes on the merely mystical identity of a were-form.

In most cases the were-animal or were-type is in some sense a 'double' or alternative identity of the person who owns it, and the area in which it moves is again a 'double' world, another existence parallel to the actual world (*kɛkpɛ*) in which people live. Most inclusively, this parallel world is the 'bush of the were-animals' (*εbə babu*), figured conceptually and sometimes in fact as the area of bush which surrounds the social, communal life of the settlements; but other were-types are thought to live in the deep pools of a river, and others again 'above the sky' (conceptualized as the roof of the house) where in a further world people who have 'thunder' live and move in their were-forms. (This cosmological replication of the social world is consistent with the replicated structure of Banyang communities as residential groups. It is extended further in the case of the 'community of the dead', believed to exist in some sense 'in the ground'.)

People are said to acquire their were-attributes from their parents when they are young, or occasionally from an older relative, or a friend. Some were-types can be purchased. Typically, however, a parent's imparting of a were-animal is thought to be consequent upon the parent's own care and concern for his (or her) child, and is part of the general instructions that a child must be given to prepare him for life in a community. The 'teaching' or 'showing' of a were-animal is often associated with the giving of medicines (usually infusions of leaves or woods which are then drunk), and I have been told by some Banyang of how their parents did in fact give them such medicines to drink when they were children. Other (hearsay) accounts describe more fanciful procedures involving the actual production of an animal. Other Banyang have told me that their parents merely asserted their own (and their children's) possession of such-and-such a were-animal. Again, there is a large area of variation and uncertainty: the distinction between ordinary therapeutic medicines and preparations that *might* have been imparting were-abilities is not always an easy one to make in retrospect, and in any case the process of instruction in Banyang society is frequently (and indeed most commonly) by example and inference rather than by any explicit deliberate explanation.

Although were-animals are taught, they are also associated with certain organic conditions. A distinction is made between were-animals that are in the 'belly' (*bεnyε*) and those 'on the surface of the body' (*amfaε mtεt*), which is in part a distinction between those that, at least potentially, are the more heinous, or harmful, and those that merely confer certain abilities (often of a physical kind). It is thus only the former that can be identified during an autopsy carried out after death, where the state of a series of internal organs (lungs, heart, intestines, liver, gall-bladder, spleen, etc.) gives evidence as to the were-animals that the dead person possessed and those that were the direct cause of his death. No comparable organic signs exist for the 'were-animals of strength' that lie 'on the surface of the body'; nor, of course, is there the same need to identify them in order to determine the moral cause of a person's death.

The abilities acquired through possession of were-animals, or the actions made by them, depend very largely upon the nature of the were-animal so owned. An underlying condition of *all* were-animals, even the most heinous, is that the owner need not have employed them to 'do evil', that is to harm other people. Were-animals that are used to 'do evil' (potentially, any of the 'were-animals of destruction', which include the owl, python, leopard, bush-pig, elephant, hippopotamus, thunder, and one or two others) may be 'caught' by one of the protective cult-agencies, nowadays usually Mfam, that Banyang use to safe-guard their communities from the worst forms of double-dealing (witchcraft, theft, and lying). It is axiomatic to Banyang belief that a were-person who attempts to do evil *must* eventually be caught by a cult-agency: 'a witch (*mu dɛbu*) will not last long in the community'. The person so 'caught' will fall seriously (and, it is expected, suddenly) sick, and if he or she does not 'confess' to his were-actions will be expected to die. On the other hand, if confession is full and if it is accompanied by due ritual appease-ment of the cult-agency, the influence of the latter (it is believed) can be removed and the patient will then recover.

Finally, at death, if the cause of death is in any way open to doubt, an autopsy can be performed and the 'truth' ascertained, according to the various organic signs. As already stated, a person's death (if he was an adult and if its cause is not old age or an accident) is almost invariably attributed to the person's own were-animals: frequently a number of animals are identified, apparently being used by their owner over a period of time.

A person who owns were-animals may still suffer through them even although he does not use them to harm others. The general principle here is the familiar one of parallel injury:

whatever befalls the were-animal in the bush (if it is caught in a trap, is shot, if it falls while running, is involved in a fight, etc.) will also leave its mark in the 'person at home' who owns the animal. This principle establishes for Banyang an elaborate system of pathology by which a whole range of standard symptoms are diagnosed: whooping cough is the panting of the leopard running off from or being chased by others in the bush; jaundiced eyes and urine are associated with the possession of thunder/lightning; sores on the legs or arms may come from any form of injury to the were-animal counterpart; the heat-stroke of a child is that it has been (mystically) struck by the *amɔ* snake; the vomiting of black vomit is the bringing up of 'gun-powder' which has shot the person's elephant or bush-cow; and so on. Again, recovery is dependent upon admission to having such a were-animal, followed by the appropriate treat-ment. If one's were-animal (usually an elephant) has been shot, it is believed that its life may be lengthened if another animal or 'young woman' (*ngɔsɔŋ*, who is typically believed to care for others) can get it to a river in time, where its injury will be cooled; alternatively, treatment may be given to substitute a different animal for the one that has been fatally injured.

I have sketched out above the broad axioms of Banyang belief in were-animals and the way in which they are used to explain events, especially of illness and death. Can one in fact speak of these as a system of 'witchcraft' belief? I would argue that one can, provided that one makes clear that the evil inten-tions or culpable actions normally identified with 'witchcraft' are contained *within* and are not coterminous with the beliefs. To put the matter in a different way, Banyang perform 'witch-craft' with their were-animals, but not all were-animals are witchcraft. Even here, however, one must be careful not to overstress the innocence of some were-animals. Just as the possibility of innocence is built into the system of belief in all its aspects, so too the possession of a were-animal is never wholly free from blame: to be other than one is seen to be, to have in some way a 'double' identity, always places one poten-tially in the position to deceive, and for Banyang the evil of witchcraft is above all the evil of deceit.

I conclude this general account with one or two instances reported to me where the beliefs have served to explain illness

or death, and have been associated with the reported confession
of the person involved.

A schoolteacher who was a young man was said to have had a
leopard and to have used the leopard to drive animals into
his traps. His leopard was shot and he himself became ill.
He would not confess that he had a leopard (in which case
another could have been given to him) and in a short time
he died – confessing finally that it was his leopard that had
been shot. There was no autopsy, because the man died in
hospital. When I protested about the explanation offered in
this case, the point emphasized was that the man had finally
confessed: how else would one know?

A wife of a man of Okorobak hamlet in Tali was believed to
have a bush-pig, with which she had eaten the farms of the
members of the hamlet. A trap was set and a bush-pig caught.
This was brought home and eaten and the wife herself ate
part. Within a few days she was dead.

On another occasion a wife of the leader of Tali became suddenly and seriously ill. It took six men to carry her to her
natal settlement, during which time she was shivering and
twitching, just as a pig which had been caught in a trap. In
both this and the previous case the women are said to have
confessed before they died that their bush-pigs had been
caught.

The explanation given for the lameness of a cripple boy who
lived in a settlement near to where I worked was that it had
been caused by a co-wife of the boy's mother to spite the
father (her husband) who had failed to do favour with her.
At her death she confessed that, using her 'python', she had
taken the boy and coiled around him, so causing the paralysis
of his legs.

When the son of a senior elder of a Tali hamlet was injured
away from home in a lorry accident, his father was said to
have travelled down 'at night' with his 'thunder' to the town
of the accident, but was stopped at a stream in the market
place and forced to return. The next day he went down in his
true 'body', but later when he returned home he became ill.

He then confessed (to what was certainly a dream), and after treatment became well.

II

I list here some examples of were-animals and describe the kinds of action or ability that are attributed to them. They are presented in decreasing order of potential harmfulness.

Ɛpɛm, the common owl, is sometimes said to be the 'leader of the were-animals' (*mfɔ babu*) and is always thought of as the most heinous in its actions. It is said to eat the flesh of others, especially of children (who have the least ability to resist the predatory actions of others, unless they are themselves protected by the were-animals of their guardians). An owl may be owned and 'not used for harm', but of all were-animals the terms by which it is described allow least possibility of non-culpable ownership. Its 'sign' at an autopsy is the presence of clots of blood in the heart, said to represent the 'persons' or 'children' consumed by the owner.

Ɛpɛm ndɛm, a further type of owl (literally the 'penis' owl), is believed to go at night to have intercourse with women, causing a miscarriage if the woman is pregnant, or barrenness. Its sign is a swollen or turgid appendix. It may be owned by men or women.

Ɛkpɔnɛn, a third distinct type of owl, carries the ambivalence characteristic of were-beliefs into this category of the potentially most evil animals. Thus the *ɛkpɔnɛn* owl is believed to be able to consume the hearts of other people; its sign at autopsy is the diseased or 'decayed' condition of its owner's heart (Mfam having deflected the action of the were-animal onto the owner himself). But also, and equally importantly, the *ɛkpɔnɛn* owl is believed to 'hear things' or know what is going on in the witchcraft world, and is especially associated with membership of the Basinjom society, whose members use their own were-animals to detect and expose the witchcraft of others.

Ngɔm, the python, is the next most heinous to the common owl and may, it is believed, work in league with it. Thus the 'owl' takes the 'shadow' of the child and gives it to the 'python' who 'sits with it' while the child falls sick and wastes away at home. Unless the python can be forced to release the shadow of the child (by the invocation of a cult-agency, which is directed to attack whoever is harming the child), the child will, it is believed, eventually die. A were-python is also sometimes cited as the cause of a crippling paralysis. The owner of a python is not uncommonly said to keep it in his (or her) house, in a physical or quasi-physical form: from here it may, or may not, have been sent out on its nefarious errands. The sign of a python at an autopsy is when the intestines are markedly swollen, or slither out of the 'opened' belly.

Njui, the bush-pig, is used by women in the ravaging of farms, and is also cited to explain failure or difficulties connected with birth. A bush-pig 'bears her children in the bush' and not 'at home' and may be used to explain why a woman regularly conceives but later miscarries. Again, during birth, extreme bleeding or the obstruction of the infant may, it is believed, be caused by the animal in the belly, which gnaws at the placenta or prevents the child from descending. Banyang descriptions of the sign of a bush-pig at autopsy would seem to refer to the Fallopian tubes (which have a somewhat 'pig-like' form) in certain states of disease.

Nkwɔ, the leopard. With this animal we approach a significant middle series of were-animals whose destructiveness is material and actual rather than mystical and whose ownership is thus contingently linked with actual events. In these cases the emphasis is less upon the actual destructiveness caused (which is sometimes trivial, e.g. in the case of trees being struck by lightning) than upon the evidence it gives of complicity in the world of were-animals. In this series also, the 'social' as distinct from the 'antisocial' characteristics of the were-animals become more marked: the personae presented embody the qualities expected especially of the 'leader' and 'elder' in Banyang society; and it is here too that we find most strongly the suggestion of a 'double' society, replicating the features of life in ordinary communities.

Thus the leopard (which in other contexts is associated with leadership and political authority) may, it is believed, seize and kill goats and other domestic animals (far less frequently, people), but, perhaps most commonly, possession of a leopard is cited to account for a number of clearly defined illnesses where the illness is attributed to parallel injury in the were-leopard rather than to intentionally destructive action on the part of its owner. Such illnesses are those with the symptoms of a 'whooping' or raucous cough, or breathlessness, and those with festering sores on the arms or legs (attributed respectively to the running of the leopard, and to its physical injury in various ways). Were-leopards are said to move in groups, and often the events that have befallen a were-leopard are thought to have arisen from its relations with others: e.g. being chased, or fighting with its peers. The physical attributes associated with a leopard-person are strength in fighting, and physical agility in running, jumping, and dancing. At an autopsy the sign of a leopard (which, it would seem, is quite frequently found) is the presence of black patches or marks on either or both lungs; if both are marked the person is said to have had two leopards.

I describe *dɛfaŋ*, 'thunder' (or 'lightning'; Banyang do not differentiate between them), as a 'were-type', although the Kenyang term remains the same, *dɛbu*. At this point it may be helpful to offer a text, for both the particular and the more general points that it illustrates:

Dɛfaŋ: this were-type is like a shadow which acts like a human being. It is in the belly and they operate on someone to see if that person died because of thunder (literally: 'had death in the form of thunder'). It is the gall-bladder (*mbi*); if it is very dark, that means that the person had trouble in the form of thunder. A person with thunder may come to have eyes that grow yellow in his head, and during the daylight hours he feels weak. His urine is a deep yellow (or red).

People believe that the sky is like a roof. It is up there, above the sky, that a thunder-person lives. Such were-types live like ordinary people. They fight and amuse themselves. Everyone has a young woman who looks after him up in the sky. Should someone fall down up there as thunder, he will also fall here at home, and will die. Father N— died some time ago because he fell in the form of thunder.

A thunder-person can do harm if he wants to. He can send thunder to strike coconut trees, even a person. When I was a

child, O—, my father's brother, sent thunder which spoilt a
coconut tree behind my mother's house because my father had
refused him food, on the very day that my father did so. That
day, I was sitting at the fire, and as the thunder fell on the
coconut tree, it came down and came into the house, and
lifted me up and threw me down.

When O— was dying (about six months later) he confessed
that it was he who had destroyed the coconut tree.

Someone who gives many commands (*asaɛ kɛnsaɛ*: the idea
is of someone who throws his weight around) up there as
thunder keeps quiet here at home.

The final statement of the text refers to the recognized fact that
a person does not always give evidence of the characteristics of
his were-animal. In fact, thunder as a were-type is associated
with a strong, dominant personality, and, while weak and ineffectual people *may* (in their shadow-world) have thunder, in
other cases the association is a direct and not an inverted one.
It is no coincidence that two of the most powerful village leaders
of the Upper Banyang in the nineteenth century were both
called Defang.

Nsok, the elephant, may cause destruction to farms but the
harm that it does is perhaps less general than that of the bush-
pig, less violent than that of thunder. On the other hand, the
quality believed to be acquired by possession of an elephant is
that of 'hearing things' or 'knowing what goes on'. In the intri-
cate web of Banyang community politics such an attribute is
highly valued. If the leopard, thunder, and the bush-cow suggest the individual qualities of a community leader, the elephant
suggests the qualities of an elder. Again, however, possession is
by no means limited to elders: like the bush-pig, the elephant is
cited as a cause for difficulties in childbirth.

Nsokonyɛn, the 'elephant of the river' or hippopotamus, like
the crocodile (*nyoŋ*), is classed with the *bo nyɛn* or 'river-people',
who are believed to live in their own social world in the deep
pools of rivers. Again, their significance lies less in the material
harm known to be done by these creatures than in the activities,
relationships, and events in which they are involved in the
'other' world of the river. In particular, this 'river-world' is

believed to correspond to the kinship (or lineage) group in the community, so that (typically) a kinsman who does not give due respect to elders of his lineage group 'at home' may be punished by them 'in the river'. A diviner who diagnoses the cause of an illness as coming from the patient's were-animal in the river may be indicating no more than an interpersonal grievance in the lineage group, to be put right by the collective performance of a kinship 'blessing'.

One passes from these to a whole series of 'animals of strength' or 'ability' whose possession is associated with some (in most cases physical) attribute, which are believed in general not to be harmful, but whose possession may be used to account for the illness or death of their owner. Strength in fighting or in carrying loads, the ability to slip out of an opponent's grip, to jolt an opponent into releasing his hold, to fly up out of a dangerous situation, to burrow out of or extricate oneself from an enclosed space, to sing or dance well, to have a strong grasp, to be successful in fishing or hunting, are all believed to be conferred by one or another were-animal, fish, bird, or type. These were-animals are more variable in their distribution than those described above and the texts that I have collected concerning them frequently link them with named individuals or lineage groups understood to possess them.

III

How far do Banyang consciously interpret their own actions or intentions in terms of these 'were'-categories that are available to them? I must immediately say that this is not something that I systematically discussed during my fieldwork and that any answer I give is drawn from observation of somewhat scattered events and from more general discussions.

The broad conclusion I would offer is that the credibility – indeed certainty – that Banyang give to their beliefs depends upon the way in which these beliefs are applied to, or suggested by, *other* people's actions and upon their connection with observed events; but that also, in a rather different way – situationally, and with far less assurance – the beliefs are used to express subjective facts of intentions, dreams, doubts, and moral conflicts.

One is indeed struck by the fact that the beliefs offer not only a system of diagnostic medicine (that in some of its pathological connections may well have a basis in fact) but also a system of psychology. The 'bush of the were-animals' appears in many respects to be very like the subconscious mind: it is the area of submerged, private identities, where physical events lose their consistency and order, where space and time are in abeyance. This shadow-world (and the metaphor is Banyang's) has a kind of autonomy: it is linked with the real world, but may be in discrepancy with it. 'Confession' rectifies the 'deceit' of such a double existence, harmonizes the submerged with the public identity.

Dreams provide some of the evidence on which Banyang base their knowledge of their own actions in the were-animal form. By no means all dreams are explained in this way (some are without significance; others may be interpreted prognostically), but if people do dream in situations of anxiety or stress it seems probable both that the dreams will relate to those situations and that they will be recognized consciously as doing so: certainly such dreams are interpreted in 'were'-terms. Thus one of the most clearly spoken confessions I have witnessed was that made by a mother whose child was sick and who had dreamt that she was before the tree of Mfam (i.e. that she had been 'caught' by Mfam in her were-form). What she had experienced was reported both as a dream and as evidence (with her child's sickness) of what had occurred in fact – and was followed the next day by the ritual appeasement of the cult-agency.

Moreover, people who are ill come under a great deal of pressure from relatives and friends to look for the cause, a pressure that increases with the severity of the illness. Their own responsibility for the outcome of their illness is stressed: 'Do you want to die? It is in your hands', they are told. The frequency of confessions made shortly before death is evidence of this kind of pressure and for Banyang is not inconsistent with the death itself, since the confession proves the guilt, but comes too late to expunge it.

Even so, actual confessions are rarely as explicit or selective as they are later reported to be. In the two cases of confession before Mfam that I witnessed (both by women) the women confessing were eventually led into stating a kind of blanket guilt:

they admitted having 'all the were-animals', and they admitted also to theft. There is every reason in fact to make such an inclusive confession since if anything *is* omitted the ritual appeasement of the cult-agency is thought to have been in vain. Yet later, when these confessions were discussed or reported, specific points were selected which fitted in with other publicly known facts or events.

Again, the fact that one should have were-animals is not for any individual person to be regarded as unusual: everyone has; why should one not oneself? In this respect the example of Basinjom society is relevant, for the members of this society (which has divinatory functions and is the only body that does today occasionally directly accuse someone specifically of witchcraft) have to confess to their own were-animals in becoming members. I may perhaps cite my own experience here, since when I became a (junior) member this requirement placed me in a quandary. In a discussion beforehand of what would in my case be appropriate, the following list was agreed to: thunder (which it is believed all Europeans possess; also someone had already confessed to meeting me 'above the sky' in the form of thunder); an elephant (who 'knows things' – a not unflattering attribute for a field anthropologist); a tortoise (regarded as clever and crafty); and a porcupine (which 'eats only ground-nuts and not people'). In point of fact I made only a general confession – 'In so far as people have were-animals I have them too....' and this was accepted. (My fellow-initiants were more explicit.)

Eventually, however, and certainly when they are suffering from the stress of sickness, I would suggest that people are not entirely clear about the were-animals they are obliged to assume they have. An incident that illustrates most clearly the general view I am advancing occurred when a diviner, during a consultation concerning the wife of an elder, said that her illness came from her own 'hippopotamus' which lived in the pool of a river with her other kinsfolk near her natal home. I knew both the elder and his wife well, and at the end of the consultation I turned directly and asked the woman: did she know about the hippopotamus? The elder interrupted to assert: 'She knows!' The woman herself shrugged her shoulders and laughed. It would be wholly in accord with Banyang reading of events to say after this incident that she had in fact agreed to possessing a hippopotamus. (She certainly did not disagree, and this is what counts.)

IV

This paper has not attempted to give a full account of Banyang were-beliefs, or to relate them to their other cosmological or value systems.[1] What it has attempted to do is to show that these beliefs, whatever else they are, provide categories for the subjective understanding of behaviour, according to the conditions and norms of Banyang society. The moral issue of what behaviour is wrong and what acceptable is posed within the beliefs and is not presupposed by them. The beliefs are certainly most clearly activated in situations of misfortune or illness and death, but the direction in which they point is to personal responsibility and personal implication, and not (directly at least) to the hostility of others. The very elaborateness of the categories available permits these questions to be asked by different people in different ways and in different situations.

How far can this analysis be made to extend to other societies? Apart from Banyang, this general complex of belief would seem to be shared by a number of other neighbouring Cross River peoples, notably the Ejagham, Efik, and Ibibio (see especially Talbot, 1912, 1923). For these peoples some verbal distinction *is* made between 'witchcraft' and 'were-animals' ('bush-souls' or 'animal affinities'), but it is clear from what Talbot says (e.g. 1923, pp. 88, 101, 107-109) that the beliefs overlap and run into each other. What is also very striking in Talbot's accounts of both Ejagham and Ibibio beliefs is the number of self-confessed were-actions he gives: indeed, he includes three photographs of were-persons, two men (one a village leader) who have a 'leopard' and an 'elephant', and a woman who has a 'snake' (a 'python'?). In these societies, accusations of witchcraft were certainly made, and in fact they gained some notoriety from an extensive use of the 'esere bean' poison ordeal in the past. Nevertheless, a very important element in this usage seems to have been the fact that the ordeal was as much a test of conscience as a proof of guilt, and that many voluntarily undertook the ordeal to assert their own innocence.[2]

Can one suggest, further, that where metamorphosis or the

'sending out' of animals appears as an adjunct to witchcraft belief one may expect to find that the witch's self-confessed identity or an actor's own implication in witchcraft is at issue? Lindskog's extensive ethnographic survey of 'The Human and the Animal' (in Lindskog, 1954) does not give sufficient details, and his sources are perhaps not selective enough, to provide an adequate answer, but his many examples do suggest that such beliefs often cohere around the 'witch-doctor' or 'diviner' and may perhaps also be related to persons holding political status. Monica Wilson's (1951) account of Nyakyusa 'python power' indicates how this can be used for good or ill, either in harming others (by the 'witches') or in protecting the community (by the 'defenders'). Similarly, among the Lele it is striking that it is the very person whose position is most critically ambivalent, the diviner who is potentially a sorcerer, who is ascribed the power of metamorphosis, being 'able to transform himself into a leopard, to meet other sorcerers at night and out-wit them on their own ground' (Douglas, 1963, p. 130). Field's (1960) extensive collection of Ashanti confessions to witchcraft does not other than incidentally make reference to animal counterparts; nevertheless, Manoukian's summary (1950, p. 61) makes it clear that Ashanti witches are believed to be able to transform themselves into a whole host of animals, and the general description Field does offer indicates a conceptualization of witchcraft which in a number of features suggests similarities with Banyang wereanimals. A 'witch' is *obayifo*, 'a person who is the abode of an evil entity, *obayi*': the effort of Ashanti is always in the direction of locating, naming, making explicit, this projected entity, the *obayi*:

> 'Every *obayi* is held to have a name. A witch cannot be freed from her *obayi* until she has disclosed its name. There are a number of traditional names for *obayi* (just as Towser, Fido and Spot are traditional names for dogs), and when asked her *obayi*'s name the self-accused witch produces one of these. Almost the only things which shrine secretaries think it important to record concerning witchcraft cases are the names of *obayi*. Sometimes a witch feels she has several *obayi*' (Field, 1960, p. 37).

And, of course, the point of Field's book is that these beliefs do provide a kind of psychology; it is an uncertain and fluid one, but its terms help to express the divisions and conflicts a person can face in his own identity.

NOTES

1. A more general account of these beliefs, which emphasizes their systematic uncertainty as a rational belief structure and the fact that they are always invoked *post hoc* and situationally (only death terminates the flow of 'situations' and it is only then that rational 'certainty' is achieved), can be found in Ruel (1965). A brief, factual description of the operation and organization of Basinjom society is contained in Ruel (1969). Further consideration of the leopard in the political context as a symbol of power may be found in Ruel (1970).

2. Any person directly accused of witchcraft had the right to demand that his accuser himself take the poison ordeal: this principle also indicates the 'conscience-testing' character of the ordeal. One might argue, indeed, that the very widespread submission to the poison ordeal at certain critical times in the past in Old Calabar – notably after the death of an important leader or 'king' – followed in part from the non-specific character of witchcraft imputations and fears, which grew in intensity at such times, leading individuals to the 'conscience-clearing' action of asserting their innocence by taking the poison ordeal. The case witnessed by Hope Waddell (1863, pp. 480-482) would lend itself to this interpretation, as also would the statement that the more recent illegal resort to the poison ordeal occurs 'when individuals desire to show their innocence of any imputation of witchcraft' (Forde, 1956, p. 22).

REFERENCES

DOUGLAS, MARY. 1963. Techniques of Sorcery Control in Central Africa. In John Middleton & E. H. Winter (eds.), *Witchcraft and Sorcery in East Africa*. London: Routledge & Kegan Paul.

EVANS-PRITCHARD, E. E. 1937. *Witchcraft, Oracles and Magic among the Azande*. Oxford: Clarendon Press.

FIELD, M. J. 1960. *Search for Security*. London: Faber.

FORDE, DARYLL (ed.). 1956. *Efik Traders of Old Calabar*. London: Oxford University Press (for the International African Institute).

LINDSKOG, BIRGER. 1954. *African Leopard Men*. Uppsala: Studia Ethnographica Upsaliensia VII.

MANOUKIAN, MADELINE. 1950. *Akan and Ga-Adangme Peoples of the Gold Coast*. Ethnographic Survey of Africa. London: Oxford University Press (for the International African Institute).

RUEL, MALCOLM. 1965. Witchcraft, Morality and Doubt. *Odu: University of Ife Journal of African Studies* **2** (1): 3-27.

RUEL, MALCOLM. 1969. *Leopards and Leaders: Constitutional Politics among a Cross River People*. London: Tavistock Publications.

—— 1970. Lions, Leopards and Rulers. *New Society*, Vol. 15, No. 380, 8 January.

TALBOT, P. A. 1912. *In the Shadow of the Bush*. London: Heinemann.

—— 1923. *Life in Southern Nigeria*. London: Macmillan.

WADDELL, HOPE M. 1863. *Twenty-nine Years in the West Indies and Central Africa*. London: Nelson. Second edition, London: Frank Cass, 1970.

WILSON, MONICA. 1951. *Good Company*. London: Oxford University Press (for the International African Institute).

© Malcolm Ruel (1970)

18

T. O. Beidelman

Towards More Open Theoretical
Interpretations

The various papers presented at this A.S.A. conference all
mention witchcraft and sorcery, and yet these terms seem labels
for social phenomena that differ radically from society to society;
furthermore, even the distinction between the two terms themselves is not always satisfactory. Taxonomic preoccupation may
sometimes distract us from recognizing ambiguities inherent in
social beliefs and acts. When applied on a cross-cultural, comparative level, such labels may conceal problematical interdependences. We feel we have explained matters away through
having imposed some nominal category.

Many of the papers show a special concern with the question
why witchcraft exists in certain societies and not in others.
My own view is that this concern may sometimes be due to a
certain predisposition towards functionalist thinking. We tend
to seek explanations for the presence of beliefs which seem to us
peculiarly destructive socially. But that they are destructive
may be an unreasonable assumption on our own part, which
derives from our functionalistic predisposition to conceive of
societies in such a way that all practices contribute to social
solidarity and continuity. It may also be that we are sometimes
misled into believing in the essentially negative effects of such
beliefs simply because we are told only of these aspects by those
within the society where such beliefs are held. Yet can we be
sure that customs come into being or persist only on such
positive functional terms? In social studies we are concerned
with both how and why certain forms of behaviour exist or
persist. While the how and the why are interrelated, the former
is far more accessible to description and demonstration. In much
of the discussion that took place during the conference, there
was a predisposition towards the problem of why. This too may
relate to our functionalistic heritage.

The complexity of the data covered in the conference meetings indicates the need for an approach combining several analytical levels. Three such analytical levels here seem of particular importance. These involve sociological, ideological, and psychological factors – though, of course, in actual analyses the interdependence of the phenomena involved makes analytical separation difficult. I am fully aware that, in actual practice, most of us mix analyses at these various levels all of the time. For example, one cannot discuss certain aspects of social norms without discussing certain ideological notions; and one cannot discuss certain aspects of adherence to, or deviation from, norms without discussing certain psychological aspects of affect, aspiration, motivation, etc. The problem is not that social anthropologists do not range freely from level to level; rather, it is that they range very freely indeed, but usually fail to explicate each of these levels in a systematic way sufficient to account for all the important features of the issues concerned.

For example, consider the problems raised by conventional analyses focusing on social roles and statuses. Robert Brain and Esther Goody emphasize the contrasting roles of chiefs and commoners in regard to various acts in witchcraft cases. Esther Goody also draws a sharp contrast between sexual roles and relates these to differences in witchcraft and sorcery accusations and the respective punishments involved. This line of analysis assumes that certain different roles and statuses are associated with various tensions and conflicts, while others are more complementary and harmonious. This assumption rests on the imputation of various motives and psychic states to certain roles and statuses.

Initially, the task seems to be that of describing the normative logic in a system of standardized social relations and of pointing out the areas of conflict or inconsistency of interests. However, this approach eventually leads to related questions less easily answered. What, for example, accounts for the absence or presence of accusations in formally similar situations? Of course, what is at issue in part is the simplicity of standard concepts about normative roles and statuses. Statistical material and detailed case-histories, especially over fairly long periods, seem the most useful means for getting at such matters. Furthermore, the entire question of stress and conflict, so crucial to

Esther Goody's paper, requires further explication as to what aggression actually means within a particular society. Most of us are familiar with the problem of defining culturally relative institutions, such as marriage and parenthood, yet few of us apply equal caution in dealing with what may appear as less formal types of institutionalized activity, such as aggression, fear, obscenity, insult, even though these may be equally important to our sociological arguments and interpretations. Thus, for the Gonja case, we still need to know far more about what the significance may be that male aggression through sorcery is allowed and even expected, whereas female aggression through reputed witchcraft is strongly condemned and punished. At this point, social psychological issues and the relativism of the symbolic expression of affect become real difficulties.

Malcolm Ruel discusses animal and human attributes and how notions about the interrelationships of body and psyche provide a folk explanation of certain acts and motivations. But the problems posed by his fascinating data go far beyond the scope of his allotted space in the conference. Ultimately, these require nothing less than an exposition of the entire field of notions about animal categories and their associated attributes, and of the folk psychology accounting for the interrelation of physical attributes and the moral and psychological qualities they are thought to reflect. Robert Brain's data suggest that certain attributes of sky, earth, twins, spiders, infants, and the aged may be part of a broader ideological system; when this is more clearly delineated, perhaps some of the apparent complexity and arbitrariness of these symbolic motifs will diminish. Esther Goody reports symbols of tails, lateral polarity, and the enshrouding of persons associated with certain affective aspects of sexual conflict and role differentiation. She goes on to remark upon the particular violence with which convicted female witches are punished. It would be useful to explore these symbolic clues regarding the emotional aspects of sexuality and how these are expressed or repressed within the field of witchcraft belief.

It may be instructive to draw parallels between alien witchcraft beliefs and our own, often non-rational, notions of mental illness and treatment as explanatory or expiatory devices both for individuals and for groups. Admittedly, our work as social anthropologists or historians cannot supplant that of trained psychologists, yet our initial advantages in perceiving a cultural and social system alien to us in space or time may give us advantages in calling such data to the attention of psychologists. Our work may also give us a socially wider and more flexible perspective than many psychologists hold. Curiously, the delusional aspects of behaviour associated with witchcraft and sorcery have received relatively little attention from social anthropologists. What is the relation between disturbed, even psychotic, persons and witchcraft behaviour? How many anthropologists have interviewed the confessed witch; or how many have compared different interpretations of the same case by the various protagonists, such as the accused, the accuser, the reputed victim, the various relatives and neighbours concerned? Such material is, admittedly, not easy to secure, but it is certainly available in some situations.

Related to this theme is the difficult task of establishing which aspects of such beliefs and behaviour are institutionalized and which represent deviancy. For example, it is reported that witchcraft accusations and suspicions are common and not especially distressing for most Azande; but then to what extent can we speak of such Azande beliefs as being comparable to those in other societies where suspected witches may be lynched? Similarly, we may speak of certain beliefs about witches or sorcerers being institutionalized or standardized within a particular society, but the confession or suspicion of witchcraft may well not represent institutionalized behaviour so much as deviancy or social breakdown. We cannot be sure until we thoroughly investigate the nature of each case. One of the strengths of the work of Ruel, Brain, and Goody is that all three try to face these difficult problems related to describing the state of mind of the witch or sorcerer himself.

What I should particularly like to see is an attempt to tackle the broader question of how the minds of witches are thought to be distinguishable from, say, those of saints or of the insane. Men tend to make beliefs out of the fabric of their available cosmology, but there *is* innovation, and witches along with prophets, witch-finders, and others are at times peripheral yet innovative persons. They are often associated with radically changing societies; unfortunately, this point is often presented as a sign of social breakdown rather than as a manifestation of new syntheses and values initiated by those persons perhaps most representative of the emerging society. To what extent, then, is a witch or a madman an unsuccessful prophet? To what extent is a prophet a socially approved deviant? And to what extent must each of these, by the very nature of his status, possess ambiguous attributes beyond the socially conventional good and bad? In many respects our current Western notions of moral responsibility, prophetic or messianic singularity, and mental aberration still form a system of profound ambiguities and non-rational features of a parallel kind. Interest in witches and sorcerers, by definition, has tended to stress the negative, antisocial aspects of such behaviour. But may this not also have, as a consequence, prevented us from utilizing such data to construct a broader analytical matrix for social beliefs and behaviour, a matrix that, by its inclusion of change and difference, would take account of those features of process, tension, and ambiguity that exist in all social life?

Analytical dichotomies are useful but, when overemphasized, they may lead to insensitivity at other levels of research and analysis, both above and below a present focus of interest. Recently, a number of social anthropologists have pointed out the limitations of analytically separating notions of purity from those of pollution, notions of the sacred from those of the profane, even though such analytical distinctions were long the stock of the most esteemed anthropologists. Our analytical notions regarding witches, sorcerers, and other malevolent beings also require a reassessment which will take considerably more account of moral ambiguities (or a moral continuum). The complex ambiguities that sometimes make it difficult to distinguish effective authority from abusive power (the monstrous quality of kingship) or the unbearable inconvenience common to both superlative selfishness and superlative altruism (e.g. Dostoevsky's idiot) are two examples of the kinds of sector where rethinking may be useful.

We have a large number of detailed accounts of certain aspects of witchcraft or sorcery institutions for various societies. But we have no detailed account for any society that provides sufficient data on all of the three levels – sociological, ideological, and psychological – to enable us to begin to chart the possible interdependences and autonomies of such factors. For that, we need a rethinking of the approach itself, rather than simply more studies, whether this means more studies of a greater depth or more studies of an even wider comparative nature. One of the values of this conference has been to underscore this need.

NOTE

1. I am grateful to Duke University for providing funds which allowed me to attend the A.S.A. conference on witchcraft. This paper represents comments on the final session of the conference, which I was asked to discuss; it therefore makes no attempt to refer to all the conference papers.

NOTES ON CONTRIBUTORS

ARDENER, EDWIN. Born 1927, England; educated at London University, B.A.; Oxford, M.A.

Treasury Studentship, 1949-52; Research Fellow, later Senior Research Fellow WAISER/NISER, University College Ibadan, Nigeria, 1952-62; Oppenheimer Student, Oxford, 1961-62; Treasury Fellowship, 1963; Lecturer in Social Anthropology, Oxford, 1963; Fellow of St John's College, 1969.

Author of *Coastal Bantu of the Cameroons*, 1956; *Divorce and Fertility*, 1962; joint author of *Plantation and Village in the Cameroons*, 1960.

BEIDELMAN, THOMAS O. Born 1931, U.S.A.; educated at University of Illinois, A.B., A.M.; University of California; University of Michigan; Oxford University, D.Phil.

Fieldwork in East Africa, 1957-58, 1961-63, 1965, 1966; Assistant Professor of Social Relations, Harvard University, 1963-65; Fellow of the Center for Advanced Study in the Behavioral Sciences, Stanford, 1965-66; Associate Professor of Anthropology, Duke University, 1966-68; Associate Professor of Anthropology, New York University, 1968- ; Visiting Lecturer in Sociology, Makerere University College, 1968.

Author of various papers on the Kaguru, Baraguyu, and Ngulu of Tanzania, East Africa.

BRAIN, ROBERT. Born 1933, Tasmania; educated at the University of Tasmania, B.A.(History), and University College, London, Ph.D.

Lecturer in Anthropology, University College, London, 1965-69; at present writing up material on the Bangwa of Cameroon.

Author of *Bangwa Kinship and Marriage*, in press; co-author (with Adam Pollock) of *Bangwa Funerary Art*, 1970.

BROWN, PETER. Born 1935, Dublin; studied Modern History at New College, Oxford, M.A.

Research Fellow at All Souls College, Oxford, from 1956.

Author of *Augustine of Hippo*, 1967; and of articles on religion and society in the Later Roman Empire.

COHN, NORMAN. Born 1915, London; educated at Oxford (Scholar), M.A. (Medieval and Modern Languages); D.Litt. (Glasgow). F.R.Hist.S.

Hugh Le May Fellow, Rhodes University, South Africa, 1950; Lecturer in French, University of Glasgow, 1946-51; Professor of French, University College, Londonderry, 1951-1960; Professor of French, University of Durham, 1960-63; Fellow, Center for Advanced Study in the Behavioral Sciences, Stanford, California, 1966; Professorial Fellow, University of Sussex, and Director, Centre for Research in Collective Psychopathology, University of Sussex, since 1966.

Author of *Gold Khan and other Siberian Legends*, 1946; *The Pursuit of the Millennium*, 1957; *Warrant for Genocide*, 1967. (Anisfield-Wolf Award in Race Relations.)

DOUGLAS, MARY. Born 1921, Italy; educated at Oxford University, B.A., B.Sc., D.Phil.

Lecturer in Social Anthropology, Oxford, 1950-51; Lecturer in Social Anthropology, University College, London, 1951-63; Reader, 1963- .

Author of *The Lele of the Kasai*, 1963; *Purity and Danger*, 1966; *Natural Symbols: Explorations in Cosmology*, 1970.

Co-editor (with Phyllis M. Kaberry) of *Man in Africa*, 1969.

FORGE, ANTHONY. Born 1929, United Kingdom; studied at Cambridge, M.A.; London School of Economics.

Horniman Scholarship, 1957-60; Part-time Research Officer, London School of Economics, 1960-61; Assistant Lecturer in Social Anthropology, London School of Economics, 1961-64; Fellow of the Bollingen Foundation, New York, 1962-63; Lecturer in Social Anthropology, London School of Economics, 1964-70; Senior Lecturer, 1970- .

Co-author (with Raymond Firth and Jane Hubert) of *Families and their Relatives*, 1969.

GOODY, ESTHER NEWCOMB. Born 1932, U.S.A.; educated at Antioch College, Yellow Springs, Ohio, B.A., and University of Cambridge, Ph.D.

Social Science Research Council (U.S.) First-year Graduate Fellowship, 1954-55; Ford Foundation Foreign Area Training Fellowship, 1956-57; Assistant Director of Studies in Archaeology and Anthropology, Newnham College, Cambridge, 1961-63; Visiting Lecturer, Institute of African Studies, University of Ghana, autumn 1964; Fellow and Lecturer in Social Anthropology, New Hall, Cambridge, 1966- .

Author of 'Terminal Separation and Divorce among the Gonja' in M. Fortes (ed.), *Marriage in Tribal Societies*, 1962; 'Kinship Fostering in Gonja' in P. Mayer (ed.), *Socialization: The Approach from Social Anthropology*, 1970; co-author (with J. R. Goody) of two comparative papers on kinship institutions in Northern Ghana, *Man* (n.s.) **1** (3), 1966, and **2** (2), 1967.

JONES, G. I. Born in Cape Town, South Africa; read History at Oxford and later Anthropology; Ph.D. (Social Anthropology), Cambridge.

District Officer, Colonial Administrative Service, Nigeria, 1927-46; Lecturer in Anthropology, Cambridge University, from 1947; Commissioner to inquire into Status of Chiefs in Eastern Region of Nigeria in 1955; further research work in this area, 1964-65 and 1966-67; Fellow of Jesus College, Cambridge.

Author of *The Trading States of the Oil Rivers*, 1963.

LEWIS, IOAN MYRDDIN. Born 1930, Scotland; studied at Glasgow University, B.Sc., and Oxford, B.Litt., D.Phil.

Research Assistant, Chatham House, 1954-55; Colonial Social Science Research Council Fellow, 1955-57; Lecturer in African Studies, University College of Rhodesia and Nyasaland, 1957-60; Lecturer in Anthropology, Glasgow University, 1960-63; Lecturer and from 1966 Reader and

Tutor in Anthropology, University College, London, 1963-69; Professor of Anthropology, London School of Economics, 1969- .

Author of *A Pastoral Democracy*, 1961; *Marriage and the Family in Northern Somaliland*, 1962; (with B. W. Andrzejewski) *Somali Poetry*, 1964; *The Modern History of Somaliland*, 1965.

Editor of *Islam in Tropical Africa*, 1966.

LIENHARDT, R. GODFREY. Born 1921, England; M.A., Cambridge University (English Tripos Pt. 1, Archaeology and Anthropology Tripos), D.Phil., Oxford University.

Lecturer in African Sociology, Oxford University, since 1949; at times Professor of Sociology and Social Anthropology, Baghdad, and Visiting Professor, University of Ghana; Research Fellow, International African Institute, 1951-53; Fieldwork, Southern Sudan, 1947-52.

Author of *Divinity and Experience: The Religion of the Dinka*, 1961; *Social Anthropology*, 1964.

Co-editor, *The Oxford Library of African Literature*.

MACFARLANE, ALAN. Born 1941, India; read History at Oxford University, M.A., D.Phil.; studied Anthropology at London School of Economics, M.Phil.

Fieldwork in Nepal, leading to Ph.D. at the School of Oriental and African Studies, London University, now in progress.

Author of *Witchcraft in Tudor and Stuart England: A Regional and Comparative Study*, 1970; *The Family Life of Ralph Josselin: An Essay in Historical Anthropology*, 1970.

PITT-RIVERS, JULIAN. Born in London, 1919; educated in Paris and Oxford, D.Phil.

Tutor to H.M. the late King Faisal II of Iraq, 1945-47; Visiting Assistant Professor, University of California, Berkeley, 1956; Visiting Professor, University of Chicago, 1957 until the present, and École Pratique des Hautes Études, Paris (VIe Section), 1964-65 and 1966 until the present.

Author of *The People of the Sierra*, 1954; various articles on the Mediterranean and Latin America; *Social and Cultural Change in Chiapas, Mexico* (forthcoming); *After the Empires: Race Relations in Middle America and the Andes* (forthcoming).

REDMAYNE, ALISON H. Born 1936, England; studied at Oxford, St Hugh's College and Nuffield College, B.A.(History), B.Litt., D.Phil.(Social Anthropology).

Field research in Tanganyika, 1961-63, 1965-66, 1968, 1969; Lecturer in Social Anthropology, University of Newcastle upon Tyne, 1967- .

RIVIÈRE, PETER G. Born 1934, London; educated at Cambridge University, M.A.; Oxford University, B.Litt., D.Phil.

Tutorial Assistant and Part-time Lecturer, Institute of Social Anthropology, Oxford University, 1965- ; Senior Research Fellow, Institute of Latin American Studies, London University, 1966-68; Visiting Professor, Harvard University, 1968-69.

Author of *Marriage among the Trio*, 1969.

Editor of J. F. McLennan's *Primitive Marriage*, 1970.

RUEL, MALCOLM J. Born 1927, Chadwell St Mary; educated at Cambridge University, M.A. (English and Social Anthropology); Oxford University, B.Litt., D.Phil.

Associate Research Fellow, West African Institute of Social and Economic Research, Ibadan, 1953-55 (field research among Banyang); Senior Research Fellow, East African Institute of Social and Economic Research, 1956-58 (field research among Kuria of Kenya and Tanzania); Assistant Lecturer, Lecturer, and Senior Lecturer, Department of Social Anthropology, University of Edinburgh, 1959-1970; Secondment to University of Ife as Lecturer, Faculty of Economics and Social Studies and Institute of African Studies, 1964-65; Lecturer in Social and Political Sciences, University of Cambridge, 1970.

Author of *Leopards and Leaders: Constitutional Politics among a Cross River People*, 1969; papers on Banyang and Kuria.

SPOONER, BRIAN. Born 1935, England; educated at Keble and St Antony's Colleges, Oxford, M.A.(Persian), D.Phil.(Social Anthropology).

Assistant Director, British Institute of Persian Studies, Teheran, 1961-68; Assistant Professor, Department of Anthropology, University of Pennsylvania, 1968- .

Author of various articles on anthropology and language in eastern Iran.

THOMAS, KEITH. Born 1933, South Wales; read Modern History at Balliol College, Oxford, M.A.

Fellow of All Souls College, Oxford, 1955-57; Fellow and Tutor in Modern History, St John's College, Oxford, 1957- .

Author of contributions to *Ideas in Cultural Perspective*, 1962; *Crisis in Europe*, 1965; *Hobbes Studies*, 1965; *Writing in England Today*, 1968; and articles in historical periodicals.

WILLIS, R. GEOFFREY. Born 1927, England; studied social anthropology at Oxford, B.Litt., D.Phil., after fifteen years in journalism and industry.

Research Assistant in Department of Anthropology, University College London, 1965-67; Lecturer in Social Anthropology, University of Edinburgh, 1967- .

Author of *The Fipa and Related Peoples of South-West Tanzania and North-East Zambia*, 1966.

Author Index

Abbott, W. C., 75n
Abel, A., 37n, 42
Abt, A., 37n, 38n, 40n, 42
Ady, T., 75-76n, 93, 98
Altmann, A., 43
Alverny, M.-T. d', 41n, 42
Amin, A., 317n, 318
Ammar, H., 317n, 318
Ammianus Marcellinus, 37n, 38n, 39n, 40n
Andersson, E., 132, 135
Andrèe, R., 311, 318
Aquina, M., 135
Arberry, A. J., 311, 318
Ardener, E., xxiv, xxvii, 145, 146, 147, 157n, 158n, 159n, 159-160, 357
Ardener, E., S. Ardener & W. A. Warmington, 157n, 160
Ardener, S., 158n, 160
Audollent, A., 37n, 38n, 39n, 40n, 42

Baëta, C. G., 132, 135
Balandier, G., 132, 135
Banton, M., 135
Barb, A., 37n, 38n, 39n, 41n, 42
Barnes, S. B., xxii, xxxvi
Barns, J., 38n, 42
Barth, F., 313, 316, 317n, 318
Bastide, R., 135
Baynes, N. H., 39n, 40n, 42
Beattie, J., 37n, 75n, 76n, 77, 302, 303, 307
Beattie, J. & J. Middleton, 308
Beidelman, T. O., xxii, 74n, 76n, 77, 357
Berkowitz, L., 244
Blackman, W. S., 318
Blumencranz, B., 41n, 42
Boëthius, 38n
Bohannan, L. & P., 135
Bohannan, P., 131, 132, 135, 203n, 205
Braimah, J. A. & J. R. Goody, 223, 244
Brain, R., xxxiv, 352, 353, 354, 357

Breckenridge, J. D., 41n, 42
Brinton, 195
Brown, G. G., 127n, 127
Brown, G. G. & A. McD. B. Hutt, 126n, 127
Brown, P., xxv, xxvii, xxxii, 37n, 38n, 39n, 40n, 41n, 42, 305, 358
Bunzel, R., 187, 188, 205
Burridge, K., 135
Butler, S., 175, 179

Cameron, A., 38n, 42
Campbell-Bonner, A., 38n, 40n, 42
Canaan, T., 314, 318
Cassiodorus, 38n
Chadwick, H., 37n, 38n, 39n, 41n, 42
Charles, R. H., 16
Church of Scotland, 127
Cohn, N., xiii, 76n, 134, 135, 305,358
Coke, E., 74n
Colson, E., 308
Comhaire, J., 135
Cooper, T., 94, 98
Cope, A., 76n
Correa, G., 205n, 205
Courcelle, P., 37n, 42
Crawford, J. R., 53, 56, 64, 69, 71, 73, 74n, 75n, 77n, 77, 135

Dawes, E. & N. H. Baynes, 39n, 40n, 42
de Bourbourg, Abbé B., 195
Dempwolff, O., 126n, 127n, 127
Des Mousseaux, G., 14, 16
Devore, P., 205
Diaz, B., 198
Dodds, E. R., 39n, 41n, 42
Dölger, F., 39n, 43
Dominic, H., 157n, 160
Donaldson, B. A., 312, 316, 318n, 318
Douglas, M., 37n, 40n, 43, 60, 64, 65, 74n, 75n, 77, 129, 131, 135, 348, 349, 358
Douglas, M. & P. A. Kaberry, 308
Doutreloux, A., 135-136
Doutté, E., 318n, 318

Earthy, E., 303, 308
East African Statistical Department, 127-128
East, R., 136
Einssler, L., 317n, 318
Eitrem, S., 37n, 38n, 43
Elvira, Council of, 39n
Elworthy, F. T., 317n, 318
Epstein, S., xxv, xxvii, xxxvi
Evans-Pritchard, E. E., xiv, xv, xvii, xxiii, xxvii, xxxvi, xxxvii, 17, 18, 37n, 39n, 43, 66, 74n, 75n, 76n, 77, 97, 98, 136, 257, 259, 275, 289, 291, 314, 318, 321, 327, 331, 333, 335, 349
Evans-Pritchard, E. E. & A. C. Beaton, 290n, 291
Ewen, C. L., 50, 51, 55, 57, 74n, 75n, 77-78, 81, 98

Fabian, J., 133, 136
Fernandez, J. W., 136
Festugière, A. J., 37n, 43
Field, M. J., 64, 78, 156, 160, 348, 349
Firth, R., 76n, 78
Forde, D., xviii, xxxvii, 326, 331, 349, 349n
Forge, A., xxvii, xxviii, 260, 275, 358
Fortes, M., 244
Fortes, M. & E. E. Evans-Pritchard, xxxvi
Fortes, M. & G. Dieterlen, xxxvii, 78, 79, 135, 138, 162, 179, 308
Foster, G. M., 195, 196, 205
Frazer, J. G., 75n, 78
Freeman, W., 75n
Fuentes y Guzman, F. A., 198, 205n, 206

Gage, T., 197, 205n
Gairdner, J., 75n
Gamitto, A. C. P., 136
Gaule, J., 75n
Gellner, E., xxi, xxxvii
Gifford, G., 76n, 81, 91, 98
Gluckman, M., xix, xxxvii, 66, 70, 75n, 76n, 77n, 78, 98, 136
Golb, N., 41n, 43
Goody, E., xxviii, xxix, 237, 244, 352, 353, 354, 359
Goody, J. R., 131, 136, 235, 244
Granqvist, H., 318
Green, M. M., 330, 331

Grégoire-Kugener, 38n, 43
Guiteras-Holmes, C., 192, 203n, 205

Hamilton, G. H., 76n
Harris, C., 307n, 308
Hastings, J., 316, 317n, 318
Haweis, J. O. W., 93, 98
Hedayat, S., 318
Hefele, D. & J. Leclercq, 41n, 43
Hermitte, M. E., 186, 200, 203n, 206
Heusch, L. de, 297, 308
Hinde, R. A., 244
Hobbes, T., 76n, 184, 203n
Hocart, A. M., 312, 318
Hofbauer, S., 127n, 128
Holas, B., 136
Holland, W., 188, 200, 203n, 204n, 206
Hopkins, K. M., 38n, 43
Horton, R., 77n, 78
Hubert, H. & M. Mauss, 204n, 206
Hulstaert, G., 78
Hunter, M., 75n, 76n, 78, 304, 308
see also Wilson, M.
Huxley, F., 158n, 160

Iliffe, J., 132, 136
Ittman, J., 158n, 160

James VI, 75n
Jarvie, I. C., 150, 160
Jaussen, A., 312, 318
Jerome, 16, 38n, 40n
Jones, A. H. M., 37n, 40n, 43
Jones, G. I., xxiv, 331, 359
Jonghe, Éd. de, 136
Junod, H. A., 308
Junod, H. P., 136

Kaberry, P. M., 273n, 275
Kayser, G., 39n, 43
Kennedy, J. G., 136
Kiev, A., 309
Kluckhohn, C., xiii, xxvi, xxxvii, 98, 229, 244
Köbben, A. J. F., 136
Koşay, H., 317n, 318
Kraus, P., 41n, 43
Krige, E. J. & J. D., 75n, 78
Kriss, R. & H. Kriss-Heinrich, 318
Kroeber, A. L., 77n, 78
Kuhn, T. S., xxii, xxiv, xxxvii

La Fontaine, J., 39n
Lane, E. W., 319
Lanternari, V., 136
Lawrence, J. B., 134n
Lawrence, P., 136
Lea, 49, 78
Leclerq, J., 40n, 43
Leonard, A. G., 332
Leroy, R., 156, 159n, 160
Less, W. A. & E. Z. Vogt, 308
Lévi-Strauss, C., xxxv, xxxvii, 156, 159n, 160, 176, 179
Levine, D. N., 305
LeVine, R., 305, 308
Lewis, I. M., xxxiii, 294, 308, 359
Libanius, 24, 26, 38n, 39n
Lieban, R., 305, 308
Lienhardt, G., xxiv, xxx, xxxiv, xxxvii, 74n, 78, 136, 279, 291, 360
Lindblom, G., 308
Lindskog, B., 348, 349
Linton, R., 136
Lonsdale, J. M., 136
Lorenz, K., 244
Lynd, H. M., 39n, 43

Macfarlane, A., xxi, xxv, xxvii, 12, 74n, 75n, 97n, 98, 360
MacMullen, R., 37n, 38n, 41n, 43
Mair, L., 137
Malinowski, B., 258, 275
Manoukian, M., 348, 349
Marçais, P. H., 314, 317n, 319
Martin, E. W., 77n, 78
Martroye, F., 37n, 43
Marwick, M. G., xviii, xxi, xxvii, xxxvii, 38n, 43, 62, 67, 69, 70-71, 74n, 75n, 76n, 77n, 78-79, 98n, 98, 137, 162, 301, 308, 327, 332
Maurice, J., 37n, 43
Maybury-Lewis, D., 250, 255n, 255
Mayer, P., xix, xx, xxxvii, 137, 275
Mazzarino, S., 39n, 44
Mead, M., 274n, 275
Medina, A., 204n, 206
Melland, F. H., 137
Middleton, J., xxi, xxiv, xxxvii, 137, 203n, 206, 302, 308
Middleton, J. & E. H. Winter, 37n, 38n, 44, 74n, 76n, 77n, 79, 98, 135, 137, 307, 308

Mitchell, J. C., xviii, xx, xxi, xxxvii, 66, 75n, 77n, 79, 137
Momigliano, A. D., 42, 43
Moore, M., 76n
Morton-Williams, P., 130, 132, 134n, 137
Murray, G. W., 313, 319
Murray, M., 195

Nadel, S., xxxiii, xxxvii, 98, 137, 236, 244, 298-299, 308
Nash, J., 183, 200, 203n, 206
Nash, M., 194, 204n, 206
National Archives of Tanzania, 127n, 128, 134n
Needham, R., 156, 160, 307n, 308
Neel, J. V., F. M. Salzano, P. C. Junquera, F. Keiter & D. Maybury-Lewis, 255n, 255
Neusner, J., 38n, 44
Nigmann, E., 126n, 127n, 128
Nilsson, M. P., 37n, 44
Nock, A. D., 37n, 44
Nordström, E., 41n, 44
Norman, A. F., 38n, 39n, 44
Notestein, W., 75n, 79, 81, 98

Odinga, O., 137
Ogot, B. A., 137
Opler, M. E., 298, 308

Pamphlets, 89, 90, 98-99
Parkin, D., 132, 137
Paul, Monk of Chartres, 9, 16
Paulme, D., 137
Pereira de Queiroz, M. I., 137
Peters, W., 274n, 275
Peterson, E., 38n, 41n, 44
Petit, P., 38n, 44
Picard, G. C., 38n, 44
Pietri, M. C., 38n, 41n, 44
Piganiol, A., 37n, 44
Pitt-Rivers, J., xxxiv, 205n, 206, 360
Poeton, E., 74n
Pollard, A. F., 75n
Poque, S., 40n, 44
Preisendanz, K., 37n, 44
Preuss, 157n

Radermacher, L., 41n, 44
Ranger, T. O., 137
Rattray, R. S., 243n, 244
Redmayne, A., xxxiv, 127n, 128, 132, 361

Reisman, D., xxxvi, xxxvii
Reynolds, B., 71, 75n, 77n, 79
Richards, A., xx, xxxvii, 75n, 79, 131, 134n, 138
Ritter, H. & M. Plessner, 41n, 44
Rivière, P., xxvi, xxvii, 255n, 255, 361
Robbins, R. H., 77n, 79
Roberts, A., 128
Rotberg, R., 138
Rubin, B., 37n, 44
Ruel, M., xxiv, xxxiv, 158n, 160, 179n, 349n, 349, 353, 354, 361

Ste Croix, G. E. M. de, 37n, 41n, 44
Saler, B., 201, 206
Savitsky, N. & S. Tarachow, 159n, 160
Schapera, I., 40n, 45n, 75n, 79
Schlimmer, J. L., 319
Schlosser, K., 138
Schmidt, L., 255n, 255
Schofield, F. D. & A. D. Parkinson, 274n, 275
Scot, R., 75n, 76n, 88, 99
Selden, J., 75n
Seligman, C. G., xvii
Seligman, S., 317n, 319
Shack, W., 297, 308
Shepperson, G., 138
Shepperson, G. & T. Price, 138
Simmons, L. W., 75n, 79
Smith, M. W., 138
Sodano, A., 41n, 45
Southall, A., 159
Spedding, J. *et al.*, 75n
Spooner, B., xxx, 361
Sprandel, R., 38n, 45
Stayt, H., 295, 296, 297, 301, 308
Stearne, J., 88, 98
Stone, B. G., 158n, 160
Summers, M., 77n, 79
Sundkler, B. G. M., 138
Szyliowicz, J. S., 319

Tait, D., 134n, 138
Talbot, D., 332
Talbot, P. A., 158n, 160, 323, 324, 332, 347, 350

Tamborino, J., 40n, 45
Tertullian, 7, 16
Theodosius II, 37n
Theuss, D., 138
Thomas, B., 319
Thomas, K., xxi, xxxiii, 12, 75n, 97, 98, 99, 362
Thompson, D. E., 205
Thompson, E. A., 41n, 45
Thompson, J. E. S., 205n, 206
Thompson, R. C., 319
Trevor-Roper, H., xxxi, xxxii, xxxvii, 49, 75n, 76n, 79, 174, 179
Turnbull, C., xxxiii, xxxvii
Turner, H. W., 138
Turner, V. W., xviii, xxi, xxxviii, 74n, 75n, 79, 138
Tylor, E. B., 123, 128

Vansina, J., xxix, xxxviii
Van Wing, J., 138
Villa-Rojas, A., 204n, 206

Waddell, H. M., 332, 349n, 350
Wallace, A. F. C., 138
Wallace-Hadrill, M., 41n, 45
Ward, B. E., xx, xxxiv, xxxviii, 130, 131, 138
Weck (Dr), 126n, 128
Welbourn, F. B., 138
Welbourn, F. B. & B. A. Ogot, 138
Wes, M. A., 45
Westermarck, E., 317n, 319
Whisson, M. G., 303, 309
White, C. M. W., xxv, xxxviii, 97n, 99
Willis, R. G., xxxiii, 75n, 79, 126n, 128, 129, 134n, 139, 362
Wilson, G. & M., xx, xxxviii, 70, 77n, 79
Wilson, M., 75n, 79, 99, 139, 348, 350 *see also* Hunter, M.
Wilson, P. J., 294, 307n, 30
Wishlade, R. L., 139
Worsley, P., 133, 139, 298, 309
Wünsch, R., 37n, 45

Zachery, 38n
Zotenburg, 41n

Subject Index

Abelam, xxviii, xxix, 259
  accusations, 265, 266, 267, 268, 271, 272
  and burial, 265-267
  and cargo cults, 275n
  ceremonial exchange, 264, 270
  cosmology, 274n
  and death, 259, 261, 262, 265, 266, 268, 269, 271, 272, 273, 274n
    malaria, 274-275n
  divination, 261, 264-267, 268, 271, 272
  location, 259
  luluai, 270
  politics, 268-273, 274n
    big-men, 263, 264, 265, 269-270, 271, 272, 273
    factions in, 271, 272, 273
    nature of, 270-271, 273
  social relations among, 274n
  sorcerer (*kwis'ndu*), 259, 260, 261, 262, 263, 264, 265, 269, 270, 273, 275n
    detection of, 264-265, 267
  sorcery, 259-267, 268-273, 273n, 275n
    enemies and, 261, 262-264, 267, 270, 271-272, 273, 274n
    politics and, 268-273
    shell ring to pay for, 262-263, 264, 265, 270, 271
  substances, sorcery
    bodily, 261-262, 274n
    'leavings', 259, 260, 261, 262, 263, 274n
    paint, xxviii, 259-260, 263-264, 265, 266, 269, 271, 273, 274n
  symbols among, 260, 266, 274n
  vengeance, 269, 272, 273
  villages
    Bengragum, 269, 272
    fission, 272-273
    Wingei, 272-273
  warfare and sorcery, 261, 273, 274n
  witch, xxvii, 259, 267-268, 273n
    curing and, 268
    witchcraft, 259, 267-268, 275n
    misfortune as, 268
  yams, 263-264, 265, 266, 268, 270, 271, 272
    magic, 269, 271
accusations
  Abelam, 265, 266, 267, 268, 271, 272
  ambiguous position and, 27, 294
  Bakweri, 145-146, 147, 148, 149, 151
  Bangwa children and, 161, 171, 175
  Banyang, 333-334
  charioteers and, 25-26
  in Chiapas, 183-184, 194, 203n
  by Chikanga, 109-110
  Christian groups and, 36, 66, 73
  at communal level, 66, 73, 91, 251-253, 254
  Evil Eye and, 311
  factions and, xxvii, xxxii, 25, 27, 251-253, 254
  Gonja, 213, 229-231, 236, 240, 242, 244n
  Hehe, 114, 116, 123-124
    structure of, 115, 125
  Ibo, 324, 326, 327
  against Jews, 13, 35, 36, 68
  in Late Roman Empire, 20, 32
    against Libanius, 24, 25
  Lugbara, 299-300, 302
  misfortune and, *see* misfortune
  Shavante, 251-252, 254
  social change and, xx, 33
  Tiv, 145-146, 230
  Trio, 248, 249, 250, 254
  in Tudor and Stuart England, 49, 52, 67
    against high office, 55
  in Tudor and Stuart Essex, 82, 84, 94-95
    number of, 83, 84, 85-88
  Venda, 301
  wealth and, 146, 147, 148, 149
  as weapon, xxv, 19, 23, 55

accusations, as weapon—*(contd.)*
   against authority, xviii, 55, 252,
     298, 299-300, 302
   for change, xxi
   political, xxiv, 25, 55, 161, 251-
     253, 298, 299-300
   widows and, xxv
   witch-cleansing movements and,
     130
   Yakö, 327
   Zuñi, 176
actors, 25
adultery, 115, 217, 247, 261-262,
   274n
Africa, xi, xiii, xix, xxxiii
   Central, xviii, 58, 130, 148, 327
   East, xxxiv, 132, 133, 134n, 148
   North, Evil Eye in, 311, 318n
   social change in, xix-xx, xxi, 65, 68
aggression
   sorcery and, 257, 258, 261-262,
     265, 267, 300
   witchcraft and, 175, 207-208, 212,
     215, 216, 220-221, 222, 226,
     231, 232, 233-236, 237, 239,
     240-243, 268, 300, 333, 353
Akẅe-Shavante, *see* Shavante, Akẅe
Albicerius of Carthage, 26, 27
allegations, Gonja, 229-230, 231, 240,
   244n
Ammianus Marcellinus, 19, 23
ancestors
   Abelam, 266
   Bangwa, 162, 178, 179n
   in Chiapas, 188, 193
   Dinka-Nuer, 281
   Ibo, 326
   Lenje, 303
   Lugbara, 302, 307
   Pondo, 305
   Venda, 295
animals
   attributes of, and men, 187, 188,
     189, 195, 196, 334, 342, 343, 344
   burial of certain hunted, 217
   categories, 353
   dog (myth of death), 281, 282, 283
   nagual, 186-187
     horse, 189, 203n
     jaguar, 188, 199
     monkey, 196
     ocelot, 188
     raccoon, 189

     tiger, 187, 190, 199, 200
     see also nagual
   tokens of, as protection, 316
   were-forms, 164, 170, 175, 334
     antelope, 166, 168
     bush-pig, 335, 338, 339, 341, 343
     crocodile, 343-344
     definition of, 335, 336
     distinguished from witchcraft,
       347
     elephant, 168, 338, 343, 346, 347
     gaining of, 336
     hippopotamus, 338, 343-344, 346-
       347
     leopard, 164, 335, 338, 339, 341-
       342, 343, 347, 348, 349
     mole, 335
     monkey, 166
     porcupine, 346
     python, 338, 339, 340-341
     range of, 334
     snake, 168, 347
     tortoise, 346
     world of, 336
   witchcraft and
     bat, 199
     boar, 247n
     cat, 9, 10, 96, 199
     cattle, 51
     chameleon, 165
     dog, 96, 164
     familiar of witch, 51, 96, 186,
       197, 200, 243n, 299, 304, 323
     farm, 48
     frog, 9
     gelding, 83
     goat, 199
     lion, 210
     snake, 165, 168, 172, 205n
     supernatural, xxxiv, 96
     toad, 9, 199
     wild, 164
     Zodiac, 197
   see also birds; natural phenomena
Anne Boleyn, accused of witchcraft,
   55
Anuak, xxx, xxxi
   acyeni, 288-289
   burial and funerary practices, 280,
     285-286
   compared with Nuer-Dinka, 279-
     283, 288, 289
   see also Dinka; Nuer

cosmology, xxxii, 281
and death
  ceremonies associated with, 285-287, 290n
  concepts of, 279, 280-281, 283-289, 290n
  mythology and, 282-283, 289
  wishes at, 283-285
and Divinity, 280, 282-283, 287, 289
diviners, 289
economy of, 279
ghostly vengeance, 287-288
inheritance, 281-282, 284, 286-287, 290n
myths
  death, 282-283, 289
  racial difference, 283
philosophy of, 279-280, 281, 289
political system of, 279-280, 286, 288-289
witchcraft, 289
Appollonius of Tyana, 34
Arapesh
  Mountain, 274n
  Plains, 260, 274n
archangels, and Chiapas indians' beliefs, 197
Ashanti, 208, 235, 348
  confessions, xxxiv, 130, 348
  hunting rituals, 243n
  witch, 348
Association of Social Anthropologists, xi, 351, 356n
astrologers, 24, 53
Athanasius of Alexandria, 26
athletes, 25
attack
  by Evil Eye, 315
  magical, 29, 129, 131, 165, 167, 171, 179, 191, 192, 208, 210, 211, 212, 225, 227, 229, 230, 233, 235, 239, 243n, 268, 273, 299, 300, 301, 302, 304-307, 324
Augustine, 26, 28, 29, 30, 31
Azande, xi, xvii, xix, xxii, xxvii, xxix, xxx, xxxvi, 51, 97, 327
  beliefs, xiv, xviii, xxviii, 60, 66, 133, 183, 259, 321, 354
  vengeance, xvi, 183
  witchcraft, xiv, xvi, 60, 259, 333, 335
Aztec beliefs, 196

Bacon, Francis, 51
Bakweri, xxiv, xxvii, xxviii
  accusations, 145-146, 147, 148, 151
  alienation of land, 142
  burial, 148
  colonial control
    British, 144
    German, 141, 142, 143, 145, 146-147, 157n, 158n
  concubinage and prostitution, 144, 147
  confessions, 151
  description of, 141-142
  economy
    bananas and, 144, 149-150, 151, 152, 153, 154, 158n
    change in, 141, 143, 144, 147, 149, 150, 151, 152, 153-154, 158n, 159n
    crops grown, 142, 158n
    division of labour, 143, 159n
    lack of confidence in, 144, 146-149, 153, 154-155, 158n
    xanthosoma (cocoyam) and, 143, 146, 154, 156
  history of, 141-157
  Njombe (*nyongo* doctor), 150-151, 152-153
  punishment for witchcraft, 145
  thought, 156, 159n
  wealth, attitudes to, 146, 147, 148, 149, 155
  witchcraft beliefs
    change in, due to economic change, 141, 147, 148, 149, 150, 152-154
    liemba, 144-147
    misfortune and, 149
    nyongo, 147-153, 156, 158n, 159n
    witch-cleansing in, 150, 152, 153, 154, 156
    zombies and, 147, 148, 150, 152, 153, 154, 155
bananas, and Bakweri economic change, 149-150, 152, 153, 154, 158n
Banda, President Hastings, and Chikanga, 124
Bangwa
  accusations, co-wives and, 167, 168, 169
  aggression, 175
  ancestors, 162, 171

Bangwa—(*contd.*)
  burial, 165, 169
  cannibalism, 173
  chiefs and witchcraft, 161, 162, 168, 169, 173, 177, 178
    leopard shape and, 164
  children
    accusations and, 161, 171, 175
    confessions by, 161, 164, 165-179
    dreams of, 171-172
    'of the gods', 162-163, 177, 178, 179n
    malnutrition and, 161, 170, 173-174
    sexual tensions and, 172-173
    'of the sky', 163, 164, 165, 173, 178
    as witches, 162, 165
  confessions, during illness, 165-167, 167-170
  cosmology, 164
  environment and witchcraft, 174-175
  illness, attitudes to, 163, 167, 170, 175-176
  missionaries and, 178-179
  political change, 177-178
  priest of the earth, 163
  social change, 177-178
  sorcery, 162
  twins, 163, 171, 178, 353
  vengeance, 162
  witches, 164, 165
  witchcraft beliefs, 164, 165, 177-179
    and Banyang beliefs, 179n
    and post-mortems, 165
    and spatial distance, 165, 166, 170, 171, 172
Banyang
  accusations, 333-334
  beliefs, xxiv, xxxiv, xxxv, 334-335, 336, 338, 344, 349n
    'river-world', 343-344, 346-347
  confessions, 334, 335, 337, 338-340, 343, 345-347
  cosmology, 336, 347
  cults/societies, 341
    Basinjom, 158, 340, 346
    Mfam, 337, 340, 345-346
  diviner, 344, 346
  dreams, 340, 344, 345

symptoms of witchcraft, 337-338, 342
were-forms (*babu*), 334-349
  animals, 334, 335, 338, 340-342, 343-344, 346, 347, 348
  birds, 335, 338, 340
  natural phenomena, 337, 339, 342-343, 346
witch, 333, 334-335
witch-cleansing, for Bakweri, 152-153
witchcraft beliefs
  introspective nature of, 333-334
  and politics, 341
  and post-mortems, 336-338, 339, 340, 341, 342
  similar to Bangwa, 179n
Banyoro
  Cwezi gods, 303
  divination, 303, 307n
  and spirit-possession, 299, 300, 302-303, 307n
Beidelman, T. O., xxv
Bekworra, 326, 331
Bemba, and witch-cleansing, 130, 134n
Benin
  Edo groups and Ibo, 330
  political inheritance in, 328
Bible
  influence of, and witchcraft, 56
  New Testament, 6
  Old Testament, 4
big-men
  Abelam, 263, 264, 265, 269-270, 271, 272, 273
  in New Guinea, 257
  see also chiefship
birds
  nagual
    chick, 187, 189, 190
    eagle, 187, 198, 199, 205n
    humming-bird, 188
    sparrow-hawk, 187
  were-forms, 344
    kite, 335
    owl, 338, 340
  witchcraft, and vultures, 218, 219, 243n
bishops
  Athanasius, 34
  Cyprian, 34
  Nuñez de la Vega, 197

blessing, 284, 344
blood, drawing of witches', 61, 95
blowing, ritual, 313
Boëthius, 24
Boki, 327, 330
boundaries
between court and aristocracy, 24
Trio concepts of, 250, 254
war group, 259, 264
Brenchley (Kent), 55
Brooks, D. H. M., 317
Browne, Sir Thomas, 90
Buea, 143, 154, 154n
Bushong, xxix
Busunu, warfare in, 223

Calabar, Old, 324, 326, 349n
see also Ibo (Cross River)
calendars, Maya and Mexican, 195, 196
Cameroon, West, xxiv, xxxv, 141, 161, 335
cannibalism, Bangwa, 173
Cardinal Wolsey, accused of witchcraft, 55
case-histories, 352
castes, spirit-possession and, 294, 298
ceremonial
dialogue (Trio), 246, 248, 255n
exchange
Abelam, 264, 270
New Guinea, 257, 259
practices at death, 285-287, 290
see also ritual
Chabannes, Adhémar de, 8
charioteers, xxv, xxvii, xxxii
accusations and, 25-26
as clients, 25
position of, 25
charms, xxxvi, 284, 314, 316
Chiapas (indians of)
accusations, 183-184, 194, 203n
ancestors, 188, 193
anti-witchcraft movement in, 197
beliefs, 183, 184, 185-186
confessions, 184, 194
cosmology, 202-203
divination in, 187, 190
misfortune in, 185, 191, 193, 194
murder of witches, 183, 184, 194, 203n
nagual, see nagual
power in, 184, 185, 194, 202

ambivalent nature of, 184, 203n
spiritual, 184, 185, 187, 189, 191, 193
sorcery, 191, 198
and witchcraft beliefs, 191
and Spaniards, 195, 196-197, 198, 201, 204n
threats of witchcraft, 184
vengeance, 184
wealth, attitudes to, 183
witch, 183, 191, 193, 194, 195, 204n
witchcraft beliefs
position in society, 184, 194
and sorcery, 191
and soul, 191-192, 204n
Chichicastenango, 187, 188
chiefship
Anuak, 280, 286, 288-289
Bangwa, 161, 162, 168, 169, 173, 177, 178
Gonja, 212, 215-216, 217, 221-228, 231, 232-236, 241-242
Shavante, 251-252, 254
Trio, 247, 254
Trobriand, 258
see also big-men
Chikanga (Lighton Chunda), xxxiv, 103, 132
accusations by, 109-110
appearance of, 108
calling of, 103
divining, 109
fall of, 124-125
Fipa beliefs and, 126n
John, case of, and, 107-110, 111
Malawi Congress Party and, 112
missionaries and, 112, 121, 124, 125
organization of, 108, 111
payment of, 118-119
President Hastings Banda and, 124
rise of, 105, 117, 120-121
success of, 120-124
wide fame of, 103, 106-107, 117-118, 120-121
witch-cleansing and, 103, 106, 119, 120, 132
as witch-finder, 103, 106, 110, 112, 119, 132
children
ashes and death, 8, 9
Bangwa
accusations by, 161, 171, 175
confessions by, 161, 164-179

371

children, Bangwa—(*contd.*)
    and gods, 162-163, 177-178
    malnutrition and, 161, 170, 173-174
    sexual tensions and, 172-173
    death of, 29, 259, 273
    witchcraft as explanation of, 54, 71, 88, 89, 147, 162, 212, 242, 268, 325, 340
    illness of, witchcraft as explanation of, 84, 89, 162, 163, 168, 175-176, 345
    murder of, by Jews, 14
    as witches, 162, 163, 164, 165, 166-179, 193
    and witchcraft, xxxiv, 161, 162, 165-179
    Zuñi, and sorcery, 176-177
Christian Church, 26, 28, 30
    accusations and, 33
    Catholic, 48, 58, 68, 87
    Central African Presbyterian, 103, 112, 125
    Protestant, 48, 63, 65
    of Scotland, 112, 121
Christianity
    and Devil beliefs, 6-16, 179, 197, 305
    and Evil Eye, 312
    and Late Roman Empire, 19, 26, 33
    and paganism, 7, 19, 24, 28, 33, 195
    Puritan, 87
    and social change, xxi, 27, 28, 31, 58, 65, 67
    in Africa, 27, 177
    in Late Antiquity, 27, 30
    and sorcery beliefs, 28-32, 193, 299, 305
class, power of, in Late Roman Empire, 21, 22, 23, 24, 26
Cole, Thomas (Archdeacon of Essex), 96
colonial control, xix, xxi, xxiii, xxxiii, 112, 131
    Australian, 267, 270, 275n
    British, 123, 127n, 144, 224, 225, 287
    German, 103, 114, 116, 141, 142, 143, 145, 146-147
        Maji-Maji uprising and, 132, 134n
communication(s), 174, 250, 251

    and Evil Eye, 314
    fame of Chikanga and, 121
confessions
    Ashanti, xxxiv, 130, 348
    Bakweri, 151
    Bangwa
        child, 161, 164, 165, 179
        during illness, 165-167, 167-169
    Banyang, 334, 335, 337, 338-340, 343, 345-347
    bribes and, xxxiv
    in Chiapas, 184, 194
    corresponding to expected behaviour, 130, 168, 170-171
    Fipa, 130
    Hehe, 115
    Knights Templars and, 10
    Tudor and Stuart England, 65, 96
    and witch-cleansing movements, 130
    Yoruba, 130
    Zuñi, 176-177
conflict
    and sorcery, 247, 249, 253, 259, 271-272
    and witchcraft, 82, 92, 95, 153, 162, 232, 301, 328, 349, 352, 353
Constantinople, racing factions of, 27
cosmologies, xxiv, xxxiv, 354
    Abelam, 274n
    Anuak, xxxii, 281
    Bakweri, xxiv
    Bangwa, 164
    Banyang, 336, 347
    in Chiapas, 201-202
    Shavante, 253-254
    and spirit-possession, 298, 301
    Trio, 253-254
    Yakö, xviii
courts
    Anuak, xxxi
    English
        Assize, 52, 53, 82, 83, 84, 85, 87, 89, 92, 96
        ecclesiastical, 53, 63, 67, 82, 84, 92, 96
        local, 54
        Quarter Sessions, 52, 54, 83
    Hehe, 118, 123-124
    records of, 53, 63, 75n, 83, 85, 87, 96, 237
    Rhodesian, 53-54

Cromwell, Oliver, accused of witchcraft, 55
Cross River, *see* Ibo (Cross River)
cults
  Banyang, 341
    Mfam, 337, 340, 345-346
  Dinka-Nuer, 280, 289
  Fijian water-baby, 297-298
  mortality, 294, 295, 297, 305, 306
  witch
    European, 195
    Mexican, 195
  witch-cleansing, *see* movements
cultivation
  Shavante, 250
  slash and burn, 245
  see also plantation agriculture
curing of illness, 103, 113, 122-123, 124, 126n, 127n, 146, 166, 184, 185, 187, 189, 190, 194, 201, 203n, 242, 268, 306, 338
curse, xxvi, 28, 52, 63, 67, 71, 92, 93, 94, 248, 249, 284, 286, 287, 288, 289, 307

Daboya, warfare in, 223
Dagomba, witch - cleansing movements, 134n
Dahomey, witch - cleansing movements, 130
dancing, 146, 151, 152, 215, 217, 218, 248, 255n, 295, 296, 342, 344
  competitive nature of, 218-219, 220, 225-227, 232
  Damba, 218, 224, 225-227, 232, 234, 243n
Dead Sea Scrolls, 5, 6
death
  Anuak
    concepts of, 279, 280-281, 283-289, 290n
    myth of, 282-283
    wishes at, 283-285
  Dinka-Nuer, concepts of, 283-285
  Evil Eye and, 313
  signs of, 281, 284
  warfare, cause of, 259, 273, 274n
  witchcraft and sorcery, explanation of, xvi, xxviii, 29, 54, 71, 109, 117, 118, 122, 131
    Abelam, 259, 261, 262, 265, 266, 268, 269, 271, 272, 273, 274n

Bakweri, 147, 150
Bangwa, 162, 166
Banyang, 334, 344
  in Chiapas, 184, 194, 203n
  Gonja, 212, 215, 219, 220, 221, 227, 229, 233, 234, 239, 241-242
  Ibo, 324, 325
  in New Guinea, 258
  Shavante-Trio, 248, 249, 253
  in Tudor and Stuart Essex, 82, 87, 88, 89, 90, 91
  see also children, death of
Dee, John (magician), 52
demonology, 5, 54, 179
  see also Devil, worship of
deprivation, and spirit-possession, 294-295
  see also roles
Descartes, xxxii
destiny, 186, 195
  see also fate
Devil, 3, 192, 198, 303
  belief in
    Christianity and, 7-16, 32, 197, 305
    as a god, 36
    history of, 3-16, 198
    Iranian influence of, 5
    Judaism and, 5-6
  human servants of the, 6-11, 15-16, 34, 193, 197, 198, 201, 305
  Jesus and, 6
  monotheism and, 4
  Negro as, 8
  Old Testament, 3-5
  St Paul and, 6
  as symbol of evil, 3, 65, 192
  worship of, 8, 10-11, 36, 49, 50, 52, 65, 68, 198
Dinka, xxx, xxxi, xxxii, 279
  burial and funerary practices, 280-281
  and cattle, 279, 281
  death, concepts of, 280, 281
  and Divinity, 280, 282, 283
  economy of, 279, 289
  inheritance, 281-282
  ghostly vengeance, 288
  myths, 282
  philosophy of, 279-280, 289
  political system, 280
  witchcraft, xxxiv, xxxv

dirt, as protection against Evil Eye, 316
see also pollution
disease
French pox, 55
among Hehe, 113
witchcraft as explanation of, 54, 71, 89, 248, 269
see also illness
disputes, settling of, 95, 248
distance
social, xxvi, 87, 145-146, 167, 175, 209, 238, 241, 261, 290n, 317n, 323, 329, 336
spatial, 164, 166, 170, 171, 172, 216, 220-253, 254, 323, 336, 337-338
see also boundaries; kinship
divination
Abelam, 261, 264-267, 268, 271, 272
Banyoro, 303, 307n
in Chiapas, 187, 190, 195
Evil Eye and, 316-317
Gonja, 227, 228, 242
Gusii, 305
illicit, 19, 20
Lenja, 303
Luo, 303
Pondo, 305
spirit-possession and witchcraft, 302-304, 305, 306
and witch-cleansing, 106, 130
diviners, xxxiv
African, 60, 61, 76n
Anuak, 289
Bangwa, 163, 164, 165, 178
Banyang, 344-346
Chikanga, *see* Chikanga
Hehe, 106, 113
see also Chikanga
Lele, 348
manipulation of, 60, 267
and power, 106, 112, 117
and spirit-possession, 113-114, 117, 295-296, 297, 302-304, 305, 306
in Tudor and Stuart England, 48, 52, 60, 61, 76n
Venda, 295-296, 297
Divinity, 280, 282-283, 287, 289
divorce, 296, 301, 304
doctors, and witchcraft, 53, 89, 90
see also astrologers; diviners

Dostoevsky, 355
dreams
Abelam, 267
Bangwa child, 171-172, 175, 177
as omens, 29, 113, 185, 190-191, 194, 203n, 340, 344, 345
Duala, and Bakweri, 148
Durkheim, E., xv, xvii

Eastern Empire, 23
economic change
among Bakweri, and witchcraft, 141, 143, 144, 147, 149, 150, 151, 152, 153-154, 158n, 159n
among Ibo, 329, 330, 331
in Tudor and Stuart Essex, 82, 84
and witch-cleansing movements, 131, 133, 152-153
economics, and witchcraft, xxiv, 15
Edo groups, 330
Efik, *see* Ibo (Cross River)
Egypt, Evil Eye in, 317n
Ejagham, 347
Ekoi, 326, 327, 331
emperors
Constantius II, 19, 23, 25, 26
Gregory the Great, 31
Justinian, 20
Valens, 23
Valentine I, 23
English witchcraft defined, 48, 61
see also Tudor and Stuart England
environment, and witchcraft, 174-175
Erasmus, xxxii
Essex, Tudor and Stuart, xxi, xxvii
accusations in, 82, 84-86, 87-88, 94-95
antisocial behaviour in, 92-93
Boreham village, 82, 83, 85, 88
confessions in, 96
conflict in, 92, 95
economic change in, 82, 84
Hatfield Peverel village, 82, 83, 87-88, 90, 96
kinship structure, 87
Little Baddow village, 82
misfortune in, 88, 89, 90, 91, 92
offences other than witchcraft, 87-88
social change in, 82, 84, 95
trials in, 83, 85, 96-97
witchcraft in, 81-98
witches in, 84-85, 87

Ethopia, Christian, 305
Europe, xiii
　Evil Eye in, 311
　witchcraft beliefs in, xxxi, 3-16, 47,
　　161, 172, 174, 186, 193, 197,
　　198-199, 200, 201, 204n, 205n,
　　299, 304, 305
　　compared with English, 12-13,
　　49, 82
Evans-Pritchard, E. E., xi, xviii,
　xxviii, 27, 257, 280
　theories of witchcraft and magic,
　　xvi, 48, 51, 153, 183, 187, 244,
　　321
Evil Breath, 314
Evil Eye, xxx
　accusations and, 311
　attack by, 315
　　people open to, 315
　belief in
　　distribution of, 311, 312, 314
　　in Persia, 311-312, 313-314,
　　　317n
　cause of, 312, 313-314, 315
　divination and, 316-317
　Koran and, 312-313, 316
　misfortune explained by, 312, 313,
　　314
　nomadism and, 314
　protection against, 313, 315-317
　　alum as, 316, 317
　　animal tokens as, 316
　　blowing as, 313
　　colour as, 313, 316
　　cross, 313
　　dirt as, 316
　　fumigation as, 315, 316, 317
　　hand as, 316
　　knotting as, 313
　　Koran as, 313, 316
　　salt as, 316
　　spitting as, 316
　　sweets as, 316
　　tattooing as, 316
　ritual against, 312, 313, 314, 315-
　　317
　witchcraft and, 311
Evil Soul, 314
Evil Tongue, 313, 314
exorcism, 31, 32, 58, 124, 152, 154,
　155, 178, 305, 306
expulsion for witchcraft, xxvi, 68,
　131, 169, 212, 213, 229

factions, xxv, xxvii
　Abelam, 271, 272, 273
　and accusations, xxvii, xxxii, 25,
　　27, 251-253, 254
　Shavante, 251-253, 254
fate, 183, 185, 195
　see also destiny
fear
　of Evil Eye, 311, 312
　of witches and sorcerers, 66, 83,
　　162, 207, 211, 234, 238, 242,
　　248, 262, 321, 323, 324, 325,
　　327, 330, 331, 349n, 353
Fernando Po, 157n
Fijian water-baby cult, 297-298
Fipa
　beliefs about Chikanga, 126n
　confessions, 130
　witch-cleansing movements (Kam-
　　cape), 121, 130, 132
Fire of London, and witchcraft, 68
Firth, R., xii
Forde, D., xii, xxiii, 290n
Fortescue, Sir John (Queen's At-
　torney), 96
freemasonry, 14
French Revolution, and Jews, 14
funerary practices
　Abelam, 265-267
　Anuak, 280, 285
　Bakweri, 148, 155, 157
　Bangwa, 165, 169
　Dinka-Nuer, 280-281
　Gonja, 211, 218
　　and hunted animals, 217, 243n
Fürer-Haimendorf, C. von, xii

Ghana, 207
　religious movements in, 132
ghosts, xxxi, 214, 216, 217, 218, 220,
　　287-288, 298
Gibbons, Edward, 26
God, as means to witchcraft, 63
Gonja, xxviii, xxix, 208
　accusations, 213, 229-230, 231, 236,
　　240, 242, 244n
　allegations, 229-230, 231, 240, 244n
　burial in, 207, 218
　　hunted animals, 217
　Damba ceremony, 218, 222, 224,
　　225-227, 232, 234, 243n
　divination in, 227, 228, 242

Gonja—(*contd.*)
horse-tail symbol, 225-226, 227, 232
Islam in, 208, 211, 225, 235
misfortune in, 230, 236
ordeals, 212-213, 232
politics
civil war, 223-224
structure of, 208, 212, 221-228
succession to office, 222-228, 232
witchcraft as weapon, 228, 229,
231-232, 236, 240
women and, 241-242
punishment, of witch, 213-215, 229,
231, 234, 239, 242
vengeance, 216, 217, 218, 233
witch(es) (*egbe*), 210, 211, 212, 213
age of, 211, 236
chiefs as, 212, 215-216, 217, 221-
228, 231, 232, 235, 241-242
differences in classification, 207,
211, 225, 229
female, 207, 209, 211, 212, 213-
214, 215, 225, 229, 231, 233,
235, 236-243
male, 207, 209, 211-228, 229,
231, 236, 241
powers of (*kegbe*), 208-211
trial of, 213, 214
witchcraft
and aggression, 207-244 *passim*
and chiefship (dominance), 208,
221, 224-228, 232, 236
counteraction against, 221, 229-
231, 234-235
and hunting, 216-217, 218-220,
233-234, 235-236, 243n
legitimate/illegitimate, 220-221,
228-236, 240-243
morality-sustaining, 235-236
protective function of, 208, 211-
215, 228, 233
and punishment, 208
and sorcery, 210
and warfare, 217-220, 233
witchcraft beliefs, 208-211, 243n,
353
carrying the 'corpse', 212-213,
215
and dancing and singing, 218-
219, 225-227, 232
and medicines, 208, 209, 210,
215, 216-221, 224-226, 227,
228, 232, 237-239, 243n
and shrines, 212-213, 216-217,
237
gossip, and witchcraft, 67, 91, 95, 123,
229-231, 236, 240, 249
Greek and Roman religion, 19
Greek science, 19
Gregory of Tours, 27
Guatemala, 194, 195, 204n
Gurage, and spirit-possession, 297,
299, 300
Gusii, 305

hair, shaving of, 114, 116, 119, 120,
124
hallucinations, 170, 174
Lilliputian, 151, 156, 159n
Hehe, 103, 106
accusations, 114, 115, 116, 123-124
beliefs, 112-114, 126n
confessions, 115
disease among, 113, 114
divination, 113, 114, 116
see also Chikanga
health of, 113
incisions and witch-cleansing, 109,
111, 113, 122, 124
ordeals, 116
paternity, 127n
and political change, 120
and social change, 120
society, development of, 115, 127n
and sorcery, 114-116, 118, 125
spirits, 114
ancestral, 113, 114, 126n
witch, 114
head-shaving of, 114, 116, 119,
120, 124
trial of, 123-124
Henry VIII, 55
heretics, 8, 9, 10
Hitler, and Jews, 13, 15
Hobbes, Thomas, 65
Holy Spirit, 31
holy water, as protection, 58, 179
Homer, 24
Hopkin, Matthew (witch-finder), 50,
58, 65, 76n
hostility, witchcraft and, xvii, xix,
66, 71, 240, 299, 301, 333
hunting
medicine, 216-217, 219, 220
taboos, 216-217, 220

and witchcraft, 216-217, 218, 219, 220, 233, 234, 235-236, 243n, 344
Hutu, and spirit-possession, 297
Huxley, F., xii

Ibibio, 321, 325, 326, 327, 330, 331, 347
accusations, 326, 347
Ibo
accusations, 324
beliefs, xxiv, 321
concept of luck, 323
distance, social and spatial, 323, 325
variations in, 325, 326
and economic change, 329, 330, 331
personality, 328
poison ordeal, 325
society, 328-329
inheritance, 328
networks, 329-330
tensions in, 326-331
variation in, and witchcraft, 326-331
sorcery, 321-324
juju, 321-322
politics and, 323
substances
magical, 321, 323
medicine, 321, 323
poison, 323, 324, 325
territorial expansion among, 330-331
unions and associations among, 329-330
vengeance, 325
witch, 323
witchcraft, 321, 323, 324, 327, 327-331
Ibo (Cross River), 321, 324, 325, 327, 328, 330, 347
accusations, 326
economics, 326
politics, 325
Ibo (Riverain and North-eastern), 321, 325, 326, 328, 330, 331
accusations, 326
see also Ibibio
idols
Baphomet, 10
nagual, 188
wax, 50-51

Ihete village, and Chikanga, 110, 111, 112, 121
Ikom, 325, 327
illness
confessions during, 166-169, 170, 334, 337, 338-340, 343, 345, 346-347
curing of, 103, 113, 122-123, 124, 126n, 127n, 146, 166, 168, 184, 185, 189, 191, 194, 201, 204n, 242, 306, 338
diviners and, xxxiv, 61, 106, 112, 117, 145, 163, 164, 165, 187, 190, 194, 289, 302, 306, 344
Evil Eye as explanation of, 313
injury to were-form and, 164-166, 338-340, 343
loss of soul as explanation of, 191-192, 204n, 208, 209
as sign of calling of diviner, 103
spirits, cause of, 295, 297
witchcraft as explanation of, 11, 57, 61, 73, 88, 89, 94, 109, 117, 118, 122, 131, 145, 163, 167, 170, 175-176, 191, 194, 212, 228, 235, 259, 271, 333
see also disease
impotence, and sorcery, 29, 65
incest, power from, 114, 301
incisions and medicines
Hehe, 113, 122
witch-cleansing, 109, 111, 122, 124
see also medicine, native
India
Northern, spirit-possession in, 298
rural, xxv
indians, of Chiapas, *see* Chiapas
Industrial Revolution, as social change, xix, xxi, 70, 77n
initiation
Basinjom society, 346
see also Banyang, cults
of witch, 209, 242, 243n, 336
see also sabbath, witches
International African Institute, xxiii
Irons, W. G., 317n
Isaiah, 4
Islam
Evil Eye and, 311, 312
Gonja, 208, 211, 225, 235
medieval, 18, 35
Islamic culture, xii, xxx

James I, 57
jealousy
    and Evil Eye, 312
    between wives, xxix, 167, 168, 169,
        240, 241, 300, 329
Jesus, as sorcerer, 26
Jews, 3, 10-15
    and Devil worship, 10
    exile in Babylon, 5
    expulsion of, 10, 35
    rabbis, 24
    and witchcraft, 13, 68
Job, 4, 57
joking relationships, 328
Judaism
    accusations against, 13-15, 35, 36
    and Evil Eye, 312

Kamba, spirit-possession, 299, 300
Kaberry, P., xii
Kikuyu, 132
kinship
    accusations and, 87
    change in structure of, 69
    politics and, 222-227, 228, 231, 235
    witchcraft and sorcery and, 87,
        209, 228, 232, 234, 237, 261,
        265, 274n, 344
    see also distance, social
Knights Templars
    in France, 9, 14
    persecution of, 10, 15
knots, binding, 52, 313
    see also symbols
Kopytoff, I., xii
Koran, Evil Eye and, 312-313, 316

labour migration, and fame of
    Chikanga, 120
Late Antique Period *see* Roman
    Empire
Lele
    diviners, 348
    ordeals among, 64
Lenje
    divination, 303
    spirit-possession, 299, 300, 303
Lévy-Bruhl, theory of magic, xv,
    xvi, xvii, xxii
Lévi-Strauss, C., xxii
    theory of totemism, 187
Leviticus, 93
Libanius, 24, 26, 28, 29, 30, 32, 33

lineage gods, 188
    see also ancestors
Lombard bankers, expulsion of, 10
London, witchcraft in, 71
love-spells, 32
Lovett, William (Chartist), 66
Lugbara, xxiv
    accusations, 299-300, 302, 307
    diviners, 302
    spirit-possession, 299, 300, 302
Luo, 133
    diviners, 303
    spirit-possession, 299, 300, 303
    and witchcraft, 299, 300
Luvale witches, xxv

magic
    counter-, 321
        see also witchcraft, as counter-
            measure
    yam, 269, 271
magicians, 7, 269
Maji-Maji uprising, 132, 134n
Malawi Congress Party, and Chik-
    anga, 112
Malinowski, B., 71, 77n
malnutrition
    in children, 161, 170, 173-174
    and witchcraft, 64
mana, xvi
Map, Walter, 9
Maquet, J., xii
Marwick, M., 53
Marx, Karl, on religion, xv
Maya, beliefs, 195, 196
Mazdean beliefs, and Judaism, 5
Mbembe, 325, 326, 327, 331
Mbo, Bangwa war against, 173
Mbuti pygmies, xxxiii
medical knowledge
    and decline of witchcraft, 70-71
    lack of, in Tudor and Stuart
        Essex, 89, 90
medicine
    European, 112, 117
    native
        cleansing, 113, 121, 131, 134n,
            152, 325, 331n, 345
        curative, 113, 122-123, 127n, 163,
            166, 191, 336
        protective, 113, 115, 116, 129,
            131, 134n, 164, 166, 214, 216,

217, 219, 220, 221, 225, 226, 227, 228, 303
war, 217-218, 219, 226
see also substances, medicines
medicine man, 103, 114, 116, 117, 129
see also diviners; shamans
medieval and Roman beliefs, 33-34
Melanesia, xiii, xxiii, 133
men
as sorcerers, 259, 273
as witches, xxviii, xxix, 115, 164, 207, 209, 211-228, 229, 231, 236, 241, 268
menstruation
Abelam beliefs about, 274n
hunting taboos and, 216-217
Mexico, 183, 186, 194
Middle East, Evil Eye in, 311
mirrors, used in detection of witch, 130, 134n
misfortune
Evil Eye as explanation of, 312, 313, 314
naguals, combat between, as explanation of, 191
sorcery as explanation of, Trio, 248
and spirit-possession, 293, 294, 299
witchcraft as explanation of, xxxiii, 11, 18, 19, 304
Abelam, 268
in Africa, 27, 129
Bakweri, 149
Bangwa, 161-162, 164, 175-176, 178
Banyang, 333, 347
in Chiapas, 185, 193, 194, 204n
Chikanga, and beliefs of, 117, 125
Gonja, 230
Hehe, 114, 115-116, 117, 118, 125
in Late Roman Empire, 27, 28, 29, 30
in Tudor and Stuart England, 48, 50, 56, 57, 58, 60, 62, 63, 67, 68, 84, 88, 89, 90, 91, 92
missionaries, xix, 169, 196, 205n
Bangwa, 178, 179
Baptist, 157n
and Chikanga, 112, 121, 124, 125
Lutheran, 124, 126n
Roman Catholic, 124
and social change, xx, 178-179, 255n

and Trio village structure, 255n
monks, Dominican, 204n
Morton-Williams, P., xxix
movements
antisemitic, 14-15
anti-witchcraft, xviii, xxiii, xxxiii
African, 31, 58
in Chiapas, 197
European, 13
Ibo, 325
in Tudor and Stuart England, 50, 58, 65
see also movements, witch-cleansing
Inquisition in Europe, 10-12
millennial, xxiii, xxxiv, 31, 58
cargo cults, 133, 275n, 297-298
Jewish, 6
medieval European, 134
Sergey Nilus and, 15
witch-cleansing compared with, 133-134
religious revivalism, in Ghana, 132
witch-cleansing (African), 129-134
accusations during, 130, 151-153
against whites, 132
aim of, 129, 152-153
ambiguity of, 132
Ashanti, 130
Banyang, 152
Bemba, 130, 134n
characteristics of, 129-130
Chikanga and, 103, 106, 118, 120, 121, 122, 132
confessions and, 130, 152
cyclical nature of, 129, 131
Dagomba, 134n
economic change and, 131-132, 151-153
Fipa (Kamcape), 121, 130, 132
Jamaa (in Katanga), 133
lack of, in some areas, 133
Lukusu (in Congo), 132
Mcape, 59, 131, 134n
millennial compared with, 133-134
social change and, 131-132
Tiv, 131, 132
Yoruba (Atinga), 130, 132, 134n
Mummolus, 24
murder, 287
witchcraft and, 66, 71, 83, 130, 183, 184, 194, 203n, 233, 255n

Mysore, xxvii
myths
of death, 282-283, 289
of racial differences, 283

nagual(s)
baby's, 188-189, 190
beliefs
distribution of, 194-195
history of, 195, 202
combat between, 191, 192, 198
distinguished from soul, 192
dreams and, 190-191, 194, 203n
King of Quiché and, 198, 205n
linguistic basis of word, 186
meaning of, 186, 189-190
origin of, 186, 195
personal, 189-202
and power, 187-188, 189, 190, 191
saints and, 192-193
Spaniards and, 195, 196, 197-198,
199, 201, 204n
and totemism, 186-187
see also animals; birds; natural
phenomena
natural phenomena
nagual and, 187, 188, 189, 190
as sign of death, 281
as were-forms
thunder/lightning, 337, 339, 342-
343, 346
as witchcraft and sorcery, 164, 268
Navaho witchcraft, xxvi, 229
Nazis, 3, 13
antisemitism, 15
Negro, as Devil, 8
networks, Ibo, 329-330
New England, witchcraft in, xiii,
76n, 161, 176
New Guinea, xiii
ceremonial exchange in, 257, 259
political types in, 257-258
big-men, 257
society, 257
vengeance, 258
witchcraft and sorcery in, 257-259
Newton, Sir Isaac, 55
Nigeria, cultural division of Ibo in,
321
night-witches, 11, 12, 65, 215, 334
Nilus, Sergey, 15
nomadic communities, Evil Eye and,
314

norms, social
and spirits, 294
witchcraft as upholding, 67, 68, 94,
162, 185, 194, 208, 230, 235,
273, 347
Nuba, shamanism, 298-299
Nuer, xiv, xvii, xxx, xxxii, 183, 279
burial and funerary practices,
280-281
and cattle, 279, 281
death
concepts of, 280, 281, 288
myths of, 282
and Divinity, 280, 282, 283
economy of, 279
ghostly vengeance, 288
inheritance, 281-282
perception of time, xvii
philosophy of, 279-280, 288, 289
political system of, 280, 289
nuns, 31
Nupe, witchcraft among, 236-237
Nyakyusa, witchcraft among, 348

Obasi Njom
Bakweri and, 150, 152-153
Banyang and, 158n
obscenity, 353
occult sciences, 18, 19, 34, 48, 227,
235
omens, 29
see also dreams
Onitsha, 330
oracles, xvii, xxii
Lugbara, 302
ordeals, xxxiii, 64, 116, 214
to clear name, 64, 116, 213-214,
347, 349n
drinking sacred water, 212, 213,
233
poison, xxiii, 73, 171, 212, 325,
347, 349n
sasswood medicine, 145, 158n, 325
torture, 10, 13
Orléans, 8

paganism
Christianity and, 7, 19, 24, 28, 32,
195
Devil and, 6-7
Paris, 9
paternity, beliefs of, 127n

perception, xiv, xv, xvii
  Bangwa, 177
  Evil Eye, and sensory, 314
  Hehe, 114
  Nuer, of time, xvii
Perkins, William, 90
Persia, Evil Eye in, 311-312, 313-314, 317n
Philip, King of France, 10
Philippines, sorcery in, 305
Pilatu (master of ceremonies), 108, 111, 118
  see also Chikanga
plantation agriculture
  Bakweri, 142, 144, 154
  see also cultivation
Pliny the Elder, 20
Plotinus, 23
politics
  Abelam, 268-273, 274n
  Anuak, 279-280, 286, 288-289
  Dinka-Nuer, 279-280, 289
  Gonja, 208, 212, 221-228, 231, 232, 240, 241-242, 243n
  in New Guinea, 257-258
  Shavante, 251-253, 254
  Trio, 245, 246, 247, 248, 254
  witch-cleansing movements and change in, 133
  witchcraft and, xiv, xvii, xxviii, xxix, 23, 24, 115, 132, 161, 177-178, 212, 221-228, 323, 341
pollution, 355
  Bangwa, 162
Pondo
  divination, 305
  spirit-possession, 299, 300, 304-305
  witches, 304
Poor Law, xxi, 67, 72
Pope Gregory IX, 9
possession, spirit, xxxiii, 17, 293
  Bangwa, parents of twins and, 171
  Banyoro, 299, 300, 302-303, 307n
  context of, 294, 295, 299-302, 304
  deprived roles and, 294-295, 297
  of diviner, 113-114, 117, 302-304, 305, 306
  Gurage and, 297, 299, 300
    Fuga carpenters and, 297
  Hutu, 297
  Ibo, 325

  Kamba, 299, 300
  Lenje, 299, 300, 303
  Lugbara, 299, 300, 302
  Luo, 299, 300, 303
  mediums, 267
  and misfortune, 293-294, 299
  Northern Indian, 298
  'peripheral', 293, 294, 295-298
    and witchcraft, 298-307
  Pondo, 299, 300, 304-305
  of prophet (*ngunza*), 132
  Rwanda, 297
  strategy of, 293-294, 301, 304-307
  Taita, 299, 300
  Thonga, 299, 300
  Tonga (Valley), 299, 300
  Venda, 295-297, 299, 300
  as weapon, domestic, 299-300, 303-304
  and witchcraft divination, 302-304, 305, 306
  and witchcraft and sorcery, 293, 298-299
  women and, 294, 302, 303-304, 307n
    Gurage, 297
    in Late Roman Empire, 31
    Venda, 295-297
  Zulu, 299, 300
'potlatch', Bakweri, 146, 155
power, xxviii, 21, 50, 93, 96, 132
  achieved, 24, 106
  acquisition of, 209, 243n
  ambivalent nature of, 164, 184, 203n, 323
  diviners, 106, 112, 117
  illegitimate, 185, 208, 211, 231, 236
  Jews and, 14
  legitimate, 184, 211, 220-221, 231, 234, 236, 240, 242, 257, 307
  nagual and, 187-188, 189, 190, 191
  political, witchcraft and, 212, 221-227, 228, 229, 231-232, 236
    see also politics
  sorcerer and, 34
  spiritual, 184, 185, 187, 189, 191, 193, 301, 305
  structure of, 194, 202
prayer, 183, 188
pregnancy and birth, witchcraft and, 324-325, 341, 343
prophets, 132, 275n, 280, 290n, 355
Protocols of the Elders of Zion, 15

psychology
  Evil Eye, explanations of, and, 314
  witchcraft, explanations of, and,
      47, 155-156, 162, 171-172, 289,
      345, 348-349, 352, 353-354, 355
punishment
  for murder, 287
  for witchcraft
    death, 11, 12, 57, 83, 92, 97, 120,
        183, 184, 193, 194, 203n, 229,
        270
    execution, 8, 10, 12, 69, 213-214,
        239
    expulsion, xxvi, 68, 131, 169, 212,
        213, 229, 242
    by God, 56-57, 185, 193
    hanging, 145
    imprisonment, 10, 91, 92, 97
    Jews and, 13
    in Late Roman Empire, 20
    legal, 70
    lynching, 73, 354
    slavery as, 214, 229

Quetzaltenango, battle of, 198, 205n

Radcliffe-Brown, A. R., xv
Reformation, Protestant, xxi, 58, 65,
    72, 73, 95
Renaissance, and change, xxxi, xxxii
residence, sorcery and, 252
Richards, A., xii
rites de passage, Evil Eye and, 315
ritual
  against Evil Eye, 312, 313, 314,
      315-317
  precautions, 165, 217, 248, 316-317
  against witchcraft
    African, 129, 130, 131, 132, 134
    Bangwa, 163, 166
    Banyang cults and, 345-346
    Catholic, 58, 73
    Gonja, 227, 235
    see also exorcism
rivalry, xxvii, xxviii, 226, 227, 228,
    229, 232, 233, 236, 243n, 271,
    272-273, 274n, 288, 300, 301,
    323
roles, xxx, xxxiii, 352, 353
  and accusations, 22
  affinal and kinship, 237, 243, 265
  see also kinship

ambiguous, 22, 27, 64, 307, 327,
    348, 355
chiefs, 212, 234, 352
  of Chikanga, 121
  and deprivation, 294-295, 307n
  Evil Eye and, 315
  male/female, *see* sex, antagonism
  and witchcraft, xvii, 54, 64, 66-73,
      207, 231, 234, 235-236, 242,
      328
Roman Empire, Late, xxv
  beliefs during and medieval beliefs,
      33-34
  and Christianity, 19-22
  social change, 20, 21
  society, xxvii, 17, 21, 22, 23, 27
  sorcery beliefs, 19, 20
  stability of, 30-31
Rwanda, spirit-possession in, 297

sabbath, witches, 12, 49, 65, 199, 209,
    243n, 325
sacrifice, 146, 166, 174, 280, 289, 325
Saint
  Ambrose, 26
  Andrew, patron of Larraínzar, 192
  Byzantine, 28
  Macedonius, 32
  Michael, patron of Pinola, 192
  Paul, 31
  Peter, as sorcerer, 26
saints, *nagual* and, 192-193
San Andrés Larraínzar, 188, 201,
    204n
sanctions, xvii, 93, 94, 193, 221, 230,
    243
  see also ordeals; punishment
Santiago el Palmar, 202
Sartre, J.-P., xxxv
Satan, *see* Devil
Schapera, I., xi, xii
Scot, Reginald, 65
sects
  Albigensian, 10
  Catharist, 10
  Christian, 28
  Dead Sea, 6
  Gnostic, 28
  heretical, 11-12
  medieval, 3, 10, 15
  Zoroastrian, 28
  see also cults
Selden, John, 54

sex
   antagonism, xxix, 231, 232, 236-237, 241, 294, 296, 300, 303-304, 352
   sorcery substances and, 261-262
   tensions of, 64, 84, 161, 171, 172-173, 353
Shakespeare, 55, 56
shaman
   female Venda as, 295-296, 297
   nagual and, 186
   Trio and, 248
shamanism, Nuba, 298-299
shame, 24
Shavante, Akw̃e, xxvii, 245, 249, 255n
   accusations, 251-252
   chiefship, 251-252, 254
   compared with the Trio, 253-254
   cosmology, 253
   economic life, 250
   location, 250
   politics, 251, 253, 254
      factions in, 251-253, 254
      power and, 251, 252
   society, 251, 253
   village structure, 250-251, 253, 254
shaving head of witch, Hehe, 114, 116, 119, 120, 124
Shona, and Venda spirit-possession, 295
Sleeping Beauty, 62
social change
   Hehe, 120
   Jews and, 14
   in Late Roman Empire, sorcery and, 20, 21
   witch-cleansing movements, 131, 132, 133, 153
   witchcraft and, xix-xx, xxi, 55, 66, 153, 177-178
      in Tudor and Stuart England, 63, 65, 66, 67, 69-70, 72, 73, 82, 84, 87
social control, xvii-xviii, 67, 251
   witchcraft and, xix, 67
   see also norms
social mobility, 21, 26, 246, 247, 248, 251, 329-330
songs, 123, 127n, 217, 242, 344
   competition of, 218-219, 220
sorcerer, 18, 248, 303, 348

Abelam (*kwis'ndu*), 259, 260, 261, 262, 263, 264, 265, 269, 270, 273, 275n
   detection of, 264-265
   Ibo, 324
   image of, 22, 37, 248-249
   Jesus as, 26
   pagan philosopher as, 34
   professional class as, 34, 52, 303
   St Peter as, 26
sorcery, 11, 17, 22, 50
   Abelam, 259-267, 268-273, 273n, 275n
   Bangwa, 162
   as belief, 18, 19, 20, 31-32
   black magic as, xxviii
   in Chiapas, 191, 198
   as counter-measure, 249, 321
   distinguished from witchcraft, xxxvin, 50, 51, 210, 259, 321
   Ibo, 321-324
   impotence and, 29
   in Late Roman Empire, 25
   in New Guinea, 258-259
   from outside, 248, 249, 254, 261, 262, 263, 267, 269, 271, 272, 273, 274n, 324
   payment for, 262-263, 264, 265, 270
   Shavante, 251-253
   social change and, 20, 21
   social context of, 20, 251
   social relations and, 18, 247-248, 249, 251, 263
   Trio, 247, 248-250, 253-254
      antisocial behaviour and, 247-248
   in Tudor and Stuart England, 51
   as weapon, political, 251-253, 258, 272-273
   Zuñi, 176-177
Spanish
   and *nagual*, 195, 196, 197-198, 199, 201, 204n
   witchcraft beliefs, 197, 198, 199, 201
spectacles, witches and, 227, 243n
spells, 50, 205n
   see also curse; substances, witchcraft and sorcery
spinsters, and witchcraft, 85
   see also witch(es), status of
spirits
   ancestral, Hehe, 113, 114, 126n

spirits—(*contd.*)
  animal, 186, 187, 243n
  Anuak, 280, 281
  in Chiapas, 185
  child, 163
  guardian
    Bangwa, 178
    nagual and, 186, 187, 193, 204n
    North American, 186
  Hehe, 114
  outside society, 294, 307n
  possession by, *see* possession, spirit
  sky, 288
  villages of, 262
  water, 154, 158n
  zombie (*nyongo*), 148, 150, 154, 155
statutory measures against witch-
    craft
  in Africa, 73, 123, 127n
  in England, 49-50, 69, 70, 72, 82, 84
substances, witchcraft and sorcery
  bodily, 261-262, 274n
    'leavings', 259, 260, 261, 262,
        263, 274n
    nail-parings, 152
  food, 94
  lettuce, 31
  medicines, xxix, 29, 50, 88, 114,
      115, 116, 118, 122, 134n, 152,
      208, 209, 210, 215, 218, 221,
      226, 227, 228, 232, 236, 237-
      239, 242, 321, 335, 336
  missiles, xxvi, 191, 219, 237, 243n
  paint, xxviii, 259-260, 263-264, 265,
      266, 269, 271, 273, 274n
  poison, 51, 114-115, 210, 237-239,
      243n, 323, 324
  potions, xxxvi
suspicion, xxxiv, 272, 312, 315, 354
symbol(s)
  analysis of, 307n, 353
  binding, 52, 313
  chief as, in Trio society, 247
  colour, 188, 313, 317n
  cross as, 58, 313
  Devil as evil, 3, 65, 192
  external, xxxvi
  hand as, 316
  heat, 185, 204n, 260, 274n, 337
  height, 185, 187, 188
  holy water as, 58, 179
  horse-tail, 225-226, 227, 232, 353
  of male authority, 296

  messages as, 265
  millennial, 133-134
  phallic, 14, 313
  rainbow as python, 148
  religious as curative, 58
  royal, 290-291n
  serpent, 14
  sexual, 172
  sorcery, 266, 274n
  warfare and power, 217
  witch-cleansing, 132-133
  witchcraft, xxv, xxvi, xxvii, xxviii
      xxx, 152
Syrian clergy, and sorcery, 26

taboos
  funerary, 266
  hunting, 216-217, 220
tabu, xvi
Taita, spirit-possession, 299, 300
tattooing, as protection against Evil
    Eye, 316
Tenejapa, 204n
tension
  political, 120
    see also rivalry
  roles and, 236-237, 240-241
  social, xvii, 67, 72, 73, 91, 92, 96,
      120, 153, 162, 167, 174, 236,
      248, 293, 301, 327-331, 355
territorial expansion, Ibo and, 330-
    331
Thomas, K., 97
Thonga, spirit-possession, 299, 300
threats, witchcraft and, xxxiv, 184
Tiv
  accusations, 145-146, 230
  power, 203n
  witch-cleansing movements, 131,
      132
Toledo, Visigothic Kings of, and
    Jews, 36
Tolkien, *Lord of the Rings*, 156
Tonga (Valley), spirit-possession, 299,
    300
totemism, 186-187, 188
towns
  Late Roman Empire, 25
    see also villages
trials, witch
  in Chiapas, 194
  Gonja, 213, 214
  Hehe, 123-124

in Tudor and Stuart England, 52,
53, 54, 55, 57, 58, 73, 76n
Essex, 83, 85, 96-97
Leicester, 57
Trigge, F. (Elizabethan preacher), 92
Trio, xxvi, 245
accusations, 248, 249, 250
chiefship, 247, 254
power of, 247
compared with the Shavante, 253-
254
cosmology, 253
economic life, 245, 248
location, 245, 246, 255n
politics, 245, 246, 247, 248, 254
ceremonial dialogue and, 246,
248, 255n
dance festival and, 248, 255n
society, 246, 248, 253
mobility of, 246, 247, 248
sorcery, 247, 248-250, 253-254
antisocial behaviour and, 247-248
misfortune as, 248
vengeance, 249-250, 254
village structure, 245-250, 253, 254
missionaries and, 255n
Trobriand chiefship, and sorcery, 258
Tudor and Stuart England
witchcraft in, 48-74, 91
social change and, 63, 65, 66, 67,
69-70, 72, 73
Tudor and Stuart Essex, xxi, 82-98
witchcraft in, 81-98
twins
Anuak myth and, 282
Bangwa, 163, 171, 178, 353

unnatural acts, 9, 10, 14, 49, 152,
172, 198-199, 210, 340
Jews and, 14
urban conditions, witchcraft and,
xx, 25, 66, 71, 133
see also towns; villages

Venda
accusations, 301
morality cult, 295
shaman or diviner, 295-296, 297
spirit-possession, 295-297, 299, 300
women and, 295-297
witch, 301
vengeance, xxvi, 57, 61, 65
Abelam, 269, 272, 273

Azande, xvi, 183
Bangwa, 162
in Chiapas, 184
ghostly
Anuak, 287-288
Dinka-Nuer, 288
Gonja, 216, 217, 218, 233
Hehe, 116
Ibo, 325
in New Guinea, 258
Trio, 249-250, 254
Vergil, 26
villages
fission of, and sorcery, 272-273
society of, Tudor and Stuart
Essex, 82-98
structure of
in New Guinea, 258
Shavante, 250-251, 253, 254
sorcery and, 245, 248-250, 251-
253, 254
Trio, 245-250, 253-254, 255n
von Gravenreuth, killed by Bakweri,
157n, 158n
von Puttkamer, governor of West
Cameroons, 142, 143
von Stetten, expedition against Bakweri, 143, 145

warfare
medicines, 217, 219, 220, 226
in New Guinea, 258-259
sorcery and, 261, 273
witchcraft and, 216, 217-218, 219,
220, 233, 234
were-forms, *see* animals; birds; natural phenomena
West Indies, zombies in, 148-149,
158n
widows, xxv, 64, 66, 85
Luvale, xxv
witch(es)
Abelam, xxvii, 259, 267-268, 273n,
274n
age of, 211, 236, 268, 326
Ashanti, 348
Bakweri, 144-157
Bangwa, 162, 163, 164-179
Banyang, 333, 334, 335
child, 162, 163, 164, 165-179, 193
in Chiapas, 183, 191, 193, 194,
195, 204n

witch(es)—(*contd.*)

in community, xxvii, 65, 66, 72, 129-134

detection of, 59-64, 73, 164, 191, 212, 243n, 324, 325, 333, 336-338, 340

by post-mortem, 145, 164, 324, 337-338, 339, 340, 341, 342

'smelling out', 171

development of belief in, 35

eating people, 114, 130, 145, 168, 173, 174, 209, 210, 219, 239, 243n, 324, 325, 340

familiar of, 51, 96, 186, 197, 200, 243n, 299, 304, 323

Gonja, 207, 208, 209, 210, 211, 225-243

Hehe, 114, 118

Ibo, 323, 324

initiation of, 209, 242, 243n

as internal enemy, xxvii, xxviii

mark of, 51, 338

Mediterranean, 35

men as, 115, 164, 207, 209, 211-216, 216-221, 221-228, 229, 231, 236, 241, 268

night, 11, 12, 65, 215, 334

as outsider, xxvi, xxvii, 230, 307n

pact with Devil, 35, 49, 52, 55, 193, 197, 198, 201, 305

Pondo, 304

power of, xxvii, xxviii, xxx, 65, 93, 96, 198

sabbath of, 12, 49, 65, 199, 209, 243n, 325

as servant of Devil, 11, 193, 197, 198, 201, 305

Spanish, 198

status of, 13, 84-85, 87, 115, 164, 205n, 236, 355

transformation of

into animal, 164, 166, 186, 195, 196, 197, 198-199, 200, 201, 208, 210, 243n, 274n, 334, 335, 348

into natural phenomena, 164, 208

see also animals; birds; natural phenomena

trial of

Gonja, 213, 214

in Tudor and Stuart England, 52, 53, 54, 55, 57, 58, 69, 73, 83, 85, 96-97

Venda, 301

women as, 48, 63, 64, 67, 72, 84, 87, 162, 164, 193, 205n, 207, 209, 211, 212, 213-214, 215, 225, 229, 233, 235, 236-243, 259, 267-268, 304, 327, 353

witch-cleansing, *see under* movements

witchcraft

Abelam, 259, 267-268, 275n

ambiguous roles and, xxv, 22, 27, 63

antisocial habits and, 62-63, 67, 72, 92-93

Anuak, 289

Azande, xiv, xvi, 60, 259, 333, 335

Bakweri, 144-157

beliefs

change in, 141, 143, 144, 147, 149, 150, 152, 154

context of, 66-67, 162, 167

inconsistency of, 333

role of, 54, 66-73, 207, 221

Ceŵa, 62, 75n

as counter-measure, xxviii, xxxiv, 57, 58, 60, 66, 73, 116, 208, 210, 211, 212, 216, 220, 221, 228, 231, 233, 240

diagnosis of, 59-64, 130, 164

see also witch(es), detection of

distinguished from sorcery, xxxvin, 50, 51, 210, 259, 321

English, defined, 48, 82

and Evil Eye, 311

function of, 176-177

Gonja, 208-211, 243n

hereditary, xvi, 51, 164, 209

and heresy, 11

Ibo, 321, 323, 324-327, 327-331

and lechery, 166

and norms, upholding of social, 67, 68, 94, 162, 185, 194, 208, 230, 235, 317, 347

Nupe, 236-237

Nyakyusa, 348

social level, xxv, 36, 65, 66, 68, 72, 130

Spanish, 197, 198-199, 201

and spirit-possession, 293, 298-307

threats, xxxiv, 184

as unconscious power, xxviii, xxx, xxxiv, 51, 333

wealth and, xxvii, 67, 146, 147, 148, 149, 325, 326

as weapon, political, 228, 229, 231-232, 236

white, 82

Witchcraft, Oracles and Magic among the Azande, xi, xiii, 17, 18

witchcraft, theories of
anthropological, xiii, xix, xxiii, xxiv, xxxiv, 67, 71, 162, 151-156
development of, xiii-xvi, xvii-xxi, xxii, xxiii
functional, xiv, xxii, xxv, 67, 69, 161, 207, 351
homeostatic control, xix, xxi, xxv
paradigms of, xxii, xxiii, xxiv
personality, 162
structural, xviii, 162, 293
historical, xiii, xix, xxxvi, 18, 47, 68, 81, 97

witch-finders
Anuak, 289
Bwanali, 59
Banyang, 150, 151, 152
Basinjom, 340, 346
Mfam, 337, 340, 345, 346
Chikanga, 103, 106, 110, 112, 118, 132
Matthew Hopkins, 50, 58, 65, 76n
Mpulumutsi, 59
Njombe, 150-151, 156, 157
see also movements

wives, jealousy between, xxix, 167, 168, 169, 240, 241, 300, 329

women
Evil Eye and, 315

witchcraft and, *see* witch(es), women as

Wordsworth, W., 290n

Wren, 55

xanthosoma (cocoyam)
Bakweri economic change and, 143, 146, 154, 156, 158n
as protection against witchcraft, 326-327

Yakö
accusations, 327
cosmology, xviii
witchcraft among, 326, 327, 331

Yao, xviii, xxvii

Yoruba, xxx
confessions, 130
political inheritance in, 328
witch-cleansing movements (Atinga), 130, 132, 134n

Zodiac, animals of, 197

zombies, xxviii, 147, 148, 150, 152, 154, 155, 159n
West Indian beliefs, 148-149, 158n

Zoroastrianism
and Evil Eye, 312
and Judaism, 5

Zulu, spirit-possession, 299, 300

Zuñi
accusations, 176
confessions, 176-177
sorcery, 176-177